Barnum Museum

Mr Mark Murrell
905 Vernon Dr
Jacksonville, NC 28540

BARNUM'S OWN STORY

The Autobiography of
P. T. BARNUM , Combined
& condensed from the various
editions published during his
lifetime by Waldo R. Browne

DOVER PUBLICATIONS, INC.
MINEOLA, NEW YORK

Bibliographical Note

This Dover edition, first published in 2017, is an unabridged and unaltered republication of the work originally published by The Viking Press, Inc., in 1927. *Barnum's Own Story* represents an editing and condensation, in one volume, of the following two books by P. T. Barnum: *The Life of P. T. Barnum,* published by Redfield in 1855, and various editions of *Struggles and Triumphs; or, Forty Years' Recollections of P. T. Barnum* that appeared from 1869 to 1888.

This Dover edition also includes forty-eight pages of illustrations not included in the 1927 edition. Grateful acknowledgment is made to Miss Elizabeth Sterling Seeley, Curator of the Barnum Museum, Bridgeport, Connecticut, and to the Museum of the City of New York for permission to reproduce illustrations in their collections.

Illustrations within the text are from the following sources: pp. 66, 83, 119, 139, 150, 233, 298, *The Life of P. T. Barnum* (Redfield); pp. 89, 132, 164, 220, 271, 321, 354, 382, 427, 433, *Struggles and Triumphs*; pp. 181, 394, *Frank Leslie's Illustrated Newspaper*; pp. 278, 285, 335, 365, 419, 448, *Harper's Weekly*; p. 169, *Illustrated London News*; p. 199, Loan Collection of Elizabeth Sterling Seeley.

International Standard Book Number
ISBN-13: 978-0-486-81187-1
ISBN-10: 0-486-81187-5

Manufactured in the United States by LSC Communications
81187501   2017
www.doverpublications.com

To

THE UNIVERSAL YANKEE NATION

of which I Am Proud to Be One

I Dedicate These Pages

P. T. Barnum

EDITOR'S NOTE

Barnum's autobiography first appeared in 1855 as "The Life of P. T. Barnum, Written by Himself." In his preface, the author wrote: "In these pages I have given the true history of my many adventures, and the numerous enterprises in which I have been engaged. . . . It will be seen that I have not covered up my so-called 'humbugs,' but have given a full account even of such schemes as 'Joice Heth,' the 'Fejee Mermaid,' and the 'Woolly Horse.' . . . Though a portion of my 'confessions' may by some be considered injudicious, I prefer frankly to 'acknowledge the corn' wherever I have had a hand in plucking it." But as he grew older and more prominent, this feeling about "acknowledging the corn" underwent a decided change. The plates used in his "Life" of 1855 were purchased and destroyed; and in 1869 he published a "new and independent" autobiography under the title, "Struggles and Triumphs; or, Forty Years' Recollections of P. T. Barnum, Written by Himself." An atmosphere of pompous self-satisfaction altogether lacking in the "Life" of 1855 makes itself felt in this later work; the story of his early career is much condensed, and the franker details either omitted altogether or so toned down as to appear innocent and respectable. This "denaturing" process was continued in several later editions, partially revised and with additional chapters or appendices, which appeared at intervals up to 1888, three years before the author's death.

The present volume is a composite reprint of the 1855 "Life" and the various editions of "Struggles and Triumphs" published from 1869 to 1888. The chief aim has been to present Barnum's own story as he himself first set it down, without regard to the qualms and tremors of respectability which gradually overcame the franker side of his nature. At the same time, the book has been subjected to a vigorous process of condensation, by the omission of many irrelevant or trivial anecdotes, public speeches, letters, laudatory press comments, and other extraneous matter which clutters up the original.

In 1888 Barnum stated that the various editions of his autobiography had sold to the extent of about half a million copies. The work has long been out of print in any form. It is hoped that the present reprint, restoring as it does the salt and savor of the original narrative and also divesting it of a heavy load of superfluous material, will be welcomed by many thousands of readers among a newer generation, to whom the name of the great showman is still a "household word" and his career one of the most picturesque and romantic in American life.

CONTENTS

x CONTENTS

ILLUSTRATIONS

BARNUM'S
OWN STORY

CHAPTER I

I was born in the town of Bethel, in the State of Connecticut, July 5, 1810. My name, Phineas Taylor, is derived from my maternal grandfather, who was a great wag in his way, and who, as I was his first grandchild, gravely handed over to my mother at my christening a gift-deed, in my behalf, of five acres of land situated in that part of the parish of Bethel known as the "Plum Trees." I was thus a real estate owner almost at my very birth; and of my property, "Ivy Island," something shall be said anon.

I think I can remember when I was not more than two years old, and the first person I recollect having seen was my grandfather. As I was his pet, and spent probably the larger half of my waking hours in his arms, during the first six years of my life, my good mother estimates that the amount of lump sugar which I swallowed from his hands, during that period, could not have been less than two barrels. My grandfather would go farther, wait longer, work harder and contrive deeper, to carry out a practical joke, than for anything else under heaven. In this one particular, as well as in many others, I am almost sorry to say I am his counterpart; for although nothing that I can conceive of delights me so much as playing off one of those dangerous things, and although I have enjoyed more hearty laughs in planning and executing them than from any one source in the world, and have generally tried to avoid giving offence, yet I have many times done so, and as often have I regretted this propensity, which was born in me, and will doubtless continue until "dust returns to dust."

3

My paternal grandfather was Captain Ephraim Barnum, of Bethel—a captain in the militia in the Revolutionary War. His son Philo was my father. He too was of a lively turn of mind, and relished a joke better than the average of mankind. These historical facts I state as some palliation for my own inclination that way. "What is bred in the bone," etc.

I am not aware that my advent created any peculiar commotion in the village, though my good mother declares that I made a great deal of noise the first hour I saw the light, and that she has never been able to discover any cessation since.

I must pass by the first seven years of my life—during which my grandfather crammed me with sugar and loaded me with pennies, to buy raisins and candies, which he always instructed me to solicit from the store-keeper at the "lowest cash price"—and proceed to talk of later events.

I commenced going to school at the age of about six years. The first date which I recollect inscribing upon my writing-book was 1818. I was generally accounted a pretty apt scholar, and as I increased in years there were but two or three in school who were considered my superiors. In arithmetic I was unusually quick, and I recollect, at the age of twelve years, being called out of bed one night by my teacher, who had laid a small wager with a neighbor that I could figure up and give the correct number of feet in a load of wood in five minutes. The neighbor stated the dimensions, and as I had no slate in the house I marked them on the stove pipe, and thereon also figured my calculations, and gave the result in less than two minutes, to the great delight of my teacher, my mother, and myself, and to the no small astonishment of our incredulous neighbor.

My father was a tailor, a farmer, and sometimes a tavernkeeper; so I was often kept out of school, and never had any "advantages" except at the common district school, and one summer at the "Academy" in Danbury, a distance of three miles, which I marched and countermarched six times per week. Like most farmers' boys, I was obliged to drive and fetch the cows, carry in firewood, shell corn, weed beets and cabbages, and, as I grew larger, I rode horse for ploughing, turned and raked hay, and in due time handled "the shovel and the hoe," as well as the plough; but I never really liked to work.

My organ of acquisitiveness must be large, or else my parents commenced its cultivation at an early period. Before I was five years of age I began to accumulate pennies and sixpennies. At the age of six years my grandfather informed me that all my little pieces of coin amounted to one dollar, and if I would go with him and take my money, he would show me something worth having. Placing all my wealth in a pocket handkerchief which was closely wound up and firmly grasped, I started with my grandfather. He took me to the village tavern, then kept by Mr. Stiles Wakelee, and approaching the landlord, he said, "Here, Mr. Wakelee, is the richest boy in this part of the country. He has a dollar in cash. I wish you to take his change and give him a silver dollar for it." The complaisant landlord took my deposits and presently handed me a silver dollar.

Never have I seen the time (nor shall I ever again) when I felt so rich, so absolutely independent of all the world, as I did when I looked at that monstrous big silver dollar, and felt that it was all my own. Talk of "cart wheels," there was never one half so large as that dollar looked to me. I believed, without the slightest reservation, that this entire earth and all its contents could be purchased by that wonderful piece of bullion, and that it would be a bad bargain at that.

But my dollar did not long remain alone. My mother taught me that I should still save my pennies, and I did so. As I grew larger, my grandfather paid me ten cents per day for riding the horse which preceded the ox-team in ploughing, and I hit upon various expedients for adding to my pile. On "training days," instead of spending money, I was earning it in the vocation of a peddler. My stock in trade consisted of a gallon of molasses, boiled down and worked into molasses candy, called in those times "cookania," and I usually found myself a dollar richer at the end of "training," than I was at the commencement. As I always had a remarkable taste for speculation, my holiday stock soon increased, and comprised "ginger-bread," cookies, sugar candies, and cherry rum. The latter article consisted of a demijohn of New England rum, in which was put a quantity of wild cherries, and I believe a little sugar. I soon learned that the soldiers were good cherry-rum customers, and no sooner did I hear the words "halt," "ground arms," than I approached the "trainers" with my decanter and wine-glass. In a few years I should have been a second Crœsus in wealth, had not my father considerately allowed me to purchase my own clothing. This arrangement kept my pile reduced to a moderate size. Always looking out for the main chance, however, I had sheep of my own, a calf of which I was the sole proprietor, and other individual property which made me feel, at twelve years of age, that I was a man of substance.

I felt at the same time that I had not reached my proper sphere. The farm was no place for me. I always disliked work. Head-work I was excessively fond of. I was always ready to concoct fun, or lay plans for money-making, but hand-work was decidedly not in my line. My father insisted that I could hoe and plough and dig in the garden as well as anybody else, but I generally contrived to shirk the work altogether, or by slighting it, get through with the day's work.

I was not quite twelve years of age when I visited the commercial metropolis for the first time. It happened as follows: My father, as before stated, kept the village tavern. Late one afternoon in January, 1822, Mr. Daniel Brown, of Southbury, Ct., arrived at our house with a drove of fat cattle which he was taking to New York for sale. The stock were put into our large barnyard, the horses ridden by himself and assistant were stabled, and Mr. Brown having partaken of a warm supper, drew off his boots, put on his slippers, and sat down by the fire to spend the evening comfortably.

I looked upon him as a great man, for he had been to "York," and to "go to York" in those days was thought quite as much of as to go to Europe is now. I listened to the relation of his adventures in city and country, my interest in the man continually increasing. At last I heard him say to my father that he expected to buy many more cattle in Ridgefield, and at other points on his way to the city, and he would be glad to hire a boy who was light of foot, to run along with him and assist in driving the cattle. I immediately besought my father (like a modern office-seeker) to intercede for me, and if possible procure me the coveted situation. He did so. Consultation with my mother resulted in her consent, and it was immediately arranged that I should visit New York. I was told to retire at once, so as to be ready to start with the drove of cattle at daylight in the morning. I went to bed, but not to sleep. Visions of all sorts haunted my imagination. A new world was about to be opened to me. I slept an hour or two towards morning, dreaming of the great city with streets paved with gold, and many castles— in the air.

At daylight I was aroused, took a few mouthfuls of breakfast, and started off on foot in the midst of a heavy snow storm, to help drive the cattle. Before reaching Ridgefield, Mr. Brown put me on his horse to gallop after a wandering ox; the horse fell, rolled upon my foot, and sprained my ankle. I suffered intensely, but dared not complain lest my employer should contrive some way to send me back, for I was not yet ten miles from home. He very considerately allowed me to ride behind him on the horse, and that night the landlady of the hotel where we stopped bathed my ankle, which was considerably swollen. The next day it was a trifle better, but as I continued to limp, Mr. Brown permitted me to ride most of the time. In three or four days we reached the city of New York, and put up at the Bull's Head tavern, kept, I think, by Mr. Givens. The drover would be busy a week selling his cattle, and then I was to return home with him in a sleigh.

That was a great week for me. My mother gave me a dollar before I left home, and I never expected to see the end of it. I supposed it would supply my every wish, and yet leave unknown quantities of small change on hand. The first outlay I made was for oranges. I was very fond of this fruit, and had often wished I could have as many as I could eat. I entered a confectionery store and inquired the price of oranges. "Four pence apiece," was the reply. Now, "four pence" in Connecticut is six cents, and I supposed it was the same the world over. Profiting by my experience in "beating down" the price, and not doubting Franklin's proverb that "a penny saved is two pence earned," I informed the lady that "I considered four pence apiece too dear, but I would give her ten cents for two." The feminine shopkeeper hesitated for a moment, but finally said that seeing it was me, and as it was probably my first visit to New York, she would let me have the two oranges for ten cents, but she should expect me to trade with her whenever I wanted any thing in her line. I thanked her, and took the oranges. I thought it was very liberal in her to make such a generous deduction from the price of her fruit, little dreaming that, owing to the difference in currency, I had paid her two cents more than she asked.

Soon dispatching my two oranges, I purchased two more, and had eighty cents left. This seemed to me sufficient for all mortal wants. I then bought for thirty-one cents a little gun, which would "go off" and send a stick some distance across the room. I intended to astonish my schoolmates with the gun when I got home, for it astonished me considerably, as I had never seen anything of the kind before. I went into the bar-room of our hotel, and began to amuse myself with the extraordinary implement. The bar-room was crowded with customers, and shooting at random, the arrow grazed one man's nose and passed on, hitting the barkeeper in the eye. Smarting under the pain it occasioned, the latter came in front of his counter, caught me by the collar, shook me sternly, boxed my ears till my head rung, and told me to put that gun out of the way or he would throw it into the stove. I felt considerably injured in my feelings, and sneaking slyly up stairs placed the precious treasure under my pillow.

Visiting the toy shop again, the good woman instructed me in the mystery of torpedoes. She threw one with considerable force on the floor, and it exploded, greatly to my delight. Would not these astonish our school-boys? I bought six cents' worth for that purpose, but could not wait to use them at home. As the guests at the hotel were passing in to dinner, and supposing that they had never seen any thing in the torpedo line and would be delighted to do so, I could not refrain from giving them the opportunity. So taking two from my pocket and throwing them with all my strength against the side of the hall through which the crowd was passing, a loud double-report followed, much to the surprise and annoyance of the guests. The landlord came rushing out in a high state of excitement, and discovering the culprit he stretched me upon the floor at a single blow with his open hand. "There, you little green-horn," he exclaimed, "see if that will teach you better than to explode your infernal crackers in my house again!" It did. I was perfectly taught in a single lesson; went up stairs and deposited the balance of the torpedoes with my gun. I ate no dinner that day. My dignity had been insulted and my appetite had vanished. I was humbled. I felt forlorn and forsaken. I however had one resource. It was the toy shop. I visited it again, bought a watch, a breast-pin, and a top. I was still a rich man. I had eleven cents left. I went to bed and dreamed of all my possessions.

The next morning, immediately after breakfast, I visited the toy shop again to "look around," and perceived many things which I had not noticed the day previously. Presently I saw a beautiful knife with two blades, besides a gimlet and cork-screw! This was a novelty. The most useful article in existence, beyond all doubt. I must possess it. My father would be delighted, for it was a carpenter shop in miniature, and was too valuable an article to leave behind me. Wouldn't old Bethel be astonished! But what was the price of this combination of all that was useful and ornamental? Only thirty-one cents. Alas, I had only eleven! I learned to my astonishment that my funds were exhausted. But have the knife I must, and so I proposed to my kind friend, the shop woman, that she should receive back the top and breast-pin at a slight deduction from what I had paid for them, and then taking my eleven cents, should let me have the knife. The kind creature consented, and thus I made my first "swop." Presently I discovered some molasses candy. It was whiter and nicer than any I had ever seen before. I must have some. So I asked the lady to take back the watch at a slight discount, and give me the worth of it in molasses candy. She did so. It was delicious. I had never tasted any thing so nice—and before night I had resigned my gun into her possession and swallowed its value in molasses candy. The next morning I swallowed all my torpedoes in the same shape, and in the course of the day even my knife followed in the sweet footsteps of its illustrious predecessors. Molasses candy was the rock on which I split. My money was all gone—my notions all swopped for it—and yet, like Oliver Twist, I cried for "more." The good woman had a son of about my size. I had no particular use for my two pocket handkerchiefs. Her boy could use them, and I gladly accepted her proposal to trade them for four sticks of molasses candy. I had an extra pair of stockings which I was sure I should never need, and they went for five more rolls of molasses candy!

When thus divested of all I possessed, I became resigned to my fate, and, turning my attention to some other source of excitement, I made the acquaintance of a young gentleman from Connecticut. He was about twenty years of age, had been in New York once before, "knew the ropes," and proposed to show me the city. I gladly accompanied him, and saw many sights that day which astonished me beyond measure.

My week was soon up. Mr. Brown took me into his one-horse sleigh immediately after dinner, drove as far as Sawpitts, now called Port Chester, stopped over night, started early the next morning, and arrived at Bethel the same evening. I had a thousand questions to answer, and found my brothers and sisters much disappointed that I had brought them none of the fruits of my dollar. My mother examined my wardrobe, and finding it two pocket-handkerchiefs and one pair of stockings short, I was whipped and sent to bed. Thus terminated my first visit to New York. I was however for a long time quite a lion among the school-boys, for I had "been to York," and seen with my own eyes many wonders which they had only "heard tell of."

CHAPTER II

My aversion to hand-work, on the farm or otherwise, continued to be manifested in various ways, all of which was generally set down to the score of laziness. I believe, indeed, I had the reputation of being the laziest boy in town, probably because I was always busy at head-work to evade the sentence of gaining bread by the sweat of the brow. In sheer despair of making any thing better of me, my father concluded to try me as a merchant. He had previously erected a suitable building in Bethel, and taking Mr. Hiram Weed as a partner, they purchased a stock of dry goods, groceries, hardware, and a thousand other "notions;" and I was duly installed as clerk in a country store.

Like many greenhorns before me, this was the height of my ambition. I felt that it was a great condescension on my part to enter into conversation with the common boys who had to work for a living. I strutted behind the counter with a pen back of my ear, was wonderfully polite to ladies, assumed a wise look when entering charges upon the day-book, was astonishingly active in waiting upon customers, whether in weighing tenpenny nails, starch, indigo, or saleratus, or drawing New England rum or West India molasses.

Ours was a cash, credit and barter store; and I drove many a sharp trade with old women who paid for their purchases in butter, eggs, beeswax, feathers, and rags, and with men who exchanged for our commodities, hats, axe-helves, oats, corn, buckwheat, hickory-nuts, and other commodities. It was something of a drawback upon my dignity that I was compelled to sweep the store, take down the window-shutters, and make the fire; nevertheless the thought of being a "merchant" fully compensated me for all such menial duties.

My propensities for money-making continued active as ever, and I asked and obtained the privilege of purchasing candies on my own account, to sell to the juvenile portion of our customers. I received a small salary for my services (my father as usual stipulating that I should clothe myself), and I intended to be faithful to my employers; but I have found, all through life, that wherever there are conflicting interests, men are very apt to think of self first, and so I fear it was with me,—for I well remember spending much time in urging indulgent mothers to buy candies for their darling children, when other customers were waiting to be served with more substantial articles of merchandise.

A country store in the evening, or upon a wet day, is a miserably dull place, so far as trade is concerned. Upon such occasions therefore I had little to do, and I will explain why the time did not hang unpleasantly upon my hands. In nearly every New England village, at the time of which I write, there could be found from six to twenty social, jolly, story-telling, joke-playing wags and wits, regular originals, who would get together at the tavern or store, and spend their evenings and stormy afternoons in relating anecdotes, describing their various adventures, playing off practical jokes upon each other, and engaging in every project out of which a little fun could be extracted by village wits whose ideas were usually sharpened at brief intervals by a "treat," otherwise known as a glass of Santa Cruz rum, old Holland gin, or Jamaica spirits.

Bethel was not an exception to this state of things. In fact no place of its size could boast more original geniuses in the way of joking and story-telling than my native village. Luckily or un-luckily, our store was the resort of all these wits, and many is the day and evening that I have hung with delight upon their stories,

and many the night that I have kept the store open until eleven
o'clock, in order to listen to the last anecdotes of the two jokers
who had remained long after their companions had gone to rest.

There is something to be learned even in a country store. We
are apt to believe that sharp trades, especially dishonest tricks and
unprincipled deceptions, are confined entirely to the city, and that
the unsophisticated men and women of the country do every thing
"on the square." I believe this to be measurably true, but know that
there are many exceptions to this rule. Many is the time I cut
open bundles of rags, brought to the store by country women in
exchange for goods, and declared to be all linen and cotton, that
contained quantities of worthless woollen trash in the interior, and
sometimes stones, gravel, ashes, etc. And sometimes, too, have I
(contrary to our usual practice) measured the load of oats, corn or
rye which our farmer-customer assured us contained a specified
number of bushels, perhaps sixty, and found it four or five bushels
short. Of course the astonished woman would impute the rag-
swindle to a servant or neighbor who had made it up without her
knowledge, and the man would charge carelessness upon his "help"
who measured the grain, and by mistake "made a wrong count."
These were exceptions to the general rule of honesty, but they
occurred with sufficient frequency to make us watchful of our customers, and to teach me the truth of the adage, "There's cheating
in all trades but ours."

Like most persons in the New England States, I was brought up
to attend church regularly on the Sabbath. Indeed, before I was
able to read, I was one of the first scholars in Sunday-school. We
had but one church or "meeting-house" in Bethel, (Presbyterian),
and here all attended. A difference in creeds and sects was scarcely
known in our little country village at that time. The old meeting-
house had neither steeple nor bell, but in summer time it was a

BARNUM AT THE TIME OF THE OPENING OF THE AMERICAN MUSEUM

Phineas Taylor, Barnum's Grandfather

comfortable place for the inhabitants to congregate. My good mother would teach me my lessons in the New Testament and the Catechism, and my highest aspiration was to get every word so perfectly as to obtain the reward of merit. This valuable pecuniary consideration consisted of a ticket which stated that the bearer was entitled to one mill "reward," so that ten tickets were worth one cent; and as this reward was not payable in cash, but in Sunday-school books at ten cents each, it follows that one hundred tickets would be required to purchase one book, so that a scholar must be successful every consecutive Sabbath (which was simply impossible) for the space of two years before he could come in possession of a tangible prize! Infinitesimal as was this recompense, it was sufficient to spur me to intense diligence.

During the Rev. Mr. Lowe's ministrations at Bethel, he formed a Bible class, of which I was a member. We used to draw promiscuously from a hat a text of scripture and write a composition on the text, which compositions were read after service in the afternoon, to such of the congregation as remained to hear the exercises of the class. Once, I remember, I drew the text, Luke x. 42: "But one thing is needful; and Mary hath chosen that good part which shall not be taken away her." *Question,* "What is the one thing needful?" My answer was nearly as follows:

"This question 'what is the one thing needful?' is capable of receiving various answers, depending much upon the persons to whom it is addressed. The merchant might answer that 'the one thing needful' is plenty of customers, who buy liberally, without beating down and pay cash for all their purchases.' The farmer might reply, that 'the one thing needful is large harvests and high prices.' The physician might answer that 'it is plenty of patients.' The lawyer might be of opinion that 'it is an unruly community, always engaged in bickerings and litigations.' The clergyman might reply, 'It is a fat salary with multitudes of sinners seeking salvation and paying large pew rents.' The bachelor might exclaim, 'It is a pretty wife who loves her husband, and who knows how to sew on buttons.' The maiden might answer, 'It is a good husband, who will love, cherish and protect me while life shall last.' But the most proper answer, and doubtless that which applied to the case of Mary, would be, 'The one thing needful is to believe on the Lord Jesus Christ, follow in his footsteps, love God and obey His commandments, love our fellow-man, and embrace every opportunity of administering to his necessities. In short, 'the one thing needful' is to live a life that we can always look back upon with satisfaction, and be enabled ever to contemplate its termination with trust in Him who has so kindly vouchsafed it to us, surrounding us with innumerable blessings, if we have but the heart and wisdom to receive them in a proper manner."

The reading of a portion of this answer occasioned some amusement in the congregation, in which the clergyman himself joined, and the name of "Taylor Barnum" was whispered in connection with the composition; but at the close of the reading I had the satisfaction of hearing Mr. Lowe say that it was a well written and truthful answer to the question, "What is the one thing needful?"

Previous to my visit to New York, I think it was in 1820, when I was ten years of age, I made my first expedition to my landed property, "Ivy Island." This, it will be remembered, was the gift of my grandfather, from whom I derived my name. From the time when I was four years old I was continually hearing of this "property." My grandfather always spoke of me (in my presence) to the neighbors and to strangers as the richest child in town, since I owned the whole of "Ivy Island," one of the most valuable farms in the State. My father and mother frequently reminded me of my wealth and hoped I would do something for the family when I attained my majority. The neighbors professed to fear that I might refuse to play with their children because I had inherited so large a property.

These constant allusions, for several years, to "Ivy Island" excited at once my pride and my curiosity and stimulated me to implore my father's permission to visit my property. At last, he promised I should do so in a few days, as we should be getting some hay near "Ivy Island." The wished for day at length arrived and my father told me that as we were to mow an adjoining meadow, I might visit my property in company with the hired man during the "nooning." My grandfather reminded me that it was to his bounty I was indebted for this wealth, and that had not my name been Phineas I might never have been proprietor of "Ivy Island." To this my mother added:

"Now, Taylor, don't become so excited when you see your property as to let your joy make you sick, for remember, rich as you are, that it will be eleven years before you can come into possession of your fortune."

She added much more good advice, to all of which I promised to be calm and reasonable and not to allow my pride to prevent me from speaking to my brothers and sisters when I returned home.

When we arrived at the meadow, which was in that part of the "Plum Trees" known as "East Swamp," I asked my father where "Ivy Island" was.

"Yonder, at the north end of this meadow, where you see those beautiful trees rising in the distance."

All the forenoon I turned grass as fast as two men could cut it, and after a hasty repast at noon, one of our hired men, a good natured Irishman, named Edmund, took an axe on his shoulder and announced that he was ready to accompany me to "Ivy Island." We started, and as we approached the north end of the meadow we found the ground swampy and wet and were soon obliged to leap from bog to bog on our route. A mis-step brought me up to my middle in water. To add to the dilemma a swarm of hornets attacked me. Attaining the altitude of another bog I was cheered by the assurance that there was only a quarter of a mile of this kind of travel to the edge of my property. I waded on. In about fifteen minutes more, after floundering through the morass, I found myself half-drowned, hornet-stung, mud-covered, and out of breath, on comparatively dry land.

"Never mind, my boy," said Edmund, "we have only to cross this little creek, and ye'll be upon your own valuable property."

We were on the margin of a stream, the banks of which were thickly covered with alders. I now discovered the use of Edmund's axe, for he felled a small oak to form a temporary bridge to my "Island" property. Crossing over, I proceeded to the centre of my domain; I saw nothing but a few stunted ivies and straggling trees. The truth flashed upon me. I had been the laughing-stock of the family and neighborhood for years. My valuable "Ivy Island" was an almost inaccessible, worthless bit of barren land, and while I stood deploring my sudden downfall, a huge black snake (one of my tenants) approached me with upraised head. I gave one shriek and rushed for the bridge.

This was my first, and, I need not say, my last visit to "Ivy Island." My father asked me how I liked my property, and I responded that I would sell it pretty cheap. My grandfather congratulated me upon my visit to my property as seriously as if it had been indeed a valuable domain. My mother hoped its richness had fully equalled my anticipations. The neighbors desired to know if I was not now glad I was named Phineas, and for five years forward I was frequently reminded of my wealth in "Ivy Island."

In the month of August, 1825, my maternal grandmother met with an accident which, although considered trivial at the time, resulted in her death. While walking in the garden she stepped upon the point of a rusty nail, which ran perhaps half an inch into her foot. It was immediately extracted, but the foot became swollen, and in a few days the most alarming symptoms were manifest. She was soon sensible that she was upon her death-bed, but she was a good Christian, and her approaching end had no terrors for her. The day before her departure, and while in full possession of her faculties, she sent for all her grandchildren to take their final leave of her. I never can forget the sensations which I experienced when my turn came to approach her bed-side, and when, taking my hand in hers, she spoke to me of her approaching dissolution, of the joys of religion, the consoling reflections that a death-bed afforded those who could feel that they had tried to live good lives and be of benefit to their fellow-men. She besought me to think seriously of religion, to read my Bible often, to pray to our Father in heaven, to be regular in my attendance at church; to use no profane nor idle language, and especially to remember that I could in no way so effectually prove my love to God, as in loving all my fellow-beings. I was affected to tears, and promised to remember her counsel. When I received from her a farewell kiss, knowing that I should never behold her again alive, I was completely overcome, and however much I may have since departed from her injunctions, the impressions received at that death-bed scene have ever been vivid among my recollections, and I trust they have proved in some degree salutary. A more sincere Christian or a more exemplary woman than my grandmother I have never seen.

CHAPTER III

AMONG the various ways which I had for making money on my own account, from the age of twelve to fifteen years, was that of lotteries. One of our neighbors, a pillar in the church, permitted his son to indulge in that line, the prizes consisting of cakes, oranges, molasses candy, etc.; and the morality of the things being thus established, I became a lottery manager and proprietor. The highest prize was generally five dollars—sometimes less, and sometimes as high as ten dollars. All the prizes in the lottery amounted to from twelve to twenty-five dollars. The cost of the entire tickets was twenty or twenty-five per cent. more than the prizes. I found no difficulty in disposing of my tickets to the workmen in the hat and comb manufactories, etc. Lotteries in those days were patronized by both Church and State. As a writer has said, "People would gamble in lotteries for the benefit of a church in which to preach against gambling."

My father was brought to his bed with a severe attack of fever in March, and departed this life, I trust for a better world, on the 7th of September, 1825, aged 48 years. I was then fifteen years of age. I stood by his bedside. The world looked dark indeed, when I realized that I was for ever deprived of my paternal protector! I felt that I was a poor inexperienced boy, thrown out on the wide world to shift for myself, and a sense of forlornness completely overcame me. My mother was left with five children. I was the oldest, and the youngest was only seven years of age. We followed the remains of husband and parent to their resting-place, and

20

returned to our desolate home, feeling that we were forsaken by the world, and that but little hope existed for us this side of the grave.

Administrators to the estate were appointed, and the fact was soon apparent that my father had not succeeded in providing any of this world's goods for the support of his family. The estate was declared insolvent, and it did not pay fifty cents upon a dollar. My mother, like many widows before her, was driven to many straits to support her little family, but being industrious, economical and persevering, she succeeded in a few years in redeeming the homestead and becoming its sole possessor. The few dollars which I had accumulated, I had loaned to my father, and held his note therefor, but it was decided that the property of a minor belonged to the father, and my claim was ruled out. I was subsequently compelled to earn as clerk in a store the money to pay for the pair of shoes that were purchased for me to wear at my father's funeral. I can truly say, therefore, that I began the world with nothing, and was barefooted at that.

I remained with Mr. Weed as clerk but a little longer, and then removed to Grassy Plain, a mile north-west of the village of Bethel, where I engaged with James S. Keeler and Lewis Whitlock, as clerk in their store, at six dollars per month and my board—my mother doing my washing. I soon entered into speculations on my own account, and by dint of economy succeeded in getting a little sum of money ahead. I boarded with Mrs. Jerusha Wheeler and her daughters, Jerusha and Mary. As nearly everybody had a nickname, the two former ladies were called "Rushia"—the old lady being designated "Aunt Rushia." They were an exceedingly nice and worthy family, and made me an excellent home. I chose my uncle Alanson Taylor as my "guardian," and was guided by his counsel. I was extremely active as a clerk, was considered a 'cute trader, and soon gained the confidence and esteem of my employers.

I remember with gratitude that they allowed me many facilities for earning money.

On one occasion a peddler called at our store with a large wagon filled with common green glass bottles of various sizes, holding from half a pint to a gallon. My employers were both absent, and I bantered him to trade his whole load of bottles in exchange for goods. Thinking me a greenhorn, he accepted my proposition, and I managed to pay him off in unsaleable goods at exorbitant prices. Soon after he departed, Mr. Keeler returned and found his little store half filled with bottles! "What under heavens have you been doing?" said he in surprise. "I have been trading goods for bottles," said I. "You have made a fool of yourself," he exclaimed, "for you have bottles enough to supply the whole town for twenty years." I begged him not to be alarmed, and promised to get rid of the entire lot within three months. "If you can do that," said he, "you can perform a miracle."

I then showed him the list of goods which I had exchanged for the bottles, with the extra prices annexed, and he found upon figuring that I had bartered a lot of worthless trash at a rate which brought the new merchandise to considerably less than one-half the wholesale price. He was pleased with the result, but wondered what could be done with the bottles. We stowed away the largest portion of them in the loft of our store.

My employers kept what was called a "barter" store. Many of the hat manufacturers traded there and paid us in hats, giving "store orders" to their numerous employees, including journeymen, apprentices, female hat trimmers, etc., etc. Of course we had a large number of customers, and I knew them all intimately. I may say that when I made the bottle trade I had a project in my head for selling them all, as well as getting rid of a large quantity of tinware which had been in the store for some years, and had become begrimed with dirt and fly-specks. That project was a lottery. On the first wet day, therefore, when there were but few customers, I spent several hours in making up my scheme. The highest prize was $25, payable in any kind of goods the customer desired. Then I had fifty prizes of $5 each, designating in my scheme what goods each prize should consist of. For instance, one $5 prize consisted of one pair cotton hose, one cotton handkerchief, two tin cups, four pint glass bottles, three tin skimmers, one quart glass bottle, six tin nutmeg graters, eleven half-pint glass bottles, etc., etc.—the glass and tinware always forming the greater portion of each prize. I had one hundred prizes of one dollar each, one hundred prizes of fifty cents each, and three hundred prizes of twenty-five cents each. There were one thousand tickets at fifty cents each. The prizes amounted to the same as the tickets—$500. I had taken an idea from the church lottery, in which my grandfather was manager, and had many prizes of only half the cost of the tickets. I headed the scheme with glaring capitals, written in my best hand, setting forth that it was a "MAGNIFICENT LOTTERY!" "$25 FOR ONLY 50 CTS.!!" "OVER 550 PRIZES!!!" "ONLY 1000 TICKETS!!!!" "GOODS PUT IN AT THE LOWEST CASH PRICES!!!!!" etc., etc., etc.

The tickets went like wildfire. Customers did not stop to consider the nature of the prizes. Journeymen hatters, boss hatters, apprentice boys, and hat trimming girls bought tickets. In ten days they were all sold. A day was fixed for the drawing of the lottery, and it came off punctually, as announced. The next day, and for several days thereafter, adventurers came for their prizes. A young lady who had drawn five dollars would find herself entitled to a piece of tape, a spool of cotton, a paper of pins, sixteen tin skimmers, cups, and nutmeg graters, and a few dozen glass bottles of various sizes! She would beg me to retain the glass and tinware and pay her in some other goods, but was informed that such a proceeding would be contrary to the rules of the establishment and could not be entertained for a moment.   One man would find all his prizes to consist of tinware.   Another would discover that out of twenty tickets, he had drawn perhaps ten prizes, and that they consisted entirely of glass bottles.   Some of the customers were vexed, but most of them laughed at the joke.   The basket loads, the arms full, and the bags full of soiled tin and glass bottles which were carried out of our store during the first few days after the lottery drawing, constituted a series of most ludicrous scenes.   Scarcely a customer was permitted to depart without one or more specimens of tin or green glass.   Within ten days every glass bottle had disappeared, and the old tinware was replaced by a smaller quantity as bright as silver.   My grandfather enjoyed my lottery speculation very much, and seemed to agree with many others, who declared that I was indeed "a chip of the old block."

On Saturday nights I usually went to Bethel to remain with my mother and attend church on the Sabbath.   My mother continued for some years to keep the village tavern.   One Saturday evening a violent thunder shower came up; it was very dark, and rained in torrents, with occasional intervals of a few minutes.   Miss Mary Wheeler (who was a milliner) sent word across to the store that there was a girl at her house from Bethel, who had come up on horseback to obtain her new bonnet, that she was afraid to return home alone, and if I was going to Bethel on horseback that night, she wished me to escort her customer.   I assented, and in a few minutes my horse was at "Aunt Rushia's" door.   I went in, and was introduced to a fair, rosy-cheeked, buxom-looking girl, with beautiful white teeth, named "Chairy" Hallett.   Of course "Chairy" was a nickname, which I subsequently learned meant "Charity."   I assisted the young lady into her saddle, was soon mounted on my own horse, and we trotted slowly towards Bethel.

The brief view that I had of this girl by candle-light had sent

BARNUM'S BIRTHPLACE IN BETHEL, CONNECTICUT

BARNUM'S STORE
IN BETHEL

all sorts of agreeable sensations through my bosom. I was in a state of feeling quite new to me, and as unaccountable as it was novel. I opened a conversation with her, and finding her affable and in no degree prim or "stuck-up," (although she was on horseback), I regretted that the distance to Bethel was not five miles instead of one. A vivid flash of lightning at that moment lighted up the horizon, and gave me a fair view of the face of my interesting companion. I then wished the distance was twenty miles at the least. I was not long in learning that she was a tailoress, working with Mr. Zerah Benedict, of Bethel. The tailoring trade stood much higher in my estimation from that moment than it ever did before. We soon arrived at Bethel, and bidding my fair companion good night, I went to my mother's. That girl's face haunted me in my dreams that night. I saw her the next day at church, and on every subsequent Sunday for some time, but no opportunity offered that season for me to renew the acquaintance.

Messrs. Keeler and Whitlock sold out their store of goods to Mr. Lewis Taylor in the summer of 1827. I remained a short time as clerk to Mr. Taylor. They have a proverb in Connecticut, that "the best school in which to have a boy learn human nature, is to permit him to be a tin peddler for a few years." I think his chances for getting "his eye-teeth cut" would be equally great in a country barter store like that in which I was clerk. As before stated, many of our customers were hatters, and we took hats in payment for goods. The large manufacturers generally dealt pretty fairly by us, but some of the smaller fry occasionally shaved us prodigiously. There probably is no trade in which there can be more cheating than in hats. If a hat was damaged "in coloring" or otherwise, perhaps by a cut of half a foot in length, it was sure to be patched up, smoothed over, and slipped in with others, to send to the store. Among the furs used for the nap of hats in those days, were beaver, Russia, nutria, otter, coney, muskrat, etc., etc. The best fur was otter, the poorest was coney.

The hatters mixed their inferior furs with a little of their best, and sold us the hats for "otter." We in return mixed our sugars, teas, and liquors, and gave them the most valuable names. It was "dog eat dog"—"tit for tat." Our cottons were sold for wool, our wool and cotton for silk and linen; in fact nearly every thing was different from what it was represented. The customers cheated us in their fabrics: we cheated the customers with our goods. Each party expected to be cheated, if it was possible. Our eyes, and not our ears, had to be our masters. We must believe little that we saw, and less that we heard. Our calicoes were all "fast colors," according to our representations, and the colors would generally run "fast" enough and show them a tub of soap-suds. Our ground coffee was as good as burned peas, beans, and corn could make, and our ginger was tolerable, considering the price of corn meal. The "tricks of trade" were numerous. If a "peddler" wanted to trade with us for a box of beaver hats worth sixty dollars per dozen, he was sure to obtain a box of "coneys" which were dear at fifteen dollars per dozen. If we took our pay in clocks, warranted to keep good time, the chances were that they were no better than a chest of drawers for that purpose—that they were like Pindar's razors, "made to sell," and if half the number of wheels necessary to form a clock could be found within the case, it was as lucky as extraordinary.

"As drunk as a hatter" has long since passed into a proverb. There were some sober hatters in the times of which I write, but there were also many drinking ones. The hatters from out of town bought their rum by the keg or barrel, while those on Grassy Plains kept a man whose almost sole duty it was to go to and from the store and shops with half a dozen rum-bottles of various sizes. Some of these bottles were replenished several times in a day.

My business, of course, included the filling of rum-bottles. I suppose I have drawn and bottled more rum than would be necessary to float a ship.

Such a school would "cut eye-teeth," but if it did not cut conscience, morals, and integrity all up by the roots, it would be because the scholars quit before their education was completed!

CHAPTER IV

IN the autumn of 1826 Mr. Oliver Taylor, who had removed from Danbury to Brooklyn, Long Island, a few years previously, offered me the position of clerk in his grocery store. He had also a large comb factory in Brooklyn and a comb store in New York. I accepted Mr. Taylor's offer. The store was at the corner of Sands and Pearl streets. Many of our customers were early ones, to buy articles for their breakfasts, and I was obliged to rise before daylight. This was so different from my previous habits, that I had much difficulty in waking in the morning. To aid me in my endeavors at diligence, I arranged with a watchman, at two shillings per week, to pull a string which hung out of my chamber-window in the third story, one end being fastened to my big toe. The arrangement fully answered the purpose, but Mr. Taylor became acquainted with it, through the watchman I believe; and on one occasion there was a more violent pulling than I had bargained for. I howled with pain, ran to the window, and bade the watchman desist, else he would pull my toe off. Not suspecting a trick, I dressed myself, went down stairs, and discovered that it was only half-past twelve o'clock! It was a long time before I ascertained who my tormentor was, though I might reasonably have suspected Oliver; but after that adventure I managed to wake without assistance, and discharged the watchman *in toto*.

I had not been long in Mr. Taylor's employment before I became conversant with the routine of the business, and the purchasing of all the goods for the store was soon intrusted to me. I bought for cash entirely, and thus was enabled to exercise my judgment in making purchases—sometimes going into all sections of the lower part of the city in search of the cheapest markets for groceries. I also frequently attended the wholesale auctions of teas, sugars, molasses, etc., so that by watching the sales, noting the prices, and recording the names of buyers, I knew what profits they were realizing, and how far I could probably beat them down for cash. At these auctions I occasionally made the acquaintance of several grocers who wanted small lots of the goods offered for sale, and we frequently clubbed together and bid off a lot which, being divided between us, gave each about the quantity he desired, and at a reduced price from what we should have been compelled to pay if the goods had passed into other hands and thus been taxed with another profit.

My employer manifested great interest in me, and treated me with the utmost kindness, but the situation did not suit me. The fact is, there are some persons so constituted that they can never be satisfied to labor for a fixed salary, let it be never so great. I am one of that sort. My disposition is, and ever was, of a speculative character, and I am never content to engage in any business unless it is of such a nature that my profits may be greatly enhanced by an increase of energy, perseverance, attention to business, tact, etc. As therefore I had no opportunity to speculate on my own account in this Brooklyn store, I soon became uneasy. Young as I was (and probably because I was so young), I began to think seriously of going into business for myself, and although I had no capital to start on, several men of means had offered to furnish the money and join me in business. I was just then at an uneasy age—in a transition state—neither boy nor man—an age when it is of the highest importance that a youth should have some discreet friend and instructor on whose good counsel he can rely.

In the summer of 1827 I caught the small-pox, which, although

I had been vaccinated successfully some eight years previously, assumed a very severe type of varioloid. This confined me to the house for several months. The expense attending my sickness made a sad inroad upon my funds. As soon as I was sufficiently recovered, I started for home to spend a few weeks in recruiting my health, taking passage on board a sloop for Norwalk. When the passengers, numbering twenty ladies and gentlemen, came on board, they were frightened at the appearance of my face, which still bore strong marks of the disease from which I had just recovered. By an unanimous vote I was requested to go on shore, and Captain Munson Hoyt, whom I well knew, having been in the habit of visiting his sloop weekly for the purchase of butter, eggs, etc., informed me that he was pained in conveying to me the wishes of the affrighted passengers. Of course I felt compelled to comply, and left the sloop with a heavy heart. I lodged that night at Holt's old hotel in Fulton street, and the next morning went to Norwalk by steamboat, reaching Bethel the same afternoon.

I spent several weeks with my mother, who was unremitting in her exertions to make me comfortable. During my convalescence I visited my old schoolmates and neighbors generally, and had several opportunities of slightly renewing the short acquaintance which I had formed with the attractive tailoress "Chairy" Hallett, while escorting her on horseback, from Grassy Plains to Bethel, in the thunder shower. These opportunities did not lessen the regard which I felt for the young lady, nor did they serve to render my sleep any sounder. However, "I did not tell my love," and the "worm in the bud" did not feed on my "pock-marked cheek."

At the end of four weeks I again left the maternal roof and departed for Brooklyn. In a short time I made arrangements for opening a porter-house on "my own hook," in the neighborhood of the grocery store; and, giving Mr. Taylor the requisite notice of my desire to leave his employment, he engaged a practised hand as my successor, and I opened the porter-house. Within a few months I found an opportunity of selling out to advantage, and as I had a good offer to engage as clerk in a similar establishment kept by Mr. David Thorp, 29 Peck Slip, New York, I sold out and removed thither. Mr. Thorp's place was a great resort of the Danbury and Bethel comb-makers, hatters, etc., and this giving me a constant opportunity of seeing my townsmen, made it very agreeable. I boarded in Mr. Thorp's family, who used me very kindly. He allowed me frequent opportunities of visiting the theatre with such of my companions as came to New York. I had much taste for the drama—soon became, in my own opinion, a close critic, and did not fail to exhibit my powers in this respect to all the juveniles from Connecticut who accompanied me to the theatre.

My habits generally were not bad. Although constantly engaged in selling liquor to others, I probably never drank a pint of liquor, wine, or cordials, before I was twenty-two years of age. I always attended church regularly, and was never without a Bible in my trunk, which I took frequent occasion to read.

In February, 1828, my grandfather wrote me that if I would come to Bethel and establish some kind of business for myself, he would allow me to occupy, rent free, one-half of his carriage-house. I had a strong desire to return to my native village, and after several weeks' reflection I accepted his offer. The carriage-house referred to was situated on the public street in Bethel, and I concluded to finish off one part of it, and open a retail fruit and confectionery store. Before leaving New York, I consulted several fruit dealers with whom I was acquainted, and made arrangements for sending them my orders. I then went to Bethel, arranged the building, put in a small stock of goods, including a barrel of ale, and opened my establishment on the first Monday morning in May, 1828, that being our military training day.

The hopes and fears which agitated me for weeks previously to this, my first grand opening, have probably never had a parallel in all my subsequent adventures. I was worth about one hundred and twenty dollars, and I invested all I possessed in this enterprise. It cost me fifty dollars to fit up my little store, and seventy dollars more purchased my stock in trade. I am suspicious that I received little good from attending church the day previously to opening my store, for I distinctly remember being greatly exercised in mind for fear it would rain the next day, and thus diminish the number of customers for my cakes, candies, nuts, raisins, etc.

I was up betimes on Monday morning, and was delighted to find the weather propitious. The country people began to flock into the village at an early hour, and the novelty of my little shop, which was set out in as good style as I was capable of, attracted their attention. I soon had plenty to do, and before noon was obliged to call in one of my old school-mates to assist me in waiting upon my numerous customers. Business continued brisk during the whole day and evening, and when I closed I had the satisfaction of counting out sixty-three dollars as my day's receipts! My entire barrel of ale was sold, but the assortment of other goods was not broken up, nor apparently very seriously diminished, so that although I had received the entire cost of my goods, less seven dollars, the stock on hand showed that my profits had been excellent.

I need not attempt to relate how gratified I was by the result of my first day's experiment. I considered my little store as a "fixed fact," and such it proved to be. I put in another barrel of ale, and proceeding to New York, expended all of my money for a small stock of fancy goods, and such articles as I thought would find a ready sale. My assortment included pocket-books, combs, beads, cheap finger-rings, pocket-knives, and a few toys. My business continued good during the summer, and in the fall I added stewed oysters to my assortment.

My grandfather had great pleasure in my success, and advised me to take the agency of some lottery dealer for the sale of lottery tickets on commission. Lotteries were at that time legal in Connecticut, and were generally considered as legitimate a branch of business as any other. I therefore adopted my grandfather's advice, and obtained an agency for selling lottery tickets on a commission of ten per cent. This business, connected with the fruit, confectionery, oyster, and toy establishment, rendered my profits quite satisfactory.

On one occasion a young man of my acquaintance called to examine some pocket-books. He inquired the prices, and finally selected one that pleased him. He said he would take it, but he desired me to give him a credit on it for a few weeks. I told him that had he wanted any article of necessity which I had for sale, I would not object to trusting him a short time, but it struck me that a pocket-book was something of a superfluity for a person who had no money. He replied that it did not strike him in that light, and that he did not see why it was not as proper to seek credit for a pocket-book as for anything else. He however failed to convince me of the necessity of his possessing such an article until he had something to put into it, and I therefore declined his proposition.

About this time I made arrangements to go to Pittsburgh, Pa., with Mr. Samuel Sherwood, of Bridgeport, on an exploring expedition. I had heard that there was a fine opening in that city for a lottery office, and Sherwood and myself concluded to try our fortunes there, provided we found the prospects equal to our anticipations. We called at the office of the New York managers, Yates & McIntyre, and had an interview with their chief business man, Mr. Dudley S. Gregory—subsequently mayor and a large proprietor in Jersey City. Mr. Gregory did not think favorably of Pittsburgh, but, after an hour's conversation with me, he offered me the entire lottery agency for the State of Tennessee, if I would go

to Nashville and open an office there.   The proposition was tempt-
ing, but I feared the distance was too great to meet the approbation
of a certain tailoress in Bethel whose wishes I felt bound to consult,
for special reasons.   I therefore declined giving an answer for two
weeks.   In the mean time, Sherwood and myself having given up
the Pittsburgh trip, concluded to go to Philadelphia for a pleasure
excursion.   We went in a morning boat to New Brunswick, where
the passengers all took stages to Bordentown, a distance of perhaps
thirty miles through the sand, where we again took steamboat to
Philadelphia, arriving there about dusk.   We put up at Congress
Hall in Chestnut street, where we experienced rather taller living
than we had ever before met with.   The array of waiters, napkins,
and other et-ceteras, as well as a frequent change of plates, was
something entirely ahead of all our former experience; but we lay
off like old stagers, and lived in clover for a week, going to the
theatre every night, and riding in our coach every day.   On Sunday, we listened to the chiming bells of Christ Church with great
satisfaction, it being the first we had ever heard.   At last we concluded to start for home.   Our hotel bill astonished us beyond
measure, and awakened serious apprehensions in regard to our
ability to raise sufficient funds to reach home.   Counting up both
our piles, we found that our fears were not without foundation.
We had been foolishly extravagant in our outlays, and after paying
our hotel bills and securing our tickets for New York, we had only
twenty-seven cents left!   This was decidedly a close shave.   Fortunately we discovered our dilemma before breakfast, and as that
meal had been included in our bill, each of us embraced the opportunity, while sipping our coffee, to pocket a few biscuits, which
sufficed us for a dinner we could not buy.   As we were about leaving
the hotel, the boot-black asked us to remember him, to which Sherwood replied that it was an imposition: he had always while travelling been accustomed to have his boot-blacking included in the bill,

and he would not stand it. I tried to look indignant also, but was overcome, and putting my hand in my pocket, drew forth a quarter dollar, and handed to the polisher of our "understandings". This reduced our capital to two cents, and with this we started, saying to the porter that, merely for the sake of the exercise, we preferred to carry our own trunks.

Living all day upon our biscuits and cold water, we reached New York, and carried our baggage to Holt's Hotel in Fulton street, a distance of about a mile. In the morning, Sherwood borrowed a couple of dollars from a Bridgeport friend, and proceeding to Newark, obtained the loan of fifty dollars from his friend and cousin, Dr. Sherwood. He loaned me one-half the amount, and after sojourning a few days in New York, we returned home. I do not know what Sherwood's feelings were, but I was forcibly reminded, as I have often been since, of the old adage, that "a fool and his money are soon parted."

Our visit to the New York lottery managers greatly enlightened me in regard to the profits of that line of business. I had been in the habit of selling tickets for Washington Yale, the editor and printer in Danbury, also for O. W. Sherwood and his cousin Samuel of Bridgeport, for a commission of 10 to 15 per cent.; but in my interviews with Mr. Gregory, I learned that the managers, taking to themselves the fifteen per cent. deducted on all prizes, furnished tickets to their agents at what was called "scheme price," which allowed the agents from 25 to 30 per cent. profit. The lotteries being drawn by combination numbers, the public generally had no knowledge whatever of the number of tickets in a lottery; the managers, therefore, made the prizes amount to less than the retail price of tickets by 25 or 30 per cent. This extra per centage was a shave additional to the 15 per cent. allowed in old-fashioned lotteries. I also learned that the process of arriving at the number of tickets in a lottery is this: Multiply the three highest combination numbers and divide by six; the quotient is the number of tickets.

After learning the profitable basis of the foregoing facts, I went to our Connecticut lottery managers, and from that time obtained my tickets directly from them at "the scheme price." In my turn I established agents all through the country, and my profits were immense. I sold from five hundred to two thousand dollars' worth of tickets per day. About this time my uncle Alanson Taylor joined me as a partner in the lottery business, and proved a very efficient salesman.

On one occasion I sold a package of quarter tickets to my aunt Laura Nichols and a neighbor of hers for $25. Before the lottery was drawn the neighbor sickened of her bargain and begged me to take the tickets back, and my aunt consented. When the mail brought the drawn numbers from Hartford, I had the package of tickets on hand. Not desiring to risk that amount of money, I induced eight of my customers to join me in the purchase of the package. We then opened the letter containing the drawn numbers, and found that we had drawn a quarter of the highest prize, $15,000. This result gave myself and eight others a profit of $350 each. The fact was duly announced, and my aunt never ceased to blame her timid neighbor nor to lament her own ill fortune. The great luck of drawing the highest prize spread like wild-fire, as usual in such cases, and the country, for miles around, was lottery-crazy. Our sales increased immensely.

Fully appreciating the powers of the press, (to which more than to any other one cause I am indebted for my success in life,) I did not fail to invoke the aid of "printer's ink." I issued handbills, circulars, etc., by tens of thousands, with striking prefixes, affixes, staring capitals, marks of wonder, pictures, etc. The newspapers throughout the region teemed with unique advertisements. Immense gold signs, and placards in inks and papers of all colors, covered my lottery office. As the curious letters of "Joe Strickland" were highly popular at that time, I advertised my office as being under the special favor and protection of "Dr. Peter Strickland," own blood cousin to the renowned Joe Strickland, etc. In my bills and advertisements, I rung all possible changes upon the renowned name. "The ever lucky Dr. Strickland," "Five more capital prizes sold by Dr. Strickland!" "A fortune for a dollar—apply to Fortune's favorite, Dr. Strickland," "Another mammoth prize!—huzza for Dr. Strickland," etc., etc. Home-made poetry was also frequently brought into requisition to set forth the inducements for patronizing my office. Customers who brought their tickets and found them blanks were told that their only wise plan was to "look for their money where they lost it,"—"it was a long lane that never turned,"—"such bad luck could not continue long," etc., etc.

The lucky drawers of the high prize before mentioned gave an oyster supper at my mother's tavern to about sixty persons, (whom I invited, knowing them to be good ticket customers) ; and after the supper was finished, I counted out the prize-money to the elated holders of the fortunate ticket. This so excited our guests, that a package of tickets, amounting to one thousand dollars, was forthwith sealed up and bought by fifty subscribers on the spot, at $20 each.

Selling so many tickets as I did, a prize of one or two thousand dollars, and numerous smaller ones, must occasionally turn up. These, being duly trumpeted, rendered mine the "lucky office" in the estimation of many. I received orders from distant parts of the country by mail, and sent out tickets on commission by post-riders and others. Among my "private customers" were a number of clergymen and deacons; and occasionally some of the weak brothers of the "Shakers," who came to Bethel to sell garden seeds, bought a few lottery tickets "on the sly."

Whenever I visited Brookfield I called on one man who was of a serious turn.   He and his wife were professors of religion, and he was a frequent exhorter at prayer meetings.   He always managed to buy a ticket or two from me, under the strictest injunction never to divulge the fact to his wife.   I usually dined with him; and when he was busy looking after my horse, or otherwise engaged out of doors, I never failed to sell a ticket to his wife, who begged me to be very careful not to let her husband have any suspicion of it, for he was opposed to such things, and would never forgive her if he should know there was a lottery ticket in the house.

I still kept a close eye upon the attractive tailoress, Charity Hallett; and although my good mother and some other relatives feared that I was not looking high enough in the world, those who knew the girl best declared that she was an industrious, excellent, sensible, and well-behaved girl, and some of them added that "she was altogether too good for Taylor Barnum."   I perfectly agreed with them in their conclusions, and in the summer of 1829 I proved it by asking her hand in marriage.   My suit was accepted, and the wedding day appointed.   In the mean time I applied myself closely to business, no person suspecting that the "event" was near at hand.

In October my sweetheart went to New York, ostensibly to visit her uncle, Nathan Beers, who resided at No. 3 Orchard street.   I left home on Saturday, November 7, for New York, having particular occasion to purchase goods for our little store.   On the next evening, by the aid of the Rev. Dr. McAuley, and in the presence of sundry relatives and friends of hers, the tailoress changed her name to Mrs. Charity Barnum, and I became the husband of one of the best women that was ever created.   I was at that time little more than nineteen years of age.   I have long felt assured, that had I waited twenty years longer, I could not have found another woman so well suited to my disposition, and so valuable as a wife, a mother,

BARNUM AT 76

CHARITY HALLETT, BARNUM'S FIRST WIFE

and a friend; yet I do not approve of nor recommend too early marriages.

The bride and bridegroom returned to Bethel the same week, and took board in the family where she had previously resided. My mother received me as if nothing had happened, and made no allusion to the wedding. She evidently felt chagrined at the clandestine manner of my marriage; but I called on her every day with the same freedom that I had ever done, and within a month she invited me to bring "my wife" and spend the following Sabbath with her. I did so; and from that day to this, I am sure that neither she nor any other person ever said or believed that I had not been extremely fortunate in the selection of my companion.

In the winter of 1829-30, I opened a lottery office in the village of Danbury, still keeping up the Bethel office, as well as branches in Norwalk, Stamford, Middletown, etc., and a host of small agencies all through the country, for thirty miles around. In June, 1830, I purchased from my grandfather three acres of land in Bethel, a few rods south of the village, for the purpose of erecting a dwelling thereon. Lewis Osborne, the builder, put me up a two-and-a-half story house, 26 by 30 feet, for ten hundred and fifty dollars, and my wife and myself moved into it and commenced housekeeping the ensuing spring.

My ticket sales were now confined in a great measure to a few large customers, who bought liberally, and to whom I gave a credit. Leaving these "large customers" in the hands of a trusty clerk, I went into a book speculation for a couple of months. I purchased books at auction and otherwise in New York, and taking them around the country, advertised and sold them at auction, I acting as auctioneer. I did tolerably well, with two exceptions. I held my auction one night at Litchfield, Ct. The law school was located there at that time. The students were among my customers, and they managed to steal a large number of the most costly books. The same thing was done in Newburgh, N. Y., and I quit the auction business in disgust.

In the same spring of 1831, I put up a building in Bethel, known as "the yellow store," making it sufficiently capacious to accommodate a family in the second and third stories. In July, 1831, my uncle Alanson and myself opened the establishment with an assortment of goods, such as are usually found in a country store, consisting of dry goods, groceries, hardware, crockery, etc., etc. Like most persons who engage in a business which they do not understand, we were unsuccessful in the enterprise, and on the 17th of October I bought out my uncle's interest, as will be seen by the following advertisement, which I cut from a newspaper dated the 20th of that month:

"DISSOLUTION.—The firm of TAYLOR & BARNUM is this day dissolved by mutual consent.

ALANSON TAYLOR,
PHINEAS T. BARNUM.

"☞The business will be conducted in future by P. T. BARNUM, who will sell all kinds of dry goods, groceries, crockery, etc., etc., 25 per cent. cheaper than any of his neighbors.

"Bethel, Oct. 17, 1831."

CHAPTER V

ABOUT this time, circumstances partly religious and partly political in their character led me into still another field of enterprise which honorably opened to me that notoriety of which in later life I surely have had a surfeit. Considering my youth, this new enterprise reflected credit upon my ability, as well as energy, and so I may be excused if I now recur to it with something like pride.

In a period of strong political excitement, I wrote several communications for the Danbury weekly paper, setting forth what I conceived to be the dangers of a sectarian interference which was then apparent in political affairs. The publication of these communications was refused and I accordingly purchased a press and types, and October 19, 1831, I issued the first number of my own paper, *The Herald of Freedom*.

I entered upon the editorship of this journal with all the vigor and vehemence of youth. The boldness with which the paper was conducted soon excited wide-spread attention and commanded a circulation which extended beyond the immediate locality into nearly every State in the Union. But lacking that experience which induces caution, and without the dread of consequences, I frequently laid myself open to the charge of libel and three times in three years I was prosecuted. A Danbury butcher, a zealous politician, brought a civil suit against me for accusing him of being a spy in a Democratic caucus. On the first trial the jury did not agree, but after a second trial I was fined several hundred dollars. Another libel suit against me was withdrawn and need not be men-

tioned further. The third was sufficiently important to warrant
the following detail:

A criminal prosecution was brought against me for stating in
my paper that a man in Bethel, prominent in the church, had "been
guilty of taking *usury* of an orphan boy," and for severely com-
menting on the fact in my editorial columns. When the case came
to trial the truth of my statement was substantially proved by several witnesses and even by the prosecuting party. But "the greater
the truth, the greater the libel," and then I had used the term
"usury," instead of extortion, or note-shaving, or some other expression which might have softened the verdict. The result was
that I was sentenced to pay a fine of one hundred dollars and to be
imprisoned in the common jail for sixty days.

The most comfortable provision was made for me in Danbury
jail. My room was papered and carpeted; I lived well; I was overwhelmed with the constant visits of my friends; I edited my paper
as usual and received large accessions to my subscription list; and
at the end of my sixty days' term the event was celebrated by a
large concourse of people from the surrounding country. The court
room in which I was convicted was the scene of the celebration.
An ode, written for the occasion, was sung; an eloquent oration on
the freedom of the press was delivered; and several hundred gentlemen afterwards partook of a sumptuous dinner followed by appropriate toasts and speeches. Then came the triumphant part of
the ceremonial, which was reported in my paper of December 12,
1832, as follows:

"P. T. BARNUM and the band of music took their seats in a coach
drawn by six horses, which had been prepared for the occasion. The
coach was preceded by forty horsemen, and a marshal, bearing the
national standard. Immediately in the rear of the coach was the carriage of the Orator and the President of the day, followed by the Committee of Arrangements and sixty carriages of citizens, which joined in
escorting the editor to his home in Bethel.

"When the procession commenced its march amidst the roar of cannon, three cheers were given by several hundred citizens who did not join in the procession. The band of music continued to play a variety of national airs until their arrival in Bethel, (a distance of three miles,) when they struck up the beautiful and appropriate tune of 'Home, Sweet Home!' After giving three hearty cheers, the procession returned to Danbury. The utmost harmony and unanimity of feeling prevailed throughout the day, and we are happy to add that no accident occurred to mar the festivities of the occasion."

My editorial career was one of continual contest. I however published the 160th number of *The Herald of Freedom* in Danbury, November 5, 1834, after which my brother-in-law, John W. Amerman, issued the paper for me at Norwalk till the following year, when the *Herald* was sold to Mr. George Taylor.

Meanwhile, I had taken Horace Fairchild into partnership in my mercantile business, in 1831, and I had sold out to him and to a Mr. Toucey, in 1833, they forming a partnership under the firm of Fairchild & Co. So far as I was concerned my store was not a success. Ordinary trade was too slow for me. I bought largely and in order to sell I was compelled to give extensive credits. Hence I had an accumulation of bad debts; and my old ledger presents a long series of accounts balanced by "death," by "running away," by "failing," and by other similarly remunerative returns. I had expended money as freely as I had gained it, for I had already learned that I could make money rapidly and in large sums when I set about it with a will, and hence I did not realize the worth of what I seemed to gain so readily. I looked forward to a future of saving when I should see the need of accumulation.

In the winter of 1834-35, I removed my family to New York, having hired a house in Hudson street. Strictly speaking, I entered that great city to "seek my fortune." Lotteries in the State of Connecticut had been prohibited by law; I had lost large amounts of money by my private customers, some of whom had gone beyond

their means in purchasing tickets, while others had put their property out of their hands, and thus defrauded me of considerable
sums. When I moved to New York I had no pecuniary resources
except such as were derived from old debts left in the hands of an
agent in Bethel for collection. I had hoped to find an opening with
some mercantile firm in New York, where for my services I could
receive a portion of the profits, for I had a disposition which ever
revolted at laboring for a fixed salary. I wanted an opportunity
where my faculties and energies could have full play, and where
the amount of profits should depend entirely upon the amount of
tact, perseverance, and energy which I contributed to the business.
But I could not find the situation I coveted. My resources began
to fail me, and, my family being in ill-health, I found it difficult to
maintain them. In order to do so, I secured the situation of "drum-
mer" to several stores, including the cap and stock store of Mr.
Chapman in Chatham street, the proprietors of which allowed me
a small commission on all sales which they made to customers whom
I introduced.

This of course was only a temporary arrangement, and, like
"Micawber," I was continually on the look-out for something better
to "turn up." Every morning at sunrise my eyes were running
over the columns of "Wants" in the New York *Sun,* hoping to hit
upon something that would suit me. Many is the wild-goose chase
which I had in pursuit of a situation so beautifully and temptingly
set forth among those "wants." Fortunes equalling that of Crœsus,
and as plenty as blackberries, were dangling from many an advertisement which mysteriously invited the reader to apply at Room
No. 16, in the fifth story of a house in some retired and uninviting
locality; but when I had wended my way up flights of dark, rickety,
greasy stairs, and through sombre, narrow passages, I would find
that my fortune depended firstly upon my advancing a certain sum
of money, from three dollars to five hundred as the case might be;

and secondly, upon my success in peddling a newly discovered patent life-pill, an ingenious mouse-trap, or something of the sort.

I remember that, on one occasion, an advertisement was headed, "IMMENSE SPECULATION on a small capital!—$10,000 easily made in one year! Apply to Professor——, at Scudder's American Museum." I had long fancied that I could succeed if I could only get hold of a public exhibition, and I hastened with all dispatch to call on the kind Professor who held forth such flattering promises at the Museum. Being ushered upon the stage of the lecture-room in the third story, I was grieved to find a dozen applicants already ahead of me. I instantly sought out the Professor, and calling him aside, took a few moments to recover myself, for I was nearly out of breath from running so fast up stairs, and then I asked him whether he had yet disposed of his speculation. "Not positively, but several customers are ready to close with me immediately," was the Professor's reply. "I beg of you to give me a chance; you will find me just the man you want," I replied with great earnestness. "Well, as you are so anxious, and seem to be a young man of energy, I will give you the first chance," replied the kind Professor. I felt exceedingly grateful, and asked him the nature of his enterprise. "I am the proprietor of the great Hydro-oxygen Microscope," said he. "It is the most extraordinary instrument now extant. Its public exhibition through the country would in a very short period secure to its owner an independence. My health is feeble, and I will sell for only two thousand dollars; one thousand cash—the balance in sixty and ninety days, on good security." My golden visions vanished, and I abruptly informed the Professor that I declined becoming a purchaser of his instrument.

One morning I found in the *Sun* an advertisement for a bar-keeper, application to be made to Wm. Niblo. I proceeded at once to Niblo's Garden, and there, for the first time in my life, saw its gentlemanly and justly-popular proprietor. Upon stating my business, Mr. Niblo informed me that he wished to employ a well-behaved and reliable man, who was competent to fill the vacant situation, who could produce the highest testimonials of his integrity, and who would bind himself to remain in the situation for three years. This last condition, of course, clashed with my arrangements, as I sought the situation only as a means of temporary relief, being determined at an early day, if possible, to secure a place such as I have before described.

All my running at the beck of advertisers finally benefited me nothing. I obtained no situation during the entire winter. Early in the spring I received several hundred dollars from my agent in Bethel, and finding no other business to suit me, I opened a small private boarding-house at No. 52 Frankfort street, on the 1st May, 1835. I intended this mostly for transient boarders, consisting of my acquaintances in Connecticut who had occasion to visit New York. We soon had a good share of custom, but not having sufficient employment for my time I purchased an interest in a grocery store, No. 156 South street, in company with Mr. John Moody.

CHAPTER VI

BY this time it was clear to my mind that my proper position in this busy world was not yet reached. I had displayed the faculty of getting money, as well as getting rid of it; but the business for which I was destined, and, I believe, made, had not yet come to me; or rather, I had not found that I was to cater for that insatiate want of human nature—the love of amusement; that I was to make a sensation on two continents; and that fame and fortune awaited me so soon as I should appear before the public in the character of a showman. These things I had not foreseen. I did not seek the position or the character. The business finally came in my way; I fell into the occupation, and far beyond any of my predecessors on this continent, I have succeeded.

The least deserving of all my efforts in the show line was the one which introduced me to the business; a scheme in no sense of my own devising; one which had been some time before the public and which had so many vouchers for its genuineness that at the time of taking possession of it I honestly believed it to be genuine; something, too, which, as I have said, I did not seek, but which by accident came in my way and seemed almost to compel my agency —such was the "Joice Heth" exhibition which first brought me forward as a showman.

In the latter part of July, 1835, Mr. Coley Bartram, of Reading, Connecticut, called at our store. He was acquainted with Mr. Moody and myself. He informed us that he had owned an interest in an extraordinary negro woman, named JOICE HETH, whom he

47

believed to be one hundred and sixty-one years of age, and whom he also believed to have been the nurse of General Washington. He had sold out his interest to his partner R. W. Lindsay, of Jefferson County, Kentucky, who was now exhibiting her in Philadelphia, but not having much tact as a showman, he was anxious to sell out and return home. Mr. Bartram also handed me a copy of *The Pennsylvania Inquirer*, of July 15, 1835, and directed my attention to the following advertisement, which I here transcribe *verbatim:*

CURIOSITY.—The citizens of Philadelphia and its vicinity have an opportunity of witnessing at the MASONIC HALL, one of the greatest natural curiosities ever witnessed, viz., JOICE HETH, a negress aged 161 years, who formerly belonged to the father of Gen. Washington. She has been a member of the Baptist Church one hundred and sixteen years, and can rehearse many hymns, and sing them according to former custom. She was born near the old Potomac River in Virginia, and has for ninety or one hundred years lived in Paris, Kentucky, with the Bowling family.

All who have seen this extraordinary woman are satisfied of the truth of the account of her age. The evidence of the Bowling family, which is respectable, is strong, but the original bill of sale of Augustine Washington, in his own handwriting, and other evidence which the proprietor has in his possession, will satisfy even the most incredulous.

A lady will attend at the hall during the afternoon and evening for the accommodation of those ladies who may call.

The New York newspapers had already furnished descriptions of this wonderful personage, and becoming considerably excited upon the subject, I proceeded at once to Philadelphia and had an interview with Lindsay at the Masonic Hall. I was favorably struck with the appearance of the old woman. So far as outward indications were concerned, she might almost as well have been called a thousand years old as any other age. She was lying upon a high lounge in the middle of the room; her lower extremities were drawn up, with her knees elevated some two feet above the top of the lounge. She was apparently in good health and spirits, but former disease or old age, or perhaps both combined, had rendered her unable to change her position; in fact, although she could move one of her arms at will, her lower limbs were fixed in their position, and could not be straightened. She was totally blind, and her eyes were so deeply sunken in their sockets that the eyeballs seemed to have disappeared altogether. She had no teeth, but possessed a head of thick bushy gray hair. Her left arm lay across her breast, and she had no power to remove it. The fingers of her left hand were drawn down so as nearly to close it, and remained fixed and immovable. The nails upon that hand were about four inches in length, and extended above her wrist. The nails upon her large toes also had grown to the thickness of nearly a quarter of an inch.

She was very sociable, and would talk almost incessantly so long as visitors would converse with her. She sang a variety of ancient hymns, and was very garrulous when speaking of her protégé "dear little George," as she termed the great father of our country. She declared that she was present at his birth, that she was formerly the slave of Augustine Washington, the father of George, and that she was the first person who put clothes upon him. "In fact," said Joice, and it was a favorite expression of hers, "I raised him." She related many interesting anecdotes of "her dear little George," and this, mixed with her conversations upon religious subjects, for she claimed to be a member of the Baptist Church, rendered her exhibition an extremely interesting one.

I asked Mr. Lindsay for the proofs of her extraordinary age, and he exhibited what purported to be a bill of sale from Augustine Washington, of the county of Westmoreland, Virginia, to "Elizabeth Atwood," of "one negro woman, named Joice Heth, aged fifty-four years, for and in consideration of the sum of thirty-three pounds lawful money of Virginia." The document bore the date "fifth day of February, one thousand seven hundred and twenty-

seven," and was "sealed and delivered in presence of Richard Buck-
ner and William Washington."

The story told by Lindsay and "Aunt Joice" was, that Mrs.
Elizabeth Atwood was a sister-in-law of Augustine Washington,
that the husband of Joice was a slave of Mrs. Atwood, and for that
reason the above sale was made. As Mrs. Atwood was a near
neighbor of Mr. Washington, Aunt Joice was present at the birth
of "little George," and she having long been the old family nurse,
was the first person called upon to clothe the new-born infant.

The story seemed plausible, and the "bill of sale" had every
appearance of antiquity. It was exhibited in a glass frame, was
very sallow in appearance, and seemed to have been folded for such
a great length of time that the folds were worn nearly through, and
in some parts entirely so.

I inquired why the existence of such an extraordinary old
woman had not been discovered and made known long ago. The
reply was that she had been lying in an out-house of John S. Bowling of Kentucky for many years, that no one knew or seemed to
care how old she was, that she had been brought thither from Virginia a long time ago, and that the fact of her extreme age had
been but recently brought to light by the discovery of this old bill
of sale in the Record office in Virginia, by the son of Mr. Bowling,
who, while looking over the ancient papers in that office, happened
to notice the paper endorsed Joice Heth, that his curiosity was
excited, and from inquiries made in that neighborhood he was convinced that the document applied to his father's old slave then living,
and who was therefore really one hundred and sixty-one years of
age; that he thereupon took the paper home, and became confirmed
in regard to the identity of Joice with the slave described in that
paper.

This whole account appeared to me satisfactory, and I inquired
the price of the negress. Three thousand dollars was the sum

named, but before leaving Philadelphia I received from Mr. Lindsay a writing, stipulating that I should have the right at any time within ten days to become her owner upon paying to him the sum of one thousand dollars.

With this paper I started for New York, determined if possible to purchase Joice Heth. I did not possess more than five hundred dollars in cash, but my glowing representations to a friend, of the golden harvest which I was sure the exhibition must produce, induced him to loan me the other five hundred dollars, and after a few days, during which time I sold my interest in the grocery store to my partner, Moody, I returned to Philadelphia with the money, and became the proprietor of the negress.

I engaged Lindsay to continue the exhibition in Philadelphia for a week, in order to allow me time to make the necessary arrangements for her reception in New York.

I applied to Mr. William Niblo, who, I believe, had seen the old negress in Philadelphia. He did not recognize me as the person who a few months previously had applied to him for the situation of bar-keeper. We soon made a bargain for the exhibition of Aunt Joice in one of the large apartments in his dwelling-house in the vicinity of his saloon, which was at that time a large, open and airy establishment where musical and light entertainments were given, the guests during the intermission, as well as at other times, being supplied with ice-cream and other refreshments, in little alcove-boxes fitted up with tables, and running nearly all the distance around his garden.

These alcoves were tastefully decorated on the outside with festoons of lamps of variegated colors, and the grand walk through the middle of the garden was illuminated on each side by chaste and pretty transparencies, about seven feet high and two feet wide, each surmounted with a large globular lamp. These transparencies were then new in the city of New York, and were very attractive.

They were gotten up by W. J. and H. Hannington, who have since become so celebrated for glass-staining and decorative painting. Mr. H. Hannington prepared me several transparencies, two feet by three in size, which I had placed upon a hollow frame and lighted from the inside. It was painted in colors with white letters, and read—

> JOICE HETH
> **161**
> YEARS OLD.

The terms of my engagement with Mr. Niblo were these: He was to furnish the room and lights, pay the expense of printing, advertising, and a ticket-seller, and retain therefor one half of the gross receipts. The result proved an average of about $1500 per week.

I engaged as an assistant in exhibiting "Aunt Joice" Mr. Levi Lyman. He was a lawyer by profession, and had been practising in Penn Yan, N. Y. He was a shrewd, sociable, and somewhat indolent Yankee; possessed a good knowledge of human nature; was polite, agreeable, could converse on most subjects, and was admirably calculated to fill the position for which I engaged him.

Of course, in carrying out my new vocation of showman, I spared no reasonable efforts to make it successful. I was aware of the great power of the public press, and I used it to the extent of my ability. Lyman wrote a brief memoir of Joice, and putting it into a pamphlet form, illustrated with her portrait, sold it to visitors on his own account, at six cents per copy. I had the same portrait printed on innumerable small bills, and also flooded the city with "posters," setting forth the peculiar attractions which "the nurse of Washington" presented.

Our exhibition usually opened with a statement of the manner in which the age of Joice Heth was discovered, as well as the account of her antecedents in Virginia, and a reading of the bill of sale. We would then question her in relation to the birth and youth of General Washington, and she always gave satisfactory answers in every particular. Individuals among the audience would also frequently ask her questions, and put her to the severest cross-examinations, without ever finding her to deviate from what had every evidence of being a plain unvarnished statement of facts.

Later, I took Joice Heth on tour through New England. In Boston we opened our exhibition in the small ball-room of Concert Hall, at the corner of Court and Hanover streets. The fame of Joice had preceded her, the city was well posted with large bills announcing her coming, and the newspapers had heralded her anticipated arrival in such a multiplicity of styles, that the public curiosity was on tip-toe. I remember that one of the papers, after giving a description of Joice Heth, and the great satisfaction which her exhibition had given in New York, added, "It *rejoice-heth* us exceedingly to know that we shall be permitted to look upon the old patriarch."

The celebrated Maelzel was exhibiting his equally celebrated "automaton chess-player" in the large ball-room of Concert Hall; but the crowd of visitors to see Aunt Joice was so great that our room could not accommodate them, and Mr. Maelzel was induced to close his exhibition, and give us his large room. I had frequent interviews and long conversations with Mr. Maelzel. I looked upon him as the great father of caterers for public amusement, and was pleased with his assurance that I would certainly make a successful showman.

"I see," said he, in broken English, "that you understand the value of the press, and that is the great thing. Nothing helps the showmans like the types and the ink. When your old woman dies," he added, "you come to me, and I will make your fortune. I will let you have my 'carousal,' my automaton trumpet-player, and many curious things which will make plenty of money." I thanked him for his generous proposals, and assured him that should circumstances render it feasible, I should apply to him.

Our exhibition room continued to attract large numbers of

visitors for several weeks before there was any visible falling off. I kept up a constant succession of novel advertisements and unique notices in the newspapers, which tended to keep old Joice fresh in the minds of the public, and served to sharpen the curiosity of the people.

When the audiences began to decrease in numbers, a short communication appeared in one of the newspapers, signed *"A Visitor,"* in which the writer claimed to have made an important discovery. He stated that Joice Heth, as at present exhibited, was a humbug, whereas if the simple truth was told in regard to the exhibition, it was really vastly curious and interesting. "The fact is," said the communication, "Joice Heth is not a human being. What purports to be a remarkably old woman is simply a curiously constructed automaton, made up of whalebone, india-rubber, and numberless springs ingeniously put together, and made to move at the slightest touch, according to the will of the operator. The exhibitor is a ventriloquist, and all the conversations apparently held with the ancient lady are purely imaginary, so far as she is concerned, for the answers and incidents purporting to be given and related by her, are merely the ventriloquial voice of the exhibitor."

Maelzel's ingenious mechanism somewhat prepared the way for this announcement, and hundreds who had not visited Joice Heth were now anxious to see the curious automaton; while many who had seen her were equally desirous of a second look, in order to determine whether or not they had been deceived. The consequence was, our audiences again largely increased.

From Boston we went to Hingham, and thence in succession to Lowell, Worcester, Springfield, and Hartford, meeting with most satisfactory success. Everywhere there appeared to be conviction of the extreme longevity of Joice.

We hastened our return to New York to fill a second engagement I had made with Mr. Niblo. The American Institute held its annual Fair at his garden, and my engagement was to commence at the same time. The great influx of visitors to the Fair caused our room to be continually crowded, insomuch that we were frequently compelled to announce to applicants that the hall was full, and no more could be admitted for the present. In those cases we would hurry up the exhibitions, cut short a hymn or two, answer questions with great rapidity, and politely open the front door as an egress to visitors, at the same time opening the entrance from the garden for the ingress of fresh customers.

From Niblo's we went to New Haven for three days, where the crowds were as large as usual. We then returned to New York and proceeded to Newark, where I met with the usual success. From Newark we returned to New York and went to Albany for one week to fill an engagement made with Mr. Meech, the proprietor of the Museum.

While exhibiting there, light evening entertainments were given in the theatre of the Museum, one part of which consisted of remarkable feats of balancing, plate spinning, stilt walking, etc., by "Signor Antonio." The balancing and spinning of crockery was nearly or quite new in this country—to me it was entirely so. It was also as surprising as it was novel. The daring feats of Antonio upon stilts, his balancing guns with the bayonets resting on his nose, and various other performances which I had never seen before, attracted my attention. I inquired of Mr. Meech where Antonio came from. He informed me that he was an Italian—had sailed from England to Canada, whence he had proceeded to Albany, and had never exhibited in any other American city. Learning that Mr. Meech did not desire his services after that week, I sought an interview with Antonio, and in ten minutes engaged him to perform for me in any portion of the United States for one year from date, at the salary of $12 per week, besides board and travelling expenses.

I did not know exactly where I should use my protégé, but I was certain that there was money in him, and thus I became interested in my second show.

Antonio, Joice Heth, Lyman and myself, left Albany for New York, stopping at the private boarding house in Frankfort street which I had taken the spring previous, but had sold out soon after engaging Aunt Joice. I left my two shows in Frankfort street while I went to join my wife and daughter, who were boarding with a Mr. Knapp, in Cherry street.

The first favor which I asked of Antonio was, that he should submit to be thoroughly washed—an operation to which he had apparently been a stranger for several years; and the second, that he should change his name. I did not think "Antonio" sufficiently "foreign," hence I named him Signor Vivalla, to both which propositions he consented. I immediately wrote a notice announcing the extraordinary qualities of Signor Vivalla, who had just arrived from Italy, elaborately setting forth the wonders of his performances. This was published as an article of news in one of the city papers, and I forwarded a dozen copies to the several theatrical managers in New York, and elsewhere.

I first called upon William Dinneford, Esq., manager of the Franklin Theatre, but he declined engaging the "eminent Italian artist." He had seen so many performances of that kind which were vastly more extraordinary than anything which Vivalla could do, he would not think of engaging him.

"Now," says I, "Mr. Dinneford, I beg your pardon, but I must be permitted to say that you are mistaken. You have no doubt seen strange things in your life, but, my dear sir, I should never have imported Signor Vivalla from Italy, unless I had authentic evidence that he was the only artist of the kind who ever left that country."

"What are your terms?" asked Dinneford, who (like many worthy young ladies, and many other republicans of the first water) was evidently beginning to melt under the magic influence of a foreign importation. "You shall have him one night for nothing," I replied. "If you like him after one trial, you shall have him the remainder of the week for fifty dollars—but, understand me, this is only that the public may be able to see what he is. After that, my terms are $50 per night."

My proposition for the one night was accepted. I invoked the powers of "printer's ink" and wood-cuts for three days and nights previous to the first appearance of "the renowned and extraordinary Italian artist, Signor Vivalla," and they were potent for my purpose. The house was crammed. I marched upon the stage as a supernumerary to assist Vivalla in arranging his plates and other "crockery ware," to hand him the gun to fire when he had divested himself of one of his stilts, and was hopping across the stage on one stilt ten feet high, and to aid him in handling his muskets, etc. This was my "first appearance on any stage."

The applause which followed each of the Italian's feats was tremendous. It was such as only a Chatham or a Bowery audience could give. Manager Dinneford was delighted, and before we left the stage he engaged Vivalla for the week. At the termination of the performances Vivalla was called before the curtain, and as I did not consider it policy for him to be able to speak English, (although he could do so very well, having travelled several years in England), I went out with him and addressed the audience in his name, thanking them for their generosity, and announcing him for the remainder of the week.

In the mean time I had opened the exhibition of Joice Heth in the large hall at the junction of the Bowery and Division street, but as I saw that Vivalla's prospects were bright, and that his success would depend in a great measure upon management, I left Lyman to exhibit Joice. After she had remained in that location for several weeks, he took her to several towns in Connecticut and elsewhere. Vivalla remained a second week at the Franklin Theatre, for which I received $150—immediately after which, I realized the same sum for his services one week in Boston; and then we proceeded to Washington city to fulfil an engagement I had made with Wemyss, my profits depending on the receipts. The theatre in Washington was a small out-of-the-way-place, and we opened, Jan. 16, 1836, to a house not exceeding $30. It was a hard beginning, for the stipulations required $50 more before I was entitled to a penny!

As this was my first visit to Washington I was much interested in visiting the capitol and other public buildings. I also satisfied my curiosity in seeing Clay, Calhoun, Benton, John Quincy Adams, Richard M. Johnson, Polk, and other leading statesmen of the time. I was also greatly gratified in calling upon Anne Royall, author of the Black Book, publisher of a little paper called "Paul Pry," and quite a celebrated personage in her day. I had exchanged *The Herald of Freedom* with her journal and she strongly sympathized with me in my persecutions. She was delighted to see me and although she was the most garrulous old woman I ever saw, I passed a very amusing and pleasant time with her. Before leaving her, I manifested my showman propensity by trying to hire her to give a dozen or more lectures on "Government," in the Atlantic cities, but I could not engage her at any price, although I am sure the speculation would have been a very profitable one. I never saw this eccentric woman again; she died at a very advanced age, October 1, 1854, at her residence in Washington.

There was incessant snow in Washington during Vivalla's engagement, and I was so unexpectedly a loser by the operation that I had not sufficient funds to return to Philadelphia. After much hesitation, and with a deep feeling of sadness and humiliation, I pawned my watch and chain for thirty-five dollars, promising to redeem it within a month. Fortunately, however, Mr. Wemyss arrived on Saturday morning, bringing with him Lucius Junius Booth and Miss Waring, afterwards Mrs. Sefton. Mr. Wemyss loaned me thirty-five dollars, and I redeemed my watch, paying a dollar for the use of the money a few hours.

Vivalla and myself proceeded to Philadelphia, and opened at the Walnut Street, on the 26th, to a slim house. "Signor Vivalla's" performances were well received. On the second night, however, I heard two or three distinct hisses from the pit. It was the first time that my protégé had received the slightest mark of disapprobation since I had engaged him, and I was surprised. Vivalla, who, under my management, had become proud of his profession, was excessively annoyed. I proceeded, therefore, to that portion of the house whence the hissing emanated, and found that it came from a circus performer named Roberts and his friends. It seems that Roberts was a balancer and juggler, and he declared he could do all that Vivalla could. I was certain he could *not,* and told him so. Some hard words ensued. I then proceeded to the ticket-office, where I wrote several copies of a "card," and proceeding to the printing-offices of various newspapers, climbing up narrow stairs and threading dark alleys for the purpose, I secured its appearance in the papers of the next morning. The card was headed "*One Thousand Dollars Reward!*" and then proceeded to state that Signor Vivalla would pay the foregoing sum to any man who would publicly accomplish his (Vivalla's) feats, at such public place as Vivalla should designate.

Roberts came out with a card the next day, accepting Vivalla's offer, calling on him to put up the thousand dollars, to name the time and place of trial, and stating that he could be found at a certain hotel near Green's Circus, of which he was a member. I borrowed a thousand dollars of my friend Oliver Taylor—went to Mr. Warren, treasurer of the Walnut, and asked him what share of the house he would give me if I would get up an excitement that should bring in four or five hundred dollars a night. (The entire receipts the night previous were but seventy-five dollars.) He replied that he would give me one-third of the gross receipts. I told him I had a crotchet in my head, and would inform him within an hour whether it would work. I then called upon Roberts and showed him my thousand dollars. "Now," says I, "I am ready to put up this money in responsible hands, to be forfeited and paid to you if you accomplish Signor Vivalla's feats."

"Very well," said Roberts, with considerable bravado; "put the money into the hands of Mr. Green, the proprietor of the circus" —to which I assented.

"Now," said I, "I wish you to sign this card, to be published in handbills and in to-morrow's newspapers." He read it. It stated that Signor Vivalla having placed one thousand dollars in hands satisfactory to himself, to be forfeited to him if he succeeded in performing the various feats of the said Vivalla, he (Roberts) would make the public trial to do so on the stage of the Walnut street Theatre, on the night of the 30th inst. "You don't expect me to perform *all* of Vivalla's feats, do you?" said Roberts, after reading the card. "No, I don't *expect* you *can*, but if you do *not*, of course you will not win the thousand dollars," I replied. "Why, I know nothing about walking on stilts, and am not fool enough to risk my neck in that way," said Roberts.

Several persons, circus-riders and others, had crowded around us, and exhibited some degree of excitement. My thousand dollars was still openly displayed in my hand. I saw that Roberts was determined to back out, and as that would not be consistent with my plans, I remarked that he and I could do our own business without the intermeddling of third parties, and I would like to see him alone. He took me up stairs to his room, and bolting the door, I thus addressed him:

"Now, Roberts, you said to the public in your card that you

accepted Vivalla's offer. What was that offer? Why, that he would give a thousand dollars to the man who could accomplish his feats. Now, you may spin a plate or two as well as Vivalla, but Vivalla spins ten plates at once, and I doubt whether you can do it—if not, you lose the reward. Again, you confess that you cannot perform on stilts. Of course, then, you don't accomplish 'his feats,' and therefore you could not receive the thousand dollars." "But I can toss balls and do tricks which Vivalla can't accomplish," said Roberts. "I have no doubt of that," I replied, "but that has nothing to do with Vivalla's offer." "Oh, I see," said Roberts, in a huff, "you have fixed up a Yankee card to suit yourself, and left a hole to sneak out of." "Not at all, Mr. Roberts. I have made a specific offer, and am ready to fulfil it. Do not fret nor be angry, for you shall find me your friend instead of an enemy." I then inquired whether he was engaged to Mr. Green. "Not at present," he replied, "as the circus is closed." "Well," I responded, "it is evident you cannot gain the thousand dollars. I did not intend you should, but I will give you $30 if you will perform under my directions one night at the Walnut street Theatre, and will keep your own counsel."

He consented to this, and I then asked him to sign the card, and give himself no uneasiness. He signed, and I had it thoroughly published, first closing my bargain with the treasurer of the Walnut for one-third of the gross receipts on the trial night, provided there was $400 in the house.

The next day I brought Roberts and Vivalla privately together, and by practising they soon discovered what tricks each could accomplish, and we then proceeded to arrange the manner in which the trial should come off, and how it should terminate.

In the mean time the excitement about the coming trial of skill was fast increasing. Suitable "notices" were inserted in the papers, bragging that Roberts was an American, and could beat the foreigner all hollow. Roberts in the mean time announced in the papers that if, as he expected, he should obtain the thousand dollars, a portion of it should be disbursed for charitable purposes. I set The Press at work lustily, in the shape of handbills, squibs, etc. Before the night of trial arrived, the excitement had reached fever heat. I knew that a crowded house was *un fait accompli.*

I was not disappointed. The pit and upper boxes were crowded to suffocation. In fact, the sales of tickets to these localities were stopped because no more persons could possibly gain admittance. The dress circle was not so full, though even that contained many more persons than had been in it at one time during the previous two or three months.

The contest was a very interesting one. Roberts of course was to be beaten, and it was agreed that Vivalla should at first perform his *easiest* feats, in order that the battle should be kept up as long as possible. Roberts successively performed the same feats that Vivalla did. Each party was continually cheered by his friends and hissed by his opponents. Occasionally some of Roberts's friends from the pit would call out, "Roberts, beat the little Frenchman," "One Yankee is too much for two Frenchmen any time," etc. The contest lasted about forty minutes, when Roberts came forward and acknowledged himself defeated. He was obliged to give up on the feat of spinning two plates at once, one in each hand. His friends urged him to try again, but on his declining, they requested him to perform his own peculiar feats (juggling, tossing the balls, etc.). This he did, and his performances, which continued for twenty minutes, were highly applauded.

As soon as the curtain fell, the two contestants were called for. Before they went out I had concluded a private arrangement with Roberts for a month—he to perform solely as I directed. When he went before the curtain, therefore, he informed the audience that he had a lame wrist, which was indeed the fact. He further informed them that he could do more feats of various kinds than Vivalla could, and he would challenge Vivalla to such a trial at any time and place he pleased, for a wager of five hundred dollars. "I accept that challenge," said Vivalla, who stood at Roberts's side, "and I name next Tuesday night in this theatre." "Bravo," cried Vivalla's friends, as vigorously as "bravo" had been shouted by the friends of Roberts.

Three hearty cheers were given by the enthusiastic audience, and the antagonists, looking daggers at each other, withdrew at opposite sides of the curtain. Before the uproar of applause had ceased, Roberts and Vivalla had met upon the stage, shaken hands, and were enjoying a hearty laugh, while little Vivalla, with thumb to his nose, was making curious gyrations to an imaginary picture on the back of the screen, or possibly to a real *tableau vivant* in front of the curtain. The receipts of the theatre on that night were $593.25, of which I received one-third—$197.75.

The contest on the Tuesday night following was nearly as profitable to me as the first one, as so indeed were several similar trials of skill brought forward in Dinneford's Franklin Theatre, New York, and various other places, during the month of Roberts's engagement.

These details may possess little interest to the general reader. They however serve to show (though it may be revealing some of the "tricks of the trade") how such matters are frequently managed in theatres and other places of amusement. The people are repeatedly wrought to excitement and take sides most enthusiastically in trials of skill, when, if the truth were known, the whole affair is a piece of management between the prominent parties. The entertainment of the time may be an offset to the "humbug" of the transaction, and it may be doubted whether managers of theatres will be losers by these revelations of mine, for the public appears disposed to be amused even when they are conscious of being deceived.

Meanwhile poor old Joice had sickened, and with her attendant, a faithful colored woman whom I hired in Boston, had gone to my brother's house in Bethel, where she was provided with warm apartments and the best medical and other assistance.

On the 21st of February, 1836, my brother's horses and sleigh stopped at the door of my boarding-house, in New York. The driver handed me a letter from my brother Philo, stating that Aunt Joice was no more. She died at his house on Friday night, the 19th, and her body was then in the sleigh, having been conveyed to New York for me to dispose of as I thought proper. I at once determined to have it returned to Bethel and interred in our village burial-ground, though for the present it was placed in a small room of which I had the key.

The next morning I called on an eminent surgeon who, upon visiting Joice at Niblo's, had expressed a desire to institute a post-mortem examination if she should die in this country. I agreed that he should have the opportunity, if unfortunately it should occur while she was under my protection. I now informed him that Aunt Joice was dead, and he reminded me of my promise. I admitted it, and immediately proceeded to arrange for the examination to take place on the following day.

In the mean time a mahogany coffin and plate were procured and taken to the hall where the examination was to take place. A large number of physicians, students, and several clergymen and editors were present. Among the last named class was Richard Adams Locke, author of the celebrated "Moon Hoax," who was at that time editor of the New York *Sun*. An absence of ossification of the arteries in the immediate region of the heart was deemed by the dissector and most of the gentlemen present an evidence against the assumed age of Joice.

When all had withdrawn excepting the surgeon, his particular friend Locke, Lyman, and myself, the surgeon remarked, addressing me, that there was surely some mistake in regard to the alleged age of Joice; that instead of being 161 years old, she was probably not over eighty. I stated to him, in reply, what was strictly true, that I had hired Joice in perfect good faith, and relied upon her appearance and the documents as evidence of the truth of her story. The same gentleman had examined her when alive on exhibition at Niblo's. He rejoined that he had no doubt I had been deceived in the matter, that her personal appearance really did indicate extreme longevity, but that the documents must either have been forged, or else they applied to some other individual. Lyman, who was always ready for a joke, no matter what the cost nor at whose expense, here made a remark regarding the inability of the faculty to decide with much precision in regard to a case of this kind. His observations wounded the feelings of the surgeon, and taking the arm of his friend Locke, they left the hall—I fear in not very good humor.

The *Sun* of the next day (February 25, 1836) contained an editorial, written of course by Locke, commencing as follows:

"Dissection of Joice Heth.—Precious Humbug Exposed.—The anatomical examination of the body of Joice Heth yesterday, resulted in the exposure of one of the most precious humbugs that ever was imposed upon a credulous community."

Mr. Locke then proceeded to give a scientific account of the dissection, and the reasons he had for doubting her story.

Here let me say a word in reply to the captious who may claim that I was over-credulous in accepting the story of Joice and her exhibitor, as a matter of fact. I assert, then, that when Joice Heth was living, I never met with six persons out of the many thousands who visited her, who seemed to doubt the claim of her age and history. Hundreds of medical men assured me that they thought the statement of her age was correct, and Dr. Rogers himself, in his parting conversation above noted, remarked to me that he expected to have spoiled half a dozen knives in severing the ossification in the arteries around the region of the heart and chest.

I will only add, that the remains of Joice were removed to Bethel, and buried respectably.

CHAPTER VII

In April, 1836, I connected myself with Aaron Turner's travelling circus company as ticket-seller, secretary and treasurer, at thirty dollars a month and one-fifth of the entire profits, while Vivalla was to receive a salary of fifty dollars. As I was already paying him eighty dollars a month, our joint salaries reimbursed me and left me the chance of twenty per cent of the net receipts. We started from Danbury for West Springfield, Massachusetts, April 26th, and on the first day, instead of halting to dine, as I expected, Mr. Turner regaled the whole company with three loaves of rye bread and a pound of butter, bought at a farm house at a cost of fifty cents, and, after watering the horses, we went on our way.

We began our performances at West Springfield, April 28th, and as our expected band of music had not arrived from Providence, I made a prefatory speech announcing our disappointment, and our intention to please our patrons, nevertheless. The two Turner boys, sons of the proprietor, rode finely. Joe Pentland, one of the wittiest, best, and most original of clowns, with Vivalla's tricks and other performances in the ring, more than made up for the lack of music. In a day or two our band arrived and our "houses" improved. My diary is full of incidents of our summer tour through numerous villages, towns, and cities in New England, New York, New Jersey, Pennsylvania, Delaware, Maryland, District of Columbia, Virginia, and North Carolina.

At Lenox, Massachusetts, one Sunday I attended church as usual, and the preacher denounced our circus and all connected with it as immoral, and was very abusive; whereupon when he had read the closing hymn I walked up the pulpit stairs and handed him a written request, signed "P. T. Barnum, connected with the circus, June 5, 1836," to be permitted to reply to him. He declined to notice it, and after the benediction I lectured him for not giving me an opportunity to vindicate myself and those with whom I was connected. The affair created considerable excitement and some of the members of the church apologized to me for their clergyman's ill-behavior. A similar affair happened afterwards at Port Deposit, on the lower Susquehanna, and in this instance I addressed the audience for half an hour, defending the circus company against the attacks of the clergyman, and the people listened, though their pastor repeatedly implored them to go home. Often have I collected our company on Sunday and read to them the Bible or a printed sermon, and one or more of the men frequently accompanied me to church. We made no pretence of religion, but we were not the worst people in the world, and we thought ourselves entitled to at least decent treatment when we went to hear the preaching of the gospel.

The proprietor of the circus, Aaron Turner, was a self-made man, who had acquired a large fortune by his industry. He believed that any man with health and common sense could become rich if he only resolved to be so, and he was very proud of the fact that he began the world with no advantages, no education, and without a shilling. Withal, he was a practical joker, as I more than once discovered to my cost. While we were at Annapolis, Maryland, he played a trick upon me which was fun to him, but was very nearly death to me.

We arrived on Saturday night, and as I felt quite "flush" I bought a fine suit of black clothes. On Sunday morning I dressed myself in my new suit and started out for a stroll. While passing through the bar-room Turner called the attention of the company present to me and said:

"I think it very singular you permit that rascal to march your streets in open day. It wouldn't be allowed in Rhode Island, and I suppose that is the reason the black-coated scoundrel has come down this way."

"Why, who is he?" asked half a dozen at once.

"Don't you know? Why that is the Rev. E. K. Avery, the murderer of Miss Cornell!"

"Is it possible!" they exclaimed, all starting for the door, eager to get a look at me, and swearing vengeance.

It was only recently that the Rev. Ephraim K. Avery had been tried in Rhode Island for the murder of Miss Cornell, whose body was discovered in a stack-yard, and though Avery was acquitted in court, the general sentiment of the country condemned him. It was this Avery whom Turner made me represent. I had not walked far in my fine clothes, before I was overtaken by a mob of a dozen, which rapidly increased to at least a hundred, and my ears were suddenly saluted with such observations as, "the lecherous old hypocrite," "the sanctified murderer," "the black-coated villain," "lynch the scoundrel," "let's tar and feather him," and like remarks which I had no idea applied to me till one man seized me by the collar, while five or six more appeared on the scene with a rail.

"Come," said the man who collared me, "old chap, you can't walk any further; we know you, and as we always make gentlemen ride in these parts, you may just prepare to straddle that rail!"

My surprise may be imagined. "Good heavens!" I exclaimed, as they all pressed around me, "gentlemen, what have I done?"

"Oh, we know you," exclaimed half a dozen voices; "you needn't roll your sanctimonious eyes; that game don't take in this country. Come, straddle the rail, and *remember the stack-yard!*"

I grew more and more bewildered; I could not imagine what

possible offence I was to suffer for, and I continued to exclaim, "Gentlemen, what have I done? Don't kill me, gentlemen, but tell me what I have done."

"Come, make him straddle the rail; we'll show him how to hang poor factory girls," shouted a man in the crowd.

The man who had me by the collar then remarked, "Come, *Mr. Avery,* it's no use, you see, we know you, and we'll give you a touch of Lynch law, and start you for home again."

"My name is *not* Avery, gentlemen; you are mistaken in your man," I exclaimed.

"Come, come, none of your gammon; straddle the rail, Ephraim." The rail was brought and I was about to be placed on it when the truth flashed upon me.

"Gentlemen," I exclaimed, "I am not Avery; I despise that villain as much as you can; my name is Barnum; I belong to the circus which arrived here last night, and I am sure Old Turner, my partner, has hoaxed you with this ridiculous story."

"If he has we'll lynch him," said one of the mob.

"Well, he has, I'll assure you, and if you will walk to the hotel with me, I'll convince you of the fact."

This they reluctantly assented to, keeping, however, a close hand upon me. As we walked up the main street, the mob received a re-enforcement of some fifty or sixty, and I was marched like a malefactor up to the hotel. Old Turner stood on the piazza ready to explode with laughter. I appealed to him for heaven's sake to explain this matter, that I might be liberated. He continued to laugh, but finally told them "he believed there was some mistake about it. The fact is," said he, "my friend Barnum has a new suit of black clothes on and he looks so much like a priest that I thought he must be Avery."

The crowd saw the joke and seemed satisfied. My new coat had been half torn from my back and I had been very roughly handled.

But some of the crowd apologized for the outrage, declaring that Turner ought to be served in the same way, while others advised me to "get even with him." I was very much offended, and when the mob dispersed I asked Turner what could have induced him to play such a trick upon me.

"My dear Mr. Barnum," he replied, "it was all for our good. Remember all we need to insure success is notoriety. You will see that this will be noised all about town as a trick played by one of the circus managers upon the other, and our pavilion will be crammed to-morrow night."

It was even so; the trick was told all over town and every one came to see the circus managers who were in a habit of playing practical jokes upon each other. We had fine audiences while we remained at Annapolis, but it was a long time before I forgave Turner for his rascally "joke."

An amusing incident occurred when we were at Hanover Court House, in Virginia. It rained so heavily that we could not perform there and Turner decided to start for Richmond immediately after dinner, when he was informed by the landlord that as our agent had engaged three meals and lodging for the whole company, the entire bill must be paid whether we went then, or next morning. No compromise could be effected with the stubborn landlord and so Turner proceeded to get the worth of his money as follows:

He ordered dinner at twelve o'clock, which was duly prepared and eaten. The table was cleared and re-set for supper at half-past twelve. At one o'clock we all went to bed, every man carrying a lighted candle to his room. There were thirty-six of us and we all undressed and tumbled into bed as if we were going to stay all night. In half an hour we rose and went down to the hot breakfast which Turner had demanded and which we found smoking on the table. Turner was very grave, the landlord was exceedingly angry, and the rest of us were convulsed with laughter at the absurdity of the whole proceeding. We disposed of our breakfast as if we had eaten nothing for ten hours and then started for Richmond with the satisfaction that we fairly settled with our unreasonable landlord.

From Richmond we proceeded to Petersburgh, thence to Warrenton, N. C., where, on the 30th October (my engagement with Turner having expired, with a clear profit to myself of twelve hundred dollars), I parted with the circus company, and taking Vivalla and a negro singer and dancer named James Sandford, with several musicians, horses, wagons, and a small canvas tent, started off with an exhibition on my own account, intending to travel as far south as Montgomery, Ala. Early in the morning my little company started. I remained behind for half an hour, receiving and reciprocating the kindly wishes of my late companions, and Mr. Turner then conveyed me in his carriage to overtake my own troupe. We rode slowly, because reluctant to part, and twenty miles of road was beguiled by pleasing conversation before we overtook those who had preceded us. My old friend wished me great success, and returned to his circus company. I felt lonely for several days, but my mind was so occupied by business that I soon became reconciled to my new position.

In Raleigh, N. C., I sold one half of my exhibition to a man whom I will here call Henry. He may be a better man *now* than he was then, and I therefore conceal his real name. He had kept along with us during the preceding week, with a wagon-load of ready-made clothing for sale, and finally bought the half-interest above named.

At Camden, S. C., Sandford abruptly left me. I had advertised negro songs; no one of my company was competent to fill his place; but being determined not to disappoint the audience, I blacked myself thoroughly, and sung the songs advertised, namely, "Zip Coon," "Gittin up Stairs," and "The Racoon Hunt, or Sitting on a Rail." It was decidedly "a hard push," but the audience supposed the singer was Sandford, and, to my surprise, my singing was applauded, and in two of the songs I was encored!

After singing my negro songs one evening, and just as I had pulled my coat off in the "dressing-room" of the tent, I heard a slight disturbance outside the canvas. Rushing to the spot, and finding a person disputing with my men, I took their part, and spoke my mind to him very freely. He instantly drew his pistol, exclaiming, "You black scoundrel! dare you use such language to a white man?" and proceeded deliberately to cock it. I saw that he supposed me to be a negro, and might perhaps blow my brains out. Quick as thought I rolled up my shirt sleeves, and replied, "I am as white as *you* are, sir." He absolutely dropped the pistol with fright! Probably he had never seen a white man blacked up before; at all events, he begged my pardon, and I re-entered my "dressing-room," fully realizing that I had incurred a narrow chance of losing my life. Nothing but a presence of mind which never yet deserted me, saved my brains. On four several occasions during my life have I had a loaded pistol pointed at my head, and on each occasion have I escaped by little less than a miracle. Several times, also, have I been in deadly peril by accidents; and now, when I look over my history, and call these things to mind, and especially when, in tracing my career, I find that so many with whom I have had intercourse are tenants of the grave, I cannot but realize that I am deeply indebted to the mercy of God. I may as well add, as one of the sections of my reflective moods, that when I consider the kinds of company into which for a number of years I was thrown, the associations with which I was connected, and the strong temptations to wrong-doing and bad habits which lay in my path, I am astonished as well as grateful that I was not utterly ruined. I honestly believe that, under God, I owe my preservation from the woe of living and dying a loafer and a vagabond, to the single fact that I was never fond of strong drink. True, I have in my time drank liquor, and have even been intoxicated, but generally I wholly abstained from the use of intoxicating beverages, and am happy to say, that for a number of years past, I have been strictly "a teetotaller."

During my absence from home, I usually wrote twice a week to my family, and nearly as often received letters from my wife. I received one from her, while in Columbia, S. C., stating it as a report current in Connecticut that I was in prison in Canada, on a charge of murder, had received my trial, and was under sentence of death! The story, I believe, originated in the fact that a circus company in Canada had gotten into difficulty with some rowdies who assaulted them. It certainly was not Turner's, for we met it in Columbia, S. C., December 5, 1836. It was shortly to be disbanded. I bought four horses and two wagons belonging to his side show, and hired Joe Pentland and Robert White to join my company. Pentland, besides being a celebrated clown, was a capital ventriloquist, balancer, comic singer, and performer of legerdemain. White was a negro-singer. This relieved me from the negro-song line, and made my exhibition (of which Henry was half owner) quite attractive. I called it "Barnum's Grand Scientific and Musical Theatre."

Henry acted as treasurer, and I received the tickets at the door. While doing this, at Augusta, Ga., a man attempted to pass. I demanded a ticket. He demurred, and upon inquiring why, he said he was a sheriff. I told him that I knew of no particular reason why a sheriff should not pay as well as anybody else, to which he replied, "You had better ask Mr. Henry about that." This startled me, so I passed him in, and hastened to ask Henry what was the matter. He reluctantly informed me that the sheriff had served a writ on him for a debt of $500. Henry had $600 of the company's money in his possession, and I saw that management would be required to prevent "sequestration of the funds." Privately hastening to a lawyer, I procured a bill of sale of all the property of the exhibition, lacking only Henry's signature, and returned to the theatre, where the performances were still in progress. The lawyer of Henry's creditor, and the creditor himself, awaited me. They demanded the keys of the stable, so as to "levy" on the horses and carriages. I declined compliance, whereupon they threatened to break down the doors and seize the property. I begged them to wait a few moments until I could consult with Henry,—and they consented. Henry desired to cheat his creditor, and immediately signed the bill of sale. Lest the sheriff should search him, he handed me $90, stating that he had $500 locked up in a safe place where the sheriff could not find it. Leaving him in the ticket office, I returned to the sheriff and the creditor, and informed them that Henry refused to compromise or to pay the claim. "Then give me the keys," said the sheriff. I declined doing so, and he again threatened to break down the stable doors. "Why will you do this?" said I.

"To attach the horses and carriages," he replied.

"Why do you wish to levy on them?"

"To secure a debt that Mr. Henry owes, and I wish to attach his interest in the property."

"You have not yet levied on the horses and carriages?" I said.

"No, I have not; but I *will* within ten minutes," replied the sheriff.

"Not exactly," said I—at the same time handing the bill of sale to my friend, Jackson O. Brown, with a request to read it. He did so. "Now, gentlemen," said I, addressing the sheriff and creditor, "you see that I am in full possession of the property as entire owner. You confess you have not yet levied on it, and if you touch my property, you do it at your peril."

I do not remember ever having seen two persons look more surprised than did these gentlemen, when they discovered they had been the victims of a "Yankee trick." The sheriff immediately seized Henry and took him to prison. It was Saturday night, December 17. I privately told Henry to keep up courage; that it was too late to find bail that night, but I would call on him in the morning.

The next morning I learned from unquestionable authority that Henry owed his creditor $1300; that he agreed, so soon as the Saturday evening performance closed, to hand over $500 in cash (belonging to the company), and a bill of sale of his interest in the horses, carriage and exhibition; and that, as a consideration, one of the horses should be "ready saddled and bridled" for Henry to decamp, leaving me in the lurch! This conspiracy happened to be defeated by the single fact (succeeded by a little management) that the sheriff sought to pass me at the door of the theatre as "a deadhead."

Under the circumstances, I could have little sympathy for Henry, and I now desired to secure the $500 which he had secreted. Vivalla obtained it from him to keep it from the sheriff, and *I* obtained it from Vivalla on Henry's order, as a means of procuring the required bail on Monday morning. I then paid the creditor the full amount received from Henry as the price of his half-interest in the establishment; received in exchange a guaranty that I should never be troubled by my quondam partner on that score, also an assignment of $500 of the creditor's claim; and thus my "lucky stars" relieved me from one of the most difficult positions of my life.

My "Diary," from which the preceding and much else has here been condensed, contains many incidents which I shall omit. I cannot, however, pass an adventure of mine as Pentland's confederate in several tricks of legerdemain.

His table had the usual trap-door for passing things to his assistant, preparatory to the magical transformations presented to the spectators. The quarters below were painfully narrow for a man of my size, but I volunteered for the occasion in the absence of the diminutive employee in that line of business. Squeezing into the allotted space, I found that my nose and my knees were likely to become acquainted by close contact—nevertheless, though heartily wishing myself out of the scrape, I held a live squirrel in my hand, ready to wind the chain of a watch around his neck and hand him up through the trap-door when needed.

Pentland's arrangements of vases, cups, balls, and divers other accompaniments of legerdemain, were on the table. In due time, he called for a watch with a gold chain. One of the spectators favored him with the article, and it was soon passed into my possession, under a vase and through the little trap-door in the top of the table. Awkwardly performing my part, the squirrel bit me severely; I shrieked with pain, straightened my neck first, then my back, then my legs, overthrew the table, smashed every breakable article upon it, and rushed behind the curtain! The squirrel galloped off with the watch around his neck. Pentland was struck speechless, but if ever there was hooting and shouting in a mass of spectators, it was heard that night.

In going from Columbus, Georgia, to Montgomery, Alabama, we were obliged to cross a thinly-settled, desolate tract, known as the "Indian Nation," and as several persons had been murdered by hostile Indians in that region, it was deemed dangerous to travel the road without an escort. Only the day before we started, the mail stage had been stopped and the passengers murdered, the driver alone escaping. We were well armed, however, and trusted that our numbers would present too formidable a force to be attacked, though we dreaded to incur the risk. Vivalla alone was fearless and was ready to encounter fifty Indians and drive them into the swamp.

Accordingly, when we had safely passed over the entire route to within fourteen miles of Montgomery, and were beyond the reach of danger, Joe Pentland determined to test Vivalla's bravery. He had secretly purchased at Mount Megs, on the way, an old Indian dress with a fringed hunting shirt and moccasins and these he put on, after coloring his face with Spanish brown. Then, shouldering his musket he followed Vivalla and the party and, approaching stealthily, leaped into their midst with a tremendous whoop.

Vivalla's companions were in the secret, and they instantly fled in all directions. Vivalla himself ran like a deer and Pentland after him, gun in hand and yelling horribly. After running a full mile the poor little Italian, out of breath and frightened nearly to death, dropped on his knees and begged for his life. The "Indian" levelled his gun at his victim, but soon seemed to relent and signified that Vivalla should turn his pockets inside out—which he did, producing and handing over a purse containing eleven dollars. The savage then marched Vivalla to an oak and with a handkerchief tied him in the most approved Indian manner to the tree, leaving him half dead with fright.

Pentland then joined us, and washing his face and changing his dress, we all went to the relief of Vivalla. He was overjoyed to see us, and when he was released his courage returned; he swore that after his companions left him the Indian had been re-enforced by six more to whom, in default of a gun or other means to defend himself, Vivalla had been compelled to surrender. We pretended to believe his story for a week and then told him the joke, which he refused to credit, and also declined to take the money which Pentland offered to return, as it could not possibly be his since seven Indians had taken his money. We had a great deal of fun over Vivalla's courage, but the matter made him so cross and surly that we were finally obliged to drop it altogether. From that time forward, however, Vivalla never boasted of his prowess.

We arrived at Montgomery, February 28th, 1837. Here I met

Henry Hawley, a legerdemain performer, about forty-five years of age, but as he was prematurely gray he looked at least seventy, and I sold him one-half of my exhibition. He had a ready wit, a happy way of localizing his tricks, was very popular in that part of the country, where he had been performing for several years, and I never saw him nonplussed but once. This was when he was performing on one occasion the well-known egg and bag trick, which he did with his usual success, producing egg after egg from the bag and finally breaking one to show that they were genuine. "Now," said Hawley, "I will show you the old hen that laid them." It happened, however, that the negro boy to whom had been intrusted the duty of supplying the bag had made a slight mistake which was manifest when Hawley triumphantly produced, not "the old hen that laid the eggs," but a rooster! The whole audience was convulsed with laughter and the abashed Hawley retreated to the dressing room cursing the stupidity of the black boy who had been paid to put a hen in the bag.

Our company performed in numerous places in Alabama, Kentucky, and Tennessee, and disbanded in Nashville, May, 1837. Vivalla went off on his own account, performed a few months in New York, and thence in the fall he sailed to Cuba, where I heard he died the year following. At a later period in my history, however, the little fellow turns up again.

Hawley remained in Tennessee to take charge of our horses, which had been "turned out to grass," and I returned to "home, sweet home," to spend a few weeks with my dear family. Early in July I returned to the West, with a new company of performers, rejoined Hawley, and recommenced operations in Kentucky. We were not successful. One of our few employees was incompetent, one was intemperate, and both were dismissed; our negro-singer was drowned in the river at Frankfort. Funds were low—I was obliged to leave a horse in *this* town, a carriage in *that,* and my watch in another, as security for tavern bills. Though these articles were afterwards redeemed by better success, I felt for several weeks that the stars were unpropitious.

Dissolving with Hawley in August, I formed a co-partnership with Z. Graves, left him in charge of the establishment, and went to Ohio in quest of Pentland, to re-engage him. I met him at Tiffin. I was a stranger in the town, but religious conversation at the hotel introduced me to several gentlemen, who solicited me to lecture on certain subjects which we had discussed. I complied, and the town school-house was crowded by an attentive congregation in the afternoon and evening of the Sabbath. A gentleman from Republic urged me to deliver two lectures in that town on the evenings of September 4th and 5th, which I did.

Having engaged Pentland and several musicians, I bought his horses and wagons, and we started for Kentucky. About thirty miles before reaching Cincinnati, we met several men with a large drove of hogs. One of the drovers made an insolent remark, because one of our drivers did not stop his wagon soon enough to prevent the swine from scattering a little. I replied rather tartly, comparing the man to his quadrupeds. Dismounting and approaching me, he drew and cocked a pistol, and, pointing it at my breast, swore he would blow me through if I did not apologize. I begged him to give me a few minutes for reflection, and told him if he would allow me a moment's consultation with a friend in the other wagon, the misunderstanding should be settled satisfactorily. He consented. That friend was a double-barrelled gun, loaded and capped. Seizing it, and approaching the hog drover, whose two mounted assistants were by his side, I said to him, "Now, sir, *you* must apologize, for your brains are in danger. You drew a weapon upon me for a trivial remark. You seem to hold human life at a cheap price; and now, sir, you have the choice between a load of shot and an apology."

He instantly apologized, and we entered into a different sort of conversation. We agreed that many a human life is sacrified in sudden anger, because one or both the parties carry deadly weapons.

The prominent points at which our company performed in that western and southern tour were Nashville (where we visited General Jackson at the Hermitage), Huntsville, Tuscaloosa, and Vicksburg—of course paying due respect to numerous intermediate places. We met with various success, though on the whole we did remarkably well.

At Vicksburg we sold all our land-conveyances, excepting four horses and the "band wagon"; bought the steamboat "Ceres" for $6000, hired the captain and crew, and proceeded down the river, stopping at desirable points to open our "budget of amusement."

At Natchez our "man-cook" left us, and I sought in vain for another. I applied to a white widow who, I had been informed, would answer the purpose. She objected, because she hoped shortly to marry a young painter. We needed a cook; our case was desperate; I called on the lover, mentioned my object, related the story, and asked him if he intended to marry the widow. He had not yet determined. "Can't you hurry up your ideas, and marry her at once?" said I.

Certainly not. He did not know that she would have *him,* and he did not know that he would have *her.* This was reasonable, but our case was desperate. "If you will marry her to-morrow morning, I will hire *her* at $25 per month as cook, and *you* at the same price as painter—boarding free for both—and a bonus of $50, cash in hand." There was a wedding on board the boat the next morning. The bride doffed her white robes, and at noon that day we had a capital dinner.

There was an alarming and yet somewhat ludicrous scene at St. Francisville, Louisiana. During the evening performance, a man attempted to pass me at the door of the tent, claiming to have paid already for admittance. He was slightly intoxicated, and when I refused him, he aimed at me with a slung-shot. The blow mashed my hat, and grazed the protuberance where phrenologists locate "the organ of caution." Perhaps this fact had something to do with what followed. The rejected party retired, and in a few minutes returned with a frightful gang of his half-drunken companions, each with a pistol, bludgeon, or other weapon. They seemed determined to assault me forthwith. Calling upon the Mayor and other respectable citizens (who were then in the "theatre"), I claimed protection from the mob. The Mayor declared his inability to afford it against such odds, but immediate violence was restrained by his intercession.

"We will let you off on one condition," said the more moderate of the ringleaders. "We will give you exactly one hour, and no help, to gather up your 'traps and plunder,' get aboard your steamboat, and be off! Hurry up, for you have no time to lose. If you are on shore one moment more than an hour, look out!"

He looked at his watch, *I* looked at the pistols and bludgeons; and I reckon that a big tent never came down with greater speed. The whole force of the company was exerted to its utmost. Not a citizen was allowed to help us, for love or money; and an occasional "Hurry up!" kept every muscle at work. Our "traps and plunder" were tumbled in confusion on the deck of the vessel; the fireman had gotten up steam; and five minutes before the hour was out, we were ready to cast off our cables and depart. The scamps who thus hurried us from the village had certainly a streak of both humor and honor. They were amused by our diligence; escorted us and our last load, waving pitch-pine torches; and when the boat swung into the current, they saluted us with a wild "hurrah!"

The New Orleans papers of March 19, 1838, announced the

arrival of the "steamer Ceres, Captain Barnum, with a theatrical company." After a week's performances, we started for the Atta-kapas country. At Opelousas we exchanged the steamer for sugar and molasses; our company was disbanded; and I started for home, arriving in New York, June 4, 1838.

CHAPTER VIII

I was thoroughly disgusted with the life of an itinerant showman; and though I felt that I could succeed in that line, I always regarded it, not as an end, but as a means to something better in due time. Aiming for a respectable, permanent business, I advertised for a partner, stating the fact that I had $2500, in cash, to invest, together with unremitting personal attention. *I received ninety-three propositions*—and *such* propositions! Whoever wishes to buy a cheap dollar's worth of knowledge how people live, or hope to live, let him spend that sum in advertising for a partner, announcing, at the same time, that four or five thousand dollars are "in the wind."

One third of my letters were from porter-house keepers. I also had applications from brokers, lottery-policy men, pawnbrokers, inventors in large numbers, patent medicine men, etc. Several of my correspondents declined naming their business, but promised, in a confidential interview, to open my eyes to mines of gold. I met several of these mysterious personages, and one of them, after much hesitation and repeated promises of secrecy, was actually a *counterfeiter,* who proposed that I should join him in the business. He showed me counterfeit coin and bank-notes; told me if I exposed him it would be certain death, but if I joined him I should reap a rich and safe harvest. He needed the $2500 to purchase paper and ink and procure new "dies."

A sedate, farmer-looking individual, dressed in Quaker costume, applied. He wished me to join him in an oat speculation. He said he was a broken-down merchant, but by dressing in the garb of a Quaker farmer, and buying a horse and wagon, he thought a profitable trade could be driven by purchasing oats at wholesale and selling them in bags from his wagon, in the neighborhood of 21 Bowery. Cartmen and livery-men, he said, would generally purchase more freely, and not be so particular about measuring the grain over again, if they thought they were trading with a Quaker farmer. "Do you mean to cheat in measuring your grain?" said I. "I should probably make it hold out," said he, with a leer which convinced me that there were better men in the State prison.

One wool merchant from Pearl Street applied. I observed that he failed in business within a month afterwards. One man had a "perpetual motion" that would make our fortunes; but unfortunately, in examining it, I discovered a main-spring slily deposited under one of the hollow posts, and so connected as to make the motion perpetual—until it ran down!

I finally entered into co-partnership with a German named Proler, who brought recommendations from a city alderman. The latter also assured me, in a personal interview, that Mr. Proler was a man of honor. He was a manufacturer of paste-blacking, waterproof paste for leather, Cologne water, and bear's grease. We took the store No. 101½ Bowery, at a rent (including the dwelling) of $600 per annum, and opened a large manufactory of the above articles. Proler manufactured and sold the goods at wholesale in Boston, Charleston, Cleveland, and various other parts of the country. I kept the accounts, and attended to sales in the store, wholesale and retail. For some months, the business seemed to be prosperous. But when all my capital had been absorbed, and our notes of hand for additional stock were falling due, our goods meanwhile having been sold on long credit, I began to see the beauties of "the credit system." I *felt* it too, for many a sleepless night did I pass, tormented by the note in the bank that would claim my acquaintance to-morrow.

Proler was a fine-looking man, of plausible manners, but he proved himself a scamp of "the first water." The details of discovery would possess little interest to the reader. Our co-partnership was dissolved in January, 1840, Proler being the purchaser of the entire interest for $2600, on "the credit system." Before his note was due, he packed up "bag and baggage," and sailed for Rotterdam, having swindled me most effectually.

During my business connection with Proler (it was in the spring of 1839) I became acquainted with a lad named John Diamond, who was really a genius in the dancing line. I entered into a contract with his father, put him in charge of an agent, called public attention to his extraordinary merits (though I did not then appear in the transaction), and he became justly celebrated as the best negro-dancer and representative of Ethiopian "break-downs" in the land. He was indeed the prototype of the numerous performers of the sort who have surprised and amused the public these many years.

In the spring of 1840, I hired from Mr. Bradford Jones the saloon in Vauxhall Garden in New York, and opened it with a variety of performances, including singing, dancing, Yankee stories, etc. Miss Mary Taylor, the celebrated actress and singer, here made her first appearance on the stage.

My enterprise in Vauxhall did not meet my expectations, and I relinquished the establishment in August. What I should do next, was now the question. No one but myself can know how earnestly I struggled against the thought of resuming the life of an itinerant showman; but I had a dependent family, my funds were low, and as nothing better appeared, I determined once more to endure the privations, vexations, and uncertainties of a tour in the West and South.

My *large* company of performers consisted of Mr. C. D. Jenkins, an admirable singer and delineator of Yankee and other eccentric characters, Master Diamond, and a fiddler! At Troy, N. Y., I added Francis Lynch, an orphan vagabond of fourteen years of age, whose talent afterwards contributed a due portion to the interest of our entertainments. My brother-in-law, Mr. John Hallett, preceded us as agent and advertiser.

Our route of travel passed through Buffalo, Toronto, in Canada, Detroit, Chicago, Ottawa, Springfield, St. Louis, and numerous intermediate places. From the latter city, we took steamer directly to New Orleans—my company of performers having been reduced, by desertions, to Master Diamond and the fiddler!

We arrived in New Orleans, January 2, 1841, and only $100 remained in my purse. I had started from New York with fully that amount—and four months of anxiety and toil had resulted, with the exception of some small remittances to my family, in nothing more than current expenses. In less than a fortnight afterwards my pockets were decidedly at "ebb-tide." A week's boarding was due to our good landlady, Mrs. Gillies, and I received notice to "pay or quit." I begged a little delay, assuring her that I should be in funds when Diamond had his benefit. He was at that time performing, but theatricals were dull and profits were yet in the dim future. Having no high opinion of "showmen," the worthy woman demanded security, and I put my watch into her hands as a pledge.

The tide began to flow on the 16th. That night I received nearly $500 as my half-share of Diamond's benefit, Mr. Manager Caldwell, of the St. Charles Theatre, retaining the other half, as per agreement. The tide continued to flow; for I received $50 the next night, and $479 the third—the latter as my share of the profits of a grand dancing match, very much on the plan of the match in Philadelphia between Vivalla and Roberts.

Engagements at Vicksburg and Jackson did not result so favorably, but on our return to New Orleans we again succeeded admirably—also subsequently in Mobile. Master Diamond, however, after extorting large sums of money from me, finally absconded, and I turned my face homeward by the route of the Mississippi and the Ohio, on the 12th of March.

When I arrived in Pittsburgh, March 30th, I learned that Jenkins, who had enticed Francis Lynch from my service in St. Louis, was exhibiting the lad at the Museum, under the assumed name of "Master Diamond." I visited the performance *incog.*, and the next day wrote Jenkins an ironical review, informing him that, on inquiry, he might possibly find me in Pittsburgh, prepared to have our law-fight forthwith, though if he preferred, I would postpone the matter until we should meet in New York!

We met the next day. He threatened suit for a libellous review, and my laughter probably instigated the revenge he attempted on the morrow. R. W. Lindsay, of whom I hired Joice Heth in Philadelphia in 1835, and whom I had not seen since that day, was at the time in Pittsburgh. By the instigation of Jenkins, Lindsay sued me for the value of a pipe of brandy, which he pretended I had promised him in addition to the purchase-money in the former transaction. The magistrate required me to give bonds of $500. I was among strangers, could not immediately find bail, and was thrown into jail! My counsel, with whom I left such securities as were then in my possession, had me liberated about four o'clock in the afternoon.

The next morning, I arrested Jenkins for trespass in regard to Francis Lynch, and the assumption of "Master Diamond's name and reputation," etc. He was sent to jail, and liberated about four o'clock in the afternoon! Each of us having had a turn in prison, we adjourned our controversy to New York—and there he got the worst of the bargain. As for Lindsay, he had been merely a tool of Jenkins, and I heard no more of his claim. Twelve years afterwards, he called upon me in Boston, with an apology. He was miserably poor, and I was highly prosperous. I hope I may be allowed to add that he did not afterwards lack a friend.

I arrived in New York, April 23, 1841, after an absence of eight months, found my family in excellent health, and re-resolved that I would never again be an itinerant showman.

CHAPTER IX

APRIL 26, 1841, I called on Robert Sears, the publisher of "Sears' Pictorial Illustrations of the Bible," and contracted for five hundred copies of the work for $500, accepted the United States agency, opened an office, May 10th, at the corner of Beekman and Nassau Streets, which was subsequently taken by Mr. Redfield as a bookstore, and is the present site of the Nassau Bank. I had thus made another effort to quit the life of a showman for ever, and settle down into a respectable calling. I advertised largely, appointed agents and sub-agents, and managed in the course of six months to sell thousands of books, and at the same time to place a sufficient number in the hands of irresponsible agents to use up all my profits and all my capital!

In the mean time I again leased Vauxhall saloon, and opened it June 14, 1841. I thought it would be compromising my dignity as a "Bible man" to be known as the lessee of a theatre, and the concern was managed, under my directions, by Mr. John Hallett, my brother-in-law. We closed the season September 25th, having cleared about two hundred dollars above expenses.

Living in the city of New York with nothing to do and a family to support, in a very short time exhausted my funds, and I became about as poor as I should ever wish to be. I looked around in vain for employment congenial to my feelings, that would serve to keep my head above water. I finally obtained the post of writing advertisements and notices for the Bowery Amphitheatre, my duties including daily visits to the upper stories of many newspaper offices to deliver what I had prepared, and see that they were inserted. For this I received $4.00 per week, and was thankful for even that. I also wrote articles for the Sunday press, for the purpose of enabling me to "keep the pot boiling" at home.

These productions afforded me a fair remuneration, but it was at best a precarious way of living, and I began to realize, seriously, that I was at the very bottom round of fortune's ladder, and that I had now arrived at an age when it was necessary to make one grand effort to raise myself above want, and to think soberly of laying up something for "a rainy day." I had hitherto been careless upon that point. I had engaged in divers enterprises, caring little what the result was, so that I made a present living for my family. I now saw that it was time to provide for the future.

About this period, I received a letter from my esteemed friend, Hon. Thomas T. Whittlesey, of Danbury. He had long held a mortgage of $500 on a piece of property which I owned in that town. He wrote to say that he was satisfied I never would lay up anything until I could "invent a riddle that would hold water," and as that was not very likely to occur, I might as well pay him now as ever. That letter strengthened the resolutions I had made, and laying it aside unanswered, I said to myself, "Now, Mr. B., no more nonsense, no more living from hand to mouth, but from this moment please to concentrate your energies upon providing permanently for *the future.*"

While engaged as outside clerk for the Bowery Amphitheatre, I casually learned that the collection of curiosities comprising Scudder's American Museum, at the corner of Broadway and Ann Street, was for sale. It belonged to the daughters of Mr. Scudder, and was conducted for their benefit by John Furzman, under the authority of Mr. John Heath, administrator. The price asked for the entire collection was $15,000. It had cost its founder, Mr. Scudder, probably $50,000, and from the profits of the establishment he had been able to leave a large competency to his children.   The Museum, however, had been for several years a losing concern, and the heirs were anxious to sell it.

It will not be considered surprising, under all the circumstances, that my speculative spirit should look in that direction for a permanent investment.   My recent enterprises had not indeed been productive, and my funds were decidedly low; but my family was in poor health, I desired to enjoy the blessing of a fixed home—and so I repeatedly visited that Museum as a thoughtful looker-on.   I saw, or believed I saw, that only energy, tact and liberality were needed, to give it life and to put it on a profitable footing; and although it might have appeared presumptuous, on my part, to dream of buying so valuable a property without having any money to do it with, I seriously determined to make the purchase, if possible.

I met a friend one day in the street, and told him my intentions. "*You* buy the American Museum?" said he with surprise, for he knew that my funds were at ebb-tide; "what do you intend buying it with?"

"*Brass*," I replied, "for silver and gold I have none."

It was even so.

The Museum building, I learned, belonged to Mr. Francis W. Olmsted, a retired merchant, who had a suite of rooms in Park Place. How to approach this great man was a question.   I was acquainted with no one who knew him, and to enter his presence without an introduction I considered equivalent to being kicked out of his house.   I therefore wrote him a letter, informing him that I desired to purchase the Museum collection, and that although I had no ready means, if it could be purchased upon a reasonable credit I was entirely confident that my tact and experience, added to a most determined devotion to business, would enable me to make the payments when due.   On this basis I asked him to purchase the collection in

BARNUM'S AMERICAN MUSEUM AT THE CORNER OF BROADWAY
AND ANN STREETS, NEW YORK CITY.

his own name—give me a writing securing it to me provided I made the payments punctually, including the rent of his building—allow me twelve dollars and a half a week on which to support my family —and if at any time I failed to meet the instalment due, I would vacate the premises and forfeit all that might have been paid to that date. "In fact, Mr. Olmsted," I continued in my earnestness, "you may bind me in any way, and as tightly as you please—only give me a chance to dig out, or scratch out, and I will either do so or forfeit all the labor and trouble which I may have incurred."

I also endeavored to show Mr. Olmsted that by making this arrangement he would secure a permanent tenant, whereas if I did not make the purchase the Museum would probably soon be closed. I added, that if he would have the goodness to grant me an interview, I should be happy to give him satisfactory references, and would also submit to any reasonable conditions which he might propose.

I took the letter myself, handed it to his servant, and in two days afterwards I received a reply, naming an hour for me to call on him. I was there at the exact moment, and Mr. Olmsted expressed himself pleased with my punctuality. He eyed me closely, and put several home questions regarding my habits and antecedents. I told him frankly my experience in the way of a caterer for public amusements—mentioned Vauxhall Garden, the circus, and several exhibitions that I had managed in the South. I was favorably impressed with Mr. Olmsted's appearance and manner. He indeed tried to assume an austere look, and to affect the aristocrat; but I thought I could see the good, open-hearted, noble *man* peering through his eyes, and a subsequent intimate acquaintance proved the correctness of my impressions respecting him.

"Who are your references?" he inquired.

"Any man in my line," I replied; "from Edmund Simpson, manager of the Park Theatre, or William Niblo, to Messrs. Welch,

June, Titus, Turner, Angevine, or other circus or menagerie proprietors; also Moses Y. Beach of the New York *Sun.*"

"Can you get any of them to call on me?" he continued.

I informed him that I could, and it was arranged that they should call on him the next day, and myself the day afterwards. My friend Niblo willingly rode down in his carriage, and had an interview with Mr. Olmsted. Mr. Beach and several others among the gentlemen named also called, and on the following morning I waited upon the arbiter of my fate.

"I don't like your references, Mr. Barnum," said Mr. Olmsted abruptly, as soon as I entered the room.

I was confused, and said I regretted to hear it.

"They all speak too well of you," he added, laughing; "in fact they talk as if they were all partners of yours, and intended to share the profits."

This intelligence, of course, pleased me. Mr. Olmsted then inquired if I could not induce some friend to give bonds as security that I should meet the instalments as they became due. I thought it was doubtful.

"Can you offer me any security in case I should make the purchase for you?" was his still more direct question.

I thought of several small pieces of land which I owned in Connecticut, but they were severely afflicted with mortgages. "I have some land and buildings in Connecticut, but there are encumbrances on them," I replied.

"Yes, yes; I don't want mortgaged property," said Mr. O.; "I should probably have to redeem it."

During further conversation, it was agreed that if he concluded to make the purchase for me, he should retain the property until it was all paid for; and should also appoint (at my expense) a ticket-receiver and accountant, who should render him a weekly statement. It was further stipulated that I should take in an apartment in the adjoining building, hitherto used as a billiard-room, and allow therefor five hundred dollars per year, making the entire rent three thousand dollars per annum, on a lease of ten years. I felt that in all this I had been liberal in my propositions and agreements, and hoped that the wealthy landlord would demand no more concessions. But he wanted something more.

"Now," said he, "if you only had a piece of unencumbered real estate that you could offer as additional security, I think I might venture to negotiate with you."

This seemed the turning-point of my fortune. Thinks I to myself, "It is now or never," and memory rapidly ran over my small possessions in search of the coveted bit of land. *Ivy Island,* in all the beauty in which my youthful imagination had pictured it, came dancing to my relief. I hesitated an instant. He is amply secured already—so I thought within myself—and without *some* piece of land, I may lose the Museum altogether. I saw no particular harm in it, and after a moment's hesitation I replied:

"I have five acres of land in Connecticut which is free from all lien or encumbrance."

"Indeed! what did you pay for it?"

"It was a present from my late grandfather, Phineas Taylor, given me on account of my name."

"Was he rich?" inquired Mr. Olmsted.

"He was considered well off in those parts," I answered.

"Very kind in him to give you the land. It is doubtless valuable. But I suppose you would not like to part with it, considering it was a present."

"I shall not have to part with it, if I make my payments punctually," I replied, "and I am sure I shall do that."

"Well," said Mr. Olmsted, "I think I will make the purchase for you. At all events, I'll think it over, and in the mean time you must see the administrator and heirs of the estate—get their best terms, and meet me here on my return to town a week hence."

I withdrew, and proceeded at once to the house of Mr. John Heath, the administrator. His price was $15,000. I offered him $10,000, payable in seven equal annual instalments, with good security. He could not think of selling at that price, and I agreed to call again.

During the week I had several interviews with Mr. Heath, and it was finally agreed that I should have it for $12,000, payable as above—possession to be given on the 15th November. Mr. Olmsted assented to this, and a morning was appointed to draw and sign the writings. Mr. Heath appeared, but said he must decline proceeding any farther in my case, as he had sold the collection to the directors of Peale's Museum (an incorporated institution) for $15,000, and had received $1000 in advance.

I was thunderstruck. I appealed to his honor. He replied that he had signed no writing with me, was not therefore legally bound, and he felt it his duty to do the best he could for the orphan girls. Mr. Olmsted said he was sorry for me, but could not help me. He would now have permanent tenants who would not require him to incur any risk, and I must necessarily be thrown overboard.

I withdrew, with feelings which I need not attempt to describe. I immediately informed myself as to the character of this Peale's Museum Company. It proved to consist of a company of speculators, headed by an unsuccessful ex-president of a bank, who had bought Peale's collection for a few thousand dollars, were now to join the American Museum with it, issue and sell stock to the amount of $50,000, pocket $30,000 profits, and permit the stockholders to look out for themselves.

I went immediately to several of the editors, including Major M. M. Noath, M. Y. Beach, my good friends, West, Herrick and Ropes, of the *Atlas,* and others, and stated my grievances. "Now," said I, "if you will grant me the use of your columns, I'll blow that speculation sky-high." They all consented, and I wrote a large number of squibs, cautioning the public against buying the Museum stock, ridiculed the idea of a board of broken-down bank directors engaging in the exhibition of stuffed monkey and gander skins, appealed to the case of the Zoological Institute, which had failed by adopting such a plan as the one now proposed, and finally told the public that such a speculation would be infinitely more unwise than Dickens's "Grand United Metropolitan Hot Muffin and Crumpet-baking and Punctual Delivery Company."

The stock was as dead as a herring! I then went to Mr. Heath and solicited a confidential conversation. He granted it. I asked him when the directors were to pay the other $14,000. "On the 26th day of December, or forfeit the $1000 already paid," was the reply. I assured him that they would never pay it, that they could not raise it, and that he would ultimately find himself with the Museum collection on his hands, and if once I started off with an exhibition for the South, I would not touch the Museum at *any* price. "Now," said I, "if you will agree with me confidentially, that in case these gentlemen do not pay you on the 26th December, I may have it on the 27th for $12,000, I will run the risk, and wait in this city until that date." He readily agreed to the proposition, but said he was sure they would not forfeit their $1000.

"Very well," said I; "all I ask of you is, that this arrangement shall not be mentioned." He assented. "On the 27th day of December, at ten o'clock A. M., I wish you to meet me in Mr. Olmsted's apartments, prepared to sign the writings, provided this incorporated company do not pay you $14,000 on the 26th." He agreed to this, and by my request put it in writing.

From that moment I felt that the Museum was mine. I saw Mr. Olmsted, and told him so. He promised secrecy, and agreed to sign the documents if the other parties did not meet their engagement.

This was about the 15th November. To all who spoke to me

about the Museum, I simply remarked that I had lost it. In the mean time the new company could not sell a dollar's worth of stock, for I kept up a perfect shower of squibs through the papers.

About the 1st of December, I received a letter from the Secretary of the Peale's Museum Company, or rather the "New York Museum Company," as it was called, desiring me to meet the directors on the following Monday morning at the Museum, when and where I should probably hear something to my advantage. I saw that the newspaper medicine was doing its office. It was evident that those gentlemen wished to purchase my silence.

I was punctual at the meeting. The "honorable board of directors" was in session. The venerable President, a gray-haired, hawk-eyed old man, who had recently been President of a broken bank, accosted me with his blandest smile and smoothest tone of language. The upshot of the matter was, they proposed to hire me to manage the united museums. I professed to take it all in earnest, and when asked to mention the salary I should expect, I specified $3000 per annum. They complimented me on my character for ability in that department, and engaged me at the sum I demanded, my salary to commence on the 1st day of January, 1842. As I was leaving the "august presence," the amiable President pleasantly remarked, "Of course, Mr. Barnum, we shall have no more of your squibs through the newspapers."

"I ever try to serve the interests of my employers," I replied. The jolly directors probably had a hearty laugh so soon as I was beyond hearing their unseemly mirth. They probably meant by thus keeping me quiet to sell their stock, and permit the stockholders to throw me overboard as soon as they pleased. They thought they had caught me securely. I *knew* that I had caught *them*.

Finding that I was now removed out of the way, those directors did not fear that any other person would attempt to buy the American Museum, and they concluded not to advertise their stock until the first of January, as that would give the people longer time to forget the attacks which I had made on it. As for their promised payment on the 26th December, unaware that Mr. Heath had contracted to me for $12,000, they thought he would cheerfully wait on them until it suited their pleasure to pay him. In fact, so unconcerned were they upon this point, that they did not even call on the administrator on the 26th inst., nor send him the slightest apology for not doing so!

On the morning of the 27th, I was at Mr. Olmsted's apartment, with my legal counsellor, Chas. T. Cromwell, Esq., at half-past nine o'clock. Mr. Heath came with his lawyer punctually at ten, and before two o'clock that day I was put in formal possession of the American Museum. The first act which I performed, after being thus installed, was to write and dispatch the following note:

AMERICAN MUSEUM, NEW YORK, Dec. 27, 1841.

To the President and Directors of the New York Museum:

GENTLEMEN:—It gives me great pleasure to inform you that you are placed upon the Free List of this establishment until further notice.

P. T. BARNUM, Proprietor.

The President was astonished beyond measure, and could scarcely believe his eyes. He called upon Mr. Heath, and learned that I had indeed bought and was in possession of the American Museum. His indignation knew no bounds. He threatened him with a prosecution, but finding that this availed him nothing, he demanded the return of the thousand dollars which had been paid on the agreement. It was refused because forfeited, and the company lost it.

No one will doubt that I now put forth all my energy. It was strictly "neck or nothing." I must either pay for the establishment within a stipulated period, or forfeit it, including all I might have paid on account, provided Mr. Olmsted should insist on the letter of the contract. Let "come what would," I was determined to *deserve* success, and brain and hands and feet were alike busy in forwarding the interests of the Museum.

The system of economy necessary to support my family in the city of New York upon $600 a year was not only assented to by my treasure of a wife, but she expressed her willingness to reduce the expenses to four hundred dollars per year, if necessary.

One day, about six months after I had purchased the Museum, my friend Mr. Olmsted happened in at my ticket office about twelve o'clock, and found me alone eating my dinner, which consisted of a few slices of corned beef and bread that I had brought from home in the morning. "Is this the way you eat your dinner?" he inquired.

"I have not eaten a warm dinner since I bought the Museum, except on the Sabbath," I replied, "and I intend never to eat another on a week-day until I am out of debt."

"Ah! you are safe, and will pay for the Museum before the year is out," he replied, clapping me familiarly on the shoulder. And he was right, for in less than a year from that period I was in full possession of the Museum as my own property, every cent having been paid out of the profits of the establishment.

In 1865 the space occupied for my Museum purposes was more than double what it was in 1842. The Lecture Room, originally narrow, ill-contrived and inconvenient, was so enlarged and improved that it became one of the most commodious and beautiful amusement halls in the City of New York. At first, my attractions and inducements were merely the collection of curiosities by day, and an evening entertainment consisting of such variety performances as were current in ordinary shows. Then Saturday afternoons, and, soon afterwards, Wednesday afternoons were devoted to entertainments and the popularity of the Museum grew so rapidly that I presently found it expedient and profitable to open the great Lecture Room every afternoon, as well as every evening, on every week-day in the year. The first experiments in this direction more than justified

Gleason's Pictorial

BARNUM'S AMERICAN MUSEUM AT THE CORNER OF BROADWAY AND ANN STREETS, NEW YORK CITY, INTERIOR VIEW

BROADWAY IN 1850, SHOWING BARNUM'S AMERICAN MUSEUM AT LEFT, ASTOR HOUSE AND ST. PAUL'S CHURCH AT RIGHT, AND

my expectations, for the day exhibitions were always more thronged than those of the evening. Of course I made the most of the holidays, advertising extensively and presenting extra inducements; nor did attractions elsewhere seem to keep the crowd from coming to the Museum. On great holidays, I gave as many as twelve performances to as many different audiences.

By degrees the character of the stage performances was changed. The transient attractions of the Museum were constantly diversified, and educated dogs, industrious fleas, automatons, jugglers, ventriloquists, living statuary, tableaux, gipsies, Albinoes, fat boys, giants, dwarfs, rope-dancers, live "Yankees," pantomime, instrumental music, singing and dancing in great variety, dioramas, panoramas, models of Niagara, Dublin, Paris, and Jerusalem; Hannington's dioramas of the Creation, the Deluge, Fairy Grotto, Storm at Sea; the first English Punch and Judy in this country, Italian Fantoccini, mechanical figures, fancy glass-blowing, knitting machines and other triumphs in the merchanical arts; dissolving views, American Indians, who enacted their warlike and religious ceremonies on the stage,—these, among others, were all exceedingly successful.

Apart from the merit and interest of these performances, and apart from every thing connected with the stage, my permanent collection of curiosities is, without doubt, abundantly worth the uniform charge of admission to all the entertainments of the establishment, and I can therefore afford to be accused of "humbug" when I add such transient novelties as increase its attractions. If I have exhibited a questionable dead mermaid in my Museum, it should not be overlooked that I have also exhibited cameleopards, a rhinoceros, grizzly bears, orang-outangs, great serpents, etc., about which there could be no mistake because they were alive; and I should hope that a little "clap-trap" occasionally, in the way of transparencies, flags, exaggerated pictures, and puffing advertisements, might find an offset in a wilderness of wonderful, instructive, and amusing realities.   Indeed I cannot doubt that the sort of "clap-trap" here referred to, is allowable, and that the public like a little of it mixed up with the great realties which I provide.   The titles of "humbug," and the "prince of humbugs," were first applied to me by myself.   I made these titles a part of my "stock in trade," and may here quote a passage from the "Fortunes of the Scattergood Family," a work by the popular English writer, Albert Smith:

> " 'It's a great thing to be a humbug,' said Mr. Rossett. 'I've been called so often. It means hitting the public in reality. Anybody who can do so, is sure to be called a humbug by somebody who can't.' "

I thoroughly understood the art of advertising, not merely by means of printer's ink, which I have always used freely, and to which I confess myself so much indebted for my success, but by turning every possible circumstance to my account.   It was my monomania to make the Museum the town wonder and town talk. I often seized upon an opportunity by instinct, even before I had a very definite conception as to how it should be used, and it seemed, somehow, to mature itself and serve my purpose.   As an illustration, one morning a stout, hearty-looking man came into my ticket-office and begged some money.   I asked him why he did not work and earn his living?   He replied that he could get nothing to do and that he would be glad of any job at a dollar a day.   I handed him a quarter of a dollar, told him to go and get his breakfast and return, and I would employ him at light labor at a dollar and a half a day. When he returned I gave him five common bricks.

"Now," said I, "go and lay a brick on the sidewalk at the corner of Broadway and Ann Street; another close by the Museum; a third diagonally across the way at the corner of Broadway and Vesey Street, by the Astor House; put down the fourth on the sidewalk in front of St. Paul's Church, opposite; then, with the fifth brick in hand, take up a rapid march from one point to the other, making the circuit, exchanging your brick at every point, and say nothing to any one."

"What is the object of this?" inquired the man.

"No matter," I replied; "all you need to know is that it brings you fifteen cents wages per hour. It is a bit of my fun, and to assist me properly you must seem to be as deaf as a post; wear a serious countenance; answer no questions; pay no attention to any one; but attend faithfully to the work and at the end of every hour by St. Paul's clock show this ticket at the Museum door; enter, walking solemnly through every hall in the building; pass out, and resume your work."

With the remark that it was "all one to him, so long as he could earn his living," the man placed his bricks and began his round. Half an hour afterwards, at least five hundred people were watching his mysterious movements. He had assumed a military step and bearing, and looking as sober as a judge, he made no response whatever to the constant inquiries as to the object of his singular conduct. At the end of the first hour, the sidewalks in the vicinity were packed with people all anxious to solve the mystery. The man, as directed, then went into the Museum, devoting fifteen minutes to a solemn survey of the halls, and afterwards returning to his round. This was repeated every hour till sundown, and whenever the man went into the Museum a dozen or more persons would buy tickets and follow him, hoping to gratify their curiosity in regard to the purpose of his movements. This was continued for several days—the curious people who followed the man into the Museum considerably more than paying his wages—till finally the policeman, to whom I had imparted my object, complained that the obstruction of the sidewalk by crowds had become so serious that I must call in my "brick man." This trivial incident excited considerable talk and amusement; it advertised me; and it materially advanced my purpose of making a lively corner near the Museum.

CHAPTER X

FROM the first, it was my study to give my patrons a superfluity of novelties, and for this I make no special claim to generosity, for it was strictly a business transaction. To send away my visitors more than doubly satisfied, was to induce them to come again and to bring their friends. I meant to make people talk about my Museum; to exclaim over its wonders; to have men and women all over the country say: "There is not another place in the United States where so much can be seen for twenty-five cents as in Barnum's American Museum." It was the best advertisement I could possibly have, and one for which I could afford to pay. I knew, too, that it was an honorable advertisement, because it was as deserved as it was spontaneous. And so, in addition to the permanent collection and the ordinary attractions of the stage, I labored to keep the Museum well supplied with transient novelties; I exhibited such living curiosities as a rhinoceros, giraffes, grizzly bears, orang-outangs, great serpents, and whatever else of the kind money would buy or enterprise secure.

Knowing that a visit to my varied attractions and genuine curiosities was well worth to any one three times the amount asked as an entrance fee, I confess that I was not so scrupulous, as possibly I should have been, about the methods used to call public attention to my establishment. The one end aimed at was to make men and women think and talk and wonder, and, as a practical result, go to the Museum. This was my constant study and occupation.

It was the world's way then, as it is now, to excite the community with flaming posters, promising almost everything for next to nothing. I confess that I took no pains to set my enterprising fellow-citizens a better example. I fell in with the world's way; and if my "puffing" was more persistent, my advertising more audacious, my posters more glaring, my pictures more exaggerated, my flags more patriotic and my transparencies more brilliant than they would have been under the management of my neighbors, it was not because I had less scruple than they, but more energy, far more ingenuity, and a better foundation for such promises.

Among my first extra exhibitions produced at the American Museum, was a model of the Falls of Niagara, belonging to Grain the artist. It was undoubtedly a fine model, giving the mathematical proportions of that great cataract, and the trees, rocks, buildings, etc., in its vicinity. But the absurdity of the thing consisted in introducing water, thus pretending to present a *fac simile* of that great wonder of nature. The falls were about eighteen inches high, every thing else being in due proportion!

I confess I felt somewhat ashamed of this myself, yet it made a good line in the bill, and I bought the model for $200. My advertisements then announced among the attractions of the Museum,

THE GREAT MODEL OF NIAGARA FALLS,
WITH REAL WATER!

A single barrel of water answered the purpose of this model for an entire season; for the falls flowed into a reservoir behind the scenes, and the water was continually re-supplied to the cataract by means of a small pump. Many visitors who could not afford to travel to Niagara were doubtless induced to visit the "model with real water," and if they found it rather "small potatoes," they had the whole Museum to fall back upon for 25 cents, and no fault was found.

One day I was peremptorily summoned to appear before the

Board of Croton Water Commissioners the next morning at ten o'clock. I was punctual.

"Sir," said the President, "you pay only $25 per annum for the Croton water at the Museum. That is simply intended to supply the ordinary purposes of your establishment. We cannot furnish water for your Niagara Falls without large extra compensation."

Begging "his honor" not to believe all he read in the papers, nor to be too literal in the interpretation of my large showbills, I explained the operation of the great cataract, and offered to pay a dollar a drop for all the water I used for Niagara Falls exceeding one barrel per month, provided my pump continued in good order! I was permitted to retire, amid a hearty burst of laughter from the Commissioners, in which his honor the President condescended to join.

On one occasion, Louis Gaylord Clark, Esq., the witty and popular editor of the *Knickerbocker,* called to view my Museum. I had never had the pleasure of seeing him before, and he introduced himself. I was extremely anxious that my establishment should receive a "first-rate notice" in his popular magazine, and therefore accompanied him through the entire Museum, taking especial pains to point out all objects of interest. We passed the entrance of the hall containing Niagara Falls just as the visitors had entered it from the performances in the Lecture Room, and hearing the pump at work, I was aware that the great cataract was at that moment in full operation.

I desired to avoid that exhibition, feeling confident that if Mr. Clark should see the model Niagara, he would be so much disgusted with the entire show that he would "blow it up" in his *Knickerbocker,* or (what I always consider much the worse for me) pass it by in *silent* contempt. Seeing him approach the entrance, I endeavored to call his attention to some object of interest in the other hall, but I was too late. He had noticed a concourse of visitors in the "Falls

Room," and his curiosity to know what was going on was excited.

"Hold on, Barnum," said Clark; "let us see what you have here."

"It is only a model of Niagara Falls," I replied.

"Oh, ah, yes, yes, I remember now. I have noticed your advertisements and splendid posters announcing Niagara Falls with real water. I have some curiosity to see the cartaract in operation," said Clark, at the same time mounting upon a chair in order to obtain a full view over the heads of the visitors.

I felt considerably sheepish as I saw this movement, and listened to the working of the old pump, whose creakings seemed to me to be worse than ever. I held my breath, expecting to hear the sagacious editor pronounce this the silliest humbug that he ever saw. I was presently, however, as much surprised as delighted to hear him say:

"Well, Barnum, I declare that is quite a new idea. I never saw the like before."

I revived in a moment; and thinking that if Louis Gaylord Clark could see any thing attractive in the old model, he must be particularly green, I determined to do all in my power to assist his verdancy. "Yes," I replied, "it is quite a new idea."

"I declare I never saw any thing of the kind before in all my life," exclaimed Clark with much enthusiasm.

"I flatter myself it is, in point of originality and ingenuity, considerably ahead of any invention of modern times," I replied with a feeling of exultation, as I saw that I had caught the great critic, and was sure of a puff of the best sort.

"Original!" exclaimed the editor. "Yes, it is certainly original. I never dreamed of such a thing; I never saw any thing of the kind before since I was born—and I hope with all my heart I never shall again!"

It is needless to say that I was completely taken in, and felt that any ordinary keyhole was considerably larger than would be necessary for me to crawl through.

We then passed to the upper stories of the Museum, and finally to the roof, where I had advertised an "aerial garden," which consisted of two tubs, each containing a stunted and faded cedar, and ten or twelve pots of wilted flowers, backed up by a dozen small tables and a few chairs for the accommodation of such partakers of ice cream as could appreciate the beauties of ever-verdant nature, as shown forth in the tubs and pots aforesaid.

The *Knickerbocker* appeared, and I felt happy to see that while it spoke of the assiduity in business manifested by the new proprietor of the Museum, and a prognostication that he would soon render his establishment highly popular, the editor had kindly refrained from making any allusion to "THE CATARACT OF NIAGARA WITH REAL WATER!"

Some months subsequent to this, Mr. Clark came rushing into the Museum almost out of breath, and with much earnestness saluted me thus: "Friend Barnum, I have come in to ask if you have got the club in the Museum that Captain Cook was killed with?"

Remembering that I had a large lot of Indian war-clubs among the collection of aboriginal curiosities, and feeling that I owed Clark a joke for his Niagara Falls catch, I instantly replied that I was the owner of the club in question.

"Well, I declare I am very glad to hear it," said he; "for do you know that I have for a long time had a singular and irrepressible desire to see that club?"

"Wait here a few minutes, and I will show it to you," I replied.

Passing up stairs, I commenced overhauling a lot of war-clubs, and finally selected a heavy one that looked as if it *might* have killed Captain Cook, or any body else whose head it came in contact with. Having affixed a small label on it, reading "The Capt.

Cook Club," I took it down to Mr. Clark, assuring him that this was the instrument of death which he had inquired for.

"Is it possible!" said he, as he took it in his hand. Presently raising it above his head, he exclaimed, "Well, I declare, this is a terrible weapon with which to take a man's life."

"Yes," I replied seriously, but feeling an inward delight that I was now paying off Mr. Clark with interest; "I believe it killed the victim at the first blow!"

"Poor Captain Cook!" exclaimed Clark with a sigh; "I wonder if he was conscious after receiving the fatal blow."

"I don't think he could have been," I responded with a well-feigned look of sorrow.

"You are sure this is the identical club?" inquired Clark.

"We have documents which place its identity beyond all question," I replied.

"Poor Cook! poor Cook!" said Clark musingly. "Well, Mr. Barnum," he continued with great gravity, at the same time extending his hand and giving mine a hearty shake, "I am really very much obliged to you for your kindness. I had an irrepressible desire to see the club that killed Captain Cook, and I felt quite confident you could accommodate me. I have been in half a dozen smaller museums, and as *they all had it,* I was sure a large establishment like yours would not be without it!"

The "Fejee Mermaid" was by many supposed to be a curiosity manufactured by myself, or made to my order. This is not the fact. I certainly had much to do in bringing it before the public, and as I am now in the confessional mood, I will "make a clean breast" of the ways and means I adopted for that purpose. I must first relate how it came into my possession and its alleged history.

Early in the summer of 1842, Moses Kimball, Esq., the popular proprietor of the Boston Museum, came to New York and exhibited to me what purported to be a mermaid. He stated that he had bought it of a sailor whose father, while in Calcutta in 1817 as captain of a Boston ship (of which Captain John Ellery was principal owner), had purchased it, believing it to be a preserved specimen of a veritable mermaid, obtained, as he was assured, from Japanese sailors. Not doubting that it would prove as surprising to others as it had been to himself, and hoping to make a rare speculation of it as an extraordinary curiosity, he appropriated $6000 of the ship's money to the purchase of it, left the ship in charge of the mate, and went to London.

He did not realize his expectations, and returned to Boston. Still believing that his curiosity was a genuine animal and therefore highly valuable, he preserved it with great care, not stinting himself in the expense of keeping it insured, though re-engaged as ship's captain under his former employers to reimburse the sum taken from their funds to pay for the mermaid. He died possessing no other property, and his only son and heir, who placed a low estimate on his father's purchase, sold it to Mr. Kimball, who brought it to New York for my inspection.

Such was the story. Not trusting my own acuteness on such matters, I requested my naturalist's opinion of the genuineness of the animal. He replied that he could not conceive how it was manufactured; for he never knew a monkey with such peculiar teeth, arms, hands, etc., nor had he knowledge of a fish with such peculiar fins.

"Then why do you suppose it is manufactured?" I inquired.

"Because I don't believe in mermaids," replied the naturalist.

"That is no reason at all," said I, "and therefore I'll believe in the mermaid, and hire it."

This was the easiest part of the experiment. How to modify general incredulity in the existence of mermaids, so far as to awaken curiosity to see and examine the specimen, was now the all-important question. Some extraordinary means must be resorted to, and I saw no better method than to "start the ball a-rolling" at some distance from the centre of attraction.

In due time a communication appeared in the New York *Herald,* dated and mailed in Montgomery, Ala., giving the news of the day, trade, the crops, political gossip, etc., and also an incidental paragraph about a certain Dr. Griffin, agent of the Lyceum of Natural History in London, recently from Pernambuco, who had in his possession a most remarkable curiosity, being nothing less than a veritable mermaid taken among the Fejee Islands, and preserved in China, where the Doctor had bought it at a high figure for the Lyceum of Natural History.

A week or ten days afterwards, a letter of similar tenor, dated and mailed in Charleston, S. C., varying of course in the items of local news, was published in another New York paper.

This was followed by a third letter, dated and mailed in Washington city, published in still another New York paper—there being in addition the expressed hope that the editors of the Empire City would beg a sight of the extraordinary curiosity before Dr. Griffin took ship for England.

A few days subsequently to the publication of this thrice-repeated announcement, Mr. Lyman (who was my employee in the case of Joice Heth) was duly registered at one of the principal hotels in Philadelphia as Dr. Griffin of Pernambuco for London. His gentlemanly, dignified, yet social manners and liberality gained him a fine reputation for a few days, and when he paid his bill one afternoon, preparatory to leaving for New York the next day, he expressed his thanks to the landlord for special attention and courtesy. "If you will step to my room," said Lyman, alias Griffin, "I will permit you to see something that will surprise you." Whereupon the landlord was shown the most extraordinary curiosity in the world—a mermaid. He was so highly gratified and interested that he earnestly begged permission to introduce certain friends of his, including several editors, to view the wonderful specimen.

"Although it is no interest of mine," said the curiosity-hunter, "the Lyceum of Natural History, of which I am agent, will not be injured by granting the courtesy you request." And so an appointment was made for the evening.

The result might easily be gathered from the editorial columns of the Philadelphia papers a day or two subsequently to that interview with the mermaid. Suffice it to say, that the plan worked admirably, and the Philadelphia press aided the press of New York in awakening a wide-reaching and increasing curiosity to see the mermaid.

I may as well confess that those three communications from the South were written by myself, and forwarded to friends of mine, with instructions respectively to mail them, each on the day of its date. This fact and the corresponding post-marks did much to prevent suspicion of a hoax, and the New York editors thus unconsciously contributed to my arrangements for bringing the mermaid into public notice.

Lyman then returned to New York with his precious treasure, and putting up at the Pacific Hotel in Greenwich Street as Dr. Griffin, it soon reached the ears of the wide-awake reporters for the press that the mermaid was in town. They called at the Pacific Hotel, and the polite agent of the British Lyceum of Natural History kindly permitted them to gratify their curosity. The New York newspapers contained numerous reports of these examinations, all of which were quite satisfactory.

I am confident that the reporters and editors who examined this animal were honestly persuaded that it was what it purported to be—a veritable mermaid. Nor is this to be wondered at, since, if it was a work of art, the monkey and fish were so nicely conjoined that no human eye could detect the point where the junction was formed. The spine of the fish proceeded in a straight and apparently unbroken line to the base of the skull—the hair of the animal was found growing several inches down on the shoulders of the fish, and the application of a microscope absolutely revealed what seemed to be minute fish scales lying in myriads amidst the hair. The teeth and formation of the fingers and hands differed materially from those of any monkey or orang-outang ever discovered, while the location of the fins was different from those of any species of the fish tribe known to naturalists. The animal was an ugly, dried-up, black-looking, and diminutive specimen, about three feet long. Its mouth was open, its tail turned over, and its arms thrown up, giving it the appearance of having died in great agony.

Assuming, what is no doubt true, that the mermaid was manufactured, it was a most remarkable specimen of ingenuity and untiring patience. For my own part I really had scarcely cared at the time to form an opinion of the origin of this creature, but it was my impression that it was the work of some ingenious Japanese, Chinaman, or other eastern genius, and that it had probably been one among the many hideous objects of Buddhist or Hindoo worship.

However, in reading myself up on the history of Japan, I found the following article in a work entitled "Manners and Customs of the Japanese in the Nineteenth Century, from the accounts of recent Dutch residents in Japan, and from the German work of Dr. Ph. Fr. Von Siebold":

"Another Japanese fisherman displayed his ingenuity in a less honorable and useful form than Kiyemon, to make money out of his countrymen's passion for whatever is odd and strange. He contrived to unite the upper half of a monkey to the lower half of a fish, so neatly as to defy ordinary inspection. He then gave out that he had caught the creature alive in his net, but that it had died shortly after being taken out of the water; and he derived considerable pecuniary profit from his device in more ways than one. The exhibition of the sea monster to Japanese curiosity paid well; but yet more productive was the assertion that the half-human fish had spoken during the few minutes it existed out of its native element, predicting a certain number of years of wonderful fertility, to be followed by a fatal epidemic, the only remedy against which would be possession of the marine prophet's likeness. The sale of these pictured mermaids was immense. Either this composite animal, or another, the offspring of the success of the first, was sold to the Dutch factory and transmitted to Batavia, where it fell into the hands of a shrewd American, who brought it to Europe, and there, in the years 1822-3, exhibited his purchase as a real mermaid, at every capital, to the admiration of the ignorant, the perplexity of the learned, and the filling of his own purse."

Is it not a plausible conjecture that this account relates to the identical mermaid exhibited in the American Museum? Certainly the method adopted to induce people to buy the likeness, as related by Siebold, fairly entitles my Japanese *confrère* to the palm and title of "Prince of Humbugs."

Smaller specimens, purporting to be mermaids, but less elaborately gotten up, have been seen in various museums. I believe they are all made in Japan. I purchased one in the Peale collection in Philadelphia. It was burnt at the time the Museum opened by me in that city was destroyed by fire in 1851.

While Lyman was preparing public opinion on mermaids at the Pacific Hotel, I was industriously at work (though of course privately) in getting up wood-cuts and transparencies, as well as a pamphlet, proving the authenticity of mermaids, all in anticipation of the speedy exhibition of Dr. Griffin's specimen. I had three several and distinct pictures of mermaids engraved, and with a peculiar description written for each, had them inserted in 10,000 copies of the pamphlet which I had printed and quietly stored away in a back office until the time came to use them.

I then called respectively on the editors of the New York *Herald,* and two of the Sunday papers, and tendered to each the free use of a mermaid cut, with a well-written description, for their papers of the ensuing Sunday. I informed each editor that I had hoped to use this cut in showing the Fejee Mermaid, but since Mr. Griffin had announced that, as agent for the Lyceum of Natural History, he could not permit it to be exhibited in America, my chance seemed dubious, and therefore he was welcome to the use of the engraving and description. The three mermaids made their appearance in the three different papers on the morning of Sunday, July 17, 1842. Each editor supposed he was giving his readers an exclusive treat in the mermaid line, but when they came to discover that I had played the same game with the three different papers, they pronounced it a *scaly* trick.

The mermaid fever was now getting pretty well up. Few city readers had missed seeing at least one of the illustrations, and as the several printed descriptions made direct allusion to *the* mermaid of Mr. Griffin now in town, a desire to see it was generally prevailing. My 10,000 mermaid pamphlets were then put into the hands of boys, and sold at a penny each (half the cost) in all the principal hotels, stores, etc., etc.

When I thought the public was thoroughly "posted up" on the subject of mermaids, I sent an agent to engage Concert Hall, Broadway, for the exhibition, and the newspapers immediately contained the following advertisement:

THE MERMAID, AND OTHER WONDERFUL SPECIMENS OF THE ANIMAL CREATION.—The public are respectfully informed that, in accordance with numerous and urgent solicitations from scientific gentlemen in this city, Mr. J. GRIFFIN, proprietor of the Mermaid, recently arrived from Pernambuco, S. A., has consented to exhibit it to the public, *positively for one week only!* For this purpose he has procured the spacious saloon known as Concert Hall, 404 Broadway, which will open on Monday, August 8, 1842, and will positively close on Saturday the 13th inst.

This animal was taken near the Fejee Islands, and purchased for a large sum by the present proprietor, for the Lyceum of Natural History in London, and is exhibited for this short period more for the gratification of the public than for gain. The proprietor having been engaged for several years in various parts of the world in collecting wonderful specimens in

Natural History, has in his possession, and will at the same time submit to public inspection, THE ORNITHORHINCHUS, from New Holland, being the connecting link between the Seal and the Duck. THE FLYING FISH, two distinct species, one from the Gulf Stream, and the other from the West Indies. This animal evidently connects the Bird with the Fish. THE PADDLE-TAIL SNAKE from South America. THE SIREN, or MUD IGUANA, an intermediate animal between the Reptile and the Fish. THE PROTEUS SANGUIHUS, a subterraneous animal from a grotto in Australia—with other animals forming connecting links in the great chain of Animated Nature. Tickets of admission 25 cents each.

A large number of visitors attended Concert Hall, and Lyman, alias Griffin, exhibited the mermaid with much dignity. I could not help fearing that some of the Joice Heth victims would discover in Professor Griffin the exhibitor of the "nurse of Washington," but happily no such catastrophe occurred. Lyman, surrounded by numerous connecting links in nature, as set forth in the advertisement, and with the hideous-looking mermaid firmly secured from the hands of visitors by a glass vase, enlightened his audiences by curious accounts of his travels and adventures, and by scientific harangues upon the works of nature in general, and mermaids in particular.

The public appeared to be satisfied, but as some persons always *will* take things literally, and make no allowance for poetic license even in mermaids, an occasional visitor, after having seen the large transparency in front of the hall, representing a beautiful creature half woman and half fish, about eight feet in length, would be slightly surprised in finding that the reality was a black-looking specimen of dried monkey and fish that a boy a few years old could easily run away with under his arm.

The mermaid remained a single week at Concert Hall, and was then advertised to be seen at the American Museum, "without extra charge." Numerous transparencies had been prepared; showbills were posted with a liberal hand; and on Monday morning, a flag representing a mermaid eighteen feet in length was streaming directly in front of the Museum. Lyman saw it as he was slowly approaching to commence operations. He quickened his pace, entered my office, and demanded, "What in the name of all conscience is that immense flag out for?"

"In order that nobody shall enter Broadway without knowing where to find the mermaid," I replied.

"Well, that flag must come in. Nobody can satisfy the public with our dried-up specimen *eighteen inches long,* after exhibiting a picture representing it as *eighteen feet.* It is preposterous."

"Oh, nonsense," I replied; "that is only to catch the eye. They don't expect to see a mermaid of that size."

"I tell you it won't do," replied Lyman, "I think I ought to know something of the public 'swallow' by this time, and I tell you the mermaid won't go down if that flag remains up."

"That flag cost me over seventy dollars, and it must remain up," I replied.

Lyman deliberately buttoned his coat, and said as he slowly walked towards the door, "Well, Mr. Barnum, if you like to fight under that flag, you can do so, but *I* won't."

"What! you are a deserter, then!" I replied, laughing.

"Yes, I desert false colors when they are too strong," said Lyman; "and *you* will desert them before night," he continued.

I could not spare "Professor Griffin," and was reluctantly compelled to take down the flag. It never saw the light again.

That her "ladyship" was an attractive feature, may be inferred from these facts and figures: The receipts of the American Museum for the four weeks immediately preceding the exhibition of the mermaid, amounted to $1272. During the first four weeks of the mermaid's exhibition, the receipts amounted to $3341.93.

I used my mermaid mainly to advertise the regular business of the Museum, and this effective indirect advertising is the only feature I can commend, in a special show of which, I confess, I am not proud. I might have published columns in the newspapers, presenting and praising the great collection of genuine specimens of natural history in my exhibition, and they would not have attracted nearly so much attention as did a few paragraphs about the mermaid which was only a small part of my show. Newspapers throughout the country copied the mermaid notices, for they were novel and caught the attention of readers. Thus was the fame of the Museum, as well as the mermaid, wafted from one end of the land to the other. I was careful to keep up the excitement, for I knew that every dollar sown in advertising would return in tens, and perhaps hundreds in a future harvest, and after obtaining all the notoriety possible by advertising and by exhibiting the mermaid at the Museum, I sent the curiosity throughout the country, directing my agent to everywhere advertise it as "From Barnum's Great American Museum, New York." The effect was immediately felt; money flowed in rapidly and was readily expended in more advertising.

While I expended money liberally for attractions for the inside of my Museum, and bought or hired everything curious or rare which was offered or could be found, I was prodigal in my outlays to arrest or arouse public attention. When I became proprietor of the establishment, there were only the words: "American Museum," to indicate the character of the concern; there was no bustle or activity about the place; no posters to announce what was to be seen; —the whole exterior was as dead as the skeletons and stuffed skins within. My experiences had taught me the advantages of advertising. I printed whole columns in the papers, setting forth the wonders of my establishment. Old "fogies" opened their eyes in amazement at a man who could expend hundreds of dollars in announcing a show of "stuffed monkey skins"; but these same old fogies paid their quarters, nevertheless, and when they saw the curiosities and novelties in the Museum halls, they, like all other visitors, were astonished as well as pleased, and went home and told their friends and neighbors and thus assisted in advertising my business.

For other and not less effective advertising, flags and banners began to adorn the exterior of the building. I kept a band of music on the front balcony and announced "Free Music for the Million." People said, "Well, that Barnum is a liberal fellow to give us music for nothing," and they flocked down to hear my outdoor free concerts. But I took pains to select and maintain the poorest band I could find—one whose discordant notes would drive the crowd into the Museum, out of earshot of my outside orchestra. Of course, the music was poor. When people expect to get "something for nothing" they are sure to be cheated, and generally deserve to be, and so, no doubt, some of my out-door patrons were sorely disappointed; but when they came inside and paid to be amused and instructed, I took care to see that they not only received the full worth of their money, but were more than satisfied. Powerful Drummond lights were placed at the top of the Museum, which, in the darkest night, threw a flood of light up and down Broadway, from the Battery to Niblo's, that would enable one to read a newspaper in the street. These were the first Drummond lights ever seen in New York, and they made people talk, and so advertise my Museum.

CHAPTER XI

THE American Museum was the ladder by which I rose to fortune. Whenever I cross Broadway at the head of Vesey Street, and see the *Herald* building and that gorgeous pile, the Park Bank, my mind's eye recalls that less solid, more showy edifice which once occupied the site and was covered with pictures of all manner of beasts, birds and creeping things, and in which were treasures that brought treasures and notoriety and pleasant hours to me. The Jenny Lind enterprise was more audacious, more immediately remunerative, and I remember it with a pride which I do not attempt to conceal; but instinctively I often go back and live over again the old days of my struggles and triumphs in the American Museum.

The Museum was always open at sunrise, and this was so well known throughout the country that strangers coming to the city would often take a tour through my halls before going to breakfast or to their hotels. I do not believe there was ever a more truly popular place of amusement. I frequently compared the annual number of visitors with the number officially reported as visiting (free of charge) the British Museum in London, and my list was invariably the larger. Nor do I believe that any man or manager ever labored more industriously to please his patrons. I furnished the most attractive exhibitions which money could procure; I abolished all vulgarity and profanity from the stage, and I prided myself upon the fact that parents and children could attend the dramatic performances in the so-called Lecture Room, and not be shocked or offended by anything they might see or hear; I introduced the "Moral Drama," producing such plays as "The Drunk-ard," "Uncle Tom's Cabin," "Moses in Egypt," "Joseph and His Brethren," and occasional spectacular melodramas produced with great care and at considerable outlay.

Mr. Sothern, who has since attained such wide-spread celebrity at home and abroad as a character actor, was a member of my dramatic company for one or two seasons. Mr. Barney Williams also began his theatrical career at the Museum, occupying, at first, quite a subordinate position, at a salary of ten dollars a week. During the past twelve or fifteen years, I presume his weekly re-ceipts, when he has acted, have been nearly $3,000. The late Miss Mary Gannon also commenced at the Museum, and many more actors and actresses of celebrity have been, from time to time, engaged there. What was once the small Lecture Room was con-verted into a spacious and beautiful theatre, extending over the lots adjoining the Museum, and capable of holding about three thousand persons. The saloons were greatly multiplied and en-larged, and the "egress" having been made to work to perfection, on holidays I advertised Lecture Room performances every hour through the afternoon and evening, and consequently the actors and actresses were dressed for the stage as early as eleven o'clock in the morning, and did not resume their ordinary clothes till ten o'clock at night. In these busy days the meals for the company were brought in and served in the dressing-rooms and green-rooms, and the company always received extra pay.

Leaving nothing undone that would bring Barnum and his Museum before the public, I often engaged some exhibition, know-ing that it would directly bring no extra dollars to the treasury, but hoping that it would incite a newspaper paragraph which would float through the columns of the American press and be copied, perhaps, abroad, and my hopes in this respect were often gratified.

I confess that I liked the Museum mainly for the opportunities it afforded for rapidly making money. Before I bought it, I weighed the matter well in my mind, and was convinced that I could present to the American public such a variety, quantity and quality of amusement, blended with instruction, "all for twenty-five cents, children half price," that my attractions would be irresistible, and my fortune certain. I myself relished a higher grade of amusement, and I was a frequent attendant at the opera, first-class concerts, lectures, and the like; but I worked for the million, and I knew the only way to make a million from my patrons was to give them abundant and wholesome attractions for a small sum of money.

About the first of July, 1842, I began to make arrangements for extra novelties, additional performances, a large amount of extra advertising, and an outdoor display for the "Glorious Fourth." Large parti-colored bills were ordered, transparencies were prepared, the free band of music was augmented by a trumpeter, and columns of advertisements, headed with large capitals, were written and put on file.

I wanted to run out a string of American flags across the street on that day, for I knew there would be thousands of people passing the Museum with leisure and pocket-money, and I felt confident that an unusual display of national flags would arrest their patriotic attention, and bring many of them within my walls. Unfortunately for my purpose, St. Paul's Church stood directly opposite, and there was nothing to which I could attach my flag-rope, unless it might be one of the trees in the church-yard. I went to the vestrymen for permission to so attach my flag rope on the Fourth of July, and they were indignant at what they called my "insulting proposition;" such a concession would be "sacrilege." I plied them with arguments, and appealed to their patriotism, but in vain.

Returning to the Museum I gave orders to have the string of flags made ready, with directions at daylight on the Fourth of

July to attach one end of the rope to one of the third story windows of the Museum, and the other end to a tree in St. Paul's churchyard. The great day arrived, and my orders were strictly followed. The flags attracted great attention, and before nine o'clock I have no doubt that hundreds of additional visitors were drawn by this display into the Museum. By half-past nine Broadway was thronged, and about that time two gentlemen in a high state of excitement rushed into my office, announcing themselves as injured and insulted vestrymen of St. Paul's Church.

"Keep cool, gentlemen," said I; "I guess it is all right."

"Right!" indignantly exclaimed one of them, "do you think it is right to attach your Museum to our Church? We will show you what is 'right' and what is law, if we live till to-morrow; those flags must come down instantly."

"Thank you," I said, "but let us not be in a hurry. I will go out with you and look at them, and I guess we can make it all right."

Going into the street I remarked: "Really, gentlemen, these flags look very beautiful; they do not injure your tree; I always stop my balcony music for your accommodation whenever you hold weekday services, and it is but fair that you should return the favor."

"We could indict your 'music,' as you call it, as a nuisance, if we chose," answered one vestryman, "and now I tell you that if these flags are not taken down in ten minutes, *I* will cut them down."

His indignation was at the boiling point. The crowd in the street was dense, and the angry gesticulation of the vestryman attracted their attention. I saw there was no use in trying to parley with him or coax him, and so, assuming an angry air, I rolled up my sleeves, and exclaimed, in a loud tone,—

"Well, Mister, I should just like to see you dare to cut down the American flag on the Fourth of July; you must be a 'Britisher' to make such a threat as that; but I'll show you a thousand pairs of Yankee hands in two minutes, if you dare to attempt to take down the stars and stripes on this great birth-day of American freedom!''

"What's that John Bull a-saying," asked a brawny fellow, placing himself in front of the irate vestryman. "Look here, old fellow," he continued, "if you want to save a whole bone in your body, you had better slope, and never dare to talk again about hauling down the American flag in the city of New York."

Throngs of excited, exasperated men crowded around, and the vestryman, seeing the effect of my ruse, smiled faintly and said, "Oh, of course, it is all right," and he and his companion quietly edged out of the crowd. The flags remained up all day and all night. The next morning I sought the vanquished vestrymen and obtained formal permission to make this use of the tree on following holidays, in consideration of my willingness to arrest the doleful strains of my discordant balcony band whenever services were held on week days in the church.

Notwithstanding my continual outlays for additional novelties and attractions, or rather I might say, because of these outlays, money poured in upon me so rapidly that I was sometimes actually embarrassed to devise means to carry out my original plan for laying out the entire profits of the first year in advertising. I meant to sow first and reap afterwards. I finally hit upon a plan which cost a large sum, and that was to prepare large oval oil paintings to be placed between the windows of the entire building, representing nearly every important animal known in zoology. These paintings were put on the building in a single night, and so complete a transformation in the appearance of an edifice is seldom witnessed. When the living stream rolled down Broadway the next morning and reached the Astor House corner, opposite the Museum, it seemed to meet with a sudden check. I never before saw so many open mouths and astonished eyes. Some people were puzzled to know what it all meant; some looked as if they thought it was an enchanted palace that had suddenly sprung up; others exclaimed, "Well, the

JENNY LIND IN SLEIGH IN FRONT OF BARNUM'S AMERICAN
MUSEUM, FROM A LITHOGRAPH

THE FIRE AT BARNUM'S AMERICAN MUSEUM, JULY 13, 1865, AS PICTURED IN *Harper's Weekly*.

RUINS OF BARNUM'S SECOND MUSEUM
AFTER THE FIRE OF MARCH, 1868

GENERAL TOM THUMB, *1844*

The celebrated American Dwarf, exhibiting every day and evening, at the Egyptian Hall, Piccadilly.

CHARLES S. STRATTON, known as General Tom Thumb, was born January 11, 1832, consequently he is now twelve years of age: he is twenty-five inches high, and weighs only fifteen pounds. The General had the honour of appearing before Her Majesty, Prince Albert, the Duchess of Kent, and several of the Nobility, at Buckingham Palace, attended by his guardian, Mr. P. T. Barnum, of New York, on Saturday, 23d of March. His various performances afforded much entertainment, and elicited the approbation of Her Majesty and the Royal Household.

The General is of the most symmetrical proportions, active, lively, intelligent, and sociable. He is robust and hearty, never having been ill in his life. His parents and a preceptor have accompanied him across the Atlantic. The extreme diminutiveness—the graceful bearing and fascinating manners of this beautiful rosy-cheeked MAN in miniature—cannot be justly conceived without seeing him. The General has been visited in America and the Canadas by nearly half a million of ladies and gentlemen of the first respectability, who unanimously pronounce him the greatest curiosity in the world.

The General shed his first set of teeth several years since; and his enormous strength, his firm and manly gait, establish his age beyond all dispute. The General amuses his Visitors with a relation of his History, Songs, Dances, Imitation of Napoleon Buonaparte, Grecian Statues, &c.

TOM THUMB PLAYBILLS

American
MUSEUM
AND PERPETUAL FAI

Cor Broadway & Ann-st.   P. T. Barnum, Manag

GRAND EXTRA WEI
FROM MONDAY, OCT. 23, to SATURDAY, OCT

In order to accommodate the great crowds which atte there will be

Two Performances Daily
AT 3 O'CLOCK & 1-2 PAST 7, P. M.

PROGRAMME.

Mr. Nellis will introduce his various, singular and ful Performances with his TOES.

Popular Song . . . . Mr. H. G. S

EXPERIMENTS IN ANIMAL MAGNETISM
By Dr. C. P. JOHNSON.

Admired Song . . . . Mr. S
To conclude with

Comic Imitations . . . . by . . . **DR. VALENT**

The last Week of

GEN. TOM THUM

The, most SURPRISING and DELIGHTFUL CURIO the world ever produced. He may be seen throughout the day and even The wonderful diminutiveness of the General, his beautiful proportions, g ful manners, sprightliness, wit, intelligence and good humor are so capti ting that none fail to be delighted and almost charmed with him. No to see him is to miss a sight of by far the MOST INTEREST ING WONDER OF THE WORLD! With all the above qualifications, the General is still

The Smallest Person that ever Walked A
He is 11 years Old, 25 Inches High, and

Weighs Only 15 Pound

MESMERISM

The time having at length arrived when Mesmerism is no longer the subject o but is believed in and practised by men of the first respectability and intell this country, the Manager is happy to announce an engagement with

Dr. C. P. Johns

the oldest MAGNETISER in this country. A committee of investigation w pointed each afternoon and evening, by the audience, chosen from among the who will take their stations on the stage, and they are particularly invited to the most rigid scrutiny in all the experiments of the afternoon and evening. son will introduce any experiments in

ANIMAL MAGNETISM

Which may be suggested by the committee or any of the audience. He will s a YOUNG LADY, and go through with a series of Extraordinary EXPERI including Clairvoyance, Sympathy, Feeling, &c all establishing beyond the tion or cavil, the truth of the *Somnambulic Condition.*

Also Engaged, for one week more, the eccentric and humorous

DR. VALENTINE

Whose Comic Delineations of American Peculiarities are unrivalled. He w introduce his

DISSERTATION on FACE
Proving that half a Face is better than a whole one.

COMIC LECTURE on Phrenology
Delivered by Ameziah Trotabout, the man of many trades.

STAGE TRAVELS!
Introducing a variety of Whimsical Characters.

FAMILY VISITS!
With specimens of old fashioned Singing.

The Mail Coach
With an imitation of the inside passengers and the stage horn. With a variety Comicalities too numerous to detail.

Mr. H. G. Sherman
The Popular Ballad Singer.

animals all seem to have 'broken out' last night," and hundreds came in to see how the establishment survived the sudden eruption. At all events, from that morning the Museum receipts took a jump forward of nearly a hundred dollars a day, and they never fell back again. Strangers would look at this great pictorial magazine and argue that an establishment with so many animals on the outside must have something on the inside, and in they would go to see. Inside, I took particular pains to please and astonish these strangers, and when they went back to the country, they carried plenty of pictorial bills and lithographs, which I always lavishly furnished, and thus the fame of Barnum's Museum became so widespread, that people scarcely thought of visiting the city without going to my establishment.

In fact, the Museum had become an established institution in the land. Now and then some one would cry out "humbug" and "charlatan," but so much the better for me. It helped to advertise me, and I was willing to bear the reputation—and I engaged queer curiosities, and even monstrosities, simply to add to the notoriety of the Museum.

On several occasions I got up "Baby shows," at which I paid liberal prizes for the finest baby, the fattest baby, the handsomest twins, for triplets, and so on. I always gave several months' notice of these intended shows and limited the number of babies at each exhibition to one hundred. Long before the appointed time, the list would be full and I have known many a fond mother to weep bitterly because the time for application was closed and she could not have the opportunity to exhibit her beautiful baby. These shows were as popular as they were unique, and while they paid in a financial point of view, my chief object in getting them up was to set the newspapers to talking about me, thus giving another blast on the trumpet which I always tried to keep blowing for the Museum. Flower shows, dog shows, poultry shows and bird shows, were held at intervals in my establishment and in each instance the same end was attained as by the baby shows. I gave prizes in the shape of medals, money and diplomas and the whole came back to me four-fold in the shape of advertising.

It will be seen that very much of the success which attended my many years' proprietorship of the American Museum was due to advertising, and especially to my odd methods of advertising. Always claiming that I had curiosities worth showing and worth seeing, and exhibited "dog cheap" at "twenty-five cents admission, children half price"—I studied ways to arrest public attention; to startle, to make people talk and wonder; in short, to let the world know that I had a Museum.

About this time, I engaged a band of Indians from Iowa. They had never seen a railroad or steamboat until they saw them on the route from Iowa to New York.   Of course they were wild and had but faint ideas of civilization.   The party comprised large and noble specimens of the untutored savage, as well as several very beautiful squaws, with two or three interesting "papooses." They lived and lodged in a large room on the top floor of the Museum, and cooked their own victuals in their own way.   They gave their war-dances on the stage in the Lecture Room with great vigor and enthusiasm, much to the satisfaction of the audiences.   But these wild Indians seemed to consider their dances as realities.   Hence when they gave a real War Dance, it was dangerous for any parties, except their manager and interpreter, to be on the stage, for the moment they had finished their war dance they began to leap and peer about behind the scenes in search of victims for their tomahawks and scalping knives!   Indeed, lest in these frenzied moments they might make a dash at the orchestra or the audience, we had a high rope barrier placed between them and the savages on the front of the stage.

After they had been a week in the Museum, I proposed a change of performance for the week following, by introducing new dances.

Among these was the Indian Wedding Dance. At that time I printed but one set of posters (large bills) per week, so that whatever was announced for Monday, was repeated every day and evening during that week. Before the Wedding Dance came off on Monday afternoon, I was informed that I was to provide a large new red woollen blanket, at a cost of ten dollars, for the bridegroom to present to the father of the bride. I ordered the purchase to be made; but was considerably taken aback, when I was informed that I must have another new blanket for the evening, inasmuch as the savage old Indian Chief, father-in-law to the bridegroom, would not consent to his daughter's being approached with the Wedding Dance unless he had his blanket present.

I undertook to explain to the chief, through the interpreter, that this was only a "make believe" wedding; but the old savage shrugged his shoulders, and gave such a terrific "Ugh!" that I was glad to make my peace by ordering another blanket. As we gave two performances per day, I was out of pocket $120 for twelve "wedding blankets," that week.

One of the beautiful squaws named Do-humme died in the Museum. The poor Indians were very sorrowful for many days, and desired to get back again to their western wilds. The father and the betrothed of Do-humme cooked various dishes of food and placed them upon the roof of the Museum, where they believed the spirit of their departed friend came daily for its supply; and these dishes were renewed every morning during the stay of the Indians at the Museum.

The president and directors of the "New York Museum Company" not only failed to buy the American Museum as they confidently expected to do, but, after my newspaper squib war and my purchase of the Museum, they found it utterly impossible to sell their stock. By some arrangement, the particulars of which I do not remember, if, indeed, I ever cared to know them, Mr. Peale was conducting Peale's Museum which he claimed was a more "scientific" establishment than mine, and he pretended to appeal to a higher class of patrons.   Mesmerism was one of his scientific attractions, and he had a subject upon whom he operated at times with the greatest seeming success, and fairly astonished his audiences. But there were times when the subject was wholly unimpressible and then those who had paid their money to see the woman put into the mesmeric state cried out "humbug," and the reputation of the establishment seriously suffered.

It devolved upon me to open a rival mesmeric performance, and accordingly I engaged a bright little girl who was exceedingly susceptible to such mesmeric influences as I could induce.   That is, she learned her lesson thoroughly, and when I had apparently put her to sleep with a few passes and stood behind her, she seemed to be duly "impressed" as I desired; raised her hands as I willed; fell from her chair to the floor; and if I put candy or tobacco into my mouth, she was duly delighted or disgusted.   She never failed in these routine performances.   Strange to say, believers in mesmerism used to witness her performances with the greatest pleasure and adduce them as positive proofs that there was something in mesmerism, and they applauded tremendously—up to a certain point.   That point was reached, when leaving the girl "asleep," I called up some one in the audience, promising to put him "in the same state" within five minutes, or forfeit fifty dollars.   Of course, all my "passes" would not put any man in the mesmeric state; at the end of three minutes he was as wide awake as ever.

"Never mind," I would say, looking at my watch; "I have two minutes more, and meantime, to show that a person in this state is utterly insensible to pain, I propose to cut off one of the fingers of the little girl who is still asleep."   I would then take out my knife and feel of the edge, and when I turned around to the girl whom I left on the chair she had fled behind the scenes to the intense amusement of the greater part of the audience and to the amazement of the mesmerists who were present.

"Why! where's my little girl?" I asked with feigned astonishment.

"Oh! she ran away when you began to talk about cutting off fingers."

"Then she was wide awake, was she?"

"Of course she was, all the time."

"I suppose so; and, my dear sir, I promised that you should be 'in the same state' at the end of five minutes, and as I believe you are so, I do not forfeit fifty dollars."

I kept up this performance for several weeks, till I quite killed Peale's "genuine" mesmerism in the rival establishment. After Peale, "Yankee" Hill undertook the management of that Museum, but in a little while he failed. It was then let to Henry Bennett, who reduced the entrance price to one shilling,—a half price which led me to characterize his concern as "cheap and nasty,"—and he began a serious rivalry with my Museum. His main reliances were burlesques and caricatures of whatever novelties I was exhibiting; thus, when I advertised an able company of vocalists, well-known as the Orphean Family, Bennett announced the "Orphan Family"; my Fejee Mermaid he offset with a figure made of a monkey and codfish joined together and called the "Fudg-ee Mermaid." These things created some laughter at my expense, but they also served to advertise my Museum.

When the novelty of this opposition died away, Bennett did a decidedly losing business. I used to send a man with a shilling to his place every night and I knew exactly how much he was doing and what were his receipts. The holidays were coming and might tide him over a day or two, but he was at the very bottom and I said to him, one day:

"Bennett, if you can keep open one week after New Year's I will give you a hundred dollars."

He made every effort to win the money, and even went to the landlord and offered him the entire receipts for a week if he would only let him stay there; but he would not do it, and the day after New Year's, January 2, 1843, Bennett shut up shop, having lost his last dollar and even failing to secure the handsome premium I offered him.

The entire collection fell into the hands of the landlord for arrearages of rent, and I privately purchased it for $7,000 cash, hired the building, and secretly engaged Bennett as my agent. We ran a very spirited opposition for a long time and abused each other terribly in public. It was very amusing when actors and performers failed to make terms with one of us and went to the other, carrying from one to the other the price each was willing to pay for an engagement. We thus used to hear extraordinary stories about each other's "liberal terms," but between the two we managed to secure such persons as we wanted at about the rates at which their services were really worth. While these people were thus running from one manager to the other, supposing we were rivals, Bennett said to me one day:

"You and I are like a pair of shears; we seem to cut each other, but we only cut what comes between."

I ran my opposition long enough to beat myself. It answered every purpose, however, in awakening public attention to my Museum, and was an advantage in preventing others from starting a genuine opposition. At the end of six months, the whole establishment, including the splendid gallery of American portraits, was removed to the American Museum and I immediately advertised the great card of a "Double attraction" and "Two Museums in One," without extra charge.

The Museum became a mania with me and I made everything possible subservient to it.   On the eve of elections, rival politicians would ask me for whom I was going to vote, and my answer invariably was, "I vote for the American Museum." In fact, at that time, I cared very little about politics, and a great deal about my business. Meanwhile the Museum prospered wonderfully, and everything I attempted or engaged in seemed at the outset an assured success.

The giants whom I exhibited from time to time were always literally great features in my establishment, and they oftentimes afforded me, as well as my patrons, food for much amusement, as well as wonder. The Quaker giant, Hales, was quite a wag in his way He went once to see the new house of an acquaintance who had suddenly become rich, but who was a very ignorant man.   When he came back he described the wonders of the mansion and said that the proud proprietor showed him everything from basement to attic; parlors, bed-rooms, dining room, and, said Hales, "what he called his 'study'—meaning, I suppose, the place where he intends to study his spelling-book!"

I had at one time two famous men, the French giant, M. Bihin, a very slim man, and the Arabian giant, Colonel Goshen.   These men generally got on together very well, though, of course, each was jealous of the other, and of the attention the rival received, or the notice he attracted.   One day they quarrelled, and a lively interchange of compliments ensued, the Arabian calling the Frenchman a "Shanghai," and receiving in return the epithet of "Nigger." From words both were eager to proceed to blows, and both ran to my collection of arms, one seizing the club with which Captain Cook or any other man might have been killed, if it were judiciously wielded, and the other laying hands on a sword of the terrific size which is supposed to have been conventional in the days of the

Crusades.   The preparation for a deadly encounter, and the high words of the contending parties brought a dozen of the Museum *attachés* to the spot, and these men threw themselves between the gigantic combatants.   Hearing the disturbance, I ran from my private office to the duelling ground, and said:

"Look here!   This is all right; if you want to fight each other, maiming and perhaps killing one or both of you, that is your affair; but my interest lies here—you are both under engagement to me, and if this duel is to come off, I and the public have a right to participate.   It must be duly advertised, and must take place on the stage of the Lecture Room.   No performance of yours would be a greater attraction, and if you kill each other, our engagement can end with your duel."

This proposition, made in apparent earnest, so delighted the giants that they at once burst into a laugh, shook hands, and quarrelled no more.

CHAPTER XII

I NOW come to the details of one of the most interesting, as well as successful, of all the show enterprises in which I have engaged— one which not only taxed all my ingenuity and industry, but which gave unqualified delight to thousands of people on two continents and put enormous sums of money into many pockets besides my own.

In November, 1842, I was in Albany on business, and as the Hudson River was frozen over, I returned to New York by the Housatonic Railroad, stopping one night at Bridgeport, Connecticut, with my brother, Philo F. Barnum, who at that time kept the Franklin Hotel. I had heard of a remarkably small child in Bridge- port, and, at my request, my brother brought him to the hotel. He was not two feet high; he weighed less than sixteen pounds, and was the smallest child I ever saw that could walk alone; but he was a perfectly formed, bright-eyed little fellow, with light hair and ruddy cheeks, and he enjoyed the best of health. He was exceed- ingly bashful, but after some coaxing he was induced to talk with me, and he told me that he was the son of Sherwood E. Stratton, and that his own name was Charles S. Stratton. After seeing him and talking with him, I at once determined to secure his services from his parents and to exhibit him in public.

He was only five years old, and to exhibit a dwarf of that age might provoke the question, How do you know that he *is* a dwarf? Some license might indeed be taken with the facts, but even with this advantage I really felt that the adventure was nothing more

133

than experiment, and I engaged him for the short term of four weeks at three dollars per week—all charges, including travelling and boarding of himself and mother, being at my expense.

They arrived in New York on Thanksgiving Day, 1842, and Mrs. Stratton was greatly astonished to find her son heralded in my Museum bills as GENERAL TOM THUMB, a dwarf of eleven years of age, just arrived from England!

This announcement contained two deceptions. I shall not attempt to justify them, but may be allowed to plead the circumstances in extenuation. The boy was undoubtedly a dwarf, and I had the most reliable evidence that he had grown little, if any, since he was six months old; but had I announced him as only five years of age, it would have been impossible to excite the interest or awaken the curiosity of the public. The thing I aimed at was, to assure them that he was *really a dwarf*—and in *this,* at least, they were not deceived.

It was of no consequence, in reality, where he was born or where he came from, and if the announcement that he was *a foreigner* answered my purpose, the people had only themselves to blame if they did not get their money's worth when they visited the exhibition. I had observed (and sometimes, as in the case of Vivalla, had taken advantage of) the American fancy for European exotics; and if the deception, practised for a season in my dwarf experiment, has done anything toward checking our disgraceful preference for foreigners, I may readily be pardoned for the offence I here acknowledge.

I took the greatest pains to educate and train my diminutive prodigy, devoting many hours to the task by day and by night, and I was very successful, for he was an apt pupil with a great deal of native talent, and a keen sense of the ludicrous. He made rapid progress in preparing himself for such performances as I wished him to undertake and he became very much attached to his teacher.

When the four weeks expired, I re-engaged him for one year at seven dollars a week, with a gratuity of fifty dollars at the end of the engagement, and the privilege of exhibiting him anywhere in the United States, in which event his parents were to accompany him and I was to pay all travelling expenses. He speedily became a public favorite, and, long before the year was out, I voluntarily increased his weekly salary to twenty-five dollars, and he fairly earned it. Sometimes I exhibited him for several weeks in succession at the Museum, and when I wished to introduce other novelties I sent him to different towns and cities, accompanied by my friend, Mr. Fordyce Hitchcock, and the fame of General Tom Thumb soon spread throughout the country.

Two years had now elapsed since I bought the Museum and I had long since paid for the entire establishment from the profits; I had bought out my only rival; I was free from debt, and had a handsome surplus in the treasury. The business had long ceased to be an experiment; it was an established success and was in such perfect running order that it could safely be committed· to the management of trustworthy and tried agents.

Accordingly, looking for a new field for my individual efforts, I entered into an agreement for General Tom Thumb's services for another year, at fifty dollars a week and all expenses, with the privilege of exhibiting him in Europe. I proposed to test the curiosity of men and women on the other side of the Atlantic. Much as I hoped for success, in my most sanguine moods I could not anticipate the half of what was in store for me; I did not foresee nor dream that I was shortly to be brought in close contact with kings, queens, lords and illustrious commoners, and that such association, by means of my exhibition, would afterwards introduce me to the great public and the public's money, which was to fill my coffers. Or, if I saw some such future, it was dreamily, dimly, and with half-opened eyes, as the man saw the "trees walking."

After arranging my business affairs for a long absence, and making every preparation for an extended foreign tour, on Thursday, January 18, 1844, I went on board the new and fine sailing ship "Yorkshire," Captain D. G. Bailey, bound for Liverpool. Our party included General Tom Thumb, his parents, his tutor, and Professor Guillaudeu, the French naturalist. We were accompanied by several personal friends, and the City Brass Band kindly volunteered to escort us to Sandy Hook.

My name has been so long associated with mirthful incidents that I presume many persons do not suppose I am susceptible of sorrowful, or even sentimental emotions; but when the bell of the steamer that towed our ship down the bay announced the hour of separation, and then followed the hastily-spoken words of farewell, and the parting grasp of friendly hands, I confess that I was very much in the "melting mood," and when the band played "Home, Sweet Home," I was moved to tears.

A voyage to Liverpool is now an old, familiar story, and I abstain from entering into details, though I have abundant material respecting my own experiences of my first sea-voyage in the first two of a series of one hundred letters which I wrote in Europe as correspondent of the New York *Atlas*. Occasional calms and adverse winds protracted our passage to nineteen days, but a better ship and a more competent captain never sailed. I was entirely exempt from sea-sickness, and enjoyed the voyage very much. Good fellowship prevailed among the passengers, the time passed rapidly, and we had a good deal of fun on board.

On our arrival at Liverpool, quite a crowd had assembled at the dock to see Tom Thumb, for it had been previously announced that he would arrive in the "Yorkshire," but his mother managed to smuggle him ashore unnoticed, for she carried him, as if he was an infant, in her arms. We went to the Waterloo Hotel, and, after an excellent dinner, walked out to take a look at the town. While

BARNUM AND TOM THUMB   Collection of Mrs. Morris S. Britto

Loan Collection of Elizabeth Sterling See

TOM THUMB AND HIS FATHER—HIS EARLIEST KNOWN PICTURE

I was viewing the Nelson monument a venerable looking, well-dressed old gentleman volunteered to explain to me the different devices and inscriptions. I looked upon him as a disinterested and attentive man of means who was anxious to assist a stranger and to show his courtesy; but when I gave him a parting bow of thanks, half ashamed that I had so trespassed on his kindness, he put out the hand of a beggar and said that he would be thankful for any remuneration I saw fit to bestow upon him for his trouble. I was certainly astonished, and I thrust a shilling into his hand and walked rapidly away.

Later in the evening, the proprietor of a cheap wax-works show, at three ha'pence admission, called upon me. He had heard of the arrival of the great American curiosity, and he seized the earliest opportunity to make the General and myself the magnificent offer of ten dollars a week if we would join ourselves to his already remarkable and attractive exhibition. I could not but think, that dwarfs must be literally at a "low figure" in England, and my prospects were gloomy indeed. I was a stranger in the land; my letters of introduction had not been delivered; beyond my own little circle, I had not seen a friendly face, nor heard a familiar voice. I was "blue," homesick, almost in despair. Next morning, there came a ray of sunshine in the following note:

"Madame CELESTE presents her compliments to Mr. Barnum, and begs to say that her private box is quite at his service, any night, for himself and friends.

"Theatre Royal, Williamson Square."

This polite invitation was thankfully accepted, and we went to the theatre that evening. Our party, including the General, who was partly concealed by his tutor's cloak, occupied Celeste's box, and in the box adjoining sat an English lady and gentleman whose appearance indicated respectability, intelligence and wealth. The

General's interest in the performance attracted their attention, and the lady remarked to me:

"What an intelligent-looking child you have! He appears to take quite an interest in the stage."

"Pardon me, madam," said I, "this is not a child. This is General Tom Thumb."

"Indeed!" they exclaimed. They had seen the announcements of our visit and were greatly gratified at an interview with the pigmy prodigy. They at once advised me in the most complimentary and urgent manner to take the General to Manchester, where they resided, assuring me that an exhibition in that place would be highly remunerative. I thanked my new friends for their counsel and encouragement, and ventured to ask them what price they would recommend me to charge for admission.

"The General is so decidedly a curiosity," said the lady, "that I think you might put it as high as tuppence!" (two-pence).

She was, however, promptly interrupted by her husband, who was evidently the economist of the family. "I am sure you would not succeed at that price," said he; "you should put admission at one penny, for that is the usual price for seeing giants and dwarfs in England."

This was worse than the ten dollars a week offer of the waxworks proprietor, but I promptly answered: "Never shall the price be less than one shilling sterling and some of the nobility and gentry of England will yet pay gold to see General Tom Thumb."

My letters of introduction speedily brought me into friendly relations with many excellent families and I was induced to hire a hall and present the General to the public, for a short season, in Liverpool. I had intended to proceed directly to London and begin operations at "head-quarters," that is, in Buckingham Palace, if possible; but I had been advised that the royal family was in mourning for the death of Prince Albert's father, and would not permit the approach of any entertainments.

Meanwhile confidential letters from London informed me that Mr. Maddox, Manager of Princess's Theatre, was coming down to witness my exhibition, with a view to making an engagement. He came privately, but I was fully informed as to his presence and object. A friend pointed him out to me in the hall, and when I stepped up to him, and called him by name, he was "taken all aback," and avowed his purpose in visiting Liverpool. An interview resulted in an engagement of the General for three nights at Princess's Theatre. I was unwilling to contract for a longer period, and even this short engagement, though on liberal terms, was acceded to only as a means of advertisement. So soon, therefore, as I could bring my short, but highly successful season in Liverpool to a close, we went to London.

CHAPTER XIII

GENERAL TOM THUMB IN LONDON

IMMEDIATELY after our arrival in London, the General came out at the Princess's Theatre and made so decided a "hit" that it was difficult to decide who was best pleased, the spectators, the manager, or myself. The spectators were delighted because they could not well help it; the manager was satisfied because he had coined money by the engagement; and I was greatly pleased because I now had a visible guaranty of success in London. I was offered far higher terms for a re-engagement, but my purpose had been already answered; the news was spread everywhere that General Tom Thumb, an unparalleled curiosity, was in the city; and it only remained for me to bring him before the public, on my own account and in my own time and way.

I took a furnished mansion in Grafton Street, Bond Street, West End, in the very centre of the most fashionable locality. The house had previously been occupied for several years by Lord Talbot, and Lord Brougham and half a dozen families of the aristocracy and many of the gentry were my neighbors. From this magnificent mansion, I sent letters of invitation to the editors and several of the nobility, to visit the General. Most of them called, and were highly gratified. The word of approval was indeed so passed around in high circles, that uninvited parties drove to my door in crested carriages, and were not admitted.

This procedure, though in some measure a stroke of policy, was neither singular nor hazardous, under the circumstances. I had not yet announced a public exhibition, and as a private American gentleman, it became me to maintain the dignity of my position. I therefore instructed my liveried servant to deny admission to see my "ward," excepting to persons who brought cards of invitation. He did it in a proper manner, and no offence could be taken, though I was always particular to send an invitation immediately to such as had not been admitted.

During our first week in London, the Hon. Edward Everett, the American Minister, to whom I had letters of introduction, called and was highly pleased with his diminutive though renowned countryman. We dined with him the next day, by invitation, and his family loaded the young American with presents. Mr. Everett kindly promised to use influence at the Palace in person, with a view to having Tom Thumb introduced to Her Majesty Queen Victoria.

A few evenings afterwards the Baroness Rothschild sent her carriage for us. Her mansion was a noble structure in Piccadilly, surrounded by a high wall, through the gate of which our carriage was driven, and brought up in front of the main entrance. Here we were received by half a dozen servants, and were ushered up the broad flight of marble stairs to the drawing-room, where we met the Baroness and a party of twenty or more ladies and gentlemen. In this sumptuous mansion of the richest banker in the world, we spent about two hours, and when we took our leave a well-filled purse was quietly slipped into my hand. The golden shower had begun to fall, and that it was no dream was manifest from the fact that, very shortly afterwards, a visit to the mansion of Mr. Drummond, another eminent banker, came to the same golden conclusion.

I now engaged the "Egyptian Hall," in Piccadilly, and the announcement of my unique exhibition was promptly answered by a rush of visitors, in which the wealth and fashion of London were liberally represented. I made these arrangements because I had little hope of being soon brought to the Queen's presence (for the reason before mentioned), but Mr. Everett's generous influence secured my object. I breakfasted at his house one morning, by invitation, in company with Mr. Charles Murray, an author of creditable repute, who held the office of Master of the Queen's Household. In the course of conversation, Mr. Murray inquired as to my plans, and I informed him that I intended going to the Continent shortly, though I should be glad to remain if the General could have an interview with the Queen—adding that such an event would be of great consequence to me.

Mr. Murray kindly offered his good offices in the case, and the next day one of the Life Guards, a tall, noble-looking fellow, bedecked as became his station, brought me a note, conveying the Queen's invitation to General Tom Thumb and his guardian, Mr. Barnum, to appear at Buckingham Palace on an evening specified. Special instructions were the same day orally given me by Mr. Murray, by Her Majesty's command, to suffer the General to appear before her, as he would appear anywhere else, without any training in the use of the titles of royalty, as the Queen desired to see him act naturally and without restraint.

Determined to make the most of the occasion, I put a placard on the door of the Egyptian Hall: "Closed this evening, General Tom Thumb being at Buckingham Palace by command of Her Majesty."

On arriving at the Palace, the Lord in Waiting put me "under drill" as to the manner and form in which I should conduct myself in the presence of royalty. I was to answer all questions by Her Majesty through him, and in no event to speak directly to the Queen. In leaving the royal presence I was to "back out," keeping my face always towards Her Majesty, and the illustrious lord kindly gave me a specimen of that sort of backward locomotion. How far I profited by his instructions and example, will presently appear.

TOM THUMB AND HIS PARENTS, MR. AND MRS. SHERWOOD
STRATTON

TOM THUMB'S CARRIAGE, NOW IN HENRY FORD MUSEUM, DEAR-
BORN, MICHIGAN

We were conducted through a long corridor to a broad flight of marble steps, which led to the Queen's magnificent picture gallery, where Her Majesty and Prince Albert, the Duchess of Kent, and twenty or thirty of the nobility were awaiting our arrival. They were standing at the farther end of the room when the doors were thrown open, and the General walked in, looking like a wax doll gifted with the power of locomotion. Surprise and pleasure were depicted on the countenances of the royal circle at beholding this remarkable specimen of humanity so much smaller than they had evidently expected to find him. The General advanced with a firm step, and as he came within hailing distance made a very graceful bow, and exclaimed, "Good evening, Ladies and Gentlemen!"

A burst of laughter followed this salutation. The Queen then took him by the hand, led him about the gallery, and asked him many questions, the answers to which kept the party in an uninterrupted strain of merriment. The General familiarly informed the Queen that her picture gallery was "first-rate," and told her he should like to see the Prince of Wales. The Queen replied that the Prince had retired to rest, but that he should see him on some future occasion. The General then gave his songs, dances, and imitations, and after a conversation with Prince Albert and all present, which continued for more than an hour, we were permitted to depart.

Before describing the process and incidents of "backing out," I must acknowledge how sadly I broke through the counsel of the Lord in Waiting. While Prince Albert and others were engaged with the General, the Queen was gathering information from me in regard to his history, etc. Two or three questions were put and answered through the process indicated in my drill. It was a round-about way of doing business not at all to my liking, and I suppose the Lord in Waiting was seriously shocked, if not outraged, when I entered directly into conversation with Her Majesty. She,

however, seemed not disposed to check my boldness, for she immediately spoke directly to me in obtaining the information which she
sought.   I felt entirely at ease in her presence, and could not avoid
contrasting her sensible and amiable manners with the stiffness and
formality of upstart gentility at home or abroad.

The Queen was modestly attired in plain black, and wore no
ornaments.   Indeed, surrounded as she was by ladies arrayed in the
highest style of magnificence, their dresses sparkling with diamonds,
she was the last person whom a stranger would have pointed out
in that circle as the Queen of England.

The Lord in Waiting was perhaps mollified toward me when
he saw me following his illustrious example in retiring from the
royal presence.   He was accustomed to the process, and therefore
was able to keep somewhat ahead (or rather aback) of me, but even
I stepped rather fast for the other member of the retiring party.   We
had a considerable distance to travel in that long gallery before reaching the door, and whenever the General found he was losing ground,
he turned around and ran a few steps, then resumed the position of
"backing out," then turned around and ran, and so continued to
alternate his methods of getting to the door, until the gallery fairly
rang with the merriment of the royal spectators.   It was really one
of the richest scenes I ever saw; running, under the circumstances,
was an offence sufficiently heinous to excite the indignation of the
Queen's favorite poodle-dog, and he vented his displeasure by barking so sharply as to startle the General from his propriety.   He,
however, recovered immediately, and with his little cane commenced
an attack on the poodle, and a funny fight ensued, which renewed
and increased the merriment of the royal party.

This was near the door of exit.   We had scarcely passed into
the ante-room, when one of the Queen's attendants came to us with
the expressed hope of Her Majesty that the General had sustained
no damage—to which the Lord in Waiting playfully added, that in

case of injury to so renowned a personage, he should fear a declaration of war by the United States!

The courtesies of the Palace were not yet exhausted, for we were escorted to an apartment in which refreshments had been provided for us. We did ample justice to the viands, though my mind was rather looking into the future than enjoying the present. I was anxious that the "Court Journal" of the ensuing day should contain more than a mere line in relation to the General's interview with the Queen, and, on inquiry, I learned that the gentleman who had charge of that feature in the daily papers was then in the Palace. He was sent for by my solicitation, and promptly acceded to my request for such a notice as would attract attention. He even generously desired me to give him an outline of what I sought, and I was pleased to see afterwards that he had inserted my notice *verbatim*.

This notice of my visit to the Queen wonderfully increased the attraction of my exhibition and compelled me to obtain a more commodious hall for my exhibition. I accordingly removed to the larger room in the same building, for some time previously occupied by our countryman, Mr. Catlin, for his great Gallery of Portraits of American Indians and Indian Curiosities, all of which remained as an adornment.

On our second visit to the Queen, we were received in what is called the "Yellow Drawing-Room," a magnificent apartment, surpassing in splendor and gorgeousness anything of the kind I had ever seen. It is on the north side of the gallery, and is entered from that apartment. It was hung with drapery of rich yellow satin damask, the couches, sofas and chairs being covered with the same material. The vases, urns and ornaments were all of modern patterns, and the most exquisite workmanship. The room was panelled in gold, and the heavy cornices beautifully carved and gilt. The tables, pianos, etc., were mounted with gold, inlaid with pearl of various hues, and of the most elegant designs.

We were ushered into this gorgeous drawing-room before the Queen and royal circle had left the dining-room, and, as they approached, the General bowed respectfully, and remarked to Her Majesty "that he had seen her before," adding, "I think this is a prettier room than the picture gallery; that chandelier is very fine."

The Queen smilingly took him by the hand, and said she hoped he was very well.

"Yes, ma'am," he replied, "I am first rate."

"General," continued the Queen, "this is the Prince of Wales."

"How are you, Prince?" said the General, shaking him by the hand; and then standing beside the Prince, he remarked, "the Prince is taller than I am, but I feel as big as anybody"—upon which he strutted up and down the room as proud as a peacock, amid shouts of laughter from all present.

The Queen then introduced the Princess Royal, and the General immediately led her to his elegant little sofa, which we took with us, and with much politeness sat himself down beside her. Then, rising from his seat, he went through his various performances, and the Queen handed him an elegant and costly souvenir, which had been expressly made for him by her order—for which, he told her, "he was very much obliged, and would keep it as long as he lived." The Queen of the Belgians (daughter of Louis Philippe) was present on this occasion. She asked the General where he was going when he left London.

"To Paris," he replied.

"Whom do you expect to see there?" she continued.

Of course all expected he would answer, "the King of the French," but the little fellow replied:

"I shall see Monsieur Guillaudeu in Paris."

The two Queens looked inquiringly to me, and when I informed them that M. Guillaudeu was my French naturalist, who had preceded me to Paris, they laughed most heartily.

On our third visit to Buckingham Palace, Leopold, King of the Belgians, was also present. He was highly pleased, and asked a multitude of questions. Queen Victoria desired the General to sing a song, and asked him what song he preferred to sing.

"Yankee Doodle," was the prompt reply.

This answer was as unexpected to me as it was to the royal party. When the merriment it occasioned somewhat subsided, the Queen good-humoredly remarked, "That is a very pretty song, General. Sing it, if you please." The General complied, and soon afterwards we retired. I ought to add, that after each of our three visits to Buckingham Palace, a very handsome sum was sent to me, of course by the Queen's command. This, however, was the smallest part of the advantage derived from these interviews, as will be at once apparent to all who consider the force of Court example in England.

The British public were now fairly excited. Not to have seen General Tom Thumb was decidedly unfashionable, and from March 20th until July 20th, the levees of the little General at Egyptian Hall were continually crowded, the receipts averaging during the whole period about five hundred dollars per day, and sometimes going considerably beyond that sum. At the fashionable hour, between fifty and sixty carriages of the nobility have been counted at one time standing in front of our exhibition rooms in Piccadilly.

Portraits of the little General were published in all the pictorial papers of the time. Polkas and quadrilles were named after him, and songs were sung in his praise. He was an almost constant theme for the London *Punch,* which served up the General and myself so daintily that it no doubt added vastly to our receipts.

Besides his three public performances per day, the little General attended from three to four private parties per week, for which we were paid eight to ten guineas each. Frequently we would visit two parties in the same evening, and the demand in that line was much greater than the supply. The Queen Dowager Adelaide requested the General's attendance at Marlborough House one afternoon. He went in his court dress, consisting of a richly embroidered brown silk-velvet coat and short breeches, white satin vest with fancy-colored embroidery, white silk stockings and pumps, wig, bag-wig, cocked hat, and a dress sword.

"Why, General," said the Queen Dowager, "I think you look very smart to-day."

"I guess I do," said the General complacently.

A large party of the nobility were present. The old Duke of Cambridge offered the little General a pinch of snuff, which he declined. The General sang his songs, performed his dances, and cracked his jokes, to the great amusement and delight of the distinguished circle of visitors.

"Dear little General," said the kind-hearted Queen, taking him upon her lap, "I see you have got no watch. Will you permit me to present you with a watch and chain?"

"I would like them very much," replied the General, his eyes glistening with joy as he spoke.

"I will have them made expressly for you," responded the Queen Dowager; and at the same moment she called a friend and desired him to see that the proper order was executed. A few weeks thereafter we were called again to Marlborough House. A number of the children of the nobility were present, as well as some of their parents. After passing a few compliments with the General, Queen Adelaide presented him with a beautiful little gold watch, placing the chain around his neck with her own hands. The little fellow was delighted, and scarcely knew how sufficiently to express his thanks. The good Queen gave him some excellent advice in regard to his morals, which he strictly promised to obey.

After giving his performances, we withdrew from the royal presence, and the elegant little watch presented by the hands of Her

Majesty the Queen Dowager was not only duly heralded, but was also placed upon a pedestal in the hall of exhibition, together with the presents from Queen Victoria, and covered with a glass vase. These presents, to which were soon added an elegant gold snuff-box mounted with turquoise, presented by his Grace the Duke of Devonshire, and many other costly gifts of the nobility and gentry, added greatly to the attractions of the exhibition. The Duke of Wellington called frequently to see the little General at his public levees. The first time he called, the General was personating Napoleon Bonaparte, marching up and down the platform, and apparently taking snuff in deep meditation. He was dressed in the well-known uniform of the Emperor. I introduced him to the "Iron Duke," who inquired the subject of his meditations. "I was thinking of the loss of the battle of Waterloo," was the little General's immediate reply. This display of wit was chronicled throughout the country, and was of itself worth thousands of pounds to the exhibition.

While we were in London the Emperor Nicholas of Russia visited Queen Victoria, and I saw him on several public occasions. I was present at the grand review of troops in Windsor Park in honor of and before the Emperor of Russia and the King of Saxony.

General Tom Thumb had visited the King of Saxony and also Ibrahim Pacha, who was then in London. At the different parties we attended, we met, in the course of the season, nearly all of the nobility. I do not believe that a single nobleman in England failed to see General Tom Thumb at his own house, at the house of a friend, or at the public levees at Egyptian Hall. The General was a decided pet with some of the first personages in the land, among whom may be mentioned Sir Robert and Lady Peel, the Duke and Duchess of Buckingham, Duke of Bedford, Duke of Devonshire, Count d'Orsay, Lady Blessington, Daniel O'Connell, Lord Adolphus Fitzclarence, Lord Chesterfield, Mr. and Mrs. Joshua Bates,

of the firm of Baring Brothers & Co., and many other persons of
distinction. We had the free entrée to all the theatres, public gardens, and places of entertainment, and frequently met the principal artists, editors, poets, and authors of the country. Albert Smith
was a particular friend of mine. He wrote a play for the General
entitled "Hop o' my Thumb," which was presented with great success at the Lyceum Theatre, London, and in several of the provincial theatres. Our visit in London and tour through the provinces
were enormously successful, and after a brilliant season in Great
Britain I made preparations to take the General to Paris.

CHAPTER XIV

BEFORE taking the little General and party to Paris, I went over alone to arrange the preliminaries for our campaign in that city. Paris was not altogether a strange place to me. Months before, when I had successfully established my exhibition in London, I ran over to Paris to see what I could pick up in the way of curiosities for my Museum in New York, for during my whole sojourn abroad, and amid all the excitements of my new career, I never forgot the interests of my many and generous patrons at home. The occasion which first called me to France was the "quinquennial exposition" in Paris. At that time, there was an assemblage, every five years, of inventors and manufacturers who exhibited specimens of their skill, especially in articles of curious and ingenious mechanism, and I went from London mainly to attend this exposition.

There I met and became well acquainted with Robert Houdin, the celebrated conjurer. He was a watchmaker by trade, but very soon displayed a wonderful ability and ingenuity which he devoted with so much assiduity to the construction of a complicated machine, that he lost all mental power for a considerable period. When he recovered, he employed himself with great success in the manufacture of mechanical toys and automata which attracted much attention, and afterwards he visited Great Britain and other countries, giving a series of juggling exhibitions which were famous throughout Europe.

At this quinquennial exposition which I attended, he received a gold medal for his automata, and the best figure which he had on exhibition I purchased at a good round price. It was an automaton writer and artist, a most ingenious little figure, which sat at a table, and readily answered with the pencil certain questions. For instance: if asked for an emblem of fidelity, the figure instantly drew a correct picture of a handsome dog; the emblem of love was shown in an exquisite drawing of a little Cupid; the automaton would also answer many questions in writing. I carried this curious figure to London and exhibited it for some time in the Royal Adelaide Gallery, and then sent it across the Atlantic to the American Museum.

During my very brief visit to Paris, Houdin was giving evening performances in the Palais Royale, in legerdemain, and I was frequently present by invitation. Houdin also took pains to introduce me to other inventors of moving figures which I purchased freely, and made a prominent feature in my Museum attractions. I managed, too, during my short stay, to see something of the surface of the finest city in the world.

I stopped at the Hotel Bedford, and securing an interpreter, began to make my arrangements. The first difficulty in the way was the government tax for exhibiting natural curiosities, which was no less than one-fourth of the gross receipts, while theatres paid only eleven per cent. This tax was appropriated to the benefit of the city hospitals. Now, I knew from my experience in London, that my receipts would be so large as to make twenty-five per cent of them a far more serious tax than I thought I ought to pay to the French government, even for the benefit of the admirable hospitals of Paris. Accordingly, I went to the license bureau and had an interview with the chief. I told him I was anxious to bring a "dwarf" to Paris, but that the percentage to be paid for a license was so large as to deter me from bringing him; but letting the usual rule go, what should I give him in advance for a two months' license?

"My dear sir," he answered, "you had better not come at all;

THE WEDDING OF MR. AND MRS. TOM THUMB AT GRACE EPISCO-
PAL CHURCH, NEW YORK CITY

Loan Collection of Elizabeth Sterling Seeley

MRS. TOM THUMB (LAVINIA WARREN)

these things never draw, and you will do nothing, or so little that the percentage need not trouble you."

I expressed my willingness to try the experiment and offered one thousand francs in advance for a license. The chief would not consent and I then offered two thousand francs. This opened his eyes to a chance for a speculation and he jumped at my offer; he would do it on his own account, he said, and pay the amount of one-quarter of my receipts to the hospitals; he was perfectly safe in making such a contract, he thought, for he had 15,000 francs in bank.

But I declined to arrange this with him individually, so he called his associates together and presented the matter in such a way that the board took my offer on behalf of the government. I paid down the 2,000 francs and received a good, strong contract and license. The chief was quite elated and handed me the license with the remark:

"Now we have made an agreement, and if you do not exhibit, or if your dwarf dies during the two months you shall not get back your money."

"All right," thought I; "if you are satisfied I am sure I have every reason to be so." I then hired, at a large rent, the Salle Musard, Rue Vivienne, in a central and fashionable quarter close by the boulevards, and engaged an interpreter, ticket-seller, and a small but excellent orchestra. In fact, I made the most complete arrangements, even to starting the preliminary paragraphs in the Paris papers; and after calling on the Honorable William Rufus King, the United States Minister at the Court of France—who assured me that after my success in London there would be no difficulty whatever in my presentation to King Louis Philippe and family—I returned to England.

I went back to Paris with General Tom Thumb and party some time before I intended to begin my exhibitions, and on the very day after my arrival I received a special command to appear at the Tuileries on the following Sunday evening. It will be remembered that Louis Philippe's daughter, the wife of King Leopold of Belgium, had seen the General at Buckingham Palace—a fact that had been duly chronicled in the French as well as English papers, and I have no doubt that she had privately expressed her gratification at seeing him. With this advantage, and with the prestige of our receptions by Queen Victoria and Prince Albert, we went to the Tuileries with full confidence that our visit and reception would be entirely satisfactory.

At the appointed hour the General and I, arrayed in the conventional court costume, were ushered into a grand saloon of the palace where we were introduced to the King, the Queen, Princess Adelaide, the Duchess d'Orleans and her son the Count de Paris, Prince de Joinville, Duke and Duchess de Nemours, the Duchess d'Aumale, and a dozen or more distinguished persons, among whom was the editor of the official *Journal des Débats*. The court circle entered into conversation with us without restraint, and were greatly delighted with the little General. King Louis Philippe was minute in his inquiries about my country and talked freely about his experiences when he wandered as an exile in America. He playfully alluded to the time when he earned his living as a tutor, and said he had roughed it generally and had even slept in Indian wigwams. General Tom Thumb then went through with his various performances to the manifest pleasure of all who were present, and at the close the King presented to him a large emerald brooch set with diamonds. The General expressed his gratitude, and the King, turning to me, said: "You may put it on the General, if you please," which I did, to the evident gratification of the King as well as the General.

King Louis Philippe was so condescending and courteous that I felt quite at home in the royal presence, and ventured upon a bit of diplomacy. The Longchamps celebration was coming—a day once devoted to religious ceremony, but now conspicuous for the display of court and fashionable equipages in the Champs Élysées and the Bois de Boulogne, and as the King was familiarly conversing with me, I ventured to say that I had hurried over to Paris to take part in the Longchamps display and I asked him if the General's carriage could not be permitted to appear in the avenue reserved for the court and the diplomatic corps, representing that the General's small but elegant establishment, with its ponies and little coachman and footman, would be in danger of damage in the general throng unless the special privilege I asked was accorded.

The King smilingly turned to one of the officers of his household and after conversing with him for a few moments he said to me:

"Call on the Prefect of Police to-morrow afternoon and you will find a permit ready for you."

Our visit occupied two hours, and when we went away the General was loaded with fine presents. The next morning all the newspaper noticed the visit, and the *Journal des Débats* gave a minute account of the interview and of the General's performances, taking occasion to say, in speaking of the character parts, that "there was one costume which the General wisely kept at the bottom of his box." That costume, however,—the uniform of Bonaparte—was once exhibited, by particular request, as will be seen anon.

Longchamps day arrived, and among the many splendid equipages on the grand avenue, none attracted more attention than the superb little carriage with four ponies and liveried and powdered coachman and footman, belonging to the General, and conspicuous in the line of carriages containing the Ambassadors to the Court of France. Thousands upon thousands rent the air with cheers for "General Tom Pouce." There never was such an advertisement; the journals next day made elaborate notices of the "turnout," and thereafter whenever the General's carriage appeared on the boulevards, as it

did daily, the people flocked to the doors of the cafés and shops
to see it pass.

Thus, before I opened the exhibition all Paris knew that General
Tom Thumb was in the city.   The French are exceedingly im-
pressible; and what in London is only excitement, in Paris becomes
furore.   Under this pressure, with the prestige of my first visit
to the Tuileries and the numberless paragraphs in the papers, I
opened my doors to an eager throng.   The élite of the city came to
the exhibition; the first day's receipts were 5,500 francs, which
would have been doubled if I could have made room for more
patrons.   There were afternoon and evening performances and
from that day secured seats at an extra price were engaged in
advance for the entire two months.   The season was more than a
success, it was a triumph.

It seemed, too, as if the whole city was advertising me.   The
papers were profuse in their praises of the General and his performances.   *Figaro*, the *Punch* of Paris, gave a picture of an
immense mastiff running away with the General's carriage and
horses in his mouth.   Statuettes of "Tom Pouce" appeared in all
the windows, in plaster, Parian, sugar and chocolate; songs were
written about him and his lithograph was seen everywhere.   A fine
café on one of the boulevards took the name of "Tom Pouce" and
displayed over the door a life-size statue of the General.   In Paris,
as in London, several eminent painters expressed their desire to
paint his portrait, but the General's engagements were so pressing that
he found little time to sit to artists.   All the leading actors and
actresses came to the General's levees and petted him and made him
many presents.   Meanwhile, the daily receipts continued to swell, and
I was compelled to take a cab to carry my bag of silver home at night.

The official who had compromised with me for a two months'
license at 2,000 francs, was amazed as well as annoyed at the
success of my "dwarf."   He came, or sent a man, to the levees to

take account of the receipts and every additional thousand francs
gave him an additional twinge. He seriously appealed to me to give
him more money, but when I reminded him of the excellent bargain
he supposed he was making, especially when he added the conditional
clause that I should forfeit the 2,000 francs if I did not exhibit or
if the General died, he smiled faintly and said something about a
"Yankee trick." I asked him if he would renew our agreement
for two months more on the same terms; and he shrugged his
shoulders and said:

"No, Monsieur Barnum; you will pay me twenty-five per cent
of your receipts when the two months of our contract expires."

But I did not; for I appealed to the authorities, claiming
that I should pay only the ordinary theatrical tax, since the General's
exhibition consisted chiefly of character imitations in various costumes, and he was more attractive as an actor than as a natural
curiosity. My view of the case was decided to be correct, and
thereafter, in Paris and throughout France, with few exceptions, I
paid only the eleven per cent theatrical tax.

Indeed, in Paris, the General made a great hit as an actor and
was elected a member of the French Dramatic Society. Besides
holding his levees, he appeared every night at the Vaudeville Theatre
in a French play, entitled "Petit Poucet," and written expressly
for him, and he afterwards repeated the part with great success in
other cities. The demands upon our time were incessant.
We were invited everywhere to dinners and entertainments,
and as many of these were understood to be private performances of the General, we were most liberally remunerated
therefor. M. Galignani invited us to a soirée and introduced us to
some of the most prominent personages, including artists, actors and
editors, in Paris. The General was frequently engaged at a large
price to show himself for a quarter of an hour at some fancy or
charitable fair, and much money was made in this way. On Sun-

days, he was employed at one or another of the great gardens in the outskirts, and thus was seen by thousands of working people who could not attend his levees. All classes became acquainted with "Tom Pouce."

We were commanded to appear twice more at the Tuileries, and we were also invited to the palace on the King's birthday to witness the display of fireworks in honor of the anniversary. Our fourth and last visit to the royal family was by special invitation at St. Cloud. On each occasion we met nearly the same persons, but the visit to St. Cloud was by far the most interesting of our interviews. On this one occasion, and by the special request of the King, the General personated Napoleon Bonaparte in full costume. Louis Philippe had heard of the General in this character, and particularly desired to see him; but the affair was quite "on the sly," and no mention was made of it in the papers, particularly in the *Journal des Débats*, which thought, no doubt, that costume was still "at the bottom of the General's box." We remained an hour, and at parting, each of the royal company gave the General a splendid present, almost smothered him with kisses, wished him a safe journey through France, and a long and happy life. After bidding them adieu, we retired to another portion of the palace to make a change of the General's costume, and to partake of some refreshments which were prepared for us. Half an hour afterwards, as we were about leaving the palace, we went through a hall leading to the front door, and in doing so passed the sitting-room in which the royal family were spending the evening. The door was open, and some of them happening to espy the General, called out for him to come in and shake hands with them once more. We entered the apartment, and there found the ladies sitting around a square table, each provided with two candles, and every one of them, including the Queen, was engaged in working at embroidery, while a young lady was reading aloud for their edification.

During my stay in Paris, a Russian Prince, who had been living in great splendor in that city, suddenly died, and his household and personal effects were sold at auction. I attended the sale for several days in succession, buying many articles of vertu, and, among others, a magnificent gold tea-set, and a silver dining-service, and many rare specimens of Sevres china. These articles bore the initials of the family name of the Prince, and his own, "P. T.," thus damaging the articles, so that the silver and gold were sold for their weight value only. I bought them, and adding "B." to the "P. T.," had a very fine table service, still in my possession, and bearing my own initials, "P. T. B."

In spite of the extraordinary attention and unbounded petting the little General received at the hands of all classes, he was in no sense a "spoiled child," but retained throughout that natural simplicity of character and demeanor which added so much to the charm of his exhibitions. He was literally the pet of Paris, and after a protracted and most profitable season we started on a tour through France. The little General's small Shetland ponies and miniature carriage would be sure to arouse the enthusiasm of the "Provincials," so I determined to take them along with us. We went first to Rouen, and from thence to Toulon, visiting all the intermediate towns, including Orleans, Nantes, Brest, Bordeaux,—where I witnessed a review by the Dukes de Nemours and d'Aumale, of 20,000 soldiers who were encamped near the city. From Bordeaux we went to Toulouse, Montpellier, Nimes, Marseilles, and many other less important places, holding levees for a longer or shorter time. While at Nantes, Bordeaux and Marseilles the General also appeared in the theatres in his French part of "Petit Poucet."

Very soon after leaving Paris for our tour through France, I found that there were many places where it would be impossible to proceed otherwise than by post. General Tom Thumb's party numbered twelve persons, and these, with all their luggage, four little ponies, and a small carriage, must be transported in posting vehicles of some description. I therefore resolved that as posting in France was as cheap, and more independent than any other method of travel, a purchase of posting vehicles should be made for the sole use of the renowned General Tom Thumb and suite. One vehicle, however large, would have been insufficient for the whole company and "effects," and, moreover, would have been against the regulations. These regulations required that each person should pay for the use of one horse, whether using it or not, and I therefore made the following arrangements: I purchased a post-chaise to carry six persons, to be drawn by six horses; a vehicle on springs, with seats for four persons, and room for the General's four ponies and carriage, to be drawn by four horses; and lastly, a third vehicle for conveying the baggage of the company, including the elegant little house and furniture set on the stage in the General's performances of "Petit Poucet" at the theatres, the whole drawn by two horses.

With such a retinue the General "cut quite a swell" in journeying through the country, travelling, indeed, in grander style than a Field Marshal would have thought of doing in posting through France. All this folly and expense, the uninitiated would say, of employing twelve horses and twelve persons, to say nothing of the General's four ponies, in exhibiting a person weighing only fifteen pounds! But when this retinue passed along the roads, and especially when it came into a town, people naturally and eagerly inquired what great personage was on his travels, and when told that it was "the celebrated General Tom Thumb and suite," everybody desired to go and see him. It was thus the best advertising we could have had, and was really, in many places, our cheapest and in some places our only mode of getting from point to point where our exhibitions were to be given.

During most of the tour I was a week or two ahead of the

company, making arrangements for the forthcoming exhibitions, and doing my entire business without the aid of an interpreter, for I soon "picked up" French enough to get along very well indeed. I did not forget that Franklin learned to speak French when he was seventy years of age, and I did not consider myself too old to learn what, indeed, I was obliged to learn in the interests of my business. As for the little General, who was accompanied by a preceptor and translator, he very soon began to give his entire speaking performances in French, and his piece "Petit Poucet" was spoken as if he were a native.

In fact, I soon became the General's *avant courier,* though not doing the duties of an *avant courier* to an ordinary exhibition, since these duties generally consist in largely puffing the "coming man" and expected show, thus endeavoring to create a public appetite and to excite curiosity. My duties were quite different; after engaging the largest theatre or saloon to be found in the town, I put out a simple placard, announcing that the General would appear on such a day. Thereafter, my whole energies were directed, apparently, to keeping the people quiet; I begged them not to get excited; I assured them through the public journals that every opportunity should be afforded to permit every person to see "the distinguished little General, who had delighted the principal monarchs of Europe, and more than a million of their subjects," and that if one exhibition in the largest audience room in the town would not suffice, two or even three would be given.

This was done quietly, and yet, as an advertisement, effectively, for, strange as it may seem, people who were told to keep quiet, would get terribly excited, and when the General arrived and opened his exhibitions, excitement would be at fever heat, the levees would be thronged, and the treasury filled!

Numerous were the word battles I had with mayors, managers of theatres, directors of hospitals, and others, relative to what I considered—justly, I think—the outrageous imposition which the laws permitted in the way of taxes upon "exhibitions." Thus the laws required, for the sake of charity, twenty-five per cent of my gross receipts for the hospitals; while to encourage a local theatre, or theatres, which might suffer from an outside show, twenty per cent more must be given to the local managers. Of course this law was nearly a dead letter; for, to have taken forty-five per cent of my gross receipts at every exhibition would soon have driven me from the provinces, so the hospitals were generally content with ten per cent, and five or ten francs a day satisfied the manager of a provincial theatre. But at Bordeaux the manager of the theatre wished to engage the General to appear in his establishment, and as I declined his offer, he threatened to debar me from exhibiting anywhere in town, by demanding for himself the full twenty per cent the law allowed, besides inducing the directors of the hospitals to compel me to pay them twenty-five per cent more.

Here was a dilemma! I must yield and take half I thought myself entitled to and permit the General to play for the manager, or submit to legal extortion, or forego my exhibitions. I offered the manager six per cent of my receipts and he laughed at me. I talked with the hospital directors and they told me that as the manager favored them, they felt bound to stand by him. I announced in the public journals that the General could not appear in Bordeaux on account of the cupidity and extortionate demands of the theatre manager and the hospital directors. The people talked and the papers denounced; but manager and directors remained as firm as rocks in their positions. Tom Thumb was to arrive in two days and I was in a decided scrape. The mayor interceded for me, but to no avail; the manager had determined to enforce an almost obsolete law unless I would permit the General to play in his theatre every night. My Yankee "dander" was up and I declared that I would exhibit the General gratis rather than submit to the demand.

Whereupon, the manager only laughed at me the more to think how snugly he had got me.

Now it happened that, once upon a time, Bordeaux, like most cities, was a little village, and the little village of Vincennes lay one mile east of it. Bordeaux had grown and stretched itself and thickly settled far beyond Vincennes, bringing the latter nearly in the centre of Bordeaux; yet, strange to say, Vincennes maintained its own identity, and had its own Mayor and municipal rights quite independent of Bordeaux. I could scarcely believe my informant who told me this, but I speedily sought out the Mayor of Vincennes, found such a personage, and cautiously inquired if there was a theatre or a hospital within his limits? He assured me there was not. I told him my story, and asked:

"If I open an exhibtion within your limits will there be any percentages to pay from my receipts?"

"Not a sou," replied the Mayor.

"Will you give me a writing to that effect?"

"With the greatest pleasure," replied the Mayor, and he did so at once.

I put this precious paper in my pocket, and in a few moments I hired the largest dancing saloon in the place, a room capable of holding over 2,000 people. I then announced, especially to the delighted citizens of Bordeaux, that the General would open his exhibitions in Vincennes, which he soon did to an overflowing house. For thirteen days we exhibited to houses averaging more than 3,000 francs per day, and for ten days more at largely increased receipts, not one sou of which went for taxes or percentages. The manager and directors, theatre and hospital, got nothing, instead of the fair allowance I would willingly have given them. Oh, yes! they got something,—that is, a lesson,—not to attempt to offset French Shylockism against Yankee shrewdness.

We were in the South of France in the vintage season. Nothing can surpass the richness of the country at that time of the year. We travelled for many miles where the eye could see nothing but vineyards loaded with luscious grapes and groves of olive trees in full bearing. It is literally a country of wine and oil. Every one who has been in the wine district knows that the wine is trodden from the grapes by the bare feet of the peasants, and while I was there, desiring a new experience, I myself trod out a half barrel or so with my own naked feet, dancing vigorously the while to the sound of a fiddle.

Our remunerative and gratifying round of mingled pleasure and profit brought us at last to Lille, capital of the department of Nord, and fifteen miles from the Belgian frontier, and from thence we proceeded to Brussels.

CHAPTER XV

In crossing the border from France into Belgium, Professor Pinte, our interpreter and General Tom Thumb's preceptor, discovered that he had left his passport behind him—at Lille, at Marseilles, or elsewhere in France, he could not tell where, for it was a long time since he had been called upon to present it. I was much annoyed and indignantly told him that he "would never make a good showman, because a good showman never forgot anything." I could see that my allusion to him as a "showman" was by no means pleasant, which leads me to recount the circumstances under which I was first brought in contact with the Professor.

He was really a "Professor" and teacher of English in one of the best educational establishments in Paris. Very soon after opening my exhibitions in that city, I saw the necessity of having a translator who was qualified to act as a medium between the General and the highly cultivated audiences that daily favored us at our levees. I had begun with a not over-cultivated interpreter, who, when the General personated Cupid, for instance, would cry out "Coopeed," to which some one would be sure to respond "Stoopeed," to the annoyance of myself and the amusement of the audience. I accordingly determined to procure the best interpreter I could find and I was directed to call upon Professor Pinte. I saw him and briefly stated what I wanted, in what capacity I proposed to employ him, and what salary I would pay him. He was highly indignant and informed me that he was "no showman," and had no desire to learn or engage in the business.

165

"But, my dear sir," said I, "it is not as a showman that I wish to employ your valuable services, but as a preceptor to my young and interesting ward, General Tom Thumb, whom I desire to have instructed in the French language and in other accomplishments you are so competent to impart. At the same time, I should expect that you would be willing to accompany my ward and your pupil and attend his public exhibitions for the purpose of translating, as may be necessary, to the cultivated people of your own class who are the principal patrons of our entertainments."

This seemed to put an entirely new face upon the matter, especially as I had offered the Professor a salary five times larger, probably, than he was then receiving. So he rapidly revolved the subject in his mind and said:

"Ah! while I could not possibly accept a situation as a showman, I should be most happy to accept the terms and the position as preceptor to your ward."

He was engaged, and at once entered upon his duties, not only as preceptor to the General, but as the efficient and always excellent interpreter at our exhibitions, and wherever we needed his services on the route. As he had lost his passport, when we came to Courtrai on the Belgian frontier, I managed to procure a permit for him which enabled him to proceed with the party. This was but the beginning of difficulties, for I had all our property, including the General's ponies and equipage, to pass through the Custom-house, and among other things there was a large box of medals, with a likeness of the General on one side and of Queen Victoria and Prince Albert on the other side, which were sold in large numbers as souvenirs at our exhibitions. They were struck off at a considerable expense in England, and commanded a ready sale.

The Custom-house officers were informed, however, that these medals were mere advertising cards, as they really were, of our exhibitions, and I begged their acceptance of as many as they pleased to put in their pockets. They were beautiful medals, and a few dozen were speedily distributed among the delighted officials, who forthwith passed our show-bills, lithographs and other property with very little trouble. They wanted, however, to charge a duty upon the General's ponies and carriage, but when I produced a document showing that the French government had admitted them duty-free, they did the same. This superb establishment led these officials to think he must be a very distinguished man, and they asked what rank he held in his own country.

"He is Prince Charles Stratton, of the Dukedom of Bridgeport, in the Kingdom of Connecticut," said one of the party.

Whereupon they all reverently raised their hats when the General entered the car. Some of the railway men who had seen the distribution of medals among the Custom-house officers came to me and begged similar "souvenirs" of their distinguished passenger, and I gave the medals very freely, till the applications became so persistent as to threaten a serious pecuniary loss. At last I handed out a final dozen in one package, and said: "There, that is the last of them; the rest are in the box, and beyond my reach."

All this while Professor Pinte was brooding over my remark to him about the loss of his passport; the word "showman" rankled, and he asked me:

"Mr. Barnum, do you consider me a showman?"

I laughingly replied, "Why, I consider you the eminent Professor Pinte, preceptor to General Tom Thumb; but, after all, we are all showmen."

Finding himself so classed with the rest of us, he ventured to inquire "what were the qualifications of a good showman," to which I replied:

"He must have a decided taste for catering for the public; prominent perceptive faculties; tact; a thorough knowledge of human nature; great suavity; and plenty of 'soft soap.' "

"Soft sup!" exclaimed the interested Professor, "what is 'soft sup?'"

I explained, as best I could, how the literal meaning of the words had come to convey the idea of getting into the good graces of people and pleasing those with whom we are brought in contact. Pinte laughed, and as he thought of the generous medal distribution, an idea struck him:

"I think those railway officials must have very dirty hands—you are compelled to use so much 'soft sup.'"

Brussels is Paris in miniature and is one of the most charming cities I ever visited. We found elegant quarters, and the day after our arrival by command we visited King Leopold and the Queen at their palace. The King and Queen had already seen the General in London, but they wished to present him to their children and to the distinguished persons whom we found assembled. After a most agreeable hour we came away—the General, as usual, receiving many fine presents.

The following day, I opened the exhibition in a beautiful hall, which on that day and on every afternoon and evening while we remained there, was crowded by throngs of the first people in the city. On the second or third day, in the midst of the exhibition, I suddenly missed the case containing the valuable presents the General had received from kings, queens, noblemen and gentlemen, and instantly gave the alarm; some thief had intruded for the express purpose of stealing these jewels, and, in the crowd, had been entirely successful in his object.

The police were notified, and I offered 2,000 francs reward for the recovery of the property. A day or two afterwards a man went into a jeweller's shop and offered for sale, among other things, a gold snuff-box, mounted with turquoises, and presented by the Duke of Devonshire to the General. The jeweller, seeing the General's initials on the box, sharply questioned the man, who became alarmed and ran out of the shop. An alarm was raised, and the man was caught. He made a clean breast of it, and in the course of a few hours the entire property was returned, to the great delight of the General and myself. Wherever we exhibited afterwards, no matter how respectable the audience, the case of presents was always carefully watched.

CHAPTER XVI

In London the General again opened his levees in Egyptian Hall with undiminished success. His unbounded popularity on the Continent and his receptions by King Louis Philippe, of France, and King Leopold, of Belgium, had added greatly to his prestige and fame. Those who had seen him when he was in London months before came to see him again, and new visitors crowded by thousands to the General's levees.

Besides giving these daily entertainments, the General appeared occasionally for an hour, during the intermissions, at some place in the suburbs; and for a long time he appeared every day at the Surrey Zoological Gardens, under the direction of the proprietor, my particular friend Mr. W. Tyler. This place subsequently became celebrated for its great music hall, in which Spurgeon, the sensational preacher, first attained his notoriety. The place was always crowded, and when the General had gone through with his performances on the little stage, in order that all might see him he was put into a balloon which, secured by ropes, was then passed around the ground just above the people's heads. Some forty men managed the ropes and prevented the balloon from rising; but, one day, a sudden gust of wind took the balloon fairly out of the hands of half the men who had hold of the ropes, while others were lifted from the ground, and had not an alarm been instantly given which called at least two hundred to the rescue the little General would have been lost.

In addition to other engagements, the General frequently performed in Douglass's Standard Theatre, in the city, in the play

"Hop o' my Thumb," which was written for him by my friend, Albert Smith, whom I met soon after my first arrival in London and with whom I became very intimate. After my arrival in Paris, seeing the decided success of "Petit Poucet," it occurred to me that I should want such a play when I returned to England and the United States. So I wrote to Mr. Albert Smith, inviting him to make me a visit in Paris, intending to have him see this play and either translate or adapt it, or write a new one in English. He came and stayed with me a week, visiting the Vaudeville Theatre to see "Petit Poucet" nearly every night, and we compared notes and settled upon a plan for "Hop o' my Thumb." He went back to London and wrote the play and it was very popular indeed.

During our stay of three months, at this time, in Egyptian Hall, we made occasional excursions and gave exhibitions at Brighton, Bath, Cheltenham, Leamington and other watering places and fashionable resorts. It was at the height of the season in these places, and our houses were very large and our profits in proportion.

In October, 1844, I made my first return visit to the United States, leaving General Tom Thumb in England, in the hands of an accomplished and faithful agent, who continued the exhibitions during my absence. One of the principal reasons for my return at this time, was my anxiety to renew the Museum building lease, although my first lease of five years had still three years longer to run. I told Mr. Olmsted that if he would not renew my lease on the same terms, for at least five years more, I would immediately put up a new building, remove my Museum, close his building during the last year of my lease, and cover it from top to bottom with placards, stating where my new Museum was to be found. Pending an arrangement, I went to Mr. A. T. Stewart, who had just purchased the Washington Hall property, at the corner of Broadway and Chambers Street, intending to erect a store on the site, and proposed to join him in building, he to take the lower floor of the new store for his business, and I to own and occupy the upper stories for my Museum. He said he would give me an answer in the course of a week. Meanwhile, Mr. Olmsted gave me the additional five years lease I asked, and I so notified Mr. Stewart. Seeing the kind of building that Mr. Stewart erected on his lots, I do not know if he seriously entertained my proposition to join him in the enterprise; but he was by no means the great merchant then he afterwards became, and neither of us then thought, probably, of the gigantic enterprises we were subsequently to undertake, and the great things we were to accomplish. Having completed my business arrangements in New York, I returned to England with my wife and daughters, and hired a house in London. My house was the scene of constant hospitality which I extended to my numerous friends in return for the many attentions shown to me. It seemed then as if I had more and stronger friends in London than in New York. I had met and had been introduced to "almost everybody who was anybody," and among them all, some of the best soon became to me much more than mere acquaintants.

Among the distinguished people whom I met, I was introduced to the poet-banker, Samuel Rogers. I saw him at a dinner party at the residence of the American Minister, the Honorable Edward Everett. The old banker was very feeble, but careful nursing and all the appliances that unbounded wealth could bring, still kept the life in him and he managed, not only to continue to give his own celebrated breakfasts, but to go out frequently to enjoy the hospitality of others. As we were going in to dinner, I stepped aside, so that Mr. Rogers who was tottering along leaning on the arm of a friend, could go in before me, when Mr. Rogers said:

"Pass in, Mr. Barnum, pass in; I always consider it an honor to follow an American."

When our three months' engagement at Egyptian Hall had expired, I arranged for a protracted provincial tour through Great

Britain. I had made a flying visit to Scotland before we went to Paris—mainly to procure the beautiful Scotch costumes, daggers, etc., which were carefully made for the General at Edinburgh, and to teach the General the Scotch dances, with a bit of the Scotch dialect, which added so much to the interest of his exhibitions in Paris and elsewhere. My second visit to Scotland, for the purpose of giving exhibitions, extended as far as Aberdeen.

In England we went to Manchester, Birmingham, and to almost every city, town, and even village of importance. We travelled by post much of the time—that is, I had a suitable carriage made for my party, and a van which conveyed the General's carriage, ponies, and such other "property" as was needed for our levees,—and we never had the slightest difficulty in finding good post horses at every station where we wanted them. This mode of travelling was not only very comfortable and independent, but it enabled us to visit many out of the way places, off from the great lines of travel, and in such places we gave some of our most successful exhibitions. We also used the railway lines freely, leaving our carriages at any station, and taking them up again when we returned.

I remember once making an extraordinary effort to reach a branch-line station, where I meant to leave my teams and take the rail for Rugby. I had a time-table, and knew at what hour exactly I could hit the train; but unfortunately the axle to my carriage broke, and as an hour was lost in repairing it, I lost exactly an hour in reaching the station. The train had long been gone, and I must be in Rugby, where we had advertised a performance. I stormed around till I found the superintendent, and told him "I must instantly have an extra train to Rugby."

"Extra train!" said he, with surprise and a half sneer, "extra train! Why, you can't have an extra train to Rugby for less than sixty pounds."

"Is that all?" I asked; "well, get up your train immediately and here are your sixty pounds. What in the world are sixty pounds to me, when I wish to go to Rugby, or elsewhere, in a hurry!"

The astonished superintendent took the money, bustled about, and the train was soon ready. He was greatly puzzled to know what distinguished person—he thought he must be dealing with some prince, or, at least, a duke—was willing to give so much money to save a few hours of time, and he hesitatingly asked whom he had the honor of serving.

"General Tom Thumb."

We reached Rugby in time to give our performance, as announced, and our receipts were £160, which quite covered the expense of our extra train and left a handsome margin for profit.

When we were in Oxford, a dozen or more of the students came to the conclusion that as the General was a little fellow, the admission fee to his entertainments should be paid in the smallest kind of money. They accordingly provided themselves with farthings, and as each man entered, instead of handing in a shilling for his ticket, he laid down forty-eight farthings. The counting of these small coins was a great annoyance to Mr. Stratton, the General's father, who was ticket seller, and after counting two or three handsful, vexed at the delay which was preventing a crowd of ladies and gentlemen from buying tickets, Mr. Stratton lost his temper and cried out:

"Blast your quarter pennies! I am not going to count them! you chaps who haven't bigger money can chuck your copper into my hat and walk in."

At Cambridge, some of the under-graduates pretended to take offence because our check-taker would not permit them to smoke in the exhibition hall, and one of them managed to involve him in a quarrel which ended with a challenge from the student to the check-taker, who was sure he must fight a duel at sunrise the next morning, and as he expected to be shot, he suffered the greatest mental agony.

About midnight, however, after he had been sufficiently scared, I brought him the gratifying intelligence that I had succeeded in settling the dispute. His gratitude at the relief thus afforded knew no bounds.

Mr. Stratton was a genuine Yankee, and thoroughly conversant with the Yankee vernacular, which he used freely. In exhibiting the General, I often said to visitors that Tom Thumb's parents and the rest of the family were persons of the ordinary size, and that the gentleman who presided in the ticket-office was the General's father. This made poor Stratton an object of no little curiosity, and he was pestered with all sorts of questions; on one occasion an old dowager said to him:

"Are you really the father of General Tom Thumb?"

"Wa'al," replied Stratton, "I have to support him!"

This evasive method of answering is common enough in New England, but the literal dowager had her doubts, and promptly rejoined:

"I rather think he supports you!"

It must not be supposed that during my protracted stay abroad I confined myself wholly to business or limited my circle of observation with a golden rim. To be sure, I ever had "an eye to business," but I had also two eyes for observation and these were busily employed in leisure hours. I made the most of my opportunities and saw, hurriedly, it is true, nearly everything worth seeing in the various places which I visited. All Europe was a great curiosity shop to me and I willingly paid my money for the show.

While in London, my friend Albert Smith, a jolly companion, as well as a witty and sensible author, promised that when I reached Birmingham he would come and spend a day with me in "sight-seeing," including a visit to the house in which Shakespeare was born.

Early one morning in the autumn of 1844, my friend Smith and myself took the box-seat of an English mail-coach, and were soon whirling at the rate of twelve miles an hour over the magnificent road leading from Birmingham to Stratford. The distance is thirty miles. At a little village four miles from Stratford, we found that the fame of the bard of Avon had travelled thus far, for we noticed a sign over a miserable barber's shop, "Shakespeare hair-dressing—a good shave for a penny." In twenty minutes more we were set down at the door of the Red Horse Hotel, in Stratford. The coachman and guard were each paid half a crown as their perquisites.

While breakfast was preparing, we called for a guide-book to the town, and the waiter brought in a book, saying that we should find in it the best description extant of the birth and burial place of Shakespeare. I was not a little proud to find this volume to be no other than the "Sketch-Book" of our illustrious countryman, Washington Irving; and in glancing over his humorous description of the place, I discovered that he had stopped at the same hotel where we were then awaiting breakfast.

After examining the Shakespeare House, as well as the tomb and the church in which all that is mortal of the great poet rests, we ordered a post-chaise for Warwick Castle. The distance to Warwick is fourteen miles. We went to the Castle, and approaching the door of the Great Hall, were informed by a well-dressed porter that the Earl of Warwick and family were absent, and that he was permitted to show the apartments to visitors. He introduced us successively into the "Red Drawing-Room," "The Cedar Drawing-Room," "The Gilt Room," "The State Bed-Room," "Lady Warwick's Boudoir," "The Compass Room," "The Chapel," and "The Great Dining-Room." As we passed out of the Castle, the polite porter touched his head (he of course had no hat on it) in a style which spoke plainer than words, "Half a crown each, if you please, gentlemen." We responded to the call, and were then placed in charge of another guide, who took us to the top of "Guy's Tower," at the bottom of which he touched his hat a shilling's worth; and placing ourselves in charge of a third conductor, an old man of seventy, we proceeded to the Greenhouse to see the Warwick Vase —each guide announcing at the end of his short tour: "Gentlemen, I go no farther," and indicating that the bill for his services was to be paid. The old gentleman mounted a rostrum at the side of the vase, and commenced a set speech, which we began to fear was interminable; so tossing him the usual fee, we left him in the middle of his oration.

Passing through the porter's lodge on our way out, under the impression that we had seen all that was interesting, the old porter informed us that the most curious things connected with the Castle were to be seen in his lodge. Feeling for our coin, we bade him produce his relics, and he showed us a lot of trumpery, which, he gravely informed us, belonged to that hero of antiquity, Guy, Earl of Warwick. Among these were his sword, shield, helmet, breast-plate, walking-staff, and tilting pole, each of enormous size—the horse armor nearly large enough for an elephant, a large pot which would hold seventy gallons, called "Guy's Porridge Pot," his flesh-fork, the size of a farmer's hay-fork, his lady's stirrups, the rib of a mastodon which the porter pretended belonged to the great "Dun Cow," which, according to tradition, haunted a ditch near Coventry, and after doing injury to many persons, was slain by the valiant Guy. The sword weighed nearly 200 pounds, and the armor 400 pounds.

I told the old porter he was entitled to great credit for having concentrated more lies than I had ever before heard in so small a compass. He smiled, and evidently felt gratified by the compliment.

"I suppose," I continued, "that you have told these marvellous stories so often, that you believe them yourself?"

"Almost!" replied the porter, with a grin of satisfaction that showed he was "up to snuff," and had really earned two shillings.

"Come now, old fellow," said I, "what will you take for the entire lot of those traps? I want them for my Museum in America."

"No money would buy these valuable historical mementoes of a by-gone age," replied the old porter with a leer.

"Never mind," I exclaimed; "I'll have them duplicated for my Museum, so that Americans can see them and avoid the necessity of coming here, and in that way I'll burst up your show."

Albert Smith laughed immoderately at the astonishment of the porter when I made this threat, and I was greatly amused, some years afterwards, when Albert Smith became a successful showman and was exhibiting his "Mont Blanc" to delighted audiences in London, to discover that he had introduced this very incident into his lecture, of course changing the names and locality. He often confessed that he derived his very first idea of becoming a showman from my talk about the business and my doings, on this charming day when we visited Warwick.

The "Warwick races" were coming off that day, within half a mile of the village, and we therefore went down and spent an hour with the multitude. There was very little excitement regarding the races, and we concluded to take a tour through the "penny shows," the vans of which lined one side of the course for the distance of a quarter of a mile. While in the showmen's vans seeking for acquisitions to my Museum in America, I was struck with the tall appearance of a couple of females who exhibited as the "Canadian giantesses, each seven feet in height." Suspecting that a cheat was hidden under their unfashionably long dresses, which reached to the floor and thus rendered their feet invisible, I attempted to solve the mystery by raising a foot or two of the superfluous covering. The strapping young lady, not relishing such liberties from a stranger, laid me flat upon the floor with a blow from her brawny hand. I was on my feet again in tolerably quick time, but not until I had discovered that she stood upon a pedestal at least eighteen inches high.

We returned to the hotel, took a post-chaise, and drove through decidedly the most lovely country I ever beheld. In less than an hour we were set down at the outer walls of Kenilworth Castle, which Scott has greatly aided to immortalize in his celebrated novel of that name. This once noble and magnificent castle is now a stupendous ruin, which has been so often described that I think it unnecessary to say anything about it here. We spent half an hour in examining the interesting ruins, and then proceeded by post-chaise to Coventry, a distance of six or eight miles. Here we remained four hours, during which time we visited St. Mary's Hall, which has attracted the notice of many antiquaries. We also took our own "peep" at the effigy of the celebrated "Peeping Tom," after which we visited an exhibition called the "Happy Family," consisting of about two hundred birds and animals of opposite natures and propensities, all living in harmony together in one cage. This exhibition was so remarkable that I bought it and hired the proprietor to accompany it to New York, and it became an attractive feature in my Museum.

We took the cars the same evening for Birmingham, where we arrived at ten o'clock, Albert Smith remarking that never before in his life had he accomplished a day's journey on the Yankee go-ahead principle. He afterwards published a chapter in *Bentley's Magazine* entitled "A Day with Barnum," in which he said we accomplished business with such rapidity, that when he attempted to write out the accounts of the day, he found the whole thing so confused in his brain that he came near locating "Peeping Tom" in the house of Shakespeare, while Guy of Warwick *would* stick his head above the ruins of Kenilworth, and the Warwick Vase appeared in Coventry.

While I was at Aberdeen, in Scotland, I met Anderson, the "Wizard of the North." I had known him for a long time, and we were on familiar terms. The General's exhibitions were to close on Saturday night, and Anderson was to open in the same hall on

Monday evening. He came to our exhibition, and at the close we went to the hotel together to get a little supper. After supper we were having some fun and jokes together, when it occurred to Anderson to introduce me to several persons who were sitting in the room, as the "Wizard of the North," at the same time asking me about my tricks and my forthcoming exhibition. He kept this up so persistently that some of our friends who were present, declared that Anderson was "too much for me," and, meanwhile, fresh introductions to strangers who came in, had made me pretty generally known in that circle as the "Wizard of the North," who was to astonish the town in the following week. I accepted the situation at last, and said:

"Well, gentlemen, as I perform here for the first time, on Monday evening, I like to be liberal, and I should be very happy to give orders of admission to those of you who will attend my exhibition."

The applications for orders were quite general, and I had written thirty or forty, when Anderson, who saw that I was in a fair way of filling his house with "dead-heads," cried out—

"Hold on! I am the 'Wizard of the North.' I'll stand the orders already given, but not another one."

Our friends, including the "Wizard" himself, began to think that I had rather the best of the joke.

With the exception of the brief time passed in making two short visits to America, I had now passed three years with General Tom Thumb in Great Britain and on the Continent. The entire period had been a season of unbroken pleasure and profit. I had immensely enlarged my business experiences and had made money and many friends. We had visited nearly every city and town in France and Belgium, all the principal places in England and Scotland, besides going to Belfast and Dublin, in Ireland. I had several times met Daniel O'Connell in private life and in the Irish capital I heard him make an eloquent and powerful public Repeal speech in Conciliation Hall. In Dublin, after exhibiting a week in Rotunda Hall, our receipts on the last day were £261, or $1,305, and the General also received £50, or $250, for playing the same evening at the Theatre Royal. Thus closing a truly triumphant tour, we set sail for New York, arriving in February, 1847.

CHAPTER XVII

AT HOME

ONE of my main objects in returning home at this time was to obtain a longer lease of the premises occupied by the American Museum. My lease had still three years to run, but Mr. Olmsted, the proprietor of the building, was dead, and I was anxious to make provision in time for the perpetuity of my establishment, for I meant to make the Museum a permanent institution in the city, and if I could not renew my lease, I intended to build an appropriate edifice on Broadway. I finally succeeded, however, in getting the lease of the entire building, covering fifty-six feet by one hundred, for twenty-five years, at an annual rent of $10,000, and the ordinary taxes and assessments. I had already hired in addition the upper stories of three adjoining buildings. My Museum receipts were more in one day than they formerly were in an entire week, and the establishment had become so popular that it was thronged at all hours from early morning to closing time at night.

On my return, I promptly made use of General Tom Thumb's European reputation. He immediately appeared in the American Museum, and for four weeks drew such crowds of visitors as had never been seen there before. He afterwards spent a month in Bridgeport, with his kindred. To prevent being annoyed by the curious, who would be sure to throng the houses of his relatives, he exhibited two days at Bridgeport. The receipts, amounting to several hundred dollars, were presented to the Bridgeport Charitable Society. The Bridgeporters were much delighted to see their old friend, "little Charlie," again. They little thought, when they saw him playing about the streets a few years previously, that he was destined to create such a sensation among the crowned heads of the old world; and now, returning with his European reputation, he was, of course, a great curiosity to his former acquaintances, as well as to the public generally. His Bridgeport friends found that he had not increased in size during the four and a half years of his absence, but they discovered that he had become sharp and witty, "abounding in foreign airs and native graces;" in fact, that he was quite unlike the little, diffident country fellow whom they had formerly known.

"We never thought Charlie much of a phenomenon when he lived among us," said one of the first citizens of the place, "but now that he has become 'Barnumized,' he is a rare curiosity."

But there was really no mystery about it; the whole change made by training and travel had appeared to me by degrees, and it came to the citizens of Bridgeport suddenly. The terms upon which I first engaged the lad showed that I had no over-sanguine expectations of his success as a "speculation." When I saw, however, that he was wonderfully popular, I took the greatest pains to engraft upon his native talent all the instruction he was capable of receiving. He was an apt pupil, and I provided for him the best of teachers. Travel and attrition with so many people in so many lands did the rest. The General left America three years before, a diffident, uncultivated little boy; he came back an educated, accomplished little man. He had seen much, and had profited much. He went abroad poor, and he came home rich.

On January 1, 1845, my engagement with the General at a salary ceased, and we made a new arrangement by which we were equal partners, the General, or his father for him, taking one-half of the profits. A reservation, however, was made of the first four weeks after our arrival in New York, during which he was to exhibit at my Museum for two hundred dollars. When we returned to

America, the General's father had acquired a handsome fortune, and settling a large sum upon the little General personally, he placed the balance at interest, secured by bond and mortgage, excepting thirty thousand dollars, with which he purchased land near the city limits of Bridgeport, and erected a large and substantial mansion, where he resided till the day of his death, and in which his only two daughters were married, one in 1850, the other in 1853. His only son, besides the General, was born in 1851. All the family, except "little Charlie," are of the usual size.

After spending a month in visiting his friends, it was determined that the General and his parents should travel through the United States. I agreed to accompany them, with occasional intervals of rest at home, for one year, sharing the profits equally, as in England. We proceeded to Washington city, where the General held his levees in April, 1847, visiting President Polk and lady at the White House—thence to Richmond, returning to Baltimore and Philadelphia. Our receipts in Philadelphia in twelve days were $5,594.91. The tour for the entire year realized about the same average. The expenses were from twenty-five dollars to thirty dollars per day. From Philadelphia we went to Boston, Lowell, and Providence. Our receipts on one day in the latter city were $976.97. We then visited New Bedford, Fall River, Salem, Worcester, Springfield, Albany, Troy, Niagara Falls, Buffalo, and intermediate places, and in returning to New York we stopped at the principal towns on the Hudson River. After this we visited New Haven, Hartford, Portland, Me., and intermediate towns.

I was surprised to find that, during my long absence abroad, I had become almost as much of a curiosity to my patrons as I was to the spinster from Maine who once came to see me and to attend the "services" in my Lecture Room. If I showed myself about the Museum or wherever else I was known, I found eyes peering and fingers pointing at me, and could frequently overhear the remark, "There's Barnum." On one occasion soon after my return, I was sitting in the ticket-office reading a newspaper. A man came and purchased a ticket of admission. "Is Mr. Barnum in the Museum?" he asked. The ticket-seller, pointing to me, answered, "This is Mr. Barnum." Supposing the gentleman had business with me, I looked up from the paper. "Is this Mr. Barnum?" he asked. "It is," I replied. He stared at me for a moment, and then, throwing down his ticket, exclaimed, "It's all right; I have got the worth of my money;" and away he went, without going into the Museum at all!

In November, 1847, we started for Havana, taking the steamer from New York to Charleston, where the General exhibited, as well as at Columbia, Augusta, Savannah, Milledgeville, Macon, Columbus, Montgomery, Mobile and New Orleans. At this latter city we remained three weeks, including Christmas and New Year's. We arrived in Havana by the schooner "Adams Gray," in January, 1848, and were introduced to the Captain-General and the Spanish nobility. We remained a month in Havana and Matanzas, the General proving an immense favorite. In Havana he was the especial pet of Count Santovania. In Matanzas we were very much indebted to the kindness of a princely American merchant, Mr. Brinckerhoff. Mr. J. S. Thrasher, the American patriot and gentleman, was also of great assistance to us, and placed me under deep obligations.

From Havana we went to New Orleans, where we remained several days, and from New Orleans we proceeded to St. Louis, stopping at the principal towns on the Mississippi river, and return-ing *via* Louisville, Cincinnati, and Pittsburgh. We reached the latter city early in May, 1848. From this point it was agreed between Mr. Stratton and myself that I should go home and henceforth travel no more with the little General. I had competent agents who could exhibit him without my personal assistance, and

I preferred to relinquish a portion of the profits, rather than continue to be a travelling showman. I had now been a straggler from home most of the time for thirteen years, and I cannot describe the feelings of gratitude with which I reflected, that having by the most arduous toil and deprivations succeeded in securing a satisfactory competence, I should henceforth spend my days in the bosom of my family. I was fully determined that no pecuniary temptation should again induce me to forego the enjoyments to be secured only in the circle of home. I reached my residence in Bridgeport, Connecticut, in the latter part of May, rejoiced to find my family and friends in good health, and delighted to find myself once more at home.

My new home, which was then nearly ready for occupancy, was the well-known Iranistan. More than two years had been employed in building this beautiful residence. In 1846, finding that fortune was continuing to favor me, I began to look forward eagerly to the time when I could withdraw from the whirlpool of business excitement and settle down permanently with my family, to pass the remainder of my days in comparative rest.

I wished to reside within a few hours of New York. I had never seen more delightful locations than there are upon the borders of Long Island Sound, between New Rochelle, New York, and New Haven, Connecticut; and my attention was therefore turned in that direction. Bridgeport seemed to be about the proper distance from the great metropolis. The enterprise which characterized the city seemed to mark it as destined to become the first in the State in size and opulence; and I was not long in deciding, with the concurrence of my wife, to fix our future residence in that vicinity.

I accordingly purchased seventeen acres of land, less than a mile west of the city, and fronting with a good view upon the

Sound. Although nominally in Bridgeport, my property was really in Fairfield, a few rods west of the Bridgeport line. In deciding upon the kind of house to be erected, I determined, first and foremost, to consult convenience and comfort. I cared little for style, and my wife cared still less; but as we meant to have a good house, it might as well, at the same time, be unique. In this, I confess, I had "an eye to business," for I thought that a pile of buildings of a novel order might indirectly serve as an advertisement of my Museum.

In visiting Brighton, in England, I had been greatly pleased with the Pavilion erected by George IV. It was the only specimen of Oriental architecture in England, and the style had not been introduced into America. I concluded to adopt it, and engaged a London architect to furnish me a set of drawings after the general plan of the Pavilion, differing sufficiently to be adapted to the spot of ground selected for my homestead. On my second return visit to the United States, I brought these drawings with me and engaged a competent architect and builder, giving him instructions to proceed with the work, not "by the job" but "by the day," and to spare neither time nor expense in erecting a comfortable, convenient, and tasteful residence. The work was thus begun and continued while I was still abroad, and during the time when I was making my tour with General Tom Thumb through the United States and Cuba. New and magnificent avenues were opened in the vicinity of my property. The building progressed slowly, but surely and substantially. Elegant and appropriate furniture was made expressly for every room in the house. I erected expensive water works to supply the premises. The stables, conservatories and out-buildings were perfect in their kind. There was a profusion of trees set out on the grounds. The whole was built and established literally "regardless of expense," for I had no desire even to ascertain the entire cost. All I cared to know was that it suited me, and that would have been a small consideration with me if it had not also suited my family.

The whole was finally completed to my satisfaction. My family removed into the premises, and, on the fourteenth of November, 1848, nearly one thousand invited guests, including the poor and the rich, helped us in the old-fashioned custom of "house-warming."

When the name "Iranistan" was announced, a waggish New York editor syllabled it, I-ran-i-stan, and gave as the interpretation that "I ran a long time before I could stan'!" Literally, however, the name signifies, "Eastern Country Place," or, more poetically, "Oriental Villa."

The years 1848 and 1849 were mainly spent with my family, though I went every week to New York to look after the interests of the American Museum. While I was in Europe, in 1845, my agent, Mr. Fordyce Hitchcock, had bought out for me the Baltimore Museum, a fully-supplied establishment, in full operation, and I placed it under the charge of my uncle, Alanson Taylor. He died in 1846, and I then sold the Baltimore Museum to the "Orphean Family," by whom it was subsequently transferred to Mr. John E. Owens, the celebrated comedian. After my return from Europe, I opened, in 1849, a Museum in Dr. Swain's fine building, at the corner of Chestnut and Seventh Streets, in Philadelphia.

This was in all respects a first-class establishment. It was elegantly fitted up, and contained, among other things, a dozen fine large paintings, such as "The Deluge," "Cain and his Family," and other similar subjects which I had ordered copied, when I was in Paris, from paintings in the gallery of the Louvre. There was also a complete and valuable collection of curiosities and I sent from New York, from time to time, my transient novelties in the way of giants, dwarfs, fat boys, animals and other attractions. There was a lecture room and stage for dramatic entertainments; but I was catering for a Quaker population, and was careful to introduce or permit nothing which could possibly be objectionable. While the Museum contained such wax-works as "The Temperate Family," "The Intemperate Family," and Mrs. Pelby's representation of "The Last Supper," the theatre presented "The Drunkard" and other moral dramas. The most respectable people in the city patronized the Museum and attended the theatre. "The Drunkard" was exceedingly well played and it made a great impression. There was a temperance pledge in the box-office, which was signed by thousands during the run of the piece. Almost every hour during the day and evening, women could be seen bringing their husbands to the Museum to sign the pledge.

I stayed in Philadelphia long enough to identify myself with this Museum and to successfully start the enterprise and then left it in the hands of different managers who profitably conducted it till 1851, when, finding that it occupied too much of my time and attention, I sold it to Mr. Clapp Spooner for $40,000. At the end of that year, the building and contents were destroyed by fire.

While my Philadelphia Museum was in full operation, Peale's Museum ran me a strong opposition at the Masonic Hall. That enterprise proved disastrous, and I purchased the collection at sheriff's sale, for five or six thousand dollars, on joint account of my friend Moses Kimball and myself. The curiosities were equally divided, one-half going to his Boston Museum and the other half to my American Museum in New York.

In 1848 I was elected President of the Fairfield County Agricultural Society in Connecticut. Although not practically a farmer, I had purchased about one hundred acres of land in the vicinity of my residence, and felt and still feel a deep interest in the cause of agriculture. In 1849 it was determined by the Society that I should deliver the annual address. I begged to be excused on the ground of incompetency, but my excuses were of no avail, and as

I could not instruct my auditors in farming, I gave them the benefit of several mistakes which I had committed. Among other things, I told them that in the fall of 1848 my head gardener reported that I had fifty bushels of potatoes to spare. I thereupon directed him to barrel them up and ship them to New York for sale. He did so, and received two dollars per barrel, or about sixty-seven cents per bushel. But, unfortunately, after the potatoes had been shipped, I found that my gardener had selected all the largest for market, and left my family nothing but "small potatoes" to live on during the winter. But the worst is still to come. My potatoes were all gone before March, and I was obliged to buy, during the spring, over fifty bushels of potatoes, at $1.25 per bushel! I also related my first experiment in the arboricultural line, when I cut from two thrifty rows of young cherry-trees any quantity of what I supposed to be "suckers," or "sprouts," and was thereafter informed by my gardener that I had cut off all his grafts!

During the year 1848, Mr. Frank Leslie, since so widely known as the publisher of several illustrated journals, came to me with letters of introduction from London, and I employed him to get up for me an illustrated catalogue of my Museum. This he did in a splendid manner, and hundreds of thousands of copies were sold and distributed far and near, thus adding greatly to the renown of the establishment.

I count these two years—1848 and 1849—among the happiest of my life. I had enough to do in the management of my business, and yet I seemed to have plenty of leisure hours to pass with my family and friends in my beautiful home of Iranistan.

CHAPTER XVIII

MANY of my most fortunate enterprises have fairly startled me by the magnitude of their success. When my sanguine hopes predicted a steady flow of fortune, I have been inundated; when I calculated upon making a curious public pay me liberally for a meritorious article, I have often found the same public eager to deluge me with compensation. Yet, I never believed in mere luck and I always pitied the simpleton who relies on luck for his success. Luck is in no sense the foundation of my fortune; from the beginning of my career I planned and worked for my success. To be sure, my schemes often amazed me with the affluence of their results, and, arriving at the very best, I sometimes "builded better than" I "knew."

For a long time I had been incubating a plan for an extraordinary exhibition which I was sure would be a success and would excite universal attention and commendation in America and abroad. This was nothing less than a "Congress of Nations"—an assemblage of representatives of all the nations that could be reached by land or sea. I meant to secure a man and woman, as perfect as could be procured, from every accessible people, civilized and barbarous, on the face of the globe. I had actually contracted with an agent to go to Europe to make arrangements to secure "specimens" for such a show. Even now, I can conceive of no exhibition which would be more interesting and which would appeal more generally to all classes of patrons. As it was, and while positively preparing for such a congress, it occurred to me that another great enterprise could be undertaken at less risk, with far less real trouble, and with more remunerative results.

And now I come to speak of an undertaking which my worst enemy will admit was bold in its conception, complete in its development, and astounding in its success. It was an enterprise never before or since equalled in managerial annals. As I recall it now, I almost tremble at the seeming temerity of the attempt. That I am proud of it I freely confess. It placed me before the world in a new light; it gained me many warm friends in new circles; it was in itself a fortune to me—I risked much but I made more.

It was in October, 1849, that I conceived the idea of bringing Jenny Lind to this country. I had never heard her sing, inasmuch as she arrived in London a few weeks after I left that city with General Tom Thumb. Her reputation, however, was sufficient for me. I usually jump at conclusions, and almost invariably find that my first impressions are correct. It struck me, when I first thought of this speculation, that if properly managed it must prove immensely profitable, provided I could engage the "Swedish Nightingale" on any terms within the range of reason. As it was a great undertaking, I considered the matter seriously for several days, and all my "cipherings" and calculations gave but one result—immense success.

Reflecting that very much would depend upon the manner in which she should be brought before the public, I saw that my task would be an exceedingly arduous one. It was possible, I knew, that circumstances might occur which would make the enterprise disastrous. "The public" is a very strange animal, and although a good knowledge of human nature will generally lead a caterer of amusements to hit the people, they are fickle, and ofttimes perverse. A slight misstep in the management of a public entertainment frequently wrecks the most promising enterprise. Taking all things into the account, I arrived at the following conclusions:

Loan Collection of Elizabeth Sterling Seeley

JENNY LIND, FROM AN OLD PRINT

JENNY LIND IN HER LATER YEARS

1st. The chances were greatly in favor of immense pecuniary success; and 2d. Inasmuch as my name has long been associated with "humbug," and the American public suspect that my capacities do not extend beyond the power to exhibit a stuffed monkey-skin or a dead mermaid, I can afford to lose fifty thousand dollars in such an enterprise as bringing to this country, in the zenith of her life and celebrity, the greatest musical wonder in the world, provided the engagement is carried out with credit to the management.

I thought that the sum above named would be amply sufficient to cover all possible loss, and, caring little for the personal anxiety and labor which I must necessarily encounter, I cast about for the purpose of finding the proper agent to dispatch to Europe to engage the "divine Jenny," if possible.

I found in Mr. John Hall Wilton, an Englishman who had visited this country with the Sax-Horn Players, the best man whom I knew for that purpose. A few minutes sufficed to make the arrangement with him, by which I was to pay but little more than his expenses if he failed in his mission, but by which also he was to be paid a large sum if he succeeded in bringing Jenny Lind to our shores, on any terms within a liberal schedule which I set forth to him in writing.

On the 6th of November, 1849, I furnished Wilton with the necessary documents, including a letter of general instructions which he was at liberty to exhibit to Jenny Lind and to any other musical notables whom he thought proper, and a private letter, containing hints and suggestions not embodied in the former. I also gave him letters of introduction to my bankers, Messrs. Baring Brothers & Co., of London, as well as to many friends in England and France.

The sum of all my instructions, public and private, to Wilton amounted to this: He was to engage her on shares, if possible. I, however, authorized him to engage her at any rate, not exceeding one thousand dollars a night, for any number of nights up to one hundred and fifty, with all her expenses, including servants, carriages, secretary, etc., besides also engaging such musical assistants, not exceeding three in number, as she should select, let the terms be what they might.   If necessary, I should place the entire amount of money named in the engagement in the hands of London bankers before she sailed. Wilton's compensation was arranged on a kind of sliding scale, to be governed by the terms which he made for me— so that the farther he kept below my utmost limits, the better he should be paid for making the engagements. He proceeded to London, and opened a correspondence with Miss Lind, who was then on the Continent. He learned from the tenor of her letters, that if she could be induced to visit America at all, she must be accompanied by Mr. Julius Benedict, the accomplished composer, pianist, and musical director, and also she was impressed with the belief that Signor Belletti, the fine baritone, would be of essential service. Wilton therefore at once called upon Mr. Benedict and also Signor Belletti, who were both then in London, and in numerous interviews was enabled to learn the terms on which they would consent to engage to visit this country with Miss Lind. Having obtained the information desired, he proceeded to Lubeck, in Germany, to seek an interview with Miss Lind herself. Upon arriving at her hotel, he sent his card, requesting her to specify an hour for an interview. She named the following morning, and he was punctual to the appointment.

In the course of the first conversation, she frankly told him that during the time occupied by their correspondence she had written to friends in London, including my friend Mr. Joshua Bates, of the house of Baring Brothers, and had informed herself respecting my character, capacity, and responsibility, which she assured him were quite satisfactory. She informed him, however, that at that time there were four persons anxious to negotiate with her for an American tour. One of these gentlemen was a well-known opera manager in London; another, a theatrical manager in Manchester; a third, a musical composer and conductor of the orchestra of Her Majesty's Opera in London; and the fourth, Chevalier Wyckoff, a person who had conducted a successful speculation some years previously by visiting America in charge of a celebrated danseuse, Fanny Ellsler. Several of these parties had called upon her personally, and Wyckoff, upon hearing my name, attempted to deter her from making any engagement with me, by assuring her that I was a mere showman, and that, for the sake of making money by the speculation, I would not scruple to put her into a box and exhibit her through the country at twenty-five cents a head.

This, she confessed, somewhat alarmed her, and she wrote to Mr. Bates on the subject. He entirely disabused her mind, by assuring her that he knew me personally, and that in treating with me she was not dealing with an "adventurer" who might make her remuneration depend entirely upon the success of the enterprise, but I was able to carry out all my engagements, let them prove never so unprofitable, and she could place the fullest reliance upon my honor and integrity.

"Now," said she to Mr. Wilton, "I am perfectly satisfied on that point, for I know the world pretty well, and am aware how far jealousy and envy will sometimes carry persons; and as those who are trying to treat with me are all anxious that I should participate in the profits or losses of the enterprise, I must prefer treating with you, since your principal is willing to assume all responsibility, and take the entire management and chances of the result upon himself."

Several interviews ensued, during which she learned from Wilton that he had settled with Messrs. Benedict and Belletti, in regard to the amount of their salaries, provided the engagement was concluded, and in the course of a week Mr. Wilton and Miss Lind had arranged the terms and conditions on which she was ready to conclude the negotiations.   As these terms were within the limits fixed in my private letter of instructions, an agreement was duly drawn in triplicate, and signed by herself and Wilton, at Lubeck, January 9, 1850; and the signatures of Messrs. Benedict and Belletti were affixed in London a few days afterwards.

I was at my Museum in Philadelphia when Wilton arrived in New York, February 19, 1850.   He immediately telegraphed to me, in the cipher we had agreed upon, that he had signed an engagement with Jenny Lind, by which she was to commence her concerts in America in the following September.   I was somewhat startled by this sudden announcement; and feeling that the time to elapse before her arrival was so long that it would be policy to keep the engagement private for a few months, I immediately telegraphed him not to mention it to any person, and that I would meet him the next day in New York.

When we reflect how thoroughly Jenny Lind, her musical powers, her character, and wonderful successes, were subsequently known by all classes in this country as well as throughout the civilized world, it is difficult to realize that, at the time this engagement was made, she was comparatively unknown on this side the water. We can hardly credit the fact that millions of persons in America had never heard of her, that other millions had merely read her name, but had no distinct idea of who or what she was.   Only a small portion of the public were really aware of her great musical triumphs in the Old World, and this portion was confined almost entirely to musical people, travellers who had visited the Old World, and the conductors of the press.

The next morning I started for New York.   On arriving at Princeton we met the New York cars, and purchasing the morning papers, I was surprised to find in them a full account of my engagement with Jenny Lind.   However, this premature announcement could not be recalled, and I put the best face on the matter.   Anxious to learn how this communication would strike the public mind, I informed the conductor, whom I well knew, that I had made an engagement with Jenny Lind, and that she would surely visit this country in the following August.

"Jenny Lind! Is she a dancer?" asked the conductor.

I informed him who and what she was, but his question had chilled me as if his words were ice. Really, thought I, if this is all that a man in the capacity of a railroad conductor between Philadelphia and New York knows of the greatest songstress in the world, I am not sure that six months will be too long a time for me to occupy in enlightening the public in regard to her merits.

I had an interview with Wilton, and learned from him that, in accordance with the agreement, it would be requisite for me to place the entire amount stipulated, $187,500, in the hands of the London bankers. I at once resolved to ratify the agreement, and immediately sent the necessary documents to Miss Lind and Messrs. Benedict and Belletti.

I then began to prepare the public mind, through the newspapers, for the reception of the great songstress. How effectually this was done, is still within the remembrance of the American public. The people soon began to talk about Jenny Lind, and I was particularly anxious to obtain a good portrait of her. Fortunately, a fine opportunity occurred. One day, while I was sitting in the office of the Museum, a foreigner approached me with a small package under his arm. He informed me in broken English that he was a Swede, and said he was an artist, who had just arrived from Stockholm, where Jenny Lind had kindly given him a number of sittings, and he now had with him the portrait of her which he had painted upon copper. He unwrapped the package, and showed me a beautiful picture of the Swedish Nightingale, inclosed in an elegant gilt frame, about fourteen by twenty inches. It was just the thing I wanted; the price was fifty dollars, and I purchased it at once. Upon showing it to an artist friend the same day, he quietly assured me that it was a cheap lithograph pasted on a tin back, neatly varnished, and made to appear like a fine oil painting. The intrinsic value of the picture did not exceed thirty-seven and one-half cents!

After getting together all my available funds for the purpose of transmitting them to London in the shape of United States bonds, I found a considerable sum still lacking to make up the amount. I had some second mortgages which were perfectly good, but I could not negotiate them in Wall Street. Nothing would answer there short of first mortgages on New York or Brooklyn city property. I went to the president of the bank where I had done all my business for eight years. I offered him, as security for a loan, my second mortgages, and as an additional inducement, I proposed to make over to him my contract with Jenny Lind, with a written guaranty that he should appoint a receiver, who, at my expense, should take charge of all the receipts over and above three thousand dollars per night, and appropriate them towards the payment of my loan. He laughed in my face and said: "Mr. Barnum, it is generally believed in Wall Street that your engagement with Jenny Lind will ruin you. I do not think you will ever receive so much as three thousand dollars at a single concert." I was indignant at his want of appreciation, and answered him that I would not at that moment take $150,000 for my contract; nor would I. I found, upon further inquiry, that it was useless in Wall Street to offer the "Nightingale" in exchange for Goldfinches. I finally was introduced to Mr. John L. Aspinwall, of the firm of Messrs. Howland & Aspinwall, and he gave me a letter of credit from his firm on Baring Brothers, for a large sum on collateral securities, which a spirit of genuine respect for my enterprise induced him to accept.

After disposing of several pieces of property for cash, I footed up the amounts, and still discovered myself five thousand short.

I felt that it was indeed "the last feather that breaks the camel's back." Happening casually to state my desperate case to the Rev. Abel C. Thomas, of Philadelphia, for many years a friend of mine, he promptly placed the requisite amount at my disposal. I gladly accepted his proffered friendship, and felt that he had removed a mountain-weight from my shoulders.

CHAPTER XIX

AFTER the engagement with Miss Lind was consummated, she declined several liberal offers to sing in London, but, at my solicitation, gave two concerts in Liverpool, on the eve of her departure for America. My object in making this request was, to add the *éclat* of that side to the excitement on this side of the Atlantic, which was already nearly up to fever heat.

The first of the two Liverpool concerts was given the night previous to the departure of the Saturday steamer for America. My agent had procured the services of a musical critic from London, who finished his account of this concert at half past one o'clock the following morning, and at two o'clock my agent was overseeing its insertion in a Liverpool morning paper, numbers of which he forwarded to me by the steamer of the same day. The republication of the criticism in the American papers, including an account of the enthusiasm which attended and followed this concert, had the desired effect.

On Wednesday morning, August 21, 1850, Jenny Lind and Messrs. Benedict and Belletti set sail from Liverpoool in the steamship "Atlantic," in which I had long before engaged the necessary accommodations, and on board of which I had shipped a piano for their use. They were accompanied by my agent, Mr. Wilton, and also by Miss Ahmansen and Mr. Max Hjortzberg, cousins of Miss Lind, the latter being her Secretary; also by her two servants, and the valet of Messrs. Benedict and Belletti.

It was expected that the steamer would arrive on Sunday, September 1, but, determined to meet the songstress on her arrival whenever it might be, I went to Staten Island on Saturday, and slept at the hospitable residence of my friend, Dr. A. Sidney Doane, who was at that time the Health Officer of the Port of New York. A few minutes before twelve o'clock, on Sunday morning, the "Atlantic" hove in sight, and immediately afterwards, through the kindness of my friend Doane, I was on board the ship, and had taken Jenny Lind by the hand.

After a few moments' conversation, she asked me when and where I had heard her sing.

"I never had the pleasure of seeing you before in my life," I replied.

"How is it possible that you dared risk so much money on a person whom you never heard sing?" she asked in surprise.

"I risked it on your reputation, which in musical matters I would much rather trust than my own judgment," I replied.

I may as well state that, although I relied prominently upon Jenny Lind's reputation as a great musical *artiste,* I also took largely into my estimate of her success with all classes of the American public, her character for extraordinary benevolence and generosity. Without this peculiarity in her disposition, I never would have dared to make the engagement which I did, as I felt sure that there were multitudes of individuals in America who would be prompted to attend her concerts by this feeling alone.

Thousands of persons covered the shipping and piers, and other thousands had congregated on the wharf at Canal Street, to see her. The wildest enthusiasm prevailed as the steamer approached the dock. So great was the rush on a sloop near the steamer's berth, that one man, in his zeal to obtain a good view, accidentally tumbled overboard, amid the shouts of those near him. Miss Lind witnessed this incident, and was much alarmed. He was, however, soon rescued, after taking to himself a cold duck instead of securing a view of the Nightingale.   A bower of green trees, decorated with beautiful flags, was discovered on the wharf, together with two triumphal arches, on one of which was inscribed, "Welcome, Jenny Lind!"   The second was surmounted by the American eagle, and bore the inscription, "Welcome to America!"   These decorations were not produced by magic, and I do not know that I can reasonably find fault with those who suspected I had a hand in their erection.   My private carriage was in waiting, and Jenny Lind was escorted to it by Captain West.   The rest of the musical party entered the carriage, and mounting the box at the driver's side, I directed him to the Irving House.   I took that seat as a legitimate advertisement, and my presence on the outside of the carriage aided those who filled the windows and sidewalks along the whole route, in coming to the conclusion that Jenny Lind had arrived.

A reference to the journals of that day will show that never before had there been such enthusiasm in the City of New York, or indeed in America.   Within ten minutes after our arrival at the Irving House, not less than twenty thousand persons had congregated around the entrance in Broadway, nor was the number diminished before nine o'clock in the evening.   At her request, I dined with her that afternoon, and when, according to European custom, she prepared to pledge me in a glass of wine, she was somewhat surprised at my saying, "Miss Lind, I do not think you can ask any other favor on earth which I would not gladly grant; but I am a teetotaler, and must beg to be permitted to drink your health and happiness in a glass of cold water."

At twelve o'clock that night, she was serenaded by the New York Musical Fund Society, numbering, on that occasion, two hundred musicians.   They were escorted to the Irving House by about three hundred firemen, in their red shirts, bearing torches.   There was a far greater throng in the streets than there was even during the day.   The calls for Jenny Lind were so vehement that I led her through a window to the balcony. The loud cheers from the crowds lasted for several minutes, before the serenade was permitted to proceed again.

I have given the merest sketch of but a portion of the incidents of Jenny Lind's first day in America. For weeks afterwards the excitement was unabated. Her rooms were thronged by visitors, including the magnates of the land in both Church and State. The carriages of the wealthiest citizens could be seen in front of her hotel at nearly all hours of the day, and it was with some difficulty that I prevented the "fashionables" from monopolizing her altogether, and thus, as I believed, sadly marring my interests by cutting her off from the warm sympathies she had awakened among the masses. Presents of all sorts were showered upon her. Milliners, mantua-makers, and shopkeepers vied with each other in calling her attention to their wares, of which they sent her many valuable specimens, delighted if, in return, they could receive her autograph acknowledgment. Songs, quadrilles and polkas were dedicated to her, and poets sung in her praise. We had Jenny Lind gloves, Jenny Lind bonnets, Jenny Lind riding hats, Jenny Lind shawls, mantillas, robes, chairs, sofas, pianos—in fact, every thing was Jenny Lind. Her movements were constantly watched, and the moment her carriage appeared at the door it was surrounded by multitudes, eager to catch a glimpse of the Swedish Nightingale.

In looking over my "scrap-books" of extracts from the New York papers of that day, in which all accessible details concerning her were duly chronicled, it seems almost incredible that such a degree of enthusiasm should have existed. An abstract of the "sayings and doings" in regard to the Jenny Lind mania for the first ten days after her arrival, appeared in the London *Times* of September 23, 1850, and although it was an ironical "showing up" of the American enthusiasm, filling several columns, it was nevertheless a faithful condensation of facts which at this late day seem even to myself more like a dream than reality.

Before her arrival I had offered $200 for a prize ode, "Greeting to America," to be sung by Jenny Lind at her first concert. Several hundred "poems" were sent in from all parts of the United States and the Canadas. The duties of the Prize Committee, in reading these effusions and making choice of the one most worthy the prize, were truly arduous. The "offerings," with perhaps a dozen exceptions, were the merest doggerel trash. The prize was awarded to Bayard Taylor. This award, although it gave general satisfaction, yet was met with disfavor by several disappointed poets, who, notwithstanding the decision of the committee, persisted in believing and declaring their own productions to be the best. This state of feeling was doubtless, in part, the cause which led to the publication, about this time, of a witty pamphlet entitled "Barnum's Parnassus; being Confidential Disclosures of the Prize Committee on the Jenny Lind song." It gave some capital hits in which the committee, the enthusiastic public, the Nightingale, and myself, were roundly ridiculed. Various extracts from this brochure were copied in the papers daily, and my agents scattered the work as widely as possible, thus efficiently aiding and advertising my enterprise and serving to keep up the public excitement.

Jenny Lind's first concert was fixed to come off at Castle Garden, on Wednesday evening, September 11th, and most of the tickets were sold at auction on the Saturday and Monday previous to the concert. John N. Genin, the hatter, laid the foundation of his fortune by purchasing the first ticket at $225. It has been extensively reported that Mr. Genin and I are brothers-in-law, but our only relations are those of business and friendship. The proprietors of the Garden saw fit to make the usual charge of one shilling to all persons who entered the premises, yet three thousand people were

CASTLE GARDEN (TOP) IN 1850; (BELOW) JENNY LIND'S CONCERT AT CASTLE GARDEN, SEPTEMBER 11, 1850, HER FIRST PUBLIC APPEARANCE IN AMERICA

BARNUM'S ROMAN HIPPODROME (TOP, EXTERIOR; BOTTOM, INTE-
RIOR), ON THE SITE AT WHICH MADISON SQUARE GARDEN LATER
STOOD

Harper's Weekly

present at the auction. One thousand tickets were sold on the first day for an aggregate sum of $10,141.

On the Tuesday after her arrival I informed Miss Lind that I wished to make a slight alteration in our agreement. "What is it?" she asked in surprise. "I am convinced," I replied, " that our enterprise will be much more successful than either of us anticipated. I wish, therefore, to stipulate that you shall receive not only $1,000 for each concert, besides all the expenses, as heretofore agreed on, but after taking $5,500 per night for expenses and my services, the balance shall be equally divided between us."

Jenny looked at me with astonishment. She could not comprehend my proposition. After I had repeated it, and she fully understood its import, she cordially grasped me by the hand, and exclaimed, "Mr. Barnum, you are a gentleman of honor: you are generous; it is just as Mr. Bates told me; I will sing for you as long as you please; I will sing for you in America—in Europe—anywhere!"

Upon drawing the new contract which was to include this entirely voluntary and liberal advance on my part, beyond the terms of the original agreement, Miss Lind's lawyer, Mr. John Jay, who was present solely to put in writing the new arrangement between Miss Lind and myself, insisted upon intruding the suggestion that she should have the right to terminate the engagement at the end of the sixtieth concert, if she should choose to do so. This proposition was so persistently and annoyingly pressed that Miss Lind was finally induced to entertain it, at the same time offering, if she did so, to refund to me all moneys paid her up to that time, excepting the $1,000 per concert according to the original agreement. This was agreed to, and it was also arranged that she might terminate the engagement at the one-hundredth concert, if she desired, upon paying me $25,000 for the loss of the additional fifty nights.

After this new arrangement was completed, I said: "Now, Miss Lind, as you are directly interested, you must have an agent to assist in taking and counting the tickets;" to which she replied, "Oh, no! Mr. Barnum; I have every confidence in you and I must decline to act upon your suggestion;" but I continued:

"I never allow myself, if it can be avoided, when I have associates in the same interests, to be placed in a position where I must assume the sole responsibility. I never even permitted an actor to take a benefit at my Museum, unless he placed a ticket-taker of his own at the door."

Thus urged, Miss Lind engaged Mr. Seton to act as her ticket-taker, and after we had satisfactorily arranged the matter, Jay, knowing the whole affair, had the impudence to come to me with a package of blank printed affidavits, which he demanded that I should fill out, from day to day, with the receipts of each concert, and swear to their correctness before a magistrate! I told him that I would see him on the subject at Miss Lind's hotel that afternoon, and going there a few moments before the appointed hour, I narrated the circumstances to Mr. Benedict and showed him an affidavit which I had made that morning to the effect that I would never directly or indirectly take any advantage whatever of Miss Lind. This I had made oath to, for I thought if there was any swearing of that kind to be done I would do it "in a lump" rather than in detail. Mr. Benedict was very much opposed to it, and arriving during the interview, Jay was made to see the matter in such a light that he was thoroughly ashamed of his proposition, and, requesting that the affair might not be mentioned to Miss Lind, he begged me to destroy the affidavit. I heard no more about swearing to our receipts.

On Tuesday, September 10th, I informed Miss Lind that, judging by present appearances, her portion of the proceeds of the first concert would amount to $10,000. She immediately resolved to devote every dollar of it to charity; and, sending for Mayor Wood-hull, she acted under his and my advice in selecting various institutions among which she wished the amount to be distributed.

My arrangements of the concert room were very complete. The great *parterre* and gallery of Castle Garden were divided by imaginary lines into four compartments, each of which was designated by a lamp of a different color. The tickets were printed in colors corresponding with the location which the holders were to occupy, and one hundred ushers, with rosettes and bearing wands tipped with ribbons of the several hues, enabled every individual to find his or her seat without the slightest difficulty. Every seat was of course numbered in color to correspond with the check, which each person retained after giving up an entrance ticket at the door. Thus, tickets, checks, lamps, rosettes, wands, and even the seat numbers were all in the appropriate colors to designate the different departments. These arrangements were duly advertised, and every particular was also printed upon each ticket. In order to prevent confusion, the doors were opened at five o'clock, while the concert did not commence until eight. The consequence was, that although about five thousand persons were present at the first concert, their entrance was marked with as much order and quiet as was ever witnessed in the assembling of a congregation at church. These precautions were observed at all the concerts given throughout the country under my administration, and the good order which always prevailed was the subject of numberless encomiums from the public and the press.

The reception of Jenny Lind on her first appearance, in point of enthusiasm, was probably never before equalled in the world. As Mr. Benedict led her towards the foot-lights, the entire audience rose to their feet and welcomed her with three cheers, accompanied by the waving of thousands of hats and handkerchiefs. This was by far the largest audience to which Jenny Lind had ever sung. She was evidently much agitated, but the orchestra commenced, and before she had sung a dozen notes of "Casta Diva," she began to recover her self-possession, and long before the *scena* was concluded, she was as calm as if she was in her own drawing-room. Towards the last portion of the *cavatina,* the audience were so completely carried away by their feelings that the remainder of the air was drowned in a perfect tempest of acclamation. Enthusiasm had been wrought to its highest pitch, but the musical powers of Jenny Lind exceeded all the brilliant anticipations which had been formed, and her triumph was complete. At the conclusion of the concert Jenny Lind was loudly called for, and was obliged to appear three times before the audience could be satisfied. They then called vociferously for "Barnum," and I reluctantly responded to their demand.

On this first night, Mr. Julius Benedict firmly established with the American people his European reputation, as a most accomplished conductor and musical composer; while Signor Belletti inspired an admiration which grew warmer and deeper in the minds of the American people, to the end of his career in this country.

It would seem as if the Jenny Lind mania had reached its culminating point before she appeared, and I confess that I feared the anticipations of the public were too high to be realized, and hence that there would be a reaction after the first concert; but I was happily disappointed. The transcendent musical genius of the Swedish Nightingale was superior to all that fancy could paint, and the furore did not attain its highest point until she had been heard. The people were in ecstasies; the powers of editorial acumen, types and ink, were inadequate to sound her praises. The Rubicon was passed. The successful issue of the Jenny Lind enterprise was established. I think there were a hundred men in New York, the day after her first concert, who would have willingly paid me $200,000 for my contract. I received repeated offers for an eighth, a tenth, or a sixteenth, equivalent to that price. But mine had been the risk, and I was determined mine should be the triumph. So elated was I with my success, in spite of all obstacles and false prophets, that I do not think half a million dollars would have tempted me to relinquish the enterprise.

Upon settling the receipts of the first concert, they were found to be somewhat less than I anticipated. The sums bid at the auction sales, together with the tickets purchased at private sale, amounted to more than $20,000. It proved, however, that several of the tickets bid off at from $12 to $25 each were not called for. In some instances, probably the zeal of the bidders cooled down when they came out from the scene of excitement, and once more breathed the fresh sea-breeze which came sweeping up from "the Narrows," while perhaps, in other instances, bids were made by parties who never intended to take the tickets. I can only say, once for all, that I was never privy to a false bid, and was so particular upon that point, that I would not permit one of my employees to bid on or purchase a ticket at auction, though requested to do so for especial friends.

The amount of money received for tickets to the first concert was $17,864.05. As this made Miss Lind's portion too small to realize the $10,000 which had been announced as devoted to charity, I proposed to divide equally with her the proceeds of the first two concerts, and not count them at all in our regular engagement. Accordingly, the second concert was given September 13th, and the receipts, amounting to $14,203.03, were, like those of the first concert, equally divided. Our third concert, but which, as between ourselves, we called the "first regular concert," was given Tuesday, September 17, 1850.

CHAPTER XX

No one can imagine the amount of head-work and hand-work which I performed during the first four weeks after Jenny Lind's arrival. Anticipating much of this, I had spent some time in August at the White Mountains to recruit my energies. Of course I had not been idle during the summer. I had put innumerable means and appliances into operation for the furtherance of my object, and little did the public see of the hand that indirectly pulled at their heart-strings, preparatory to a relaxation of their purse-strings; and these means and appliances were continued and enlarged throughout the whole of that triumphal musical campaign.

The first great assembly at Castle Garden was not gathered by Jenny Lind's musical genius and powers alone. She was effectually introduced to the public before they had seen or heard her. She appeared in the presence of a jury already excited to enthusiasm in her behalf. She more than met their expectations, and all the means I had adopted to prepare the way were thus abundantly justified.

As a manager, I worked by setting others to work. Biographies of the Swedish Nightingale were largely circulated; "Foreign Correspondence" glorified her talents and triumphs by narratives of her benevolence; and "printer's ink" was invoked in every possible form, to put and keep Jenny Lind before the people. I am happy to say that the press generally echoed the voice of her praise from first to last.

After the first month the business became thoroughly systematized, and by the help of such agents as my faithful treasurer, L. C. Stewart, and the indefatigable Le Grand Smith, my personal labors were materially relieved; but from the first concert on the 11th of September, 1850, until the ninety-third concert on the 9th of June, 1851, a space of nine months, I did not know a waking moment that was entirely free from anxiety.

I could not hope to be exempted from trouble and perplexity in managing an enterprise which depended altogether on popular favor, and which involved great consequences to myself; but I did not expect the numerous petty annoyances which beset me, especially in the early period of the concerts. Miss Lind did not dream, nor did any one else, of the unparalleled enthusiasm that would greet her; and the first immense assembly at Castle Garden somewhat prepared her, I suspect, to listen to evil advisers. It would seem that the terms of our revised contract were sufficiently liberal to her and sufficiently hazardous to myself, to justify the expectation of perfectly honorable treatment; but certain envious intermeddlers appeared to think differently. "Do you not see, Miss Lind, that Mr. Barnum is coining money out of your genius," said they; of course she saw it, but the high-minded Swede despised and spurned the advisers who recommended her to repudiate her contract with me at all hazards, and take the enterprise into her own hands— possibly to put it into theirs. I, however, suffered much from the unreasonable interference of her lawyer, Mr. John Jay. Benedict and Belletti behaved like men, and Jenny afterwards expressed to me her regret that she had for a moment listened to the vexatious exactions of her legal counsellor.

It is not my purpose to enter into full details of all of the Lind concerts, though I have given elsewhere a transcript from the account books of my treasurer, presenting a table of the places and exact receipts of the concerts. This will gratify curiosity, and at the same time indicate our route of travel. Meanwhile, I devote a few pages to interesting incidents connected with Miss Lind's visit to America.

Jenny Lind's character for benevolence became so generally known that her door was beset by persons asking charity, and she was in the receipt, while in the principal cities, of numerous letters, all on the same subject. Her secretary examined and responded favorably to some of them. He undertook at first to answer them all, but finally abandoned that course in despair. I know of many instances in which she gave sums of money to applicants, varying in amount from $20, $50, $500, to $1,000, and in one instance she gave $5,000 to a Swedish friend.

One night, while giving a concert in Boston, a girl approached the ticket-office, and laying down $3 for a ticket, remarked, "There goes half a month's earnings, but I am determined to hear Jenny Lind." Miss Lind's secretary heard the remark, and a few minutes afterwards coming into her room, he laughingly related the circumstance. "Would you know the girl again?" asked Jenny, with an earnest look. Upon receiving an affirmative reply, she instantly placed a $20 gold-piece in his hand, and said, "Poor girl! give her that with my best compliments." He at once found the girl, who cried with joy when she received the gold-piece, and heard the kind words with which the gift was accompanied.

The night after Jenny's arrival in Boston, a display of fireworks was given in her honor, in front of the Revere House, after which followed a beautiful torch-light procession by the Germans of that city.

On her return from Boston to New York, Jenny, her companion, and Messrs. Benedict and Belletti, stopped at Iranistan, my residence in Bridgeport, where they remained until the following day. The morning after her arrival, she took my arm and proposed a promenade through the grounds. She seemed much pleased, and said, "I am astonished that you should have left such a beautiful place for the sake of travelling through the country with me."

The same day she told me, in a playful mood, that she had heard a most extraordinary report. "I have heard that you and I are about to be married," said she; "now how could such an absurd report ever have originated?"

"Probably from the fact that we are 'engaged.'" I replied. She enjoyed a joke, and laughed heartily.

"Do you know, Mr. Barnum," said she, "that if you had not built Iranistan, I should never have come to America for you?"

I expressed my surprise, and asked her to explain.

"I had received several applications to visit the United States," she continued, "but I did not much like the appearance of the applicants, nor did I relish the idea of crossing 3,000 miles of ocean; so I declined them all. But the first letter which Mr. Wilton, your agent, addressed me, was written upon a sheet headed with a beautiful engraving of Iranistan. It attracted my attention. I said to myself, a gentleman who has been so successful in his business as to be able to build and reside in such a palace cannot be a mere 'adventurer.' So I wrote to your agent, and consented to an interview, which I should have declined if I had not seen the picture of Iranistan!"

"That, then, fully pays me for building it," I replied; "for I intend and expect to make more by this musical enterprise than Iranistan cost me."

"I really hope so," she replied; "but you must not be too sanguine, you know, 'man proposes but God disposes.'"

Jenny Lind always desired to reach a place in which she was to sing, without having the time of her arrival known, thus avoiding the excitement of promiscuous crowds. As a manager, however, I knew that the intersts of the enterprise depended in a great degree upon these excitements. Although it frequently seemed inconceivable to her how so many thousands should have discovered her secret and consequently gathered together to receive her, I was not so much astonished, inasmuch as my agent always had early telegraphic intelligence of the time of her anticipated arrival, and was not slow in communicating the information to the public.

On reaching Philadelphia, a large concourse of persons awaited the approach of the steamer which conveyed her. With difficulty we pressed through the crowd, and were followed by many thousands to Jones's Hotel. The street in front of the building was densely packed by the populace, and poor Jenny, who was suffering from a severe headache, retired to her apartments. I tried to induce the crowd to disperse, but they declared they would not do so until Jenny Lind should appear on the balcony. I would not disturb her, and knowing that the tumult might prove an annoyance to her, I placed her bonnet and shawl upon her companion, Miss Ahmansen, and led her out on the balcony. She bowed gracefully to the multitude, who gave her three hearty cheers and quietly dispersed. Miss Lind was so utterly averse to anything like deception, that we never ventured to tell her the part which her bonnet and shawl had played in the absence of their owner.

Jenny was in the habit of attending church whenever she could do so without attracting notice. She always preserved her nationality, also, by inquiring out and attending Swedish churches wherever they could be found. She gave $1,000 to a Swedish church in Chicago.

While in Boston, a poor Swedish girl, a domestic in a family at Roxbury, called on Jenny. She detained her visitor several hours, talking about home, and other matters, and in the evening took her in her carriage to the concert, gave her a seat, and sent her back to Roxbury in a carriage, at the close of the performances.

My eldest daughter, Caroline, and her friend, Mrs. Lyman, of Bridgeport, accompanied me on the tour from New York to Havana, and thence home, *via* New Orleans and the Mississippi.

We were at Baltimore on the Sabbath, and my daughter, accompanying a friend, who resided in the city, to church, took a seat with her in the choir, and joined in the singing. A number of the congregation, who had seen Caroline with me the day previous, and supposed her to be Jenny Lind, were yet laboring under the same mistake, and it was soon whispered through the church that Jenny Lind was in the choir! The excitement was worked to its highest pitch when my daughter rose as one of the musical group. Every ear was on the alert to catch the first notes of her voice, and when she sang, glances of satisfaction passed through the assembly. Caroline, quite unconscious of the attention she attracted, continued to sing to the end of the hymn. Not a note was lost upon the ears of the attentive congregation. "What an exquisite singer!" "Heavenly sounds!" "I never heard the like!" and similar expressions were whispered through the church.

At the conclusion of the services, my daughter and her friend found the passage way to their carriage blocked by a crowd who were anxious to obtain a nearer view of the "Swedish Nightingale," and many persons that afternoon boasted, in good faith, that they had listened to the extraordinary singing of the great songstress. The pith of the joke is that we have never discovered that my daughter has any extraordinary claims as a vocalist.

Our orchestra in New York consisted of sixty. When we started on our southern tour, we took with us permanently as the orchestra twelve of the best musicians we could select, and in New Orleans augmented the force to sixteen. We increased the number to thirty-five, forty or fifty, as the case might be, by choice of musicians residing where the concerts were given. On our return to New York from Havana, we enlarged the orchestra to one hundred performers.

The morning after our arrival in Washington, President Fillmore called, and left his card, Jenny being out. When she returned and found the token of his attention, she was in something of a flurry. "Come," said she, "we must call on the President immediately."

"Why so?" I inquired.

"Because he has called on me, and of course that is equivalent to a command for me to go to his house."

I assured her that she might make her mind at ease, for whatever might be the custom with crowned heads, our Presidents were not wont to "command" the movements of strangers, and that she would be quite in time if she returned his call the next day. She did so, and was charmed with the unaffected bearing of the President, and the warm kindnesses expressed by his amiable wife and daughter, and consented to spend the evening with them in conformity with their request. She was accompanied to the "White House" by Messrs. Benedict, Belletti and myself, and several happy hours were spent in the private circle of the President's family.

Mr. Benedict, who engaged in a long quiet conversation with Mr. Fillmore, was highly pleased with the interview. A foreigner, accustomed to court etiquette, is generally surprised at the simplicity which characterizes the Chief Magistrate of this Union. In 1852 I called on the President with my friend the late Mr. Brettell, of London, who resided in St. James Palace, and was quite a worshipper of the Queen, and an ardent admirer of all the dignities and ceremonies of royalty. He expected something of the kind in visiting the President of the United States, and was highly pleased with his disappointment.

Both concerts in Washington were attended by the President and his family, and every member of the Cabinet. I noticed, also, among the audience, Henry Clay, Benton, Foote, Cass and General Scott, and nearly every member of Congress. On the following morning, Miss Lind was called upon by Mr. Webster, Mr. Clay, General Cass, and Colonel Benton, and all parties were evidently gratified. I had introduced Mr. Webster to her in Boston. Upon hearing one of her wild mountain songs in New York, and also in Washington, Mr. Webster signified his approval by rising, drawing himself up to his full height, and making a profound bow. Jenny was delighted by this expression of praise from the great statesman. When I first introduced Miss Lind to Mr. Webster, at the Revere House, in Boston, she was greatly impressed with his manners and conversation, and after his departure, walked up and down the room in great excitement, exclaiming: "Ah! Mr. Barnum, that is a man; I have never before seen such a man!"

We visited the Capitol while both Houses were in session. Miss Lind took the arm of Hon. C. F. Cleveland, representative from Connecticut, and was by him escorted into various parts of the Capitol and the grounds, with all of which she was much pleased.

During the week I was invited with Miss Lind and her immediate friends to visit Mount Vernon, with Colonel Washington, the then proprietor, and Mr. Seaton, ex-Mayor of Washington, and Editor of the *Intelligencer*. Colonel Washington chartered a steamboat for the purpose. We were landed a short distance from the tomb, which we first visited. Proceeding to the house, we were introduced to Mrs. Washington, and several other ladies. Much interest was manifested by Miss Lind in examining the mementoes of the great man whose home it had been. A beautiful collation was spread out and arranged in fine taste. Before leaving, Mrs. Washington presented Jenny with a book from the library, with the name of Washington written by his own hand. She was much overcome at receiving this present, called me aside, and expressed her desire to give something in return. "I have nothing with me," she said, "excepting this watch and chain, and I will give that if you think it will be acceptable." I knew the watch was very valuable, and told her that so costly a present would not be expected, nor would it be proper. "The expense is nothing, compared to the value of that book," she replied, with deep emotion; "but as the watch was a present from a dear friend, perhaps I should not give it away." Jenny Lind, I am sure, never forgot the pleasurable emotions of that day.

At Richmond, half an hour previous to her departure, hundreds of young ladies and gentlemen had crowded into the halls of the house to secure a glimpse of her at parting. I informed her that she would find difficulty in passing out. "How long is it before we must start?" she asked. "Half an hour," I replied. "Oh, I will clear the passages before that time," said she, with a smile; whereupon she went into the upper hall, and informed the people that she wished to take the hands of every one of them, upon one condition, viz.: they should pass by her in rotation, and as fast as they had shaken hands proceed down stairs, and not block up the passages. They joyfully consented to the arrangement, and in fifteen minutes the course was clear. Poor Jenny had shaken hands with every person in the crowd, and I presume she had a feeling remembrance of the incident for an hour or two at least. She was waited on by many members of the Legislature while in Richmond, that body being in session while we were there.

The voyage from Wilmington to Charleston was an exceedingly rough and perilous one. We were about thirty-six hours in making the passage, the usual time being seventeen. There was really great danger of our steamer being swamped, and we were all apprehensive that we should never reach the Port of Charleston alive. Some of the passengers were in great terror. Jenny Lind exhibited more calmness upon this occasion than any other person, the crew excepted. We arrived safely at last, and I was grieved to learn that for twelve hours the loss of the steamer had been considered certain, and had even been announced by telegraph in the Northern cities.

We remained at Charleston about ten days, to take the steamer "Isabella" on her regular trip to Havana. Jenny had been through so much excitement at the North that she was determined to have quiet here, and therefore declined receiving any calls. This disappointed many ladies and gentlemen. One young lady, the daughter of a wealthy planter near Augusta, was so determined upon seeing her in private, that she paid one of the servants to allow her to put on a cap and white apron, and carry in the tray for Jenny's tea. I afterwards told Miss Lind of the joke, and suggested that after such an evidence of admiration, she should receive a call from the young lady. "It is not admiration—it is only curiosity," replied Jenny, "and I will not encourage such folly."

Christmas was at hand, and Jenny Lind determined to honor it in the way she had often done in Sweden. She had a beautiful Christmas tree privately prepared, and from its boughs depended a variety of presents for members of the company. The night before New Year's day was spent in her apartment with great hilarity. Enlivened by music, singing, dancing and story-telling, the hours glided swiftly away. Miss Lind asked me if I would dance with her. I told her my education had been neglected in that line, and that I had never danced in my life. "That is all the better," said she; "now dance with me in a cotillion. I am sure you can do it." She was a beautiful dancer, and I never saw her laugh more heartily than she did at my awkwardness. She said she would give me the credit of being the poorest dancer she ever saw!

I had arranged with a man in New York to transport furniture to Havana, provide a house, and board Jenny Lind and our immediate party during our stay. When we arrived, we found the building converted into a semi-hotel, and the apartments were anything but comfortable. Jenny was vexed. Soon after dinner, she took a volante and an interpreter, and drove into the suburbs. She was absent four hours. Whither or why she had gone, none of us knew. At length she returned and informed us that she had hired a commodious furnished house in a delightful location outside the walls of the city, and invited us all to go and live with her during our stay in Havana, and we accepted the invitation. She was now freed from all annoyances; her time was her own, she received no calls, went and came when she pleased, had no meddlesome advisers about her, legal or otherwise, and was as merry as a cricket. We had a large court-yard in the rear of the house, and here she would come and romp and run, sing and laugh, like a young school-girl. "Now, Mr. Barnum, for another game of ball," she would say half a dozen times a day; whereupon, she would take an india-rubber ball (of which she had two or three), and commence a game of throwing and catching, which would be kept up until, being completely tired out, I would say, "I give it up." Then her rich, musical laugh would be heard ringing through the house, as she exclaimed, "Oh, Mr. Barnum, you are too fat and too lazy; you cannot stand it to play ball with me!"

Her celebrated countrywoman, Miss Frederika Bremer, spent a few days with us very pleasantly, and it is difficult to conceive of a more delightful month than was passed by the entire party at Jenny Lind's house in the outskirts of Havana.

CHAPTER XXI

SOON after arriving in Havana, I discovered that a strong prejudice existed against our musical enterprise. I might rather say that the Habaneros, not accustomed to the high figure which tickets had commanded in the States, were determined on forcing me to adopt their opera prices, whereas I paid one thousand dollars per night for the Tacon Opera House, and other expenses being in proportion, I was determined to receive remunerating prices, or give no concerts. This determination on my part annoyed the Habaneros, who did not wish to be thought penurious, though they really were so. Their principal spite, therefore, was against me; and one of their papers politely termed me a "Yankee pirate," who cared for nothing except their doubloons. They attended the concert, but were determined to show the great songstress no favor. I perfectly understood this feeling in advance, but studiously kept all knowledge of it from Miss Lind. I went to the first concert, therefore, with some misgivings in regard to her reception. The following, which I copy from the Havana correspondence of the *New York Tribune,* gives a correct account of it:

"Jenny Lind soon appeared, led on by Signor Belletti. Some three or four hundred persons clapped their hands at her appearance, but this token of approbation was instantly silenced by at least two thousand five hundred decided hisses. Thus, having settled the matter that there should be no forestalling of public opinion, and that if applause was given to Jenny Lind in that house it should first be incontestably earned, the most solemn silence prevailed. I have heard the Swedish Nightingale often in Europe as well as in America and have ever noticed a distinct tremulousness attending her first appearance in any city. Indeed this feeling was plainly manifested in her countenance as she neared the foot-lights; but when she witnessed the kind of reception in store for her—so different from anything she had reason to expect—her countenance changed in an instant to a haughty self-possession, her eye flashed defiance, and, becoming immovable as a statue, she stood there, perfectly calm and beautiful. She was satisfied that she now had an ordeal to pass and a victory to gain worthy of her powers. In a moment her eye scanned the immense audience, the music began and then followed—how can I describe it?—such heavenly strains as I verily believe mortal never breathed except Jenny Lind, and mortal never heard except from her lips. Some of the oldest Castilians kept a frown upon their brow and a curling sneer upon their lip; their ladies, however, and most of the audience began to look surprised. The gushing melody flowed on increasing in beauty and glory. The *caballeros,* the *senoras* and *senoritas* began to look at each other; nearly all, however, kept their teeth clenched and their lips closed, evidently determined to resist to the last. The torrent flowed deeper and faster, the lark flew higher and higher, the melody grew richer and grander; still every lip was compressed. By and by, as the rich notes came dashing in rivers upon our enraptured ears, one poor critic involuntarily whispered a 'brava.' This outbursting of the soul was instantly hissed down. The stream of harmony rolled on till, at the close, it made a clean sweep of every obstacle, and carried all before it. Not a vestige of opposition remained, but such a tremendous shout of applause as went up I never before heard.

"The triumph was most complete. And how was Jenny Lind affected? She who stood a few moments previous like adamant, now trembled like a reed in the wind before the storm of enthusiasm which her own simple notes had produced. Tremblingly, slowly, and almost bowing her face to the ground, she withdrew. The roar and applause of victory increased. '*Encore! encore! encore!*' came from every lip. She again appeared, and, courtsying low, again withdrew, but again, again, and again did they call her out and at every appearance the thunders of applause rang louder and louder. Thus five times was Jenny Lind called out to receive their unanimous and deafening plaudits."

I cannot express what my feelings were as I watched this scene from the dress circle. Poor Jenny! I deeply sympathized with her when I heard that first hiss. I indeed observed the resolute bearing which she assumed, but was apprehensive of the result. When I witnessed her triumph, I could not restrain the tears of joy that rolled down my cheeks; and rushing through a private box, I reached the stage just as she was withdrawing after the fifth encore.

"God bless you, Jenny, you have settled them!" I exclaimed. "Are you satisfied?" said she, throwing her arms around my neck. She, too, was crying with joy, and never before did she look so beautiful in my eyes as on that evening.

One of the Havana papers, notwithstanding the great triumph, continued to cry for low prices. This induced many to absent themselves, expecting soon to see a reduction. It had been understood that we would give twelve concerts in Havana; but when they saw, after the fourth concert, which was devoted to charity, that no more were announced, they became uneasy. Committees waited upon us requesting more concerts, but we peremptorily declined. Some of the leading Dons, among whom was Count Penalver, then offered to guarantee us $25,000 for three concerts. My reply was, that there was not money enough on the island of Cuba to induce me to consent to it. That settled the matter, and gave us a pleasant opportunity for recreation.

We visited, by invitation, Mr. Brinckerhoff, the eminent American merchant at Matanzas, whom I had met at the same place three years previously, and who subsequently had visited my family in Connecticut. The gentlemanly host did everything in his power to render our stay agreeable; and Miss Lind was so delighted with his attentions and the interesting details of sugar and coffee plantations which we visited through his kindness, that as soon as she returned to Havana she sent on the same tour of pleasure Mr. Benedict, who had been prevented by illness from accompanying us.

I found my little Italian plate-dancer, Vivalla, in Havana. He called on me frequently. He was in great distress, having lost the use of his limbs on the left side of his body by paralysis. He was thus unable to earn a livelihood, although he still kept a performing dog, which turned a spinning-wheel and performed some curious tricks. One day, as I was passing him out of the front gate, Miss Lind inquired who he was. I briefly recounted to her his history.

She expressed deep interest in his case, and said something should be set apart for him in the benefit which she was about to give for charity. Accordingly, when the benefit came off, Miss Lind appropriated $500 to him, and I made the necessary arrangements for his return to his friends in Italy. At the same benefit $4,000 were distributed between two hospitals and a convent.

A few mornings after the benefit our bell was rung, and the servant announced that I was wanted. I went to the door and found a large procession of children, neatly dressed and bearing banners, attended by ten or twelve priests, arrayed in their rich and flowing robes. I inquired their business, and was informed that they had come to see Miss Lind, to thank her in person for her benevolence. I took their message, and informed Miss Lind that the leading priests of the convent had come in great state to see and thank her. "I will not see them," she replied; "they have nothing to thank me for. If I have done good, it is no more than my duty, and it is my pleasure. I do not deserve their thanks, and I will not see them." I returned her answer, and the leaders of the grand procession went away in disappointment.

The same day Vivalla called, and brought her a basket of the most luscious fruit that he could procure. The little fellow was very happy and extremely grateful. Miss Lind had gone out for a ride.

"God bless her! I am so happy; she is such a good lady. I shall see my brothers and sisters again. Oh, she is a very good lady," said poor Vivalla, overcome by his feelings. He begged me to thank her for him, and give her the fruit. As he was passing out of the door, he hesitated a moment, and then said, "Mr. Barnum, I should like so much to have the good lady see my dog turn a wheel; it is very nice; he can spin very good. Shall I bring the dog and wheel for her? She is such a good lady, I wish to please her very much." I smiled, and told him she would not care for the dog; that he was quite welcome to the money; and that she refused to see the priests from the convent that morning, because she never received thanks for favors.

When Jenny came in I gave her the fruit, and laughingly told her that Vivalla wished to show her how his performing dog could turn a spinning-wheel.

"Poor man, poor man, do let him come; it is all the good creature can do for me," exclaimed Jenny, and the tears flowed thick and fast down her cheeks. "I like that, I like that," she continued; "do let the poor creature come and bring his dog. It will make him so happy."

I confess it made me happy, and I exclaimed, for my heart was full, "God bless you, it will make him cry for joy; he shall come to-morrow."

I saw Vivalla the same evening, and delighted him with the intelligence that Jenny would see his dog perform the next day, at four o'clock precisely.

"I will be punctual," said Vivalla, in a voice trembling with emotion; "but I was *sure* she would like to see my dog perform."

For full half an hour before the time appointed did Jenny Lind sit in her window on the second floor and watch for Vivalla and his dog. A few minutes before the appointed hour, she saw him coming. "Ah, here he comes! here he comes!" she exclaimed in delight, as she ran downstairs and opened the door to admit him. A negro boy was bringing the small spinning-wheel while Vivalla led the dog. Handing the boy a silver coin, she motioned him away, and taking the wheel in her arms, she said, "This is very kind of you to come with your dog. Follow me. I will carry the wheel upstairs." Her servant offered to take the wheel, but no, she would let no one carry it but herself. She called us all up to her parlor, and for one full hour did she devote herself to the happy Italian. She went down on her knees to pet the dog and to ask Vivalla all sorts of questions about his performances, his former course of life, his friends in Italy, and his present hopes and determinations. Then she sang and played for him, gave him some refreshments, finally insisted on carrying his wheel to the door, and her servant accompanied Vivalla to his boarding-house.

Poor Vivalla! He was probably never so happy before, but his enjoyment did not exceed that of Miss Lind. That scene alone would have paid me for all my labors during the entire musical campaign. A few months later, however, the Havana correspondent of the *New York Herald* announced the death of Vivalla and stated that the poor Italian's last words were about Jenny Lind and Mr. Barnum.

In the party which accompanied me to Havana was Mr. Henry Bennett, who formerly kept Peale's Museum in New York, afterwards managing the same establishment for me when I purchased it, and he was now with me in the capacity of a ticket-taker. He was as honest a man as ever lived, and a good deal of a wag. With all his waggery he was subject at times to moods of the deepest despondency, bordering on insanity. Madness ran in his family. His brother, in a fit of frenzy, had blown his brains out. Henry himself had twice attempted his own life while in my employ in New York. Some time after our present journey to Havana, I sent him to London. He conducted my business precisely as I directed, writing up his account with me correctly to a penny. Then handing it to a mutual friend with directions to give it to me when I arrived in London the following week, he went to his lodgings and committed suicide.

While we were in Havana, Bennett was so despondent at times that we were obliged to watch him carefully, lest he should do some damage to himself or others. When we left Havana for New Orleans, on board the steamer "Falcon," Mr. James Gordon Bennett, editor of the *New York Herald,* and his wife were also passengers. After permitting one favorable notice in his paper, Bennett had turned around, as usual, and had abused Jenny Lind and bitterly attacked me. There was an estrangement, no new thing, between the editor and myself. The *Herald*, in its desire to excite attention, has a habit of attacking public men and I had not escaped. I was always glad to get such notices, for they served as inexpensive advertisements to my Museum, and brought custom to me free of charge.

Ticket-taker Bennett, however, took much to heart the attacks of Editor Bennett upon Jenny Lind, and while in New York had threatened personal violence (a resort, it must be confessed, of doubtful expediency), but I restrained him. When Editor Bennett came on board the "Falcon," his violent namesake said to a bystander:

"I would willingly be drowned if I could see that old scoundrel go to the bottom of the sea."

Several of our party overheard the remark and I turned laughingly to Bennett and said: "Nonsense; he can't harm any one, and there is an old proverb about the impossibility of drowning those who are born to another fate."

That very night, however, as I stood near the cabin door, conversing with my treasurer and other members of my company, Henry Bennett came up to me with a wild air, and hoarsely whispered:

"Old Bennett has gone forward alone in the dark—and I am going to throw him overboard!"

We were all startled, for we knew the man and he seemed terribly in earnest. Knowing how most effectively to address him at such times, I exclaimed:

"Ridiculous! you would not do such a thing."

"I swear I will," was his savage reply. I expostulated with him, and several of our party joined me.

"Nobody will know it," muttered the maniac, "and I shall be doing the world a favor."

I endeavored to awaken him to a sense of the crime he contemplated, assuring him that it could not possibly benefit any one, and that from the fact of the relations existing between the editor and myself, I should be the first to be accused of his murder. I implored him to go to his stateroom, and finally he did so, accompanied by some of the gentlemen of our party. I took pains to see that he was carefully watched that night, and, indeed, for several days, till he became calm again. He was a large, athletic man, quite able to pick up his namesake and drop him overboard. The matter was too serious for a joke, and we made little mention of it; but more than one of my party said then, and has said since, what I really believe to be true, that "James Gordon Bennett would have been drowned that night had it not been for P. T. Barnum."

In New Orleans the wharf was crowded by a great concourse of persons, as the steamer "Falcon" approached. Jenny Lind had enjoyed a month of quiet, and dreaded the excitement which she must now again encounter.

"Mr. Barnum, I am sure I can never get through that crowd," said she, in despair.

"Leave that to me. Remain quiet for ten minutes, and there shall be no crowd here," I replied.

Taking my daughter on my arm, she threw her veil over her face, and we descended the gangway to the dock. The crowd pressed around. I had beckoned for a carriage before leaving the ship.

"That's Barnum, I know him," called out several persons at the top of their voices.

"Open the way, if you please, for Mr. Barnum and Miss Lind!" cried Le Grand Smith over the railing of the ship, the deck of which he had just reached from the wharf.

"Don't crowd her, if you please, gentlemen," I exclaimed, and by dint of pushing, squeezing and coaxing, we reached the carriage, and drove for the Montalba buildings, where Miss Lind's apartments had been prepared, and the whole crowd came following at our heels. In a few minutes afterwards, Jenny and her companion came quietly in a carriage, and were in the house before the ruse was discovered. In answer to incessant calls, she appeared a moment upon the balcony, waved her handkerchief, received three hearty cheers, and the crowd dispersed.

A poor blind boy, residing in the interior of Mississippi, a flute-player and an ardent lover of music, visited New Orleans expressly to hear Jenny Lind. A subscription had been taken up among his neighbors to defray the expenses. This fact coming to the ears of Jenny, she sent for him, played and sang for him, gave him many words of joy and comfort, took him to her concerts, and sent him away considerably richer than he had ever been before.

I made arrangements with the captain of the splendid steamer "Magnolia," of Louisville, to take our party as far as Cairo, the junction of the Mississippi and Ohio rivers, stipulating for sufficient delay in Natchez, Mississippi, and in Memphis, Tennessee, to give a concert in each place. It was no unusual thing for me to charter a steamboat or a special train of cars for our party. With such an enterprise as that, time and comfort were paramount to money.

The time on board the steamer was whiled away in reading, viewing the scenery of the Mississippi, and other diversions. One day we had a pleasant musical festival in the ladies' saloon for the gratification of the passengers, at which Jenny volunteered to sing without ceremony. It seemed to us she never sang so sweetly before. I also did my best to amuse my fellow passengers with anecdotes and the exhibition of sundry legerdemain tricks which I had been obliged to learn and use in the South years before and under far different circumstances than those which attended the performance now.

According to agreement, the "Magnolia" waited for us at Natchez and Memphis, and we gave profitable concerts at both places. The concert at Memphis was the sixtieth in the list since Miss Lind's arrival in America, and the first concert in St. Louis would be the sixty-first. When we reached that city, on the morning of the day when our first concert was to be given, Miss Lind's secretary came to me, commissioned, he said, by her, and announced that as sixty concerts had already taken place, she proposed to avail herself of one of the conditions of our contract, and cancel the engagement next morning. As this was the first intimation of the kind I had received, I was somewhat startled, though I assumed an entirely placid demeanor, and asked:

"Does Miss Lind authorize you to give me this notice?"

"I so understand it," was the reply.

I immediately reflected that if our contract was thus suddenly cancelled, Miss Lind was bound to repay to me all I had paid her over the stipulated $1,000 for each concert, and a little calculation showed that the sum thus to be paid back was $77,000, since she had already received from me $137,000 for sixty concerts. In this view, I could not but think that this was a ruse of some of her advisers, and, possibly, that she might know nothing of the matter. So I told her secretary that I would see him again in an hour, and meanwhile I went to my old friend, Mr. Sol. Smith, for his legal and friendly advice.

I showed him my contract and told him how much I had been annoyed by the selfish and greedy hangers-on and advisers, legal and otherwise, of Jenny Lind. I talked to him about the "wheels within wheels" which moved this great musical enterprise, and asked and gladly accepted his advice, which mainly coincided with my own views of the situation. I then went back to the secretary and quietly told him that I was ready to settle with Miss Lind and to close the engagement.

"But," said he, manifestly taken aback, "you have already advertised concerts in Louisville and Cincinnati, I believe."

"Yes," I replied; "but you may take my contracts for halls and printing off my hands at cost." I further said that he was welcome to the assistance of my agent who had made these arrangements, and, moreover, that I would cheerfully give my own services to help them through with these concerts, thus giving them a good start "on their own hook."

My liberality, which he acknowledged, emboldened him to make an extraordinary proposition:

"Now suppose," he asked, "Miss Lind should wish to give some fifty concerts in this country, what would you charge as manager, per concert?"

"A million dollars each, not one cent less," I replied. I was now thoroughly aroused; the whole thing was as clear as daylight, and I continued:

"Now we might as well understand each other; I don't believe Miss Lind has authorized you to propose to me to cancel our contract; but if she has, just bring me a line to that effect over her signature and her check for the amount due me by the terms of that contract, some $77,000, and we will close our business connections at once."

"But why not make a new arrangement," persisted the secretary, "for fifty concerts more, by which Miss Lind shall pay you liberally, say $1,000 per concert?"

"Simply because I hired Miss Lind, and not she me," I replied, "and because I never ought to take a farthing less for my risk and trouble than the contract gives me. I have voluntarily paid Miss Lind more than twice as much as I originally contracted to pay her, or as she expected to receive when she first engaged with me.

Now, if she is not satisfied, I wish to settle instantly and finally. If you do not bring me her decision to-day, I shall go to her for it to-morrow morning."

I met the secretary soon after breakfast next morning and asked him if he had a written communication for me from Miss Lind. He said he had not and that the whole thing was a "joke." He merely wanted, he added, to see what I would say to the proposition. I asked him if Miss Lind was in the "joke," as he called it? He hoped I would not inquire, but would let the matter drop. I went on, as usual, and gave four more concerts in St. Louis, and followed out my programme as arranged in other cities for many weeks following; nor at that time, nor at any time afterwards, did Miss Lind give me the slightest intimation that she had any knowledge of the proposition of her secretary to cancel our agreement or to employ me as her manager.

With all her excellent and even extraordinarily good qualities, Jenny Lind was human, though the reputation she bore in Europe for her many charitable acts led me to believe, till I knew her, that she was nearly perfect. I think now that her natural impulses were more simple, childlike, pure and generous than those of almost any other person I ever met. But she had been petted, almost worshipped, so long, that it would have been strange indeed if her unbounded popularity had not in some degree affected her to her hurt, and it must not be thought extraordinary if she now and then exhibited some phase of human weakness.

Like most persons of uncommon talent, she had a strong will which, at times, she found ungovernable; but if she was ever betrayed into a display of ill-temper she was sure to apologize and express her regret afterwards. Le Grand Smith, who was quite intimate with her, and who was my right-hand man during the entire Lind engagement, used sometimes to say to me:

"Well, Mr. Barnum, you have managed wonderfully in always keeping Jenny's 'angel' side outside with the public."

More than one Englishman—I may instance Mr. Dolby, Mr. Dickens's agent during his last visit to America—expressed surprise at the confirmed impression of "perfection" entertained by the general American public in regard to the Swedish Nightingale. These things are written with none but the kindest feelings towards the sweet songstress, and only to modify the too current ideas of superhuman excellence which cannot be characteristic of any mortal being.

CHAPTER XXII

AFTER five concerts in St. Louis, we went to Nashville, where we gave our sixty-sixth and sixty-seventh concerts in this country. At the first ticket auction in that city, the excitement was considerable and the bidding spirited, as was generally the case. After the auction was over, one of my men, happening in at a dry-goods store in the town, heard the proprietor say, "I'll give five dollars to any man who will take me out and give me a good horse-whipping! I deserve it, and am willing to pay for having it done. To think that I should have been such a fool as to have paid forty-eight dollars for four tickets for my wife, two daughters, and myself, to listen to music for only two hours, makes me mad with myself, and I want to pay somebody for giving me a thundering good horse-whipping!" I am not sure that others have not experienced a somewhat similar feeling, when they became cool and rational, and the excitement of novelty and competition had passed away.

While at Nashville, Jenny Lind, accompanied by my daughter Mrs. Lyman, and myself, visited "the Hermitage," the late residence of General Jackson. On that occasion, for the first time that season, we heard the wild mocking-birds singing in the trees. This gave Jenny Lind great delight, as she had never before heard them sing except in their wire-bound cages.

From Nashville, Jenny Lind and a few friends went by way of the Mammoth Cave to Louisville, while the rest of the party proceeded by steamboat.

While in Havana, I engaged Signor Salvi for a few months, to begin about the 10th of April. He joined us at Louisville, and sang in the three concerts there, with great satisfaction to the public. Mr. George D. Prentice, of the Louisville *Journal,* and his beautiful and accomplished lady, who had contributed much to the pleasure of Miss Lind and our party, accompanied us to Cincinnati.

A citizen of Madison had applied to me, on our first arrival in Louisville, for a concert in that place. I replied that the town was too small to afford it, whereupon he offered to take the management of it into his own hands, and pay me $5,000 for the receipts. The last concert at Louisville and the concerts at Natchez and Wheeling were given under a similar agreement, though with better pecuniary results than at Madison. As the steamer from Louisville to Cincinnati would arrive at Madison about sundown, and would wait long enough for us to give a concert, I agreed to his proposition.

We were not a little surprised to learn upon arriving that the concert must be given in a "pork house"—a capacious shed which had been fitted up and decorated for the occasion. We concluded, however, that if the inhabitants were satisfied with the accommodations we ought not to object. The person who had contracted for the concert came $1,300 short of his agreement, which I consequently lost, and at ten o'clock we were again on board the fine steamer "Ben Franklin" bound for Cincinnati.

The next morning the crowd upon the wharf was immense. I was fearful that an attempt to repeat the New Orleans ruse with my daughter would be of no avail, as the joke had been published in the Cincinnati papers; so I gave my arm to Miss Lind, and begged her to have no fears, for I had hit upon an expedient which would save her from annoyance. We then descended the plank to the shore, and as soon as we had touched it, Le Grand Smith called out from the boat, as if he had been one of the passengers. "That's

no go, Mr. Barnum; you can't pass your daughter off for Jenny
Lind this time."

The remark elicited a peal of merriment from the crowd, several
persons calling out, "That won't do, Barnum! you may fool the
New Orleans folks, but you can't come it over the 'Buckeyes.' We
intend to stay here until you bring out Jenny Lind!" They readily
allowed me to pass with the lady whom they supposed to be my
daughter, and in five minutes afterwards the Nightingale was complimenting Mr. Coleman upon the beautiful and commodious apartments which were devoted to her in the Burnett House. The crowd
remained an hour on the wharf before they would be convinced
that the person whom they took for my daughter was in fact the
veritable Swede. When this was discovered, a general laugh followed the exclamation from one of the victims, "Well, Barnum has
humbugged us after all!"

In passing up the river to Pittsburgh, the boat waited for hours
to enable us to give a concert in Wheeling. It was managed by a
couple of gentlemen in that city, who purchased it for five thousand
dollars in advance, by which they made a handsome profit for their
trouble. The concert was given in a church.

At Pittsburgh, the open space surrounding the concert room became crowded with thousands of persons, who, foolishly refusing
to accommodate each other by listening to the music, disturbed the
concert and determined us to leave the next morning for Baltimore,
instead of giving a second concert that had been advertised.

We reached New York early in May, 1851, and gave fourteen
concerts in Castle Garden and Metropolitan Hall. The last of
these made the ninety-second regular concert under our engagement.
Jenny Lind had now again reached the atmosphere of her legal and
other "advisers," and I soon discovered the effects of their influence.
I, however, cared little what course they advised her to pursue. I
indeed wished they would prevail upon her to close with her hun-

dredth concert, for I had become weary with constant excitement and unremitting exertions. I was confident that if she undertook to give concerts on her own account, she would be imposed upon and harassed in a thousand ways; yet I felt it would be well for her to have a trial at it, if she saw fit to credit her advisers' assurance that I had not managed the enterprise as successfully as it might have been done.

At about the eighty-fifth concert, therefore, I was most happy to learn from her lips that she had concluded to pay the forfeiture of $25,000, and terminate the concerts with the one hundredth.

We went to Philadelphia, where I had advertised the ninety-second, ninety-third, and ninety-fourth concerts, and had engaged the large National Theatre on Chestnut Street. It had been used for equestrian and theatrical entertainments, but was now thoroughly cleansed and fitted up by Max Maretzek for Italian opera. It was a convenient place for our purpose. One of her "advisers," a subordinate in her employ, who was already itching for the position of manager, made the selection of this building a pretext for creating dissatisfaction in the mind of Miss Lind. I saw the influences which were at work, and not caring enough for the profits of the remaining seven concerts to continue the engagement at the risk of disturbing the friendly feelings which had hitherto uninterruptedly existed between that lady and myself, I wrote her a letter offering to relinquish the engagement, if she desired it, at the termination of the concert which was to take place that evening, upon her simply allowing me a thousand dollars per concert for the seven which would yet remain to make up the hundred, besides paying me the sum stipulated as a forfeiture for closing the engagement at the one-hundredth concert. Towards evening I received the following reply:

"To P. T. BARNUM, ESQ.

"MY DEAR SIR:—I accept your proposition to close our contract to-night, at the end of the ninety-third concert, on condition of my paying you seven thousand dollars, in addition to the sum I forfeit under the condition of finishing the engagement at the end of one hundred concerts.

"I am, dear Sir, yours truly,

"JENNY LIND.

"PHILADELPHIA, 9th of June, 1851."

I met her at the concert in the evening, and she was polite and friendly as ever. Between the first and second parts of the concert, I introduced General Welch, the lessee of the National Theatre, who informed her that he was quite willing to release me from my engagement of the building, if she did not desire it longer. She replied that, upon trial, she found it much better than she expected, and she would therefore retain it for the remainder of the concerts.

In the meantime, her advisers had been circulating the story that I had compelled her to sing in an improper place, and when they heard she had concluded to remain there they beset her with arguments against it, until at last she consented to remove her concerts to a smaller hall.

I had thoroughly advertised the three concerts, in the newspapers within a radius of one hundred miles from Philadelphia, and had sent admission tickets to the editors. On the day of the second concert, one of the new agents, who had indirectly aided in bringing about the dissolution of our engagement, refused to recognize these tickets. I urged upon him the injustice of such a course, but received no satisfaction. I then stated the fact to Miss Lind, and she gave immediate orders that these tickets should be received. Country editors' tickets which were offered after I left Philadelphia were however refused by her agents (contrary to Miss Lind's wish and knowledge), and the editors, having come from a distance with their wives, purchased tickets, and I subsequently remitted the money to numerous gentlemen whose complimentary tickets were thus repudiated.

Jenny Lind gave several concerts with varied success, and then retired to Niagara Falls and afterwards to Northampton, Massachusetts. While sojourning at the latter place, she visited Boston and was married to Mr. Otto Goldschmidt, a German composer and pianist, to whom she was much attached, and who had studied music with her in Germany. He played several times in our concerts. He was a very quiet, inoffensive gentleman, and an accomplished musician.

I met her several times after our engagement terminated. She was always affable. On one occasion, while passing through Bridgeport, she told me that she had been sadly harassed in giving her concerts. "People cheat me and swindle me very much," said she, "and I find it very annoying to give concerts on my own account."

I was always supplied with complimentary tickets when she gave concerts in New York, and on the occasion of her last appearance in America I visited her in her room back of the stage, and bade her and her husband adieu, with my best wishes. She expressed the same feeling to me in return. She told me she should never sing much, if any more, in public; but I reminded her that a good Providence had endowed her with a voice which enabled her to contribute in an eminent degree to the enjoyment of her fellow beings, and if she no longer needed the large sums of money which they were willing to pay for this elevating and delightful entertainment, she knew by experience what a genuine pleasure she would receive by devoting the money to the alleviation of the wants and sorrows of those who needed it.

"Ah! Mr. Barnum," she replied, "that is very true, and it would be ungrateful in me to not continue to use for the benefit of the poor and lowly that gift which our kind Heavenly Father has so graciously bestowed upon me. Yes, I will continue to sing so long as my voice lasts, but it will be mostly for charitable objects, for I am thankful to say I have all the money which I shall ever need." Pursuant to this resolution, the larger portion of the concerts which this noble lady has given since her return to Europe have been for objects of benevolence.

After so many months of anxiety, labor and excitement, in the Jenny Lind enterprise, it will readily be believed that I desired tranquillity. I spent a week at Cape May, and then came home to Iranistan, where I remained during the entire summer.

RECEIPTS OF THE JENNY LIND CONCERTS.

NEW YORK .	35 CONCERTS. .	RECEIPTS,	$286,216 64 .	AVERAGE,	$8,177 50
PHILADELPHIA	8 "	. "	48,884 41 .	"	6,110 55
BOSTON . .	7 "	. "	70,388 16 .	"	10,055 45
PROVIDENCE .	1 "	. "	6,525 54 .	"	6,525 54
BALTIMORE. .	4 "	. "	32,101 88 .	"	8,000 47
WASHINGTON .	2 "	. "	15,385 60 .	"	7,692 80
RICHMOND .	1 "	. "	12,385 21 .	"	12,385 21
CHARLESTON .	2 "	. "	10,428 75 .	"	5,214 37
HAVANA . .	3 "	. "	10,436 04 .	"	3,478 68
NEW ORLEANS	12 "	. "	87,646 12 .	"	7,303 84
NATCHEZ . .	1 "	. "	5,000 00 .	"	5,000 00
MEMPHIS . .	1 "	. "	4,539 56 .	"	4,539 56
ST. LOUIS . .	5 "	. "	30,613 67 .	"	6,122 73
NASHVILLE .	2 "	. "	12,034 30 .	"	6,017 15
LOUISVILLE .	3 "	. "	19,429 50 .	"	6,476 50
MADISON . .	1 "	. "	3,693 25 .	"	3,693 25
CINCINNATI .	5 "	. "	44,242 13 .	"	8,848 43
WHEELING .	1 "	. "	5,000 00 .	"	5,000 00
PITTSBURGH .	1 "	. "	7,210 58 .	"	7,210 58
TOTAL . .	95 CONCERTS.	RECEIPTS,	$712,161 34	AVERAGE,	$7,496 43

JENNY LIND'S RECEIPTS.

From the Total Receipts of Ninety-five Concerts . $712,161 34
Deduct the receipts of the first two, which, as between P. T. Barnum and Jenny Lind, were aside
from the contract 32,067 08

Total Receipts of Concerts from No. 1 to No. 93 $680,094 26

Deduct the receipts of the 28 Concerts,
    each of which fell short of $5,500 . $123,311 15
Also deduct $5,500 for each of the re-
    maining 65 Concerts 357,500 00 480,811 15

     Leaving the total excess, as above $199,283 11
Being equally divided, Miss Lind's portion was $99,641 55
I paid her $1,000 for each of the 93 Concerts 93,000 00
Also one-half the receipts of the first two Concerts 16,033 54

    Amount paid to Jenny Lind $208,675 09
She refunded to me as forfeiture, per contract, in
    case she withdrew after the 100th Concert . . $25,000
She also paid me $1,000 each for the seven Concerts
    relinquished   7,000
                               32,000 00

JENNY LIND's net avails of 95 Concerts $176,675 09
P. T. BARNUM's gross receipts, after paying Miss Lind . . . 535,486 25

    TOTAL RECEIPTS OF 95 Concerts $712,161 34

PRICE OF TICKETS.—The highest prices paid for tickets were at auction as follows:—John N. Genin, in New York, $225; Ossian E. Dodge, in Boston, $625; Col. William C. Ross, in Providence, $650; M. A. Root, in Philadelphia, $625; Mr. D'Arcy, in New Orleans, $240; a keeper of a refreshment saloon in St. Louis, $150; a Daguerrotypist, in Baltimore, $100. I cannot now recall the names of the last two. After the sale of the first ticket, the premium usually fell to $20, and so downward in the scale of figures. The fixed price of tickets ranged from $7 to $3. Promenade tickets were from $2 to $1 each.

CHAPTER XXIII.

OTHER ENTERPRISES —"WOOLLY HORSE"—"BUFFALO HUNT"

WHILE I was managing the Lind concerts, in addition to the American Museum I had other business matters in operation which were more than enough to engross my entire attention and which, of course, I was compelled to commit to the hands of associates and agents.

In 1849 I had projected a great traveling museum and menagerie, and, as I had neither time nor inclination to manage such a concern, I induced Mr. Seth B. Howes, justly celebrated as a "showman," to join me, and take the sole charge. Mr. Sherwood E. Stratton, father of General Tom Thumb, was also admitted to partnership, the interest being in thirds. In carrying out a portion of the plan, we chartered the ship "Regatta," Captain Pratt, and despatched her, together with our agents, Messrs. June and Nutter, to Ceylon. The ship left New York in May, 1850, and was absent one year. Their mission was to procure, either by capture or purchase, twelve or more living elephants, besides such other wild animals as they could secure. In order to provide sufficient drink and provender for a cargo of these huge animals, we purchased a large quantity of hay in New York. Five hundred tons were left at the Island of St. Helena, to be taken on the return trip of the ship, and staves and hoops of water-casks were also left at the same place.

As our agents were unable to purchase the required number of elephants, either in Columbo or Kandy, the principal towns of the island (Ceylon), they took one hundred and sixty native assistants, and plunged into the jungles, where, after many most exciting

242

adventures, they succeeded in securing thirteen elephants of a suitable size for their purpose, with a female and her calf, or "baby" elephant, only six months old. In the course of the expedition, Messrs. Nutter and June killed large numbers of the huge beasts, and had numerous encounters of the most terrific description with the formidable animals, one of the most fearful of which took place near Anarajah Poora, while they were endeavoring, by the aid of the natives and trained elephants, to drive the wild herd of beasts into an Indian kraal.

They arrived in New York in 1851 with ten of the elephants, and these, harnessed in pairs to a chariot, paraded up Broadway past the Irving House, while Jenny Lind was staying at that hotel, on the occasion of her second visit to New York. Messrs. Nutter and June also brought with the elephants a native who was competent to manage and control them. We added a caravan of wild animals and many museum curiosities, the entire outfit, including horses, vans, carriages, tent, etc., costing $109,000, and commenced operations, with the presence and under the "patronage" of General Tom Thumb, who travelled nearly four years as one of the attractions of "Barnum's Great Asiatic Caravan, Museum and Menagerie," returning us immense profits.

At the end of that time, after exhibiting in all sections of the country, we sold out the entire establishment—animals, cages, chariots and paraphernalia, excepting one elephant, which I retained in my own possession two months for agricultural purposes. It occurred to me that if I could put an elephant to plowing for a while on my farm at Bridgeport, it would be a capital advertisement for the American Museum, which was then, and always during my proprietorship of that establishment, foremost in my thoughts.

So I sent him to Connecticut in charge of his keeper, whom I dressed in Oriental costume, and keeper and elephant were stationed on a six-acre lot which lay close beside the track of the New York and New Haven Railroad. The keeper was furnished with a time-table of the road, with special instructions to be busily engaged in his work whenever passenger trains from either way were passing through. Of course, the matter soon appeared in the papers and went the entire rounds of the press in this country and even in Europe, and it was everywhere announced that P. T. Barnum, "Proprietor of the celebrated American Museum in New York"—and here is where the advertisement came in—"had introduced elephants upon his farm, to do his plowing and heavy draft work." Hundreds of people came many miles to witness the novel spectacle. The six acres were plowed over at least sixty times before I thought the advertisement sufficiently circulated, and I then sold the elephant to Van Amburgh's menagerie.

In 1851 I became a part owner of the steamship "North America." Our intention in buying it was to run it to Ireland as a passenger and freight ship. The project was, however, abandoned, and Commodore Cornelius Vanderbilt bought one half of the steamer, while the other half was owned by three persons, of whom I was one. The steamer was sent around Cape Horn to San Francisco, and was put into the Vanderbilt line. I later sold out my share in the steamship to Mr. Daniel Drew. The day after closing with Mr. Drew, I discovered an error of several hundred dollars (a matter of interest on some portion of the purchase money, which had been overlooked). I called on Mr. Drew, and asked him to correct it, but could get no satisfaction. I then wrote him a threatening letter, but received no response. I was on the eve of suing him for the amount due me, when the news came that the steamship "North America" was lying at the bottom of the Pacific. It turned out that she was sunk several days before I sold .out, and as the owners were mulcted in the sum of many thousands of dollars damages by their passengers, besides suffering a great loss in their steamship, I said no more to the millionaire Drew about the few hundreds which he had withheld from the showman.

Some reference to the various enterprises and "side shows" connected with and disconnected from my Museum is necessary to show how industriously I have catered for the public's amusement, not only in America but abroad. When I was in Paris in 1844, in addition to the purchase of Robert Houdin's ingenious automaton writer, and many other costly curiosities for the Museum, I ordered, at an expense of $3,000, a panoramic diorama of the obsequies of Napoleon. Every event of that grand pageant, from the embarkation of the body at St. Helena to its entombment at the Hotel des Invalides, amid the most gorgeous parade ever witnessed in France, was wonderfully depicted. This exhibition, after having had its day at the American Museum, was sold, and extensively and profitably exhibited elsewhere.

Having heard, while in London, 1844, of a company of "Campanalogians, or Lancashire Bell Ringers," performing in Ireland, I induced them to meet me in Liverpool, and there engaged them for an American tour. One of my stipulations was, that they should suffer their moustaches to grow, assume a picturesque dress, and be known as the "Swiss Bell Ringers." They at first objected, in the broad and almost unintelligible dialect of Lancashire, because, as they said, they spoke only the English language, and could not pass muster as Swiss people; but the objection was withdrawn when I assured them that if they continued to speak in America as they had just spoken to me, they might safely claim to be Swiss, or anything else, and no one would be any the wiser. As in other cases, so in this, the deception as to birth-place was of small account, and did no injury. Those seven men were really admirable performers, and by means of their numerous bells, of various sizes, they produced the most delicious music. They attracted much attention in various parts of the United States, in Canada, and in Cuba.

As a compensation to England for the loss of the Bell Ringers, I despatched an agent to America for a party of Indians, including squaws. He proceeded to Iowa, and returned to London with a company of sixteen. They were exhibited by Mr. Catlin on our joint account, and were finally left in his sole charge.

On my first return to America from Europe, I engaged Mr. Faber, an elderly and ingenious German, who had constructed an automaton speaker. It was of life-size, and when worked with keys similar to those of a piano, it really articulated words and sentences with surprising distinctness. My agent exhibited it for several months in Egyptian Hall, London, and also in the provinces. This was a marvellous piece of mechanism, though for some unaccountable reason it did not prove a success. The Duke of Wellington visited it several times, and at first he thought that the "voice" proceeded from the exhibitor, whom he assumed to be a skilful ventriloquist. He was asked to touch the keys with his own fingers, and after some instruction in the method of operating, he was able to make the machine speak, not only in English, but also in German, with which language the Duke seemed familiar. Thereafter, he entered his name on the exhibitor's autograph book, and certified that the "Automaton Speaker" was an extraordinary production of mechanical genius.

During my first visit to England I obtained, verbally, through a friend, the refusal of the house in which Shakespeare was born, designing to remove it in sections to my Museum in New York; but the project leaked out, British pride was touched, and several English gentlemen interfered and purchased the premises for a Shakespearian Association. Had they slept a few days longer, I should have made a rare speculation, for I was subsequently assured that the British people, rather than suffer that house to be removed to America, would have bought me off with twenty thousand pounds.

CHANG AND ENG, BARNUM'S SIAMESE TWINS

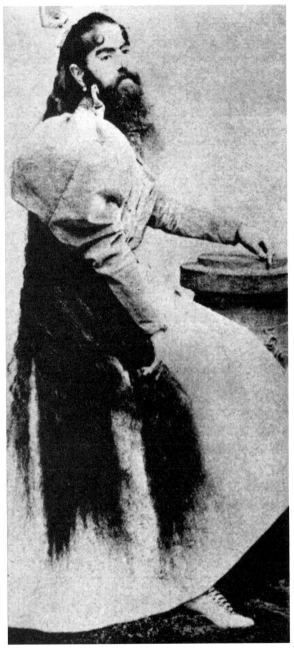

MADAME JOSEPHINE CLOFULLIA,
BARNUM'S BEARDED LADY

Four of Barnum's Freaks: (top left) Anna Swan at 17; (top right) Barnum's Fat Boy; (bottom, left) Mrs. Anna Bates; (and right) Her Husband

The Fejee Mermaid (above) as Pictured in the New York
Mercury, July 17, 1842, and, More Realistically (bottom),
in the New York *Sunday Herald*.

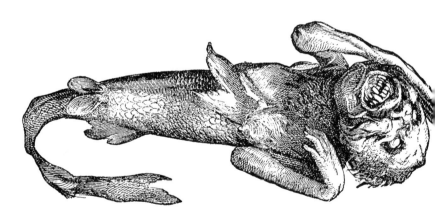

I did not hesitate to engage, or attempt to secure anything, at any expense, to please my patrons in the United States, and I made an effort to transfer Madame Tussaud's world-wide celebrated wax-work collection entire to New York. The papers were actually drawn up for this engagement, but the enterprise finally fell through.

The models of machinery exhibited in the Royal Polytechnic Institution in London pleased me so well that I procured a duplicate; also duplicates of the "Dissolving Views," the Chromatrope and Physioscope, including many American scenes painted expressly to my order, at an aggregate cost of $7,000. After they had been exhibited in my Museum, they were sold to itinerant showmen, and some of them were afterwards on exhibition in various parts of the United States.

In June, 1850, I added the celebrated Chinese Collection to the attractions of the American Museum. I also engaged the Chinese Family, consisting of two men, two "small-footed" women and two children. My agent exhibited them in London during the World's Fair. It may be stated here that I subsequently sent to London the celebrated artist De Lamano to paint a panorama of the Crystal Palace, in which the World's Fair was held, and Colonel John S. Dusolle, an able and accomplished editor, whom I sent with De Lamano, wrote an accompanying descriptive lecture. Like most panoramas, however, the exhibition proved a failure.

The giants whom I sent to America were not the greatest of my curiosities, though the dwarfs might have been the least. The "Scotch Boys" were interesting, not so much on account of their weight, as for the mysterious method by which one of them, though blindfolded, answered questions put by the other respecting objects presented by persons who attended the surprising exhibition. The mystery, which was merely the result of patient practice, consisted wholly in the manner in which the question was propounded; in fact, the question invariably carried its own answer. For instance:

"What is this?" meant gold; "Now what is this?" silver; "Say
what is this?" copper; "Tell me what this is," iron; "What is the
shape?" long; "Now what shape?" round; "Say what shape,"
square; "Please say what this is," a watch; "Can you tell what is in
this lady's hand?" a purse; "Now please say what this is?" a key;
"Come now, what is this?" money; "How much?" a penny; "Now
how much?" sixpence; "Say how much," a quarter of a dollar;
"What color is this?" black; "Now what color is this?" red; "Say
what color," green; and so on, *ad infinitum*. To such perfection was
this brought that it was almost impossible to present any object that
could not be quite closely described by the blindfolded boy. This is
the key to all exhibitions of what is called "second sight."

In 1850 the celebrated Bateman children acted for several
weeks at the American Museum, and in June of that year I sent
them to London with their father and Mr. Le Grand Smith, where
they played in the St. James Theatre, and afterwards in the principal
provincial theatres. The elder of these children, Miss Kate Bateman, subsequently attained the highest histrionic distinction in
America and abroad, and reached the very head of her profession.

In October, 1852, having stipulated with Mr. George A. Wells
and Mr. Bushnell that they should share in the enterprise and take
the entire charge, I engaged Miss Catherine Hayes and Herr Begnis
to give a series of sixty concerts in California, and the engagement
was fulfilled to our entire satisfaction. Mr. Bushnell afterwards
went to Australia with Miss Hayes and they were subsequently married. Both of them are dead.

In the summer of 1848, while in Cincinnati with General Tom
Thumb, my attention was arrested by handbills announcing the
exhibition of a "woolly horse." Being always on the *qui vive* for
everything curious with which to amuse or astonish the public, I
visited the exhibition, and found the animal to be a veritable curios-

ity. It was a well-formed horse of rather small size, without any mane or the slightest portion of hair upon his tail. The entire body and limbs were covered with a thick fine hair or wool curling tight to his skin. He was foaled in Indiana, was a mere freak of nature, and withal a very curious-looking animal. I purchased him and sent him to Bridgeport, Connecticut, where he was placed quietly away in a retired barn, until I might have use for him.

The occasion at last occurred. Colonel Fremont was lost among the trackless snows of the Rocky Mountains. The public mind was excited. Serious apprehensions existed that the intrepid soldier and engineer had fallen a victim to the rigors of a severe winter. At last the mail brought intelligence of his safety. The public heart beat quick with joy. I now saw a chance for the "woolly horse." He was carefully covered with blankets and leggings, so that nothing could be seen excepting his eyes and hoofs, conveyed to New York, and deposited in a rear stable, where no eye of curiosity could reach him.

The next mail was said to have brought intelligence that Colonel Fremont and his hardy band of warriors had, after a three days' chase, succeeded in capturing, near the river Gila, a most extraordinary nondescript, which somewhat resembled a horse, but which had no mane nor tail, and was covered with a thick coat of wool. The account further added that the Colonel had sent this wonderful animal as a present to the U. S. Quartermaster.

Two days after this announcement, the following advertisement appeared in the New York papers:

"COL. FREMONT'S NONDESCRIPT OR WOOLLY HORSE will be exhibited for a few days at the corner of Broadway and Reade street, previous to his departure for London. Nature seems to have exerted all her ingenuity in the production of this astounding animal. He is extremely complex—made up of the Elephant, Deer, Horse, Buffalo, Camel, and Sheep. It is the full size of a Horse, has the haunches of the Deer, the tail of the Elephant, a fine curled wool of camel's hair color, and easily bounds twelve or fifteen feet high. Naturalists and the oldest trappers assured Col. Fremont that it was never known previous to his discovery. It is undoubtedly 'Nature's last,' and the richest specimen received from California. To be seen every day this week. Admittance 25 cents; children half price."

The building where he was exhibited, exactly opposite Stewart's immense dry-goods store, was mounted by several large transparencies representing the "Nondescript" in full flight, pursued by the brave Fremont and his hardy handful of soldiers. The streets were also lined with handbills and posters, illustrating in wood-cuts the same thrilling event. The public appetite was craving something tangible from Colonel Fremont. The community was absolutely famishing. They were ravenous. They could have swallowed anything, and like a good genius, I threw them, not a "bone," but a regular tit-bit, a bon-bon—and they swallowed it at a single gulp!

My agent tried "Old Woolly" in several of the provincial towns with tolerable success, and finally he was taken to Washington city, to see if the wool could be pulled over the eyes of politicians. It was successfully done for several days, when Colonel Benton, regardful of the reputation of his son-in-law, caused my agent to be arrested on a grand-jury complaint of obtaining from him twenty-five cents under false pretences, and the Senator from Missouri testified that, having no mention of this horse in any of the numerous letters received from his son-in-law, he was sure Colonel Fremont never saw the animal. Such testimony could not prove a negative. The complaint was ruled out, and "Old Woolly" came off victorious. The excitement which Colonel Benton unconsciously produced added materially to the receipts for the succeeding few days. But, always entertaining the greatest respect for "Old Bullion," and out of regard to his feelings, I ordered the horse back to Bridgeport, where in due time he gave his last kick. For some time, however, he was turned loose in a field lying on the public road, where occasional New York patrons recognized their woolly friend in his retirement.

I attended the great Bunker Hill celebration, June 17, 1843, and heard Mr. Webster's oration. I found exhibiting near the monument, under an old canvas tent, a herd of calf buffaloes a year old. There were fifteen in number, and I purchased the lot for $700. I had an idea in my head which, if I could carry it out, would make buffaloes a profitable investment, and I was determined to try it. The animals were poor and remarkably docile, having been driven from the plains of the Great West. I had them brought to New York, and placed in a farmer's barn in New Jersey, near Hoboken. Mr. C. D. French, of whom I purchased them, understood throwing the *lasso,* and I hired him for $30 per month to take care of the buffaloes, until such time as I had matured my plans.

Paragraphs were soon started in the papers announcing that a herd of wild buffaloes, caught by the lasso when quite young, were now on their way from the Rocky Mountains to Europe, *via* New York, in charge of the men who captured them. In a few days communications appeared in several papers, suggesting that if the buffaloes could be safely secured in some race course, and a regular buffalo chase given by their owners, showing the use of the *lasso,* etc., it would be a treat worth going many miles to see. One correspondent declared it would be worth a dollar to see it; another asserted that fifty thousand persons would gladly pay to witness it, etc. One suggested the Long Island Race Course; another thought a large plot of ground at Harlem, inclosed expressly for the purpose, would be better; and a third suggested Hoboken as just the place. In due time, the following advertisement appeared in the public prints, and handbills and posters of the same purport, illustrated by a picture of wild buffaloes pursued by Indians on horseback, were simultaneously circulated, far and near, with a liberal hand:

"GRAND BUFFALO HUNT, FREE OF CHARGE.—At Hoboken, on Thursday,

August 31, at 3, 4, and 5 o'clock P. M. ☞Mr. C. D. French, one of the most daring and experienced hunters of the West, has arrived thus far on his way to Europe, with a HERD OF BUFFALOES, captured by himself, near Santa Fé. He will exhibit the method of hunting the Wild Buffaloes, and throwing the lasso, by which the animals were captured in their most wild and untamed state. This is perhaps one of the most exciting and difficult feats that can be performed, requiring at the same time the most expert horsemanship and the greatest skill and dexterity. Every man, woman and child can here witness *the wild sports of the Western Prairies,* as the exhibition is to be free to all, and will take place on the extensive grounds and Race Course of the Messrs. Stevens, within a few rods of the Hoboken Ferry, where at least fifty thousand ladies and gentlemen can conveniently witness the interesting sport. The Grand Chase will be repeated at three distinct hours. At 3 o'clock P. M., from twelve to twenty Buffaloes will be turned loose, and Mr. French will appear dressed as an Indian, mounted on a Prairie Horse and Mexican saddle, chase the Buffaloes around the Race Course, and capture one with the lasso. At 4 and 5 o'clock, the race will be repeated, and the intervals of time will be occupied with various other sports. The City Brass Band is engaged.

"No possible danger need be apprehended, as a double railing has been put around the whole course, to prevent the possibility of the Buffaloes approaching the multitude. Extra ferry-boats will be provided, to run from Barclay, Canal, and Christopher streets. If the weather should be stormy, the sport will come off at the same hours the first fair day."

The mystery of a free exhibition of the sort, though not understood at the time, is readily explained. I had engaged all the ferry-boats to Hoboken, at a stipulated price, and all the receipts on the day specified were to be mine.

The assurance that no danger need be apprehended from the buffaloes was simply ridiculous. The poor creatures were so weak and tame that it was doubtful whether they would run at all, notwithstanding my man French had been cramming them with oats to get a little extra life into them.

The eventful day arrived. Taking time by the forelock, multitudes of people crossed to Hoboken before ten o'clock, and by noon the ferry-boats were constantly crowded to their utmost capacity. An extra boat, the "Passaic," was put on, and the rush of passengers continued until five o'clock. Twenty-four thousand persons went

Living Curiosities at Barnum's Museum.

Since Mr. P. T. BARNUM re-purchased the Museum last Spring, it has become more than ever a popular place of resort for Ladies, Children and Families, and the energies of this world-renowned "Prince of Showmen," seem to increase in a corresponding ratio with his patronage. Our artist has sketched the above from a host of other curiosities now on exhibition in the Museum at all hours, day and evening.

The two centre figures in the foreground of the above cut represent the celebrated AZTEC CHILDREN, found in one of the long lost cities of Central America. It will be observed that their cast of features, and very small heads, bear a striking resemblance to the sculpture found in those cities by Stephens and other travelers, which fact seems to indicate that the race of men to which they belong were the original type of these sculptures.

The figure on the right represents a creature, found in the wilds of Africa, and is supposed to be a mixture of the wild native African and the Orang Outang, a kind of Man-Monkey, but for want of a positive name is called "WHAT IS IT?" The two WHITE FIGURES represent two ALBINO GIRLS, and the black ones their black mother and sister. These Girls, though of black parentage, are a PURE WHITE, WITH WHITE WOOL AND PINK EYES, but with every other feature and characteristic of the real African. No one can look upon them without feeling the conviction that they are beyond all doubt WHITE NEGROES. All these extraordinary living wonders are on exhibition at

Barnum's American Museum,

in this city, where everything novel and curious is sure to be found. In addition to the above, the Museum presents a combination of wonders and curiosities, unequaled in any part of the world. The GRAND AQUARIA alone constitutes an attraction which well repays a visit. Here, in miniature Oceans, are to be found almost every variety of living Fish and other aquatic animals disporting in their native element, from a noble specimen of a living Seal, down to the tiny Stickleback, which builds its nest on the rocks and in the weeds. The HAPPY FAMILY, consists of beasts and birds of opposite natures, as Dogs, Cats, Rats, Hawks, Chickens, Pigeons, &c., &c., all living in peace and harmony, and the whole made amusing and interesting by a number of lively and playful Monkeys, which always keep spectators in capital humor by their inimitable sports. A monster den of mammoth Serpents, 30 in number, has just been added to the

850,000 Other Interesting Curiosities

contained in this wonderful Museum. How so much can be afforded for the low price of twenty-five cents admission is only explained by the fact that an average of nearly four thousand persons visit the Museum daily; on holidays the number of visitors frequently exceeds twenty thousand.

ADVERTISEMENT IN *Harper's Weekly*, DECEMBER 15, 1860

ELEPHANT PLOWING, AN EXAMPLE OF BARNUM'S PROMOTION

by the ferryboats to Hoboken that day. Each paid six and a quarter cents going, and as much returning, and the aggregate receipts, including the ferriage of carts and carriages, and the hire for refreshment-stands on the ground, were $3500. Many thousand persons were present from various parts of New Jersey, and these, though bringing "grist to my mill," of course escaped my "toll" at the ferries.

The band of music engaged for the occasion did its best to amuse the immense crowd until three o'clock. At precisely that hour the buffaloes emerged from a shed in the center of the inclosure—my man French having previously administered a punching with a sharp stick, hoping to excite them to a trot on their first appearance. He immediately followed them, painted and dressed as an Indian, mounted on a fiery steed, with lasso in one hand and a sharp stick in the other, but the poor little calves huddled together, and refused to move! This scene was so wholly unexpected, and so perfectly ludicrous, that the spectators burst into uncontrollable uproarious laughter. The shouting somewhat startled the buffaloes, and goaded by French and his assistants, they started off in a slow trot. The uproar of merriment was renewed, and the multitude swinging their hats and hallooing in wild disorder, the buffaloes broke into a gallop, ran against a panel of the low fence, (consisting of two narrow boards), tumbled over, and scrambled away as fast as they could. The crowd in that quarter offered no obstruction. Seeing the animals approach, and not being sufficiently near to discover how harmless they were, men, women and children scattered pell-mell! Such a scampering I never saw before. The buffaloes, which were as badly frightened as the people, found shelter in a neighboring swamp, and all efforts to disengage them proved ineffectual. French, however, captured one of them with his lasso, and afterwards amused the people by lassoing horses and riders—and good-humor prevailed.

No one seemed to suspect the ferry-boat arrangement—the projector was *incog.*—the exhibition had been free to the public—there had been much amusement for twelve and a half cents each, and no one complained. It was, however, nearly midnight before all the visitors found ferry accommodations to New York.

N. P. Willis, of the *Home Journal,* wrote an article illustrating the perfect good nature with which the American public submits to a clever humbug. He said that he went to Hoboken to witness the Buffalo Hunt. It was nearly four o'clock when the boat left the foot of Barclay Street, yet it was so densely crowded that many persons were obliged to stand upon the railings and hold on to the awning posts. When they reached the Hoboken side, a boat equally crowded was leaving that wharf. The passengers of the boat just arriving cried out to those in the boat just returning, "Is the Buffalo Hunt over?" To which came the reply, "Yes, and it was the biggest humbug you ever heard of!" Willis added, that the passengers on the boat with him were so delighted that they instantly gave three cheers for the author of the humbug, whoever he might be.

The same experiment was subsequently tried successfully at Camden, N. J., opposite Philadelphia; after which a number of the buffaloes were sent to England and sold, and the rest were fattened and disposed of in steaks in Fulton Market at fifty cents per pound.

It is but justice to myself to remind the reader that, at the time of their occurrence, the public did not suspect that I had any connection whatever with the exhibition of the Woolly Horse, or the herd of Buffaloes. The entire facts in these cases came to light only through my own voluntary admissions.

CHAPTER XXIV

In 1851, 1852, and 1853, I spent much of my time at my beautiful home in Bridgeport, going very frequently to New York, to attend to matters in the Museum, but remaining in the city only a day or two at a time. I resigned the office of President of the Fairfield County Agricultural Society in 1853, but the members accepted my resignation, only on condition that it should not go into effect until after the fair of 1854. During my administration, the society held six fairs and cattle-shows,—four in Bridgeport and two in Stamford,—and the interest in these gatherings increased from year to year.

Pickpockets are always present at these country fairs, and every year there were loud complaints of the depredations of these operators. In 1853 a man was caught in the act of taking a pocket-book from a country farmer, nor was this farmer the only one who had suffered in the same way. The scamp was arrested, and proved to be a celebrated English pickpocket. As the Fair would close the next day, and as most persons had already visited it, we expected our receipts would be light.

Early in the morning the detected party was legally examined, plead guilty, and was bound over for trial. I obtained consent from the sheriff that the culprit should be put in the Fair room for the purpose of giving those who had been robbed an opportunity to identify him. For this purpose he was handcuffed, and placed in a conspicuous position, where of course he was "the observed of all observers." I then issued handbills, stating that as it was the last day of the Fair, the managers were happy to announce that they had secured extra attractions for the occasion, and would accordingly exhibit, safely handcuffed, and without extra charge, a live pick-pocket, who had been caught in the act of robbing an honest farmer the day previous. Crowds of people rushed in "to see the show." Some good mothers brought their children ten miles for that purpose, and our treasury was materially benefited by the operation.

At the close of my presidency in 1854, I was requested to deliver the opening speech at our County Fair, which was held at Stamford. As I was not able to give agricultural advice, I delivered a portion of my lecture on the "Philosophy of Humbug." The next morning, as I was being shaved in the village barber's shop, which was at the time crowded with customers, the ticket-seller to the Fair came in.

"What kind of a house did you have last night?" asked one of the gentlemen in waiting.

"Oh, first-rate, of course. Barnum always draws a crowd," was the reply of the ticket-seller, to whom I was not known.

Most of the gentlemen present, however, knew me, and they found much difficulty in restraining their laughter.

"Did Barnum make a good speech?" I asked.

"I did not hear it. I was out in the ticket-office. I guess it was pretty good, for I never heard so much laughing as there was all through his speech. But it makes no difference whether it was good or not," continued the ticket-seller, "the people will go to see Barnum."

"Barnum must be a curious chap," I remarked.

"Well, I guess he is up to all the dodges."

"Do you know him?" I asked.

"Not personally," he replied; "but I always get into the Museum for nothing. I know the doorkeeper, and he slips me in free."

"Barnum would not like that, probably, if he knew it," I remarked.

"But it happens he don't know it," replied the ticket-seller, in great glee.

"Barnum was on the cars the other day, on his way to Bridge-port," said I, "and I heard one of the passengers blowing him up terribly as a humbug. He was addressing Barnum at the time, but did not know him. Barnum joined in lustily, and indorsed every-thing the man said. When the passenger learned whom he had been addressing, I should think he must have felt rather flat."

"I should think so, too," said the ticket-seller.

This was too much, and we all indulged in a burst of laughter; still the ticket-seller suspected nothing. After I had left the shop, the barber told him who I was. I called into the ticket-office on busi-ness several times during the day, but the poor ticket-seller kept his face turned from me, and appeared so chap-fallen that I did not pretend to recognize him as the hero of the joke in the barber's shop.

This incident reminds me of numerous similar ones which have occurred at various times. On one occasion—it was in 1847—I was on board the steamboat from New York to Bridgeport. As we approached the harbor of the latter city, a stranger desired me to point out "Barnum's house" from the upper deck. I did so, whereupon a bystander remarked, "I know all about that house, for I was engaged in painting there for several months while Barnum was in Europe." He then proceeded to say that it was the meanest and most ill-contrived house he ever saw. "It will cost old Barnum a mint of money, and not be worth two cents after it is finished," he added.

"I suppose old Barnum don't pay very punctually," I remarked.

"Oh, yes, he pays punctually every Saturday night—there's no trouble about that; he has made half a million by exhibiting a little boy whom he took from Bridgeport, and whom we never considered any great shakes till Barnum took him and trained him."

Soon afterwards one of the passengers told him who I was,

whereupon he secreted himself, and was not seen again while I remained on the boat.

Late in August, 1851, I was visited at Bridgeport by a gentleman who was interested in an English invention patented in this country, and known as Phillips' Fire Annihilator. He showed me a number of certificates from men of eminence and trustworthiness in England, setting forth the merits of the invention in the highest terms. The principal value of the machine seemed to consist in its power to extinguish flame, and thus prevent the spread of fire when it once broke out. Besides, the steam or vapor generated in the Annihilator was not prejudicial to human life. Now, as water has no effect whatever upon flame, it was obvious that the Annihilator would at the least prove a great *assistant* in extinguishing conflagrations, and that, especially in the incipient stage of a fire, it would extinguish it altogether, without damage to goods or other property, as is usually the case with water.

Hon. Elisha Whittlesey, First Comptroller of the United States Treasury at Washington, was interested in the American patent, and the gentleman that called upon me desired that I should also take an interest in it. I had no disposition to engage in any speculation; but, believing this might prove a beneficent invention, and be the means of saving a vast amount of human life as well as property, I visited Washington City for the purpose of conferring with Mr. Whittlesey, Hon. J. W. Allen and other parties interested.

I was there shown numerous certificates of fires having been extinguished by the machine in Great Britain, and property to the amount of many thousands of pounds saved. I also saw that Lord Brougham had proposed in Parliament that every Government vessel should be compelled to have the Fire Annihilator on board. Mr. Whittlesey expressed his belief in writing, that "if there is any reliance to be placed on human testimony, it is one of the greatest discoveries of this most extraordinary age." I fully agreed with him, and have never yet seen occasion to change that opinion.

I agreed to join in the enterprise. Mr. Whittlesey was elected President, and I was appointed Secretary and General Agent of the Company. I opened the office of the Company in New York, and sold and engaged machines and territory in a few months to the amount of $180,000. I refused to receive more than a small portion of the purchase money until a public experiment had tested the powers of the machine, and I voluntarily delivered to every purchaser an agreement, signed by myself, in the following words:

"If the public test and demonstration are not perfectly succesful, I will at any time when demanded, within ten days after the public trial, refund and pay back every shilling that has been paid into this office for machines or territory for the sale of the patent."

The public trial came off in Hamilton Square on the 18th December, 1851. It was an exceedingly cold and inclement day. Mr. Phillips, who conducted the experiment, was interfered with and knocked down by some rowdies who were opposed to the invention, and the building was ignited and consumed after he had extinguished the previous fire. Subsequently to this unexpected and unjust opposition, I refunded every cent which I had received, sometimes against the wishes of those who had purchased, for they were willing to wait the result of further experiments; but I was utterly disgusted with the course of a large portion of the public upon a subject in which they were much more deeply interested than I was.

The arrangements of the Annihilator Company with Mr. Phillips, the inventor, predicated all payments which he was to receive on *bona fide* sales which we should actually make; therefore he really received nothing, and the entire losses of the American Company, which were merely for advertising and the expense of trying the experiments, hire of an office, etc., amounted to nearly $30,000, of which my portion was less than $10,000.

In the spring of 1851 the Connecticut Legislature chartered the

Pequonnock Bank of Bridgeport, with a capital of two hundred thousand dollars. I had no interest whatever in the charter, and did not even know that an application was to be made for it. The stock-books were opened under the direction of State Commissioners, according to the laws of the Commonwealth, and nearly double the amount of capital was subscribed on the first day. Circumstances unexpectedly occurred which induced me to accept the presidency of the bank, in compliance with the unanimous vote of its directors. Feeling that I could not, from my many avocations, devote the requisite personal attention to the duties of the office, C. B. Hubbell, Esq., then Mayor of Bridgeport, was at my request appointed Vice-President of the institution.

In the fall of 1852 a proposition was made by certain parties to commence the publication of an illustrated weekly newspaper in the City of New York. The field seemed to be open for such an enterprise, and I invested twenty thousand dollars in the concern, as special partner, in connection with two other gentlemen, who each contributed twenty thousand dollars, as general partners. Within a month after the publication of the first number of the *Illustrated News,* which was issued on the first day of January, 1853, our weekly circulation had reached seventy thousand. Numerous and almost insurmountable difficulties, for novices in the business, continued however to arise, and my partners becoming weary and disheartened with constant over-exertion, were anxious to wind up the enterprise at the end of the first year. The good-will and the engravings were sold to *Gleason's Pictorial,* in Boston, and the concern was closed without loss.

In 1851, when the idea of opening a World's Fair in New York was first broached, I was waited upon by Mr. Riddell and the other originators of the scheme, and invited to join in getting it up. I declined, giving as a reason that such a project was, in my opinion, premature. I felt that it was following quite too closely upon its

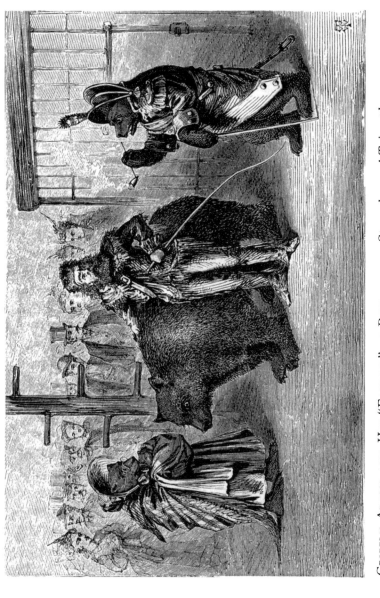

GRIZZLY ADAMS AND HIS "FAMILY," AS PICTURED IN *Struggles and Triumphs*

London prototype, and assured the projectors that I could see in it nothing but certain loss. The plan, however, was carried out, and a charter obtained from the New York Legislature. The building was erected on a plot of ground upon Reservoir Square, leased to the association, by the City of New York, for one dollar per annum. The location, being four miles distant from the City Hall, was enough of itself to kill the enterprise. The stock was readily taken up, however, and the Crystal Palace opened to the public in July, 1853. Many thousands of strangers were brought to New York, and however disastrous the enterprise may have proved to the stockholders, it is evident that the general prosperity of the city has been promoted far beyond the entire cost of the whole speculation.

In February, 1854, numerous stockholders applied to me to accept the Presidency of the Crystal Palace, or, as it was termed, "The Association for the Exhibition of the Industry of all Nations." I utterly declined listening to such a project, as I felt confident that the novelty had passed away, and that it would be difficult to revive public interest in the affair. Shortly afterwards, however, I was waited upon by numerous influential gentlemen, and strongly urged to allow my name to be used. I repeatedly objected to this, and at last consented, much against my own judgment. Having been elected one of the directors, I was by that body chosen President. I acceqted the office conditionally, reserving the right to decline if I thought, upon investigation, that there was no vitality left in the institution. Upon examining the accounts said to exist against the Association, many were pronounced indefensible by those who I supposed knew the facts in the case, while various debts existing against the concern were not exhibited when called for, and I knew nothing of their existence until after I accepted the office of President. I finally accepted it, only because no suitable person could be found who was willing to devote his entire time and services to the enterprise, and because I was frequently urged by directors and stockholders to take hold of it for the benefit of the city at large, inasmuch as it was settled that the Palace would be permanently closed early in April, 1854, if I did not take the helm.

These considerations moved me, and I entered upon my duties with all the vigor which I could command. To save it from bankruptcy, I advanced large sums of money for the payment of debts, and tried by every legitimate means to create an excitement and bring it into life. By extraneous efforts, such as the Re-inauguration, the Monster Concerts of Jullien, the Celebration of Independence, etc., it was temporarily galvanized, and gave several life-like kicks, generally without material results, except prostrating those who handled it too familiarly; but it was a corpse long before I touched it, and I found, after a thorough trial, that my first impression was correct, and that so far as my ability was concerned, "the dead could not be raised." I therefore resigned the presidency and the concern soon went into liquidation.

CHAPTER XXV

THE JEROME CLOCK COMPANY ENTANGLEMENT

I NOW come to a series of events which, all things considered, constitute one of the most remarkable experiences of my life—an experience which brought me much pain and many trials; which humbled my pride and threatened me with hopeless financial ruin; and yet, nevertheless, put new blood in my veins, fresh vigor in my action, warding off all temptation to rust in the repose which affluence induces, and developed, I trust, new and better elements of manliness in my character. This trial carried me through a severe and costly discipline, and now that I have passed through it and have triumphed over it, I can thank God for sending it upon me, though I feel no special obligations to the human instruments employed in the severe chastening.

When the blow fell upon me, I thought that I could never recover; the event has shown, however, that I have gained both in character and fortune, and what threatened, for years, to be my ruin, has proved one of the most fortunate happenings of my career. The "Bull Run" of my life's battle was a crushing defeat, which, unknown to me at the time, only presaged the victories which were to follow.

In my general plan of presenting the facts and incidents of my life in chronological order, I shall necessarily introduce in the history of the next seven years an account of my entanglement in the "Jerome Clock Company,"—how I was drawn into it, how I got out of it, and what it did to me and for me. The great notoriety given to my connection with this concern—the fact that the journals throughout the country made it the subject of news, gossip, sympathy, abuse, and advice to and about me, my friends, my persecutors, and the public generally—seems to demand that the story should be briefly but plainly told. The event itself has passed away and with it the passions and excitements that were born of it; and I certainly have no desire now to deal in personalities or to go into the question of the motives which influenced those who were interested, any farther than may be strictly essential to a fair and candid statement of the case.

It is vital to the narrative that I should give some account of the new city, East Bridgeport, and my interests therein, which led directly to my subsequent complications with the Jerome Clock Company.

In 1851, I purchased from Mr. William H. Noble, of Bridgeport, the undivided half of his late father's homestead, consisting of fifty acres of land, lying on the east side of the river, opposite the City of Bridgeport. We intended this as the nucleus of a new city, which we concluded could soon be built up, in consequence of many natural advantages that it possesses.

Before giving publicity to our plans, however, we purchased one hundred and seventy-four acres contiguous to that which we already owned, and laid out the entire property in regular streets, and lined them with trees, reserving a beautiful grove of six or eight acres, which we inclosed, and converted into a public park. We then commenced selling alternate lots, at the same price which the land cost us by the acre. Our sales were always made on the condition that a suitable dwelling-house, store, or manufactory should be erected upon the land, within one year from the date of purchase; that every building should be placed at a certain distance from the street, in a style of architecture approved by us; that the grounds should be enclosed with acceptable fences, and kept clean and neat, with other conditions which would render the locality a desirable one for respectable residents, and operate for the mutual benefit of all persons who should become settlers in the new city.

This entire property consists of a beautiful plateau of ground, lying within less than half a mile of the centre of Bridgeport city. A new footbridge was built, connecting this place with the City of Bridgeport, and a public toll-bridge which belonged to us was thrown open to the public free. We also obtained from the State Legislature a charter for erecting a toll-bridge between the two bridges already existing, and under that charter we put up a fine covered draw-bridge at a cost of $16,000 which also we made free to the public for several years. We built and leased to a union company of young coach makers a large and elegant coach manufactory, which was one of the first buildings erected there, and which went into operation on the first of January, 1852, and was the beginning of the extensive manufactories which were subsequently built in East Bridgeport.

Besides the inducement which we held out to purchasers to obtain their lots at a merely nominal price, we advanced one half, two-thirds, and frequently all the funds necessary to erect their buildings, permitting them to repay us in sums as small as five dollars, at their own convenience. This arrangement enabled many persons to secure and ultimately pay for homes which they could not otherwise have obtained. We looked for our profits solely to the rise in the value of the reserved lots, which we were confident must ensue. Of course, these extraordinary inducements led many persons to build in the new city, and it began to develop and increase with a rapidity rarely witnessed in this section of the country. Indeed, our speculation, which might be termed a profitable philanthropy, soon promised to be so remunerative that I offered Mr. Noble for his interest in the estate $60,000 more than the prime cost, which offer he declined.

It will thus be seen that, in 1851, my pet scheme was to build up a city in East Bridgeport. I had made a large fortune and was anxious to be released from the harassing cares of active business. But I could not be idle, and if I could be instrumental in giving value to land comparatively worthless, if I could by the judicious invest- ment of a portion of my capital open the way for new industries and new homes, I should be of service to my fellow men and find grateful employment for my energies and time. I saw that in case of success there was profit in my project, and I was enough like mankind in general to look upon the enlargement of my means as a consummation devoutly and legitimately to be wished.

Yet, I can truly say that mere money-making was a secondary consideration in my scheme. I wanted to build a city on the beau- tiful plateau across the river; in the expressive phrase of the day, I "had East Bridgeport on the brain." Whoever approached me with a project which looked to the advancement of my new city, touched my weak side and found me an eager listener. The serpent that beguiled me was any plausible proposition that promised pros- perity to East Bridgeport, and it was in this way that the coming city connected me with that source of so many annoyances and woes, the Jerome Clock Company.

There was a small clock manufactory in the town of Litchfield, Connecticut, in which I became a stockholder to the amount of six or seven thousand dollars, and my duties as a director in the com- pany called me occasionally to Litchfield and made me somewhat acquainted with the clock business. Thinking of plans to forward my pet East Bridgeport enterprise, it occurred to me that if the Litchfield clock concern could be transferred to my prospective new city, it would necessarily bring many families, thus increasing the growth of the place and the value of the property. Negotiations were at once commenced and the desired transfer of the business was the result. A new stock company was formed under the name of the "Terry & Barnum Manufacturing Company," and in 1852 a factory was built in East Bridgeport.

In 1855 I received a suggestion from a citizen of New Haven that the Jerome Clock Company, then reputed to be a wealthy concern, should be removed to East Bridgeport, and shortly afterwards I was visited at Iranistan by Mr. Chauncey Jerome, the President of that company. The result of this visit was a proposition from the agent of the company, who also held power of attorney for the president, that I should lend my name as security for $110,000 in aid of the Jerome Clock Company, and the proffered compensation was the transfer of this great manufacturing concern, with its seven hundred to one thousand operatives, to my beloved East Bridgeport. It was just the bait for the fish; I was all attention; yet I must do my judgment the justice to say that I called for proofs, strong and ample, that the great company deserved its reputation as a substantial enterprise that might safely be trusted.

Accordingly, I was shown an official report of the directors of the company, exhibiting a capital of $400,000, and a surplus of $187,000, in all, $587,000. The need for $110,000 more was on account of a dull season, and the market glutted with the goods, and immediate money demands which must be met. I was also impressed with the pathetic tale that the company was exceedingly loth to dismiss any of the operatives, who would suffer greatly if their only dependence for their daily food was taken away.

The official statement seemed satisfactory, and I cordially sympathized with the philanthropic purpose of keeping the workmen employed, even in the dull season. The company was reputed to be rich; the President, Mr. Chauncey Jerome, had built a church in New Haven, at a cost of $40,000, and proposed to present it to a congregation; he had given a clock to a church in Bridgeport, and these things showed that he, at least, thought he was wealthy. The Jerome clocks were for sale all over the world, even in China, where the Celestials were said to take out the "movements," and use the cases for little temples for their idols, thus proving that faith was possible without "works." So wealthy and so widely-known a company would surely be a grand acquisition to my city.

Further testimony came in the form of a letter from the cashier of one of the New Haven banks, expressing the highest confidence in the financial strength of the concern, and much satisfaction that I contemplated giving temporary aid which would keep so many workmen and their families from suffering, and perhaps starvation. I had not, at that time, the slightest suspicion that my voluntary correspondent had any interest in the transfer of the Jerome Company from New Haven to East Bridgeport, though I was subsequently informed that the bank, of which my correspondent was the cashier, was almost the largest, if not the largest, creditor of the clock company.

Under all the circumstances, and influenced by the rose-colored representations made to me, not less than by my mania to push the growth of my new city, I finally accepted the proposition and consented to an agreement that I would lend the clock company my notes for a sum not to exceed $50,000, and accept drafts to an amount not to exceed $60,000. It was thoroughly understood that I was in no case to be responsible for one cent in excess of $110,000. I also received the written guaranty of Chauncey Jerome that in no event should I lose by the loan, as he would become personally responsible for the repayment. I was willing that my notes, when taken up, should be renewed, I cared not how often, provided the stipulated maximum of $110,000 should never be exceeded. I was weak enough, however, under the representation that it was impossible to say exactly when it would be necessary to use the notes, to put my name to several notes for $3,000, $5,000, and $10,000, leaving the date of payment blank; but it was agreed that the blanks should be filled to make the notes payable in five, ten, or even sixty days from date, according to the exigencies of the case, and I was careful to keep a memorandum of the several amounts of the notes.

On the other side it was agreed that the Jerome Company should exchange its stock with the Terry & Barnum stockholders and thus absorb that company and unite the entire business in East Bridgeport. It was scarcely a month before the secretary wrote me that the company would soon be in condition to "snap its fingers at the banks."

Nevertheless, three months after the consolidation of the companies, a reference to my memoranda showed that I had already become responsible for the stipulated sum of $110,000. I was then called upon in New York by the agent, who wanted five notes of $5,000 each, and I declined to furnish them unless I should receive in return an equal amount in my own cancelled notes, since he assured me they were cancelling these "every week." The cancelled notes were brought to me next day and I renewed them. This I did frequently, receiving cancelled notes, till finally my confidence in the company became so established that I did not ask to see the notes that had been taken up, but furnished new accommodation paper as it was called for.

By and by I heard that the banks began to hesitate about discounting my paper, and knowing that I was good for $110,000 several times over, I wondered what was the matter, till the discovery came at last that my notes had not been taken up as was represented, and that some of the blank date notes had been made payable in twelve, eighteen, and twenty-four months. Further investigation revealed the frightful fact that I had endorsed for the clock company to the extent of more than half a million dollars, and most of the notes had been exchanged for old Jerome Company notes due to the banks and other creditors. My agent who made these startling discoveries came back to me with the refreshing intelligence that I was a ruined man!

Not quite; I had the mountain of Jerome debts on my back,

but I found means to pay every claim against me at my bank, all my store and shop debts, notes to the amount of $40,000, which banks in my neighborhood, relying upon my personal integrity, had discounted for the Clock Company, and then I—failed!

What a dupe had I been! Here was a great company pretending to be worth $587,000, asking temporary assistance to the amount of $110,000, coming down with a crash, so soon as my helping hand was removed, and sweeping me down with it. It failed; and even after absorbing my fortune, it paid but from twelve to fifteen per cent of its obligations, while, to cap the climax, it never removed to East Bridgeport at all, notwithstanding this was the only condition which ever prompted me to advance one dollar to the rotten concern!

If at any time my vanity had been chilled by the fear that after my retirement from the Jenny Lind enterprise the world would forget me, this affair speedily reassured me; I had notice enough to satisfy the most inordinate craving for notoriety. All over the country, and even across the ocean, "Barnum and the Jerome Clock Bubble" was the great newspaper theme. I was taken to pieces, analyzed, put together again, kicked, "pitched into," tumbled about, preached to, preached about, and made to serve every purpose to which a sensation-loving world could put me. Well! I was now in training, in a new school, and was learning new and strange lessons.

Yet, these new lessons conveyed the old, old story. There were those who fawned upon me in my prosperity, who now jeered at my adversity; people whom I had specially favored, made special efforts to show their ingratitude; papers which, when I had the means to make it an object for them to be on good terms with me, over-loaded me with adulation, now attempted to overwhelm me with abuse; and then the immense amount of moralizing over the "insta-bility of human fortunes" and especially the retributive justice that is sure to follow "ill-gotten gains," which my censors assumed to be the sum and substance of my honorably acquired and industriously worked for property. I have no doubt that much of this kind of twaddle was believed by the twaddlers to be sincere; and thus my case was actual capital to certain preachers and religious editors who were in want of fresh illustrations wherewith to point their morals.

As for myself, I was in the depths, but I did not despond. I was confident that with energetic purpose and divine assistance I should, if my health and life were spared, get on my feet again; and events have since fully justified and verified the expectation and the effort.

CHAPTER XXVI

CLOUDS AND SUNSHINE

HAPPILY, there is always more wheat than there is chaff. While my enemies and a few envious persons and misguided moralists were abusing and traducing me, my very misfortunes revealed to me hosts of hitherto unknown friends who tendered to me something more than mere sympathy. Funds were offered to me in unbounded quantity for the support of my family and to re-establish me in business. I declined these tenders because, on principle, I never accepted a money favor, unless I except the single receipt of a small sum which came to me by mail at this time and anonymously so that I could not return it. Even this small sum I at once devoted to charity towards one who needed the money far more than I did.

The generosity of my friends urged me to accept "benefits" by the score, the returns of which would have made me quite independent. There was a proposition among leading citizens in New York to give a series of benefits which I felt obliged to decline though the movement in my favor deeply touched me.

And with other offers of assistance from far and near, came the following from a little gentleman who did not forget his old friend and benefactor in the time of trial:

JONES' HOTEL, PHILADELPHIA, May 12, 1856.

MY DEAR MR. BARNUM,—I understand your friends, and that means "all creation," intend to get up some benefits for your family. Now, my dear sir, just be good enough to remember that I belong to that mighty crowd, and I must have a finger (or at least a "thumb") in that pie. I am bound to appear on all such occasions in some shape, from "Jack the Giant Killer," up stairs, to the doorkeeper down, whichever may serve you best; and there are some feats that I can perform as well as any other man of my inches. I have just started out on my western tour, and have my carriage, ponies and assistants all here, but I am ready to go on to New York, bag and baggage, and remain at Mrs. Barnum's service as long as I, in my small way, can be useful. Put me into any "heavy" work, if you like. Perhaps I cannot lift as much as some other folks, but just take your pencil in hand and you will see I can draw a tremendous load. I drew two hundred tons at a single pull to-day, embracing two thousand persons, whom I hauled up safely and satisfactorily to all parties, at one exhibition. Hoping that you will be able to fix up a lot of magnets that will attract all New York, and volunteering to sit on any part of the loadstone, I am, as ever, your little but sympathizing friend,

Gen. Tom Thumb.

Even this generous offer from my little friend I felt compelled to refuse. But kind words were written and spoken which I could not prevent, nor did I desire to do so, and which were worth more to me than money. I should fail to find space, if I wished it, to copy one-tenth part of the cordial and kind articles and paragraphs that appeared about me in newspapers throughout the country. The following sentence from an editorial article in a prominent New York journal was the key-note to many similar kind notices in all parts of the Union: "It is a fact beyond dispute that Mr. Barnum's financial difficulties have accumulated from the goodness of his nature; kind-hearted and generous to a fault, it has ever been his custom to lend a helping hand to the struggling; and honest industry and enterprise have found his friendship prompt and faithful." The *Boston Journal* dwelt especially upon the use I had made of my money in my days of prosperity in assisting deserving laboring men and in giving an impulse to business in the town where I resided. It seems only just that I should make this very brief allusion to these things, if only as an offset to the unbounded abuse of those who believed in kicking me merely because I was down; nor can I refrain from copying the following from the *Boston Saturday Evening Gazette,* of May 3, 1856:

BARNUM REDIVIVUS

A WORD FOR BARNUM

BARNUM, your hand! Though you are "down,"
    And see full many a frigid shoulder,
Be brave, my brick, and though they frown,
    Prove that misfortune makes you bolder.
There's many a man that sneers, my hero,
    And former praise converts to scorning,
Would worship—when he fears—a Nero,
    And bend "where thrift may follow fawning."

You humbugged us—that we have seen,
    We got our money's worth, old fellow,
And though you thought our *minds* were *green,*
    We never thought your *heart* was *yellow.*
We knew you liberal, generous, warm,
    Quick to assist a falling brother,
And, with such virtues, what's the harm
    All memories of your faults to smother?

We had not heard the peerless Lind,
    But for your spirit enterprising,
You were the man to raise the wind,
    And make a *coup* confessed surprising.
You're reckoned in your native town
    A friend in need, a friend in danger,
You ever keep the latchstring down,
    And greet with open hand the stranger.

Stiffen your upper lip. You know
    Who are your friends and who your foes now;
We pay for knowledge as we go;
    And though you get some sturdy blows now,
You've a fair field,—no favors crave,—
    The storm once passed will find you braver,—
In virtue's cause long may you wave,
    And on the right side, never waver.

But the manifestations of sympathy which came to me from Bridgeport, where my home had been for more than ten years, were the most gratifying of all, because they showed unmistakably that my best friends, those who were most constant in their friendship and most emphatic in their esteem, were my neighbors and associates who, of all people, knew me best. With such support I could easily endure the attacks of traducers elsewhere. The *New York Times*, April 25, 1856, under the head of "Sympathy for Barnum," published a full report of the meeting of my fellow-citizens of Bridgeport, the previous evening, to take my case into consideration.

In response to a call headed by the mayor of the city, and signed by several hundred citizens, this meeting was held in Washington Hall "for the purpose of sympathizing with P. T. Barnum, Esq., in his recent pecuniary embarrassments, and of giving some public expression to their views in reference to his financial misfortunes." It was the largest public meeting which, up to that time, had ever been held in Bridgeport. Several prominent citizens made addresses, and resolutions were adopted declaring "that respect and sympathy were due to P. T. Barnum in return for his many acts of liberality, philanthropy and public spirit," expressing unshaken confidence in his integrity, admiration for the "fortitude and composure with which he has met reverses into which he has been dragged through no fault of his own except a too generous confidence in pretended friends," and hoping that he would "yet return to that wealth which he has so nobly employed, and to the community he has so signally benefited."

Shortly after this sympathetic meeting, a number of gentlemen in Bridgeport offered me a loan of $50,000 if that sum would be instrumental in extricating me from my entanglement. I could not say that this amount would meet the exigency; I could only say, "wait, wait, and hope."

Meanwhile, my eyes were fully opened to the entire magnitude of the deception that had been practised upon my too confiding nature. I not only discovered that my notes had been used to five times the amount I stipulated or expected, but that they had been applied, not to relieving the company from temporary embarrassment after my connection with it, but almost wholly to the redemption of old and rotten claims of years and months gone by. To show the extent to which the fresh victim was deliberately bled, it may be stated that I was induced to become surety to one of the New Haven banks in the sum of $30,000 to indemnify the bank against future losses it might incur from the Jerome company after my connection with it, and by some legerdemain this bond was made to cover past obligations which were older even than my knowledge of 'the existence of the company. In every way it seemed as if I had been cruelly swindled and deliberately defrauded.

As the clock company had gone to pieces and was paying but from twelve to fifteen per cent for its paper, I sent two of my friends to New Haven to ask for a meeting of the creditors and I instructed them to say in substance for me as follows:

"Gentlemen: This is a capital practical joke! Before I negotiated with your clock company at all, I was assured by several of you, and particularly by a representative of the bank which was the largest creditor of the concern, that the Jerome Company was eminently responsible and that the head of the same was uncommonly pious. On the strength of such representations solely, I was induced to agree to indorse and accept paper for that company to the extent of $110,000—no more. That sum I am now willing to pay for my own verdancy, with an additional sum of $40,000 for your 'cuteness, making a total of $150,000, which you can have if you cry 'quits' with the fleeced showman and let him off."

Many of the old creditors favored this proposition; but it was found that the indebtedness was so scattered it would be impracticable to attempt a settlement by an unanimous compromise of the creditors. It was necessary to liquidation that my property should go into the hands of assignees; I therefore at once turned over my

Bridgeport property to Connecticut assignees and I removed my family to New York, where I also made an assignment of all my real and personal estate, excepting what had already been transferred in Connecticut.

About this time I received a letter from Philadelphia proffering $500 in case my circumstances were such that I really stood in need of help. The very wording of the letter awakened the suspicion in my mind that it was a trick to ascertain whether I really had any property, for I knew that banks and brokers in that city held some of my Jerome paper which they refused to compound or compromise. So I at once wrote that I did need $500, and, as I expected, the money did not come, nor was my letter answered; but, as a natural consequence, the Philadelphia bankers who were holding the Jerome paper for a higher percentage at once acceded to the terms which I had announced myself able and willing to pay.

Every dollar which I honestly owed on my own account I had already paid in full or had satisfactorily arranged. For the liabilities incurred by the deliberate deception which had involved me I offered such a percentage as I thought my estate, when sold, would eventually pay; and my wife, from her own property, advanced from time to time money to take up such notes as could be secured upon these terms. It was, however, a slow process. More than one creditor would hold on to his note, which possibly he had "shaved" at the rate of two or three per cent a month, and say:

"Oh! you can't keep Barnum down; he will dig out after a while; I shall never sell my claim for less than par and interest."

Of course, I knew very well that if all the creditors took this view I should never get out of the entanglement in which I had been involved by the old creditors of the Jerome Company, who had so ingeniously managed to make me take their place. All I could do was to take a thorough survey of the situation, and consider, now that I was down, how I could get up again.

We were now living in a very frugal manner in a hired furnished house in Eighth Street, near Sixth Avenue, in New York, and our landlady and her family boarded with us.　At the age of forty-six, after the acquisition and the loss of a handsome fortune, I was once more nearly at the bottom of the ladder, and was about to begin the world again.　The situation was disheartening, but I had energy, experience, health and hope.

CHAPTER XXVII

IN the summer of 1855, previous to my financial troubles, feeling that I was independent and could retire from active business, I sold the American Museum collection and good will to Messrs. John Greenwood, Junior, and Henry D. Butler. They paid me double the amount the collection had originally cost, giving me notes for nearly the entire amount secured by a chattel mortgage, and hired the premises from my wife, who owned the Museum property lease, and on which, by the agreement of Messrs. Greenwood and Butler, she realized a profit of $19,000 a year. The chattel mortgage of Messrs. Greenwood and Butler was, of course, turned over to the New York assignee with the other property.

And now there came to me a new sensation which was at times terribly depressing and annoying. My wide-spread reputation for shrewdness as a showman had induced the general belief that my means were still ample, and certain outside creditors who had bought my clock notes at a tremendous discount and entirely on speculation, made up their minds that they must be paid at once without waiting for the slow process of the sale of my property by the assignees.

They therefore took what are termed "supplementary proceedings," which enabled them to haul me any day before a judge for the purpose, as they phrased it, of "putting Barnum through a course of sprouts," and which meant an examination of the debtor under oath, compelling him to disclose everything with regard to his property, his present means of living, and so on.

I repeatedly answered all questions on these points; and reports of the daily examinations were published. Still another and another, and yet another creditor would haul me up; and his attorney would ask me the same questions which had already been answered and published half a dozen times. This persistent and unnecessary annoyance created considerable sympathy for me, which was not only expressed by letters I received daily from various parts of the country, but the public press, with now and then an exception, took my part, and even the Judges, before whom I appeared, said to me on more than one occasion, that as men they sincerely pitied me, but as judges of course they must administer the law. After a while, however, the judges ruled that I need not answer any question propounded to me by an attorney, if I had already answered the same question to some other attorney in a previous examination in behalf of other creditors. In fact, one of the judges, on one occasion, said pretty sharply to an examining attorney:

"This, sir, has become simply a case of persecution. Mr. Barnum has many times answered every question that can properly be put to him to elicit the desired information; and I think it is time to stop these examinations. I advise him to not answer one interrogatory which he has replied to under any previous inquiries."

These things gave me some heart, so that at last I went up to the "sprouts" with less reluctance, and began to try to pay off my persecutors in their own coin.

On one occasion, a dwarfish little lawyer, who reminded me of "Quilp," commenced his examination in behalf of a note-shaver who held a thousand dollar note, which it seemed he had bought for seven hundred dollars. After the oath had been administered the little "limb of the law" arranged his pen, ink and paper, and in a loud voice, and with a most peremptory and supercilious air, asked:

"What is your name, sir?"

I answered him, and his next question, given in a louder and more peremptory tone, was:

"What is your business?"

"Attending bar," I meekly replied.

"Attending bar!" he echoed, with an appearance of much surprise. "Attending bar! Why, don't you profess to be a temperance man—a teetotaler?"

"I do," I replied.

"And yet, sir, do you have the audacity to assert that you peddle rum all day, and drink none yourself?"

"I doubt whether that is a relevant question," I said in a low tone of voice.

"I will appeal to his honor the judge, if you don't answer it instantly," said Quilp in great glee.

"I attend bar, and yet never drink intoxicating liquors," I replied.

"Where do you attend bar, and for whom?" was the next question.

"I attend the bar of this court, nearly every day, for the benefit of two-penny, would-be lawyers and their greedy clients."

A loud tittering in the vicinity only added to the vexation which was already visible on the countenance of my interrogator, and he soon brought his examination to a close.

On another occasion, a young lawyer was pushing his inquiries to a great length, when, in a half laughing, apologetic tone, he said:

"You see, Mr. Barnum, I am searching after the small things; I am willing to take even the crumbs which fall from the rich man's table!"

"Which are you, Lazarus, or one of the dogs?" I asked.

"I guess a blood-hound would not smell out much on this trail," he said good-naturedly, adding that he had no more questions to ask.

I still continued to receive many offers of pecuniary assistance, which, whenever proposed in the form of a gift, I invariably refused. In a number of instances, personal friends tendered me their checks for $500, $1,000, and other sums, but I always responded in substance: "Oh, no, I thank you; I do not need it; my wife has considerable property, besides a large income from her Museum lease. I want for nothing; I do not owe a dollar for personal obligations that is not already secured, and when the clock creditors have fully investigated and thought over the matter, I think they will be content to divide my property among themselves and let me up."

Just after my failure, and on account of the ill-health of my wife, I spent a portion of the summer with my family in the farmhouse of Mr. Charles Howell, at Westhampton, on Long Island. The place is a mile west of Quogue, and was then called "Ketchebonneck." The thrifty and intelligent farmers of the neighborhood were in the habit of taking summer boarders, and the place had become a favorite resort. Mr. Howell's farm lay close upon the ocean and I found the residence a cool and delightful one. Surf bathing, fishing, shooting and fine roads for driving made the season pass pleasantly and the respite from active life and immediate annoyance from my financial troubles was a very great benefit to me.

One morning we discovered that the waves had thrown upon the beach a young black whale some twelve feet long. It was dead, but the fish was hard and fresh and I bought it for a few dollars from the men who had taken possession of it. I sent it at once to the Museum, where it was exhibited in a huge refrigerator for a few days, creating considerable excitement, the general public considering it "a big thing on ice," and the managers gave me a share of the profits, which amounted to a sufficient sum to pay the entire board bill of my family for the season.

This incident both amused and amazed my Long Island landlord. "Well, I declare," said he, "that beats all; you are the luckiest man

I ever heard of. Here you come and board for four months with your family, and when your time is nearly up, and you are getting ready to leave, out rolls a black whale on our beach, a thing never heard of before in this vicinity, and you take that whale and pay your whole bill with it! I wonder if that ain't 'providential'?" This was followed by such a laugh as only Charles Howell could give, and like one of his peculiar sneezes, it resounded, echoed, and re-echoed through the whole neighborhood.

Soon after my return to New York, something occurred which I foresaw, I thought, at the time, was likely indirectly to lead me out of the wilderness into a clear field again, and, indeed, it eventually did so. Strange to say, my new city which had been my ruin was to be my redemption, and dear East Bridgeport which plunged me into the slough was to bring me out again. "Dear" as the place had literally proved to me, it was to be yet dearer, in another and better sense, hereafter.

The now gigantic Wheeler & Wilson Sewing Machine Company was then doing a comparatively small, yet rapidly growing business at Watertown, Connecticut. The Terry & Barnum clock factory was standing idle, almost worthless, in East Bridgeport, and Wheeler & Wilson saw in the empty building, the situation, the ease of communication with New York, and other advantages, precisely what they wanted, provided they could procure the premises at a rate which would compensate them for the expense and trouble of removing their establishment from Watertown. It is enough to say here, that the clock factory was sold for a trifle and the Wheeler & Wilson Company moved into it and speedily enlarged it. I felt then that this was providential; the fact that the empty building could be cheaply purchased was the main motive for the removal of this Watertown enterprise to East Bridgeport, and was one of the first indications that my failure might prove a "blessing in disguise." It was a fresh impulse towards the building up of the new city and the consequent increase of the value of the land belonging to my estate.

This important movement of the Wheeler & Wilson Company gave me the greatest hope, and moreover, Mr. Wheeler kindly offered me a loan of $5,000, without security, and as I was anxious to have it used in purchasing the East Bridgeport property, when sold at public auction by my assignees, and also in taking up such clock notes as could be bought at a reasonable percentage, I accepted the offer and borrowed the $5,000. This sum, with many thousand dollars more belonging to my wife, was devoted to these purposes.

It seemed as if I had now got hold of the thread which would eventually lead me out of the labyrinth of financial difficulty in which the Jerome entanglement had involved me. Though the new plan promised relief, and actually did succeed, even beyond my most sanguine expectations, eventually putting more money into my pocket than the Jerome complication had taken out—yet I also foresaw that the process would necessarily be very slow. In fact, two years afterwards I had made very little progress. But I concluded to let the new venture work out itself and it would go on as well without my personal presence and attention, perhaps even better. Growing trees, money at interest, and rapidly rising real estate, work for their owners all night as well as all day, Sundays included, and when the proprietors are asleep or away; and with the design of cooperating in the new accumulation and of saving something to add to the amount, I made up my mind to go to Europe again. I was anxious for a change of scene and for active employment, and equally desirous of getting away from the immediate pressure of troubles which no effort on my part could then remove. While my affairs were working out themselves in their own way and in the speediest manner possible, I might be doing something for myself and for my family.

Accordingly, leaving all my business affairs at home in the hands of my friends, early in 1857 I set sail once more for England, taking with me General Tom Thumb, and also little Cordelia Howard and her parents. This young girl had attained an extended reputation for her artistic personation of "Little Eva," in the play of "Uncle Tom," and she displayed a precocious talent in her rendering of other juvenile characters. With these attractions, and with what else I might be able to do myself, I determined to make as much money as I could, intending to remit the same to my wife's friends, for the purpose of repurchasing a portion of my estate, when it was offered at auction, and of redeeming such of the clock notes as could be obtained at reasonable rates.

CHAPTER XXVIII

ABROAD AGAIN

On arriving at Liverpool, I found that my old friends, Mr. and Mrs. Lynn, of the Waterloo Hotel, had changed very little during my ten years' absence from England. Even the servants in the hotel were mainly those whom I left there when I last went away from Liverpool—which illustrates, in a small way, how much less changeable and more "conservative" the English people are than we are. The old head-waiter, Thomas, was still head-waiter, as he had been for full twenty years. His hair was more silvered, his gait was slower, his shoulders had rounded, but he was as ready to receive, as I was to repeat, the first order I ever gave him, to wit: "Fried soles and shrimp sauce."

And among my many friends in Liverpool and London, but one death had occurred, and with only two exceptions they all lived in the same buildings and pursued the same vocations as when I left them in 1847. When I reached London, I found one of these exceptions to be Mr. Albert Smith, who, when I first knew him, was a dentist, a literary hack, a contributor to *Punch,* and a writer for the magazines,—and who was now transformed to a first-class showman in the full tide of success, in my own old exhibition quarters in Egyptian Hall, Piccadilly.

When the late William M. Thackeray made his first visit to the United States, I think in 1852, he called on me at the Museum with a letter of introduction from our mutual friend Albert Smith. He spent an hour with me, mainly for the purpose of asking my advice in regard to the management of the course of lectures on "The

English Humorists of the Eighteenth Century," which he proposed to deliver, as he did afterwards, with very great success, in the principal cities of the Union. I gave him the best advice I could as to management, and the cities he ought to visit, for which he was very grateful, and he called on me whenever he was in New York. I also saw him repeatedly when he came to America the second time with his admirable lectures on "The Four Georges," which, it will be remembered, he delivered in the United States in the season of 1855-56, before he read these lectures to audiences in Great Britain. My relations with this great novelist, I am proud to say, were cordial and intimate; and now, when I called upon him, in 1857, at his own house, he grasped me heartily by the hand and said:

"Mr. Barnum, I admire you more than ever. I have read the accounts in the papers of the examinations you underwent in the New York courts, and the positive pluck you exhibit under your pecuniary embarrassments is worthy of all praise. You would never have received credit for the philosophy you manifest, if these financial misfortunes had not overtaken you."

I thanked him for his compliment, and he continued:

"But tell me, Barnum, are you really in need of present assistance? for if you are you must be helped."

"Not in the least," I replied, laughing; "I need more money in order to get out of bankruptcy and I intend to earn it; but so far as daily bread is concerned, I am quite at ease, for my wife is worth £30,000 or £40,000."

"Is it possible?" he exclaimed, with evident delight; "well, now, you have lost all my sympathy; why, that is more than I ever expect to be worth; I shall be sorry for you no more."

During my stay in London, I met Thackeray several times, and on one occasion I dined with him. He was a most genial, noble-hearted gentleman. In our conversations he spoke with the warmest appreciation of America, and of his numerous friends in this country, and he repeatedly expressed his obligations to me for the advice and assistance I had given him on the occasion of his first lecturing visit to the United States.

The late Charles Kean, then manager of the Princess's Theatre, in London, was also exceedingly polite and friendly to me. He placed a box at my disposal at all times, and took me through his theatre to show me the stage, dressing rooms, and particularly the valuable "properties" he had collected. Among other things, he had twenty or more complete suits of real armor and other costumes and appointments essential to the production of historical plays, in the most complete and authentic manner. In the mere matter of stage-setting, Charles Kean has never been surpassed.

Otto Goldschmidt, the husband of Jenny Lind, also called on me in London. He and his wife were then living in Dresden, and he said the first thing his wife desired him to ask me was, whether I was in want. I assured him that I was not, although I was managing to live in an economical way and my family would soon come over to reside in London. He then advised me to take them to Dresden, saying that living was very cheap there; and, he added, "my wife will gladly look up a proper house for you to live in." I thankfully declined his proffered kindness, as Dresden was too far away from my business. A year subsequent to this, a letter was generally published in the American papers, purporting to have been written to me by Jenny Lind, and proffering me a large sum of money. I immediately pronounced the letter a forgery, and I soon afterwards received a communication from a young reporter in Philadelphia acknowledging himself as the author, and saying that he wrote it from a good motive, hoping it would benefit me. On the contrary it annoyed me exceedingly. My old friends Julius Benedict and Giovanni Belletti called on me and we had some very pleasant dinners together, when we talked over incidents of their travels in America.

I had numerous offers from professional friends on both sides of the Atlantic who supposed me to be in need of employment. Mr. Barney Williams, who had not then acted in England, proposed in the kindest manner to make me his agent for a tour through Great Britain, and to give me one-third of the profits which he and Mrs. Williams might make by their acting. Mr. S. M. Pettengill, of New York, the newspaper advertising agent, offered me the fine salary of $10,000 a year to transact business for him in Great Britain. These offers, both from Mr. Williams and Mr. Pettengill, I was obliged to decline.

Mr. Lumley, manager of Her Majesty's Theatre, used to send me an order for a private box for every opera night, and I frequently availed myself of his courtesy. I had an idea that much money might be made by transferring his entire opera company, which then included Piccolomini and Titjiens, to New York for a short season. The plan included the charter of a special steamer for the company and the conveyance of the entire troupe, including the orchestra, with their instruments, and the chorus, costumes, scores, and properties of the company. It was a gigantic scheme, which would no doubt have been pecuniarily successful, and Mr. Lumley and I went so far as to draw up the preliminaries of an arrangement, in which I was to share a due proportion of the profits for my assistance in the management; but after a while, and to the evident regret of Mr. Lumley, the scheme was given up.

Meanwhile, I was by no means idle. Cordelia Howard as "Little Eva," with her mother as the inimitable "Topsy," were highly successful in London and other large cities, while General Tom Thumb, returning after so long an absence, drew crowded houses wherever he went. These were strong spokes in the wheel that was moving slowly but surely in the effort to get me out of debt, and, if possible, to save some portion of my real estate. Of course, it was not generally known that I had any interest whatever in either of these exhibitions; if it had been, possibly some of the clock creditors would have annoyed me; but I busied myself in these and in other ways, working industriously and making much money, which I constantly remitted to my trusty agent at home.

After a pleasant and successful season of several weeks in London and in the provinces, I took the little General into Germany, going from London to Paris and from thence to Strasbourg and Baden-Baden. I had not been in Paris since the times of King Louis Philippe, and while I noticed great improvements in the city, in the opening of the new boulevards and the erection of noble buildings, I could see also with sorrow that there was less personal liberty under the Emperor Napoleon III., than there was under the "Citizen King." The custom-house officials were overbearing and unnecessarily rigid in their exactions; the police were overwatchful and intolerant; the screws were turned on everywhere. I had a lot of large pictorial placards of General Tom Thumb, which were merely *in transitu,* as I wished only to forward them to Germany to be used as advertisements of the forthcoming exhibitions. These the French custom-house officers determined to examine in detail, and when they discovered that one of the pictures represented the General in the costume of the First Napoleon, the whole of the bills were seized and sent to the Prefecture of Police. I was compelled to stay three days in Paris before I could convince the Prefect of Police that there was no treason in the Tom Thumb pictures. I was very glad to get out of Paris with my baggage and taking a seat in the express train on the Paris and Strasbourg railway I soon forgot my custom-house annoyances.

From Strasbourg we went to Baden-Baden, and in due time, when our preliminary arrangements were completed, the General's attendants, carriage, ponies and liveried coachman and footmen were seen in the streets. The excitement was intense and increased from day to day. Several crowned heads, princes, lords and ladies who were spending the season at Baden-Baden, with a vast number of wealthy pleasure seekers and travellers, crowded the saloon in which the General exhibited during the entire time we remained in the place. The charges for admission were much higher than had been demanded in any other city.

From Baden-Baden we went to other celebrated German Spas, including Ems, Homburg and Weisbaden. These are all fashionable gambling as well as watering places, and during our visits they were crowded with visitors from all parts of Europe. Our exhibitions were attended by thousands who paid the same high prices that were charged for admission at Baden-Baden, and at Wiesbaden, among many distinguished persons, the King of Holland came to see the little General. These exhibitions were among the most profitable that had ever been given, and I was able to remit thousands of dollars to my agents in the United States to aid in re-purchasing my real estate and to assist in taking up such clock notes as were offered for sale. A short but very remunerative season at Frankfort-on-the-Main, the home and starting-place of the great house of the Rothschilds, assisted me largely in carrying out these purposes.

We exhibited at Mayence and several other places in the vicinity, reaping golden harvests everywhere, and then went down the Rhine to Cologne. The journey down the river was very pleasant and we duly "did" the scenery and lions on the way. The slowness of the boat was a great annoyance and on one occasion I said to the captain :

"Look here! confound your slow old boat. I have a great mind to put on an opposition American line and burst up your business."

He knew me, and knew something of Yankee enterprise, and he was evidently alarmed, but a thought came to his relief :

"You cannot do it," he triumphantly exclaimed; "the government will not permit you to run more than nine miles an hour."

We remained at Cologne only long enough to visit the famous cathedral and to see other curiosities and works of art, and then pushed on to Rotterdam and Amsterdam.

CHAPTER XXIX

HOLLAND gave me more genuine satisfaction than any other foreign country I have ever visited, if I except Great Britain. Redeemed as a large portion of the whole surface of the land has been from the bottom of the sea by the wonderful dykes, which are monuments of the industry of whole generations of human beavers, Holland seems to me the most curious as well as interesting country in the world. The people, too, with their quaint costumes, their extraordinary cleanliness, their thrift, industry and frugality, pleased me very much. It is the universal testimony of all travellers that the Hollanders are the neatest and most economical people among all nations. So far as cleanliness is concerned, in Holland it is evidently not next to, but far ahead of godliness. It is rare, indeed, to meet a ragged, dirty, or drunken person. The people are very temperate and economical in their habits; and even the very rich—and there is a vast amount of wealth in the country—live with great frugality, though all of the people live well.

As for the scenery, I cannot say much for it, since it is only diversified by thousands of windmills, which are made to do all kinds of work, from grinding grain to pumping water from the inside of the dykes back to the sea again. As I exhibited the General only in Rotterdam and Amsterdam, and to no great profit in either city, we spent most of our time in rambling about to see what was to be seen. In the country villages it seemed as if every house was scrubbed twice and white-washed once every day in the week, excepting Sunday. Some places were almost painfully pure, and I was in one village where horses and cattle were not allowed to go through the streets, and no one was permitted to wear their boots or shoes in the houses. There is a general and constant exercise of brooms, pails, floor brushes and mops all over Holland, and in some places even, this kind of thing is carried so far, I am told, that the only trees set out are scrub-oaks.

The reason, I think, why our exhibitions were not more successful in Rotterdam and Amsterdam, is that the people are too frugal to spend much money for amusement, but they and their habits and ways afforded us so much amusement that we were quite willing they should give our entertainment the "go by," as they generally did. We were in Amsterdam at the season of "Kremis," or the annual Fair which is held in all the principal towns, and where shows of all descriptions are open, at prices for admission ranging from one to five pennies, and are attended by nearly the whole population. For the people generally, this one great holiday seems all-sufficient for the whole year. I went through scores of booths, where curiosities and monstrosities of all kinds were exhibited, and was able to make some purchases and engagements for the American Museum. Among these was the Albino family, consisting of a man, his wife, and son, who were by far the most interesting and attractive specimens of their class I had ever seen.

We visited The Hague, the capital and the finest city in Holland. It is handsomely and regularly laid out, and contains a beautiful theatre, a public picture-gallery, which contains some of the best works of Vandyke, Paul Potter, and other Dutch masters, while the museum is especially rich in rarities from China and Japan. When we arrived at The Hague, Mr. August Belmont, who had been the United States Minister at that court, had just gone home; but I heard many encomiums passed upon him and his family, and I was told some pretty good stories of his familiarity with the king, and of the "jolly times" these two personages frequently enjoyed together. I did not miss visiting the great government museum, as I wished particularly to see the rich collection of Japan ware and arms, made during the many years when the Dutch carried on almost exclusively the entire foreign trade with the Japanese. I spent several days in minutely examining these curious manufactures of a people who were then almost as little known to nations generally as are the inhabitants of the planet Jupiter.

On the first day of my visit to this museum, I stood for an hour before a large case containing a most unique and extraordinary collection of fabulous animals, made from paper and other materials, and looking as natural and genuine as the stuffed skins of any animals in the American Museum. There were serpents two yards long, with a head and pair of feet at each end; frogs as large as a man, with human hands and feet; turtles with three heads; monkeys with two heads and six legs; scores of equally curious monstrosities; and at least two dozen mermaids, of all sorts and sizes. Looking at these "sirens" I easily divined from whence the Fejee mermaid originated.

While I was standing near this remarkable cabinet the superintendent of the Museum came, and, introducing himself to me, asked me from what country I came and how I liked the Museum. I told him that I was an American and that the collection was interesting and remarkable, adding:

"You seem to have a great variety of mermaids here."

"Yes," he replied; "the Japanese exercise great ingenuity in manufacturing fabulous animals, especially mermaids; and by the way," he added, "your great showman, Barnum, is said to have succeeded in humbugging the Americans to a very considerable extent, by means of what he claimed to be a veritable mermaid."

I said that such was the story, though I believed that Barnum only used the mermaid as an advertisement for his Museum.

"Perhaps so," responded the superintendent, "but he is a shrewd and industrious manager. We have had frequent applications from his European agents for duplicates from our collection and have occasionally sold some to them to be sent to America."

After a truly delightful visit in Holland, we went back to England; and, proceeding to Manchester, opened our exhibition. For several days the hall was crowded to overflowing at each of the three, and sometimes four, entertainments we gave every day. By this time, my wife and two youngest daughters had come over to London, and I hired furnished lodgings in the suburbs where they could live within the strictest limits of economy. It was necessary now for me to return for a few weeks to America, to assist personally in forwarding a settlement of the clock difficulties. So leaving the little General in the hands of trusty and competent agents to carry on the exhibitions in my absence, I set my face once more towards home and the west, and took steamer at Liverpool for New York.

The trip, like most of the passages which I have made across the Atlantic, was an exceedingly pleasant one. These frequent voyages were to me the rests, the reliefs from almost unremitting industry, anxiety, and care, and I always managed to have more or less fun on board ship every time I crossed the ocean. During the present trip, for amusement and to pass away the time, the passengers got up a number of mock trials which afforded a vast deal of fun. A judge was selected, jurymen drawn, prisoners arraigned, counsel employed, and all the formalities of a court established. I have the vanity to think that if my good fortune had directed me to that profession I should have made a very fair lawyer, for I have always had a great fondness for debate and especially for the cross-examination of witnesses, unless that witness was P. T. Barnum in examination under supplementary proceedings at the instance of some note-shaver who had bought a clock note at a discount of thirty-six per cent. In this mock court, I was unanimously chosen as prosecuting attorney, and as the court was established expressly to convict, I had no difficulty in carrying the jury and securing the punishment of the prisoner. A small fine was generally imposed, and the fund thus collected was given to a poor sailor boy who had fallen from the mast and broken his leg.

After my arrival in New York, oftentimes in passing up and down Broadway I saw old and prosperous friends coming, but before I came anywhere near them, if they espied me they would dodge into a store, or across the street, or opportunely meet some one with whom they had pressing business, or they would be very much interested in something that was going on over the way or on top of the City Hall. I was delighted at this, for it gave me at once a new sensation and a new experience. "Ah, ha!" I said to myself; "my butterfly friends, I know you now; and what is more to the point, if ever I get out of this bewilderment of broken clock-wheels, I shall not forget you"; and I heartily thanked the old clock concern for giving me the opportunity to learn this sad but most needful lesson. I had a very few of the same sort of experiences in Bridgeport, and they proved valuable to me.

Mr. James D. Johnson, of Bridgeport, one of my assignees, who had written to me that my personal presence might facilitate a settlement of my affairs, told me soon after my arrival that there was no probability of disposing of Iranistan at present, and that I might as well move my family into the house. I had arrived in August and my family followed me from London in September, and October 20, 1857, my second daughter, Helen, was married in the house of her elder sister, Mrs. D. W. Thompson, in Bridgeport, to Mr. Samuel H. Hurd.

Meanwhile, Iranistan, which had been closed and unoccupied for more than two years, was once more opened to the carpenters

IRANISTAN, WHICH BARNUM COPIED FROM GEORGE IV's ORIENTAL PAVILION

Loan Collection of Elizabeth Sterling Seeley

Struggles and Triumph.

DOMICILES PLAYED AN IMPORTANT PART IN THE LIVES OF NINE-
TEENTH-CENTURY AMERICANS. HERE ARE THREE WHICH, WITH
IRANISTAN (PREVIOUS PAGE), WERE MOST IMPORTANT IN BAR-
NUM'S: (ABOVE) WALDEMERE, BEFORE AND AFTER RESTORATION;
(OPPOSITE PAGE, TOP) LINDENCROFT, BARNUM'S HOME IN BRIDGE-
PORT; (BOTTOM) MARINA, BARNUM'S HOME AFTER 1888

The Barnum Museum

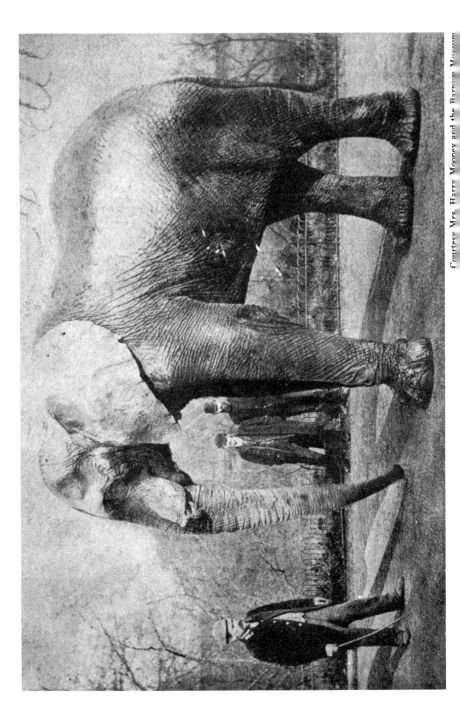

and painters whom Mr. Johnson sent there to put the house in order. He agreed with me that it was best to keep the property as long as possible, and in the interval, till a purchaser for the estate appeared, or till it was forced to auction, to take up the clock notes whenever they were offered. The workmen who were employed in the house were specially instructed not to smoke there, but nevertheless it was subsequently discovered that some of the men were in the habit occasionally of going into the main dome to eat their dinners which they brought with them, and that they stayed there awhile after dinner to smoke their pipes. In all probability, one of these lighted pipes was left on the cushion which covered the circular seat in the dome and ignited the tow with which the cushion was stuffed. It may have been days and even weeks before this smouldering tow fire burst into flame.

I was staying at the Astor House, in New York, when, on the morning of December 18, 1857, I received a telegram from my brother Philo F. Barnum, dated at Bridgeport and informing me that Iranistan was burned to the ground that morning. The alarm was given at eleven o'clock on the night of the 17th, and the fire burned till one o'clock on the morning of the 18th. My beautiful Iranistan was gone! This was not only a serious loss to my estate, for it had probably cost at least $150,000, but it was generally regarded as a public calamity. It was the only building in its peculiar style of architecture, of any pretension, in America, and many persons visited Bridgeport every year expressly to see Iranistan. The insurance on the mansion had usually been about $62,000, but I had let some of the policies expire without renewing them, so that at the time of the fire there was only $28,000 insurance on the property. Most of the furniture and pictures were saved, generally in a damaged state.

Subsequently, my assignees sold the grounds and outhouses of

Iranistan to the late Elias Howe, Jr., the celebrated inventor of the needle for sewing-machines. The property brought $50,000, which, with the $28,000 insurance, went into my assets to satisfy clock creditors. It was Mr. Howe's intention to erect a splendid mansion on the estate, but his untimely and lamented death prevented the fulfilment of the plan.

CHAPTER XXX

SEEING the necessity of making more money to assist in extricating me from my financial difficulties, and leaving my affairs in the hands of Mr. James D. Johnson—my wife and youngest daughter, Pauline, boarding with my eldest daughter, Mrs. Thompson, in Bridgeport— early in 1858, I went back to England, and took Tom Thumb to all the principal places in Scotland and Wales, giving many exhibitions and making much money which was remitted, as heretofore, to my agents and assignees in America.

Finding, after a while, that my personal attention was not needed in the Tom Thumb exhibitions and confiding him almost wholly to agents who continued the tour through Great Britain, under my general advice and instruction, I turned my individual attention to a new field. At the suggestion of several American gentlemen, resident in London, I prepared a lecture on "The Art of Money Getting." I told my friends that, considering my clock complications, I thought I was more competent to speak on "The Art of Money Losing"; but they encouraged me by reminding me that I could not have lost money if I had not previously possessed the faculty of making it. They further assured me that my name having been intimately associated with the Jenny Lind concerts and other great money-making enterprises, the lecture would be sure to prove attractive and profitable.

The old clocks ticked in my ear the reminder that I should improve every opportunity to "turn an honest penny," and my lecture was duly announced for delivery in the great St. James'

Hall, Regent Street, Piccadilly. It was thoroughly advertised—a feature I never neglected—and, at the appointed time, the hall, which would hold three thousand people, was completely filled, at prices of three and two shillings (seventy-five and fifty cents) per seat, according to location. It was the evening of December 29, 1858. Since my arrival in Great Britain the previous spring, I had spent months in travelling with General Tom Thumb, and now I was to present myself in a new capacity to the English public as a lecturer. I could see in my audience all my American friends who had suggested this effort; all my theatrical and literary friends; and as I saw several gentlemen whom I knew to be connected with the leading London papers, I felt sure that my success or failure would be duly chronicled next morning. There was, moreover, a general audience that seemed eager to see the "showman" of whom they had heard so much, and to catch from his lips the "art" which, in times past, had contributed so largely to his success in life. Stimulated by these things, I tried to do my best, and I think I did it.

Nearly every paper in London had something to say about my lecture, and in almost every instance the matter and manner of the lecturer were unqualifiedly approved. Indeed, the profusion of praise quite overwhelmed me. My own lavish advertisements were as nothing to the notoriety which the London newspapers voluntarily and editorially gave to my new enterprise. The weekly and literary papers followed in the train; and even *Punch,* which had already done so much to keep Tom Thumb before the public, gave me a half-page notice, with an illustration, and thereafter favored me with frequent paragraphs. The city thus prepared the provinces to give me a cordial reception.

During the year 1859, I delivered this lecture nearly one hundred times in different parts of England, returning occasionally to London to repeat it to fresh audiences, and always with pecuniary success. Every provincial paper had something to say about Barnum and

"The Art of Money Getting," and I was never more pleasantly or profusely advertised. The tour, too, made me acquainted with many new people and added fresh and fast friends to my continually increasing list. My lecturing season is among my most grateful memories of England.

Remembering my experiences, some years before, with General Tom Thumb at Oxford and Cambridge, and the fondness of the undergraduates for practical joking, I was quite prepared when I made up my mind to visit those two cities, to take any quantity of "chaff" and lampooning which the University boys might choose to bring. I was sure of a full house in each city, and as I was anxious to earn all the money I could, so as to hasten my deliverance from financial difficulties, I fully resolved to put up with whatever offered—indeed, I rather liked the idea of an episode in the steady run of praise which had followed my lecture everywhere, and I felt, too, in the coming encounter that I might give quite as much as I was compelled to take.

I commenced at Cambridge, and, as I expected, to an overflowing house, largely composed of undergraduates. Soon after I began to speak, one of the young men called out: "Where is Joice Heth?" to which I very coolly replied:

"Young gentleman, please to restrain yourself till the conclu-sion of the lecture, when I shall take great delight in affording you, or any others of her posterity, all the information I possess concerning your deceased relative."

This reply turned the laugh against the youthful and anxious inquirer and had the effect of keeping other students quiet for a half hour. Thereafter, questions of a similar character were occasionally propounded, but as each inquirer generally received a prompt Roland for his Oliver, there was far less interruption than I had anticipated. The proceeds of the evening were more than one hundred pounds sterling, an important addition to my treasury at that time.

At the close of the lecture, several students invited me to a sumptuous supper where I met, among other undergraduates, a nephew of Lord Macaulay, the historian. This young gentleman insisted upon my breakfasting with him at his rooms next morning, but as I was anxious to take an early train for London, I only called to leave my card, and after his "gyp" had given me a strong cup of coffee, I hastened away, leaving the young Macaulay, whom I did not wish to disturb, fast asleep in bed.

At Oxford the large hall was filled half an hour before the time announced for the lecture to begin and the sale of tickets was stopped. I then stepped upon the platform, and said: "Ladies and Gentlemen: As every seat is occupied and the ticket-office is closed, I propose to proceed with my lecture now, and not keep you waiting till the advertised hour."

"Good for you, old Barnum," said one; "Time is money," said another; "Nothing like economy," came from a third, and other remarks and exclamations followed which excited much laughter in the audience. Holding up my hand as a signal that I was anxious to say something so soon as silence should be restored, I thus addressed my audience:

"Young gentlemen, I have a word or two to say, in order that we may have a thorough understanding between ourselves at the outset. I see symptoms of a pretty jolly time here this evening, and you have paid me liberally for the single hour of my time which is at your service. I am an old traveller and an old showman, and I like to please my patrons. Now, it is quite immaterial to me; you may furnish the entertainment for the hour, or I will endeavor to do so, or we will take portions of the time by turns—you supplying a part of the amusement, and I a part;—as we say sometimes in America, 'you pays your money, and you takes your choice.'"

My auditors were in the best of humor from the beginning, and my frankness pleased them, "Good for you, old Barnum," cried their leader; and I went on with my lecture for some fifteen minutes, when a voice called out:

"Come, old chap! you must be tired by this time; hold up now till we sing 'Yankee Doodle,'" whereupon they all joined in that pleasing air with a vigor which showed that they had thoroughly prepared themselves for the occasion, and meanwhile I took a chair and sat down to show them that I was quite satisfied with their manner of passing the time. When the song was concluded, the leader of the party said: "Now, Mr. Barnum, you may go ahead again."

I looked at my watch and quietly remarked, "Oh! there is time for lots of fun yet; we have nearly forty minutes of the hour remaining," and I proceeded with my lecture, or rather a lecture, for I began to adapt my remarks to the audience and the occasion. At intervals of ten minutes, or so, came interruptions which I, as my audience saw, fully enjoyed as much as the house did. When this miscellaneous entertainment was concluded, and I stopped short at the end of the hour, crowds of the young men pressed forward to shake hands with me, declaring that they had had a "jolly good time," while the leader said: "Stay with us a week, Barnum, and we will dine you, wine you, and give you full houses every night." But I was announced to lecture in London the next evening and I could not accept the pressing invitation, though I would gladly have stayed through the week. They asked me all sorts of questions about America, the Museum, my various shows and successes, and expressed the hope that I would come out of my clock troubles all right.

At least a score of them pressed me to breakfast with them next morning, but I declined, till one young gentleman put it on this purely personal ground: "My dear sir, you must breakfast with me; I have almost split my throat in screaming here to-night and it is only fair that you should repay me by coming to see me in the morning." This appeal was irresistible, and at the appointed time I met him and half a dozen of his friends at his table and we spent a very pleasant hour together. They complimented me on the tact and equanimity I had exhibited the previous evening, but I replied: "Oh! I was quite inclined to have you enjoy your fun, and came fully prepared for it."

But they liked better, they said, to get the party angry. A fortnight before, they told me, my friend Howard Paul had left them in disgust, because they insisted upon smoking while his wife was on the stage, adding that the entertainment was excellent and that Howard Paul could have made a thousand pounds if he had not let his anger drive him away. My new-found friends parted with me at the railway station, heartily urging me to come again, and my ticket seller returned £169 as the immediate result of an evening's good-natured fun with the Oxford boys.

After delivering my lecture many times in different places, a prominent publishing house in London offered me £1,200 ($6,000), for the copyright. This offer I declined, not that I thought the lecture worth more money, but because I had engaged to deliver it in several towns and cities, and I thought the publication would be detrimental to the public delivery of my lecture. It was a source of very considerable emolument to me, bringing in much money, which went towards the redemption of my pecuniary obligations, so that the lecture itself was an admirable illustration of "The Art of Money Getting."

CHAPTER XXXI

RICHARD'S HIMSELF AGAIN

In 1859 I returned to the United States. During my last visit abroad I had secured many novelties for the Museum, including the Albino Family, which I engaged at Amsterdam, and Thiodon's mechanical theatre, which I found at Southampton, beside purchasing many curiosities. These things all afforded me a liberal commission, and thus, by constant and earnest effort, I made much money, besides what I derived from the Tom Thumb exhibitions, my lectures, and other enterprises. All of this money, as well as my wife's income and a considerable sum raised by selling a portion of her property, was faithfully devoted to the one great object of my life at that period—my extrication from those crushing clock debts. I worked and I saved. When my wife and youngest daughter were not boarding in Bridgeport, they lived frugally in the suburbs, in a small one-story house which was hired at the rate of $150 a year. I had now been struggling about four years with the difficulties of my one great financial mistake, and the end still seemed to be far off. I felt that the land purchased by my wife in East Bridgeport at the assignees' sale would, after a while, increase rapidly in value; and on the strength of this expectation more money was borrowed for the sake of taking up the clock notes, and some of the East Bridgeport property was sold in single lots, the proceeds going to the same object.

At last, in March, 1860, all the clock indebtedness was satisfactorily extinguished, excepting some $20,000 which I had bound myself to take up within a certain number of months, my friend,

James D. Johnson, guaranteeing my bond to that effect. Mr. Johnson was by far my most effective agent in working me through these clock troubles, and in aiding to bring them to a successful conclusion. Another man, however, who pretended to be my friend, and whom I liberally paid to assist in bringing me out of my difficulties, gained my confidence, possessed himself of a complete knowledge of the situation of my affairs, and then coolly proposed to Mr. Johnson to counteract all my efforts to get out of debt, and to divide between them what could be got out of my estate. Failing in this, the scoundrel, taking advantage of the confidence reposed in him, slyly arranged with the owners of clock notes to hold on to them, and share with him whatever they might gain by adopting his advice, he assuming that he knew all my secrets and that I would soon come out all right again. Thus I had to contend with foes from within as well as without; but the "spotting" of this traitor was worth something, for it opened my eyes in relation to former transactions in which I had intrusted large sums of money to his hands, and it put me on guard for the future. But I bear no malice towards him; I only pity him, as I do any man who knows so little of the true road to contentment and happiness as to think that it lies in the direction of dishonesty.

I need not dwell upon the details of what I suffered from the doings of those heartless, unscrupulous men who fatten upon the misfortunes of others. It is enough to say that I triumphed over them and all my troubles. I was once more a free man. At last I was able to make proclamation that "Richard's himself again"; that Barnum was once more on his feet. The Museum had not flourished greatly in the hands of Messrs. Greenwood & Butler, and so, when I was free, I was quite willing to take back the property upon terms that were entirely satisfactory to them. I had once retired from the establishment a man of independent fortune; I was now ready to return, to make, if possible, another fortune.

On the 17th of March, 1860, Messrs. Butler & Greenwood signed an agreement to sell and deliver to me on the following Saturday, March 24th, their good will and entire interest in the Museum collection. This fact was thoroughly circulated and it was everywhere announced in blazing posters, placards and advertisements which were headed, "Barnum on his feet again." It was furthermore stated that the Museum would be closed, March 24th, for one week for repairs and general renovation, to be reopened, March 31st, under the management and proprietorship of its original owner. It was also announced that on the night of closing I would address the audience from the stage.

The American Museum, decorated on that occasion, as on holidays, with a brilliant display of flags and banners, was filled to its utmost capacity, and I experienced profound delight at seeing hundreds of old friends of both sexes in the audience. I lacked but four months of being fifty years of age; but I felt all the vigor and ambition that fired me when I first took possession of the premises twenty years before; and I was confident that the various experiences of that score of years would be valuable to me in my second effort to secure an independence.

At the rising of the curtain and before the play commenced, I stepped on the stage and was received by the large and brilliant audience with an enthusiasm far surpassing anything of the kind I had ever experienced or witnessed in a public career of a quarter of a century. Indeed, this tremendous demonstration nearly broke me down, and my voice faltered and tears came to my eyes as I thought of this magnificent conclusion to the trials and struggles of the past four years. Recovering myself, however, I bowed my grateful acknowledgments for the reception, and addressed the audience in an off-hand speech which was received with almost tumultuous applause. At nearly fifty years of age, I was now once more before the public with the promise to put on a full head of steam, to "rush things," to give double or treble the amount of attractions ever before offered at the Museum, and to devote all my own time and services to the enterprise. In return, I asked that the public should give my efforts the patronage they merited, and the public took me at my word. The daily number of visitors at once more than doubled, and my exertions to gratify them with rapid changes and novelties never tired.

The announcement that "Richard's himself again"—that I was at last out of the financial entanglement—was variously received in the community. That portion of the press which had followed me with abuse when I was down, under the belief that my case was past recovery, were chary in allusions to the new state of things, or passed them over without comment. The sycophants always knew I would get up again, "and said so at the time"; the many and noble journals which had stood by me and upheld me in my misfortunes, were of course rejoiced, and their words of sincere congratulations gave me a higher satisfaction than I have power of language to acknowledge. Letters of congratulation came in upon me from every quarter. Friendly hands that had never been withheld during the long period of my misfortune, were now extended with a still heartier grip. I never knew till now the warmth and number of my friends.

My editorial friend, Mr. Robert Bonner, of the New York *Ledger,* sincerely congratulated me upon my full and complete restoration. I had some new plays which were adapted from very popular stories which had been written for Mr. Bonner's paper, and I went to him to purchase, if I could, the large cuts he had used to advertise these stories in his street placards. He at once generously offered to lend them to me as long as I wished to use them and tendered me his services in any way. Mr. Bonner was the boldest of advertisers, following me closely in the field in which I was the pioneer, and to his judicious use of printer's ink he owes the fine fortune which he so worthily deserves and enjoys.

Nor must I neglect to state that a large number of my creditors who held the clock notes proved very magnanimous in taking into consideration the gross deception which had put me in their power. Not a few of them said to me in substance: "You never supposed you had made yourself liable for this debt; you were deluded into it; it is not right that it should be held over you to keep you hopelessly down; take it, and pay me such percentage as, under the circumstances, it is possible for you to pay." But for such men and such consideration I fear I should never have got on my feet again; and of the many who rejoiced in my bettered fortune, not a few were of this class of my creditors.

My old friend, the Boston *Saturday Evening Gazette,* which printed a few cheering poetical lines of consolation and hope when I was down, now gave me the following from the same graceful pen, conveying glowing words of congratulation at my rise again:

ANOTHER WORD FOR BARNUM.

BARNUM, your hand! The struggle o'er,
  You face the world and ask no favor;
You stand where you have stood before,
  The old salt hasn't lost its savor.
You now can laugh with friends, at foes,
  Ne'er heeding Mrs. Grundy's tattle;
You've dealt and taken sturdy blows,
  Regardless of the rabble's prattle.

Not yours the heart to harbor ill
  'Gainst those who've dealt in trivial jesting;
You pass them with the same good will
  Erst shown when they their wit were testing.
You're the same Barnum that we knew,
  You're good for years, still fit for labor,
Be as of old, be bold and true,
  Honest as man, as friend, as neighbor.

CHAPTER XXXII

I was now fairly embarked on board the good old ship American Museum, to try once more my skill as captain, and to see what fortune the voyage would bring me. Curiosities began to pour into the Museum halls, and I was eager for enterprises in the show line, whether as part of the Museum itself, or as outside accessories or accompaniments. Among the first to give me a call, with attractions sure to prove a success, was James C. Adams, of hard-earned, grizzly-bear fame. This extraordinary man was eminently what is called "a character." He was universally known as "Grizzly Adams," from the fact that he had captured a great many grizzly bears, at the risk and cost of fearful encounters and perils. He was brave, and with his bravery there was enough of the romantic in his nature to make him a real hero. For many years a hunter and trapper in the Rocky and Sierra Nevada Mountains, he acquired a recklessness, which, added to his natural invincible courage, rendered him one of the most striking men of the age, and he was emphatically a man of pluck. A month after I had re-purchased the Museum, he arrived in New York with his famous collection of California animals, captured by himself, consisting of twenty or thirty immense grizzly bears, at the head of which stood "Old Sampson," together with several wolves, half a dozen different species of California bears, California lions, tigers, buffalo, elk, and "Old Neptune," the great sea-lion from the Pacific.

Old Adams had trained all these monsters so that with him they were as docile as kittens, though many of the most ferocious among them would attack a stranger without hesitation, if he came within their grasp. In fact the training of these animals was no fool's play, as Old Adams learned to his cost, for the terrific blows which he received from time to time, while teaching them "docility," finally cost him his life.

Adams called on me immediately on his arrival in New York. He was dressed in his hunter's suit of buckskin, trimmed with the skins and bordered with the hanging tails of small Rocky Mountain animals; his cap consisting of the skin of a wolf's head and shoulders, from which depended several tails, and under which appeared his stiff, bushy, gray hair and his long, white, grizzly beard; in fact Old Adams was quite as much of a show as his beasts. They had come around Cape Horn on the clipper ship "Golden Fleece," and a sea voyage of three and a half months had probably not added much to the beauty or neat appearance of the old bear-hunter. During our conversation, Grizzly Adams took off his cap, and showed me the top of his head. His skull was literally broken in. It had on various occasions been struck by the fearful paws of his grizzly students; and the last blow, from the bear called "General Fremont," had laid open his brain so that its workings were plainly visible. I remarked that I thought it was a dangerous wound and might possibly prove fatal.

"Yes," replied Adams, "that will fix me out. It had nearly healed, but old Fremont opened it for me, for the third or fourth time, before I left California, and he did his business so thoroughly, I'm a used-up man. However I reckon I may live six months or a year yet." This was spoken as coolly as if he had been talking about the life of a dog. The immediate object of old Adams in calling upon me was this: I had purchased, a week previously, one-half interest in his California menagerie, from a man who had come by way of the Isthmus from California, and who claimed to own an equal interest with Adams in the show. Adams declared that the man had only advanced him some money, and did not possess the right to sell half of the concern. However, the man held a bill of sale for half of the "California Menagerie," and old Adams finally consented to accept me as an equal partner in the speculation, saying that he guessed I could do the managing part, and he would show up the animals. I obtained a canvas tent, and erecting it on the present site of Wallack's Theatre, Adams there opened his novel California Menagerie. On the morning of opening, a band of music preceded a procession of animal cages down Broadway and up the Bowery, old Adams dressed in his hunting costume, heading the line, with a platform wagon on which were placed three immense grizzly bears, two of which he held by chains, while he was mounted on the back of the largest grizzly, which stood in the centre and was not secured in any manner whatever. This was the bear known as "General Fremont," and so docile had he become that Adams said he had used him as a pack-bear to carry his cooking and hunting apparatus through the mountains for six months, and had ridden him hundreds of miles. But apparently docile as were many of these animals, there was not one among them that would not occasionally give Adams a sly blow or a sly bite when a good chance offered; hence old Adams was but a wreck of his former self, and expressed pretty nearly the truth when he said:

"Mr. Barnum, I am not the man I was five years ago. Then I felt able to stand the hug of any grizzly living, and was always glad to encounter, single handed, any sort of an animal that dared present himself. But I have been beaten to a jelly, torn almost limb from limb, and nearly chawed up and spit out by these treacherous grizzly bears. However, I am good for a few months yet, and by that time I hope we shall gain enough to make my old woman comfortable, for I have been absent from her some years."

His wife came from Massachusetts to New York and nursed him. Dr. Johns dressed his wounds every day, and not only told

Adams he could not recover, but assured his friends that probably a very few weeks would lay him in his grave. But Adams was as firm as adamant and as resolute as a lion. Among the thousands who saw him dressed in his grotesque hunter's suit, and witnessed the seeming vigor with which he "performed" the savage monsters, beating and whipping them into apparently the most perfect docility, probably not one suspected that this rough, fierce looking, powerful demi-savage, as he appeared to be, was suffering intense pain from his broken skull and fevered system, and that nothing kept him from stretching himself on his death-bed but his most indomitable and extraordinary will.

Old Adams liked to astonish others, as he often did, with his astounding stories, but no one could astonish him; he had seen everything and knew everything, and I was anxious to get a chance of exposing this weak point to him. A fit occasion soon presented itself. One day, while engaged in my office at the Museum, a man with marked Teutonic features and accent approached the door and asked if I would like to buy a pair of living golden pigeons.

"Yes," I replied, "I would like a flock of golden pigeons, if I could buy them for their weight in silver; for there are no 'golden' pigeons in existence, unless they are made from the pure metal."

"You shall see some golden pigeons alive," he replied, at the same time entering my office, and closing the door after him. He then removed the lid from a small basket which he carried in his hand, and sure enough, there were snugly ensconsed a pair of beautiful, living ruff-necked pigeons, as yellow as saffron, and as bright as a double-eagle fresh from the mint.

I confess I was somewhat staggered at this sight and quickly asked the man where those birds came from. A dull, lazy smile crawled over the sober face of my German visitor, as he replied in a slow, guttural tone of voice:

"What you think yourself?"

Catching his meaning, I quickly said: "I think it is a humbug."

"Of course, I know you will say so; because you 'forstha' such things; so I shall not try to humbug you; I have color them myself."

On further inquiry I learned that this German was a chemist, and that he possessed the art of coloring birds any hue desired, and yet retain a natural gloss on the feathers, which gave every shade the appearance of reality.

"I can paint a green pigeon or a blue pigeon, a gray pigeon or a black pigeon, a brown pigeon or a pigeon half blue or half green," said the German; "and if you prefer it, I can paint them pink or purple, or give you a little of each color, and make you a rainbow pigeon."

The "rainbow pigeon" did not strike me as particularly desirable; but thinking here was a good chance to catch "Grizzly Adams," I bought the pair of golden pigeons for ten dollars, and sent them up to the "Happy Family" (where I knew Adams would soon see them), marked, "Golden Pigeons, from California." Mr. Taylor, the great pacificator, who had charge of the Happy Family, soon came down in a state of excitement.

"Really, Mr. Barnum," said he, "I could not think of putting those elegant golden pigeons into the Happy Family,—they are too valuable a bird, and they might get injured; they are by far the most beautiful pigeons I ever saw; and as they are so rare, I would not jeopardize their lives for anything."

"Well," said I, "you may put them in a separate cage, properly labelled."

Monsieur Guillaudeu, the naturalist and taxidermist of the Museum, had been attached to that establishment since the year it was founded, in 1810. He is a Frenchman, and has read everything upon natural history that was ever published in his own or in the English language. When he saw the "Golden Pigeons from California," he was considerably astonished. He examined them with great delight for half an hour, expatiating upon their beautiful color and the near resemblance which every feature bore to the American ruff-necked pigeon. He soon came to my office, and said:

"Mr. Barnum, these golden pigeons are superb, but they cannot be from California. Audubon mentions no such bird in his work upon American Ornithology."

I told him he had better take Audubon home with him that night, and perhaps by studying him attentively he would see occasion to change his mind.

The next day, the old naturalist called at my office and remarked:

"Mr. Barnum, those pigeons are a more rare bird than you imagine. They are not mentioned by Linnæus, Cuvier, Goldsmith, or any other writer on natural history, so far as I have been able to discover. I expect they must have come from some unexplored portion of Australia."

"Never mind," I replied, "we may get more light on the subject, perhaps, before long. We will continue to label them 'California Pigeons' until we can fix their nativity elsewhere."

The next morning, "Old Grizzly Adams" passed through the Museum when his eyes fell on the "Golden California Pigeons." He looked a moment and doubtless admired. He soon after came to my office.

"Mr. Barnum," said he, "you must let me have those California pigeons."

"I can't spare them," I replied.

"But you must spare them. All the birds and animals from California ought to be together. You own half of my California menagerie, and you must lend me those pigeons."

"Mr. Adams, they are too rare and valuable a bird to be hawked about in that manner."

"Oh, don't be a fool," replied Adams. "Rare bird, indeed! Why they are just as common in California as any other pigeon! I could have brought a hundred of them from San Francisco, if I had thought of it."

"But why did you not think of it?" I asked, with a suppressed smile.

"Because they are so common there," said Adams, "I did not think they would be any curiosity here. I have eaten them in pigeon-pies hundreds of times, and have shot them by the thousands!"

I was ready to burst with laughter to see how readily Adams swallowed the bait, but maintaining the most rigid gravity, I replied:

"Oh well, Mr. Adams, if they are really so common in California, you had probably better take them, and you may write over and have half a dozen pairs sent to me for the Museum."

"All right," said Adams, "I will send over to a friend in San Francisco, and you shall have them here in a couple of months."

I told Adams that, for certain reasons, I would prefer to have him change the label so as to have it read: "Golden Pigeons from Australia."

"Well, I will call them what you like," said Adams; "I suppose they are probably about as plenty in Australia as they are in California."

Six or eight weeks after this incident, I was in the California Menagerie, and I noticed that the "Golden Pigeons" had assumed a frightfully mottled appearance. Their feathers had grown out and they were half white. Adams had been so busy with his bears that he had not noticed the change. I called him up to the pigeon cage, and remarked:

"Mr. Adams, I fear you will lose your Golden Pigeons; they must be very sick; I observe they are turning quite pale."

Adams looked at them a moment with astonishment, then turning to me, and seeing that I could not suppress a smile, he indignantly exclaimed:

"Blast the Golden Pigeons! You had better take them back to the Museum. You can't humbug me with your painted pigeons!"

This was too much, and "I laughed till I cried," to witness the mixed look of astonishment and vexation which marked the grizzly features of old Adams.

After the exhibition on Thirteenth Street and Broadway had been open six weeks, the doctor insisted that Adams should sell out his share in the animals and settle up all his worldly affairs, for he assured him that he was growing weaker every day, and his earthly existence must soon terminate. "I shall live a good deal longer than you doctors think for," replied Adams doggedly; and then, seeming after all to realize the truth of the doctor's assertion, he turned to me and said: "Well, Mr. Barnum, you must buy me out." He named his price for his half of the "show," and I accepted his offer. We had arranged to exhibit the bears in Connecticut and Massachusetts during the summer, in connection with a circus, and Adams insisted that I should hire him to travel for the season and exhibit the bears in their curious performances. He offered to go for $60 per week and travelling expenses of himself and wife. I replied that I would gladly engage him as long as he could stand it, but I advised him to give up business and go to his home in Massachusetts; "for," I remarked, "you are growing weaker every day, and at best cannot stand it more than a fortnight."

"What will you give me extra if I will travel and exhibit the bears every day for ten weeks?" added old Adams, eagerly.

"Five hundred dollars," I replied, with a laugh.

"Done!" exclaimed Adams, "I will do it, so draw up an agreement to that effect at once. But mind you, draw it payable to my wife, for I may be too weak to attend to business after the ten weeks are up, and if I perform my part of the contract, I want her to get the $500 without any trouble."

I drew up a contract to pay him $60 per week for his services, and if he continued to exhibit the bears for ten consecutive weeks I was then to hand him, or his wife, $500 extra.

"You have lost your $500!" exclaimed Adams on taking the contract, "for I am bound to live and earn it."

"I hope you may, with all my heart, and a hundred years more if you desire it," I replied.

"Call me a fool if I don't earn the $500!" exclaimed Adams, with a triumphant laugh.

The "show" started off in a few days, and at the end of a fortnight I met it at Hartford, Connecticut.

"Well," said I, "Adams, you seem to stand it pretty well. I hope you and your wife are comfortable?"

"Yes." he replied, with a laugh; "and you may as well try to be comfortable, too, for your $500 is a goner."

"All right," I replied, "I hope you will grow better every day."

But I saw by his pale face and other indications that he was rapidly failing. In three weeks more, I met him again at New Bedford, Massachusetts. It seemed to me, then, that he could not live a week, for his eyes were glassy and his hands trembled, but his pluck was as great as ever.

"This hot weather is pretty bad for me," he said, "but my ten weeks are half expired, and I am good for your $500, and, probably, a month or two longer."

This was said with as much bravado as if he was offering to bet upon a horse-race. I offered to pay him half of the $500 if he would give up and go home; but he peremptorily declined making any compromise whatever. I met him the ninth week in Boston. He had failed considerably since I last saw him, but he still continued to exhibit the bears although he was too weak to lead them in, and he chuckled over his almost certain triumph. I laughed in return, and sincerely congratulated him on his nerve and probable success. I remained with him until the tenth week was finished, and handed him his $500. He took it with a leer of satisfaction, and remarked that he was sorry I was a teetotaler, for he would like to stand treat!

After the death of Adams, the grizzly bears and other animals were added to the collection in my Museum, and I employed Herr Driesbach, the celebrated lion-tamer, as an exhibitor. Some time afterwards the bears were sold to a menagerie company, but I kept "Old Neptune," the sea-lion, for several years, sending him occasionally for exhibition in other cities, as far west as Chicago. This noble and ferocious animal was a very great curiosity and attracted great attention. He was kept in a large tank, which was supplied with salt water every day from the Fall River steamboats, whose deck hands filled my barrels on every passage to the city with salt water from the deepest part of Long Island Sound. On his tours through the country the sea-lion lived very well in fresh water.

It was at one time my serious intention to engage in an American Indian Exhibition on a stupendous scale. I proposed to secure at the far West not less than one hundred of the best specimens of full-blood Indians, with their squaws and papooses, their paint, ponies, dresses and weapons, for a general tour throughout the United States and Europe. The plan comprehended a grand entry at every town and city where the Indians were to exhibit—the Indians in all the glory of paint and feathers, beads and bright blankets, riding on their ponies, followed by tame buffaloes, elks and antelopes; then an exhibition on a lot large enough to admit of a display of all the Indian games and dances, their method of hunting, their style of cooking, living, etc. Such an exhibition is perfectly practicable now to any one who has the capital and tact to undertake it, and a sure fortune would follow the enterprise.

On the 13th of October, 1860, the Prince of Wales, then making a tour in the United States, in company with his suite, visited the American Museum. This was a very great compliment, since it was the only place of amusement the Prince attended in this country. Unfortunately, I was in Bridgeport at the time and the Museum was in charge of my manager, Mr. Greenwood. Knowing that the name of the American Museum was familiar throughout Europe, I was quite confident of a call from the Prince, and from regard to his filial feelings I had, a day or two after his arrival in New York, ordered to be removed to a dark closet a frightful wax figure of his royal mother, which, for nineteen years, had excited the admiration of the million and which bore a placard with the legend, "An exact likeness of Her Majesty Queen Victoria, taken from life." Mr. Greenwood, who was an Englishman, was deeply impressed with the condescension of the Prince, and backed his way through the halls, followed by the Prince, the Duke of Newcastle, and other members of the royal suite, and he actually trembled as he attempted to do the reception honors. On leaving the Museum the Prince asked to see Mr. Barnum, and when he was told that I was out of town, he remarked: "We have missed the most interesting feature of the establishment." A few days afterwards, when the Prince was in Boston, happening to be in that city, I sent my card to him at the Revere House, and was cordially received. He smiled when I reminded him that I had seen him when he was a little boy, on the occasion of one of my visits to Buckingham Palace with General Tom Thumb. The Prince told me that he was much pleased with his recent inspection of my Museum, and that he and his suite had left their autographs in the establishment, as mementos of their visit.

When I arrived in Boston, by the by, on this visit, the streets were thronged with the military and citizens assembled to receive the Prince of Wales, and I had great difficulty, in starting from the depot to the Revere House, in getting through the assembled crowd. At last, a policeman espied me, and taking me for Senator Stephen

A. Douglas, he cried out, at the top of his voice: "Make way there for Judge Douglas's carriage." The crowd opened a passage for my carriage at short notice, and shouted out "Douglas, Douglas, hurrah for Douglas." I took off my hat and bowed, smiling from the windows on each side of my carriage; the cheers and enthusiasm increased as I advanced, and all the way to the Revere House I continued to bow Judge Douglas's grateful acknowledgments for the enthusiastic reception. There must have been at least fifty thousand people who joined in this spontaneous demonstration in honor of Judge Douglas.

Meanwhile, the Museum flourished better than ever; and I began to make large holes in the mortgages which covered the property of my wife in New York and in Connecticut. Still, there was an immense amount of debts resting upon all her real estate, and nothing but time, economy, industry and diligence would remove the burdens.

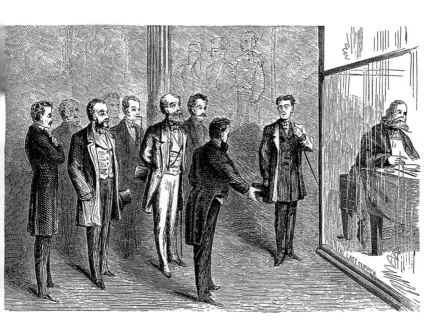

CHAPTER XXXIII

On the 13th of October, 1860, the American Museum was the scene of another re-opening, which was, in fact, the commencement of the fall dramatic season, the summer months having been devoted to pantomime. A grand flourish of trumpets in the way of newspaper advertisements and flaming posters drew a crowded house. Among other attractions, it was announced that Mr. Barnum would introduce a mysterious novelty never before seen in that establishment. I appeared upon the stage behind a small table, in front of which was nailed a white sack, on which was inscribed, in large letters, "The cat let out of the bag." I then stated that, having spent two of the summer months in the country, leaving the Museum in charge of Mr. Greenwood, he had purchased a curiosity with which he was not satisfied; but, for my part, I thought he had received his money's worth, and I proposed to exhibit it to the audience, for the purpose of getting their opinion on the subject. I stated that a farmer came in from the country, and said he had got a "cherry-colored cat" at home which he would like to sell; that Mr. Greenwood gave him a writing promising to pay him twenty-five dollars for such a cat delivered in good health, provided it was not artificially colored; and that the cat was then in the bag in front of the table, ready for exhibition. Whereupon, my assistant drew from the bag a common black cat, and informed the audience that when the farmer brought his "cherry-colored cat," he quietly remarked to Mr. Greenwood that, of course, he meant "a cat of the color of black cherries." The laughter that followed this narration was uproarious, and the audience unanimously voted that the "cherry-colored cat," all things considered, was well worth twenty-five dollars. The cat, adorned with a collar bearing the inscription, "The Cherry-colored Cat," was then placed in the cage of the "Happy Family," and the story getting into the newspapers, it became another advertisement of the Museum.

In 1861, I learned that some fishermen at the mouth of the St. Lawrence had succeeded in capturing a living white whale, and I was also informed that a whale of this kind, if placed in a box lined with sea-weed and partially filled with salt water, could be transported by land to a considerable distance, and be kept alive. It was simply necessary that an attendant, supplied with a barrel of salt water and a sponge, should keep the mouth and blow-hole of the whale constantly moist. It seemed incredible that a living whale could be "expressed" by railroad on a five days' journey, and although I knew nothing of the white whale or its habits, since I had never seen one, I determined to experiment in that direction. Landsman as I was, I believed that I was quite as competent as a St. Lawrence fisherman to superintend the capture and transportation of a live white whale.

When I had fully made up my mind to attempt the task, I made every provision for the expedition, and took precaution against every conceivable contingency. I determined upon the capture and transport to my Museum of at least two living whales, and prepared in the basement of the brick building a brick and cement tank, forty feet long, and eighteen feet wide, for the reception of the marine monsters. When this was done, taking two trusty assistants, I started upon my whaling expedition. Going by rail to Quebec, and thence by the Grand Trunk Railroad, ninety miles, to Wells River, where I chartered a sloop to Elbow Island (Isle au Coudres), in the St. Lawrence River, and found the place populated by Canadian French people of the most ignorant and dirty description. They were hospitable, but frightfully filthy, and they gained their livelihood by farming and fishing. Immense quantities of maple sugar are made there, and in exploring about the island, we saw hundreds of birch-bark buckets suspended to the trees to catch the sap. After numerous consultations, extending over three whole days, with a party of twenty-four fishermen, whose gibberish was almost as untranslatable as it was unbearable, I succeeded in contracting for their services to capture for me, alive and unharmed, a couple of white whales, scores of which could at all times be discovered by their "spouting" within sight of the island. I was to pay these men a stipulated price per day for their labor, and if they secured the whales they were to have a liberal bonus.

The plan decided upon was to plant in the river a "kraal," composed of stakes driven down in the form of a V, leaving the broad end open for the whales to enter. This was done in a shallow place, with the point of the kraal towards shore; and if by chance one or more whales should enter the trap at high water, my fishermen were to occupy the entrance with their boats, and keep up a tremendous splashing and noise till the tide receded, when the frightened whales would find themselves nearly "high and dry," or with too little water to enable them to swim, and their capture would be the next thing in order. This was to be effected by securing a slip-noose of stout rope over their tails, and towing them to the sea-weed lined boxes in which they were to be transported to New York.

All this was simple enough "on paper"; but several days elapsed before a single spout was seen inside the kraal, though scores of whales were constantly around and near it. In time, it became exceedingly aggravating to see the whales glide so near the trap without going into it, and our patience was sorely tried. One day a whale actually went into the kraal, and the fishermen proposed to capture it; but I wanted another, and while we waited for number two to go in, number one, knowing the proverb, probably, and having an eye to his own interests, went out.   Two days afterwards, I was awakened at daylight by a great noise, and amid the clamor of many voices I caught the cheering news that two whales were even then within the kraal, and hastily dressing myself, I took a boat for the exciting scene.   The real difficulty, which was to get the whales into the trap, was now over, and the details of capture and transportation could safely be left to my trusty assistants and the fishermen.   What they were to do until the tide went out and thereafter was once more fully explained; and after depositing money enough to pay the bill, if the capture was successsful, I started at once for Quebec.   There I learned by telegraph that both whales had been caught, boxed, and put on board sloop for the nearest point where they could be transshipped in the cars.   I had made every arrangement with the railway officials, and had engaged a special car for the precious and curious freight.

Elated as I was at the result of this novel enterprise, I had no idea of hiding my light under a bushel, and I immediately wrote a full account of the expedition, its intention, and its success, for publication in the Quebec and Montreal newspapers.   I also prepared a large number of brief notices which I left at every station on the line, instructing telegraph operators to "take off" all "whaling messages" that passed over the wires to New York, and to inform their fellow townsmen at what hour the whales would pass through each place.   The result of these arrangements may be imagined; at every station crowds of people came to the cars to see the whales which were travelling by land to Barnum's Museum, and those who did not see the monsters with their own eyes, at least saw some one who had seen them, and I thus secured a tremendous advertisement, seven hundred miles long, for the American Museum.

When I arrived in New York, a dozen despatches had come from the "whaling expedition," and they continued to come every few hours.   These I bulletined in front of the Museum and sent copies to the papers. The excitement was intense, and when at last these marine monsters arrived and were swimming in the tank that had been prepared for them, anxious thousands literally rushed to see the strangest curiosities ever exhibited in New York.

Thus was my first whaling expedition a great success; but I did not know how to feed or to take care of the monsters, and, moreover, they were in fresh water, and this, with the bad air in the basement, may have hastened their death, which occurred a few days after their arrival, but not before thousands of people had seen them. Not at all discouraged, I resolved to try again. My plan now was to connect the water of New York bay with the basement of the Museum by means of iron pipes under the street, and a steam engine on the dock to pump the water. This I actually did at a cost of several thousand dollars, with an extra thousand to the aldermanic "ring" for the privilege, and I constructed another tank in the second floor of the building. This tank was built of slate and French glass plates six feet long, five feet broad, and one inch thick, imported expressly for the purpose, and the tank, when completed, was twenty-four feet square, and cost $4,000. It was kept constantly supplied with what would be called Hibernically, "fresh" salt water, and inside of it I soon had two white whales, caught, as the first had been, hundreds of miles below Quebec, to which city they were carried by a sailing vessel, and from thence were brought by railway to New York.

Of this whole enterprise, I confess I was very proud that I had originated it and brought it to such successful conclusion. It was a very great sensation, and it added thousands of dollars to my treasury. The whales, however, soon˙ died—their sudden and immense popularity was too much for them—and I then despatched agents to the coast of Labrador, and not many weeks thereafter I had two more live whales disporting themselves in my monster aquarium. Certain envious people started the report that my whales were only porpoises, but this petty malice was turned to good account, for Professor Agassiz, of Harvard University, came to see them, and gave me a certificate that they were genuine white whales, and this indorsement I published far and wide.

The tank which I had built in the basement served for a yet more interesting exhibition. On the 12th of August, 1861, I began to exhibit the first and only genuine hippopotamus that had ever been seen in America, and for several weeks the Museum was thronged by the curious who came to see the monster. I advertised him extensively and ingeniously, as "the great behemoth of the Scriptures," giving a full description of the animal and his habits, and thousands of cultivated people, biblical students, and others, were attracted to this novel exhibition. There was quite as much excitement in the city over this wonder in the animal creation as there was in London when the first hippopotamus was placed in the zoölogical collection in Regent's Park.

Having a stream of salt water at my command at every high tide, I was enabled to make splendid additions to the beautiful aquarium, which I was the first to introduce into this country. I not only procured living sharks, porpoises, sea horses, and many rare fish from the sea in the vicinity of New York, but in the summer of 1861 I despatched a fishing smack and crew to the Island of Bermuda and its neighborhood, whence they brought scores of specimens of the beautiful "angel fish," and numerous other tropical fish of brilliant colors and unique forms. These fish were a great attraction to all classes, and especially to naturalists and others, who commended me for serving the ends of science as well as amusement. But as cold weather approached, these tropical fish began to die, and before the following spring they were all gone. I, therefore, replenished this portion of my aquaria during the summer, and for several summers in succession, by sending a special vessel to the Gulf for specimens. These operations were very expensive, but I really did not care for the cost, if I could only secure valuable attractions.

In the same year, I bought out the Aquarial Gardens in Boston, and soon after removed the collection to the Museum. I had now the finest assemblage of fresh as well as salt water fish ever exhibited, and with a standing offer of one hundred dollars for every living brook-trout, weighing four pounds or more, which might be brought to me, I soon had three or four of these beauties, which trout-fishermen from all parts of the country came to New York to see. But the trout department of my Museum required so much care, and was attended with such constant risks, that I finally gave it up.

In December, 1861, I made one of my most "palpable hits." I was visited at the Museum by a most remarkable dwarf, who was a sharp, intelligent little fellow, with a deal of drollery and wit. He had a splendid head, was perfectly formed, was very attractive, and, in short, for a "showman" he was a perfect treasure. His name, he told me, was George Washington Morrison Nutt, and his father was Major Rodnia Nutt, a substantial farmer, of Manchester, New Hampshire. I was not long in despatching an efficient agent to Manchester, and in overcoming the competition with other showmen who were equally eager to secure this extraordinary pigmy. The terms upon which I engaged him for three years were so large that he was christened the $30,000 Nutt; I, in the meantime, conferring upon him the title of Commodore. As soon as I engaged him, placards, posters and the columns of the newspapers proclaimed the presence of "Commodore Nutt," at the Museum. I also procured for the Commodore a pair of Shetland ponies, miniature coachman and footman in livery, gold-mounted harness and an elegant little carriage which, when closed, represented a gigantic English walnut. The little Commodore attracted great attention and grew rapidly in public favor. General Tom Thumb was then travelling in the South and West. For some years he had not been exhibited in New York, and during these years he had increased considerably in rotundity and had changed much in his general appearance. It was a singular fact, however, that Commodore Nutt was almost a *fac-simile* of General Tom Thumb as he looked half-a-dozen years before. Consequently, very many of my patrons, not making allowance for the time which had elapsed since they had last seen the General, declared that I was trying to play "Mrs. Gamp" with my "Mrs. Harris"; that there was, in fact, no such person as "Commodore Nutt"; and that I was exhibiting my old friend Tom Thumb under a new name. The mistake was very natural, and to me it was very laughable, for the more I tried to convince people of their error the more they winked and looked wise, and said, "It's pretty well done, but you can't take me in."

Commodore Nutt enjoyed the joke very much. He would sometimes half admit the deception, simply to add to the bewilderment of the doubting portion of my visitors. After he had been in the Museum a few weeks, I took the Commodore to Bridgeport to spend a couple of days by way of relaxation. Many of the citizens of Bridgeport, who had known Tom Thumb from his birth, would salute the Commodore as General Tom Thumb. The little fellow would return these salutes, for he delighted in keeping up the illusion.

It was evident that here was an opportunity to turn all doubts into hard cash by simply bringing the two dwarf Dromios together, and showing them on the same platform. I therefore induced Tom Thumb to bring his Western engagements to a close, and to appear for four weeks, beginning with August 11, 1862, in my Museum. Announcements headed "The Two Dromios," and "Two Smallest Men, and Greatest Curiosities Living," as I expected, drew large crowds to see them, and many came especially to solve their doubts with regard to the genuineness of the "Nutt." But here I was considerably nonplussed, for astonishing as it may seem, the doubts of many of the visitors were confirmed! The sharp people who were determined "not to be humbugged, anyhow," still declared that Commodore Nutt was General Tom Thumb, and that the little fellow whom I was trying to pass off as Tom Thumb was no more like the General than he was like the man in the Moon. It is very amusing to see how people will sometimes deceive themselves by being too incredulous.

In 1862, I sent the Commodore to Washington, and joining him there, I received an invitation from President Lincoln to call at the White House with my little friend. Arriving at the appointed hour I was informed that the President was in a special cabinet meeting, but that he had left word if I called to be shown in to him with the Commodore. These were dark days in the rebellion and I felt that my visit, if not ill-timed, must at all events be brief. When we were admitted Mr. Lincoln received us cordially, and introduced us to the members of the cabinet. When Mr. Chase was introduced as the Secretary of the Treasury, the little Commodore remarked:

"I suppose you are the gentleman who is spending so much of Uncle Sam's money?"

"No, indeed," said Secretary of War Stanton, very promptly: "I am spending the money."

"Well," said Commodore Nutt, "it is in a good cause, anyhow, and I guess it will come out all right."

His apt remark created much amusement. Mr. Lincoln then bent down his long, lank body, and taking Nutt by the hand, he said:

"Commodore, permit me to give you a parting word of advice. When you are in command of your fleet, if you find yourself in danger of being taken prisoner, I advise you to wade ashore."

The Commodore found the laugh was against him, but placing himself at the side of the President, and gradually raising his

eyes up the whole length of Mr. Lincoln's very long legs, he replied:
"I guess, Mr. President, you could do better than I could."

Commodore Nutt and the Nova Scotia giantess, Anna Swan,
illustrate the old proverb sufficiently to show how extremes occasionally met in my Museum. He was the shortest of men and she was
the tallest of women. I first heard of her through a quaker who
came into my office one day and told me of a wonderful girl, seventeen years of age, who resided near him at Pictou, Nova Scotia, and
who was probably the tallest girl in the world. I asked him to
obtain her exact height, on his return home, which he did and sent
it to me, and I at once sent an agent who in due time came back
with Anna Swan. She was an intelligent and by no means ill-looking
girl, and during the long period while she was in my employ she
was visited by thousands of persons. After the burning of my
second Museum, she went to England, where she attracted great
attention.

For many years I had been in the habit of engaging parties of
American Indians from the far West to exhibit at the Museum, and
had sent two or more Indian companies to Europe, where they were
regarded as very great "curiosities." In 1864, ten or twelve chiefs
of as many different tribes visited the President of the United
States at Washington. By a pretty liberal outlay of money, I succeeded in inducing the interpreter to bring them to New York, and
to pass some days at my Museum. Of course, getting these Indians
to dance, or to give any illustration of their games or pastimes, was
out of the question. They were real chiefs of powerful tribes, and
would no more have consented to give an exhibition of themselves
than the Chief Magistrate of our own nation would have done.
Their interpreter could not therefore promise that they would remain
at the Museum for any definite time; "for," said he, "you can only
keep them just so long as they suppose all your patrons come to pay

them visits of honor. If they suspected that your Museum was a place where people paid for entering," he continued, "you could not keep them a moment after the discovery."

On their arrival at the Museum, therefore, I took them upon the stage and personally introduced them to the public. The Indians liked this attention from me, as they had been informed that I was the proprietor of the great establishment in which they were invited and honored guests. My patrons were of course pleased to see these old chiefs, as they knew they were the "*real* thing," and several of them were known to the public, either as being friendly or cruel to the whites. After one or two appearances upon the stage, I took them in carriages and visited the Mayor of New York in the Governor's room at the City Hall. Here the Mayor made them a speech of welcome, which being interpreted to the savages was responded to by a speech from one of the chiefs, in which he thanked the great "Father" of the city for his pleasant words, and for his kindness in pointing out the portraits of his predecessors hanging on the walls of the Governor's room.

On another occasion, I took them by special invitation to visit one of the large public schools up town. The teachers were pleased to see them, and arranged an exhibition of special exercises by the scholars, which they thought would be most likely to gratify their barbaric visitors. At the close of these exercises, one old chief arose, and simply said, "This is all new to us. We are mere unlearned sons of the forest, and cannot understand what we have seen and heard."

On other occasions, I took them to ride in Central Park, and through different portions of the city. At every street corner which we passed, they would express their astonishment to each other, at seeing the long rows of houses which extended both ways on either side of each cross-street. Of course, between each of these outside visits I would return with them to the Museum, and secure two or three appearances upon the stage to receive the people who had there congregated "to do them honor."

As they regarded me as their host, they did not hesitate to trespass upon my hospitality. Whenever their eyes rested upon a glittering shell among my specimens of conchology, especially if it had several brilliant colors, one would take off his coat, another his shirt, and insist that I should exchange my shell for their garment. When I declined the exchange, but on the contrary presented them with the coveted article, I soon found I had established a dangerous precedent. Immediately, they all commenced to beg for everything in my vast collection which they happened to take a liking to. This cost me many valuable specimens, and often "put me to my trumps" for an excuse to avoid giving them things which I could not part with.

The chief of one of the tribes one day discovered an ancient shirt of chain-mail which hung in one of my cases of antique armor. He was delighted with it, and declared he must have it. I tried all sorts of excuses to prevent his getting it, for it had cost me a hundred dollars and was a great curiosity. But the old man's eyes glistened, and he would not take "no" for an answer. "The Utes have killed my little child," he told me through the interpreter; and now he must have this steel shirt to protect himself; and when he returned to the Rocky Mountains he would have his revenge. I remained inexorable until he finally brought me a new buckskin Indian suit, which he insisted upon exchanging. I felt compelled to accept his proposal; and never did I see a man more delighted than he seemed to be when he took the mailed shirt into his hands. He fairly jumped up and down with joy. He ran to his lodging room, and soon appeared again with the coveted armor upon his body, and marched down one of the main halls of the Museum, with folded arms, and head erect, occasionally patting his breast with his right hand, as much as to say, "Now, Mr. Ute, look sharp, for I will soon be on the war path!"

Among these Indians were War Bonnet, Lean Bear, and Hand-in-the-water, chiefs of the Cheyennes; Yellow Buffalo, of the Kiowas; Yellow Bear, of the same tribe; Jacob, of the Caddos; and White Bull, of the Apaches. The little wiry chief known as Yellow Bear had killed many whites as they had travelled through the "far West." He was a sly, treacherous, blood-thirsty savage, who would think no more of scalping a family of women and children than a butcher would of wringing the neck of a chicken. But now he was on a mission to the "Great Father" at Washington, seeking for presents and favors for his tribe, and he pretended to be exceedingly meek and humble, and continually urged the interpreter to announce him as a "great friend to the white man." He would fawn about me, and although not speaking or understanding a word of our language, would try to convince me that he loved me dearly.

In exhibiting these Indian warriors on the stage, I explained to the large audiences the names and characteristics of each. When I came to Yellow Bear I would pat him familiarly upon the shoulder, which always caused him to look up to me with a pleasant smile, while he softly stroked down my arm with his right hand in the most loving manner. Knowing that he could not understand a word I said, I pretended to be complimenting him to the audience, while I was really saying something like the following:

"This little Indian, ladies and gentlemen, is Yellow Bear, chief of the Kiowas. He has killed, no doubt, scores of white persons, and he is probably the meanest, black-hearted rascal that lives in the far West." Here I patted him on the head, and he, supposing I was sounding his praises, would smile, fawn upon me, and stroke my arm, while I continued: "If the blood-thirsty little villain understood what I was saying, he would kill me in a moment; but as he thinks

I am complimenting him, I can safely state the truth to you, that he is a lying, thieving, treacherous, murderous monster. He has tortured to death poor, unprotected women, murdered their husbands, brained their helpless little ones; and he would gladly do the same to you or to me, if he thought he could escape punishment. This is but a faint description of the character of Yellow Bear." Here I gave him another patronizing pat on the head, and he, with a pleasant smile, bowed to the audience, as much as to say that my words were quite true, and that he thanked me very much for the high encomiums I had so generously heaped upon him.

After they had been about a week at the Museum, one of the chiefs discovered that visitors paid money for entering. This information he soon communicated to the other chiefs, and I heard an immediate murmur of discontent. Their eyes were opened, and no power could induce them to appear again upon the stage. Their dignity had been offended, and their wild, flashing eyes were anything but agreeable. Indeed, I hardly felt safe in their presence, and it was with a feeling of relief that I witnessed their departure for Washington the next morning.

CHAPTER XXXIV

In 1862 I heard of an extraordinary dwarf girl, named Lavinia Warren, who was residing with her parents at Middleboro', Massachusetts, and I sent an invitation to her and her parents to come and visit me at Bridgeport. They came, and I found her to be a most intelligent and refined young lady, well educated, and an accomplished, beautiful and perfectly developed woman in miniature. I succeeded in making an engagement with her for several years, during which she contracted—as dwarfs are said to have the power to do—to visit Great Britain, France, and other foreign lands.

Having arranged the terms of her engagement, I took her to the house of one of my daughters in New York, where she remained quietly, while I was procuring her wardrobe and jewelry, and making arrangements for her *début*. She was then placed on exhibition at the Museum and from the day of her *début* she was an extraordinary success. Commodore Nutt was on exhibition with her, and although he was several years her junior he evidently took a great fancy to her. One day I presented to Lavinia a diamond and emerald ring, and as it did not exactly fit her finger, I told her I would give her another one and that she might present this one to the Commodore in her own name. She did so, and an unlooked-for effect was speedily apparent; the little Commodore felt sure that this was a love-token, and poor Lavinia was in the greatest trouble, for she considered herself quite a woman, and regarded the Commodore only as a nice little boy. But she did not like to offend him, and while she did not encourage she did not openly repel his attentions. Miss Lavinia Warren, however, was never destined to be Mrs. Commodore Nutt.

It was by no means an unnatural circumstance that I should be suspected of having instigated and brought about the marriage of Tom Thumb with Lavinia Warren. Had I done this, I should at this day have felt no regrets, for it has proved, in an eminent degree, one of the "happy marriages." I only say, what is known to all of their immediate friends, that from first to last their engagement was an affair of the heart—a case of "love at first sight"—that the attachment was mutual, and that it only grows with the lapse of time. But I had neither part nor lot in instigating or in occasioning the marriage. And as I am anxious to be put right before the public, and so to correct whatever of false impression may have gained ground, I have procured the consent of all the parties to a sketch of the wooing, winning and nuptials. Of course I should not lay these details before the public except with the sanction of those most interested. In this they consent to pay the penalty of distinction. And if the wooings of kings and queens must be told, why not the courtship and marriage of General and Mrs. Tom Thumb? The story is an interesting one, and shall be told alike to exonerate me from the suspicion named, and to amuse those—and they count by scores of thousands—who are interested in the welfare of the distinguished couple.

In the autumn of 1862, when Lavinia Warren was on exhibition at the Museum, Tom Thumb had no business engagement with me; in fact, he was not on exhibition at the time at all; he was taking a "vacation" at his house in Bridgeport. Whenever he came to New York he naturally called upon me, his old friend, at the Museum. He happened to be in the city at the time referred to, and one day he called, quite unexpectedly to me, while Lavinia was holding one of her levees. Here he now saw her for the first time, and very naturally made her acquaintance. He had a short interview with her, after which he came directly to my private office and desired to see me alone. Of course I complied with his request, but without the remotest suspicion as to his object. I closed the door, and the General took a seat. His first question let in the light. He inquired about the family of Lavinia Warren. I gave him the facts, which I clearly perceived gave him satisfaction of a peculiar sort. He then said, with great frankness, and with no less earnestness:

"Mr. Barnum, that is the most charming little lady I ever saw, and I believe she was created on purpose to be my wife! Now," he continued, "you have always been a friend of mine, and I want you to say a good word for me to her. I have got plenty of money, and I want to marry and settle down in life, and I really feel as if I must marry that young lady."

The little General was highly excited, and his general manner betrayed the usual anxiety, which, I doubt not, most of my readers will understand without a description. I could not repress a smile, nor forget my joke; and I said:

"Lavinia is engaged already."

"To whom—Commodore Nutt?" asked Tom Thumb, with much earnestness, and some exhibition of the "green-eyed monster."

"No, General, to me," I replied.

"Never mind," said the General, laughing, "you can exhibit her for a while, and then give up the engagement; but I do hope you will favor my suit with her."

I told the General that this was too sudden an affair; that he must take time to think of it; but he insisted that years of thought would make no difference, for his mind was fully made up.

"Well, General," I replied, "I will not oppose you in your suit, but you must do your own courting. I tell you, however, the Commodore will be jealous of you, and more than that, Miss Warren is nobody's fool, and you will have to proceed very cautiously if you can succeed in winning her affections."

The General thanked me, and promised to be very discreet. A change now came suddenly over him in several particulars. He had been (much to his credit) very fond of his country home in Bridgeport, where he spent his intervals of rest with his horses, and especially with his yacht, for his fondness for the water was his great passion. But now he was constantly having occasion to visit the city, and horses and yachts were strangely neglected. He had a married sister in New York, and his visits to her multiplied, for, of course, he came to New York "to see his sister!" His mother, who resided in Bridgeport, remarked that Charles had never before shown so much brotherly affection, nor so much fondness for city life.

His visits to the Museum were very frequent, and it was noticeable that new relations were being established between him and Commodore Nutt. The Commodore was not exactly jealous, yet he strutted around like a bantam rooster whenever the General approached Lavinia. One day he and the General got into a friendly scuffle in the dressing-room, and the Commodore threw the General upon his back in "double quick" time. The Commodore is lithe, wiry, and quick in his movements, but the General is naturally slow, and although he was considerably heavier than the Commodore, he soon found that he could not stand before him in a personal encounter. Moreover, the Commodore is naturally quick-tempered, and when excited brags about his knowledge of the "manly art of self-defence," and sometimes talks about pistols and bowie knives, etc. Tom Thumb, on the contrary, is by natural disposition decidedly a man of peace; hence, in this, agreeing with Falstaff as to what constituted the "better part of valor," he was strongly inclined to keep his distance, if the little Commodore showed any belligerent symptoms.

In the course of several weeks the General found numerous opportunities to talk with Lavinia, while the Commodore was performing on the stage, or was otherwise engaged; and, to a watchful discerner, it was evident he was making encouraging progress in the affair of the heart. He also managed to meet Lavinia on Sunday afternoons and evenings, without the knowledge of the Commodore; but he assured me he had not yet dared to suggest matrimony.

He finally returned to Bridgeport, and privately begged that on the following Saturday I would take Lavinia up to my house, and also invite him.

His immediate object in this was, that his mother might get acquainted with Lavinia, for he feared opposition from that source whenever the idea of his marriage should be suggested. I could do no less than accede to his proposal, and on the following Friday, while Lavinia and the Commodore were sitting in the greenroom, I said:

"Lavinia, you may go up to Bridgeport with me to-morrow morning, and remain until Monday."

"Thank you," she replied; "it will be quite a relief to get into the country for a couple of days."

The Commodore immediately pricked up his ears, and said:

"Mr. Barnum, I should like to go to Bridgeport to-morrow."

"What for?" I asked.

"I want to see my little ponies; I have not seen them for several months," he replied.

I whispered in his ear, "you little rogue, that is the pony you want to see," pointing to Lavinia.

He insisted I was mistaken. When I remarked that he could not well be spared from the Museum, he said:

"Oh! I can perform at half past seven o'clock, and then jump on to the eight o'clock evening train, and go up by myself, reaching Bridgeport before eleven, and return early Monday morning."

I feared there would be a clashing of interests between the rival pigmies; but wishing to please him, I consented to his request, especially as Lavinia also favored it. I wished I could then fathom that little woman's heart, and see whether she (who must have discovered the secret of the General's frequent visits to the Museum) desired the Commodore's visit in order to stir up the General's ardor, or whether, as seemed to me the more likely, she was seeking in this way to prevent a *dénouement* which she was not inclined to favor. Certain it is, that though I was the General's confidant, and knew all his desires upon the subject, no person had discovered the slightest evidence that Lavinia Warren had ever entertained the remotest suspicion of his thoughts regarding marriage. If she had made the discovery, as I assume, she kept the secret well. In fact, I assured Tom Thumb that every indication, so far as any of us could observe, was to the effect that his suit would be rejected. The little General was fidgety, but determined; hence he was anxious to have Lavinia meet his mother, and also see his possessions in Bridgeport, for he owned considerable land and numerous houses there.

The General met us at the depot in Bridgeport, on Saturday morning, and drove us to my house in his own carriage—his coachman being tidily dressed, with a broad velvet ribbon and silver buckle placed upon his hat expressly for the occasion. Lavinia was duly informed that this was the General's "turn out"; and after resting half an hour at Lindencroft, he took her out to ride. He stopped a few moments at his mother's house, where she saw the apartments which his father had built expressly for him, and filled with the most gorgeous furniture—all corresponding to his own diminutive size. Then he took her to East Bridgeport, and undoubtedly took occasion to point out in great detail all of the houses which he owned, for he depended much upon having his wealth make some impression upon her. They returned, and the General stayed to lunch. I asked Lavinia how she liked her ride; she replied:

"It was very pleasant, but," she added, "it seems as if you and Tom Thumb owned about all of Bridgeport!"

The General took his leave and returned at five o'clock to dinner, with his mother. Mrs. Stratton remained until seven o'clock. She expressed herself charmed with Lavinia Warren; but not a suspicion passed her mind that little Charlie was endeavoring to give her this accomplished young lady as a daughter-in-law. The General had privately asked me to invite him to stay over night, for, said he, "If I get a chance, I intend to 'pop the question' before the Commodore arrives." So I told his mother I thought the General had better stop with us over night, as the Commodore would be up in the late train, adding that it would be more pleasant for the little folks to be together. She assented, and the General was happy.

After tea Lavinia and the General sat down to play back-gammon. As nine o'clock approached, I remarked that it was about time to retire, but somebody would have to sit up until nearly eleven o'clock, in order to let in the Commodore. The General replied:

"I will sit up with pleasure, if Miss Warren will remain also."

Lavinia carelessly replied that she was accustomed to late hours, and she would wait and see the Commodore. A little supper was placed upon the table for the Commodore, and the family retired.

Now it happened that a couple of mischievous young ladies were visiting at my house, one of whom was to sleep with Lavinia. They were suspicious that the General was going to propose to Lavinia that evening, and, in a spirit of ungovernable curiosity, they determined, notwithstanding its manifest impropriety, to witness the operation, if they could possibly manage to do so on the sly. Of course this was inexcusable, the more so as so few of my readers, had they been placed under the same temptation, would have been guilty of such an impropriety! Perhaps I should hesitate to use the testimony of such witnesses, or even to trust it. But a few weeks after, they told the little couple the whole story, were forgiven, and all had a hearty laugh over it.

It so happened that the door of the sitting room, in which the General and Lavinia were left at the backgammon board, opened into the hall just at the side of the stairs, and these young misses, turning out the lights in the hall, seated themselves upon the stairs in the dark, where they had a full view of the cosy little couple, and were within easy ear-shot of all that was said.

The house was still. The General soon acknowledged himself vanquished at backgammon, and gave it up. After sitting a few moments, he evidently thought it was best to put a clincher on the financial part of his abilities; so he drew from his pocket a policy of insurance, and handing it to Lavinia, he asked her if she knew what it was.

Examining it, she replied, "It is an insurance policy. I see you keep your property insured."

"But the beauty of it is, it is not my property," replied the General, "and yet I get the benefit of the insurance in case of fire. You will see," he continued, unfolding the policy, "this is the property of Mr. Williams, but here, you will observe, it reads 'loss, if any, payable to Charles C. Stratton, as his interest may appear.' The fact is, I loaned Mr. Williams three thousand dollars, took a mortgage on his house, and made him insure it for my benefit. In this way, you perceive, I get my interest, and he has to pay the taxes."

"That is a very wise way, I should think," remarked Lavinia.

"That is the way I do all my business," replied the General, complacently, as he returned the huge insurance policy to his pocket. "You see," he continued, "I never lend any of my money without taking bond and mortgage security, then I have no trouble with taxes; my principal is secure, and I receive my interest regularly."

The explanation seemed satisfactory to Lavinia, and the General's courage began to rise. Drawing his chair a little nearer to hers, he said:

"So you are going to Europe, soon?"

"Yes," replied Lavinia, "Mr. Barnum intends to take me over in a couple of months."

"You will find it very pleasant," remarked the General; "I have been there twice, in fact I have spent six years abroad, and I like the old countries very much."

"I hope I shall like the trip, and I expect I shall," responded Lavinia; "for Mr. Barnum says I shall visit all the principal cities, and he has no doubt I will be invited to appear before the Queen of England, the Emperor and Empress of France, the King of Prussia, the Emperor of Austria, and at the courts of any other countries which we may visit. Oh! I shall like that, it will be so new to me."

"Yes, it will be very interesting indeed. I have visited most of the crowned heads," remarked the General, with an evident feeling of self-congratulation. "But are you not afraid you will be lonesome in a strange country?" asked the General.

"No, I think there is no danger of that, for friends will accompany me," was the reply.

"I wish I was going over, for I know all about the different countries, and could explain them all to you," remarked Tom Thumb.

"That would be very nice," said Lavinia.

"Do you think so?" said the General, moving his chair still closer to Lavinia's.

"Of course," replied Lavinia, coolly, "for I, being a stranger to all the habits and customs of the people, as well as to the country, it would be pleasant to have some person along who could answer all my foolish questions."

"I should like it first rate, if Mr. Barnum would engage me," said the General.

"I thought you remarked the other day that you had money

enough, and was tired of travelling," said Lavinia, with a slightly mischievous look from one corner of her eye.

"That depends upon my company while travelling," replied the General.

"You might not find my company very agreeable."

"I would be glad to risk it."

"Well, perhaps Mr. Barnum would engage you, if you asked him," said Lavinia.

"Would you really like to have me go?" asked the General, quietly insinuating his arm around her waist, but hardly close enough to touch her.

"Of course I would," was the reply.

The little General's arm clasped the waist closer as he turned his face nearer to hers, and said:

"Don't you think it would be pleasanter if we went as man and wife?"

The little fairy quickly disengaged his arm, and remarked that the General was a funny fellow to joke that way.

"I am not joking at all," said the General, earnestly, "it is quite too serious a matter for that."

"I wonder why the Commodore don't come?" said Lavinia.

"I hope you are not anxious for his arrival, for I am sure *I* am not," responded the General, "and what is more, I do hope you will say 'yes,' before he comes at all!"

"Really, Mr. Stratton," said Lavinia, with dignity, "if you are in earnest in your strange proposal, I must say I am surprised."

"Well, I hope you are not *offended*," replied the General, "for I was never more in earnest in my life, and I hope you will consent. The first moment I saw you I felt that you were created to be my wife."

"But this is so sudden."

"Not so very sudden; it is several months since we first met, and you know all about me, and my family, and I hope you find nothing to object to in me."

"Not at all; on the contrary, I have found you very agreeable, in fact I like you very much as a friend, but I have not thought of marrying, and—"

"And what? my dear," said the General, giving her a kiss. "Now, I beg of you, don't have any 'buts' or 'ands' about it. You say you like me as a friend, why will you not like me as a husband? You ought to get married; I love you dearly, and I want you for a wife. Now, deary; the Commodore will be here in a few minutes, I may not have a chance to see you again alone; do say that we will be married, and I will get Mr. Barnum to give up your engagement."

Lavinia hesitated, and finally said:

"I think I love you well enough to consent, but I have always said I would never marry without my mother's consent."

"Oh! I'll ask your mother. May I ask your mother? Come, say yes to that, and I will go and see her next week. May I do that, pet?"

"Yes, Charles, you may ask my mother. Now, don't whisper this to a living soul; let us keep our own secrets for the present."

"All right," said the General, "I will say nothing; but next Tuesday I shall start to see your mother."

"Perhaps you may find it difficult to obtain her consent," said Lavinia.

At that moment a carriage drove up to the door, and immediately the bell was rung, and the little Commodore entered.

"*You* here, General?" said the Commodore, as he espied his rival.

"Yes," said Lavinia, "Mr. Barnum asked him to stay, and we were waiting for you; come, warm yourself."

"I am not cold," said the Commodore; "where is Mr. Barnum?"

"He has gone to bed," remarked the General, "but a nice supper has been prepared for you."

"I am not hungry, I thank you; I am going to bed. Which room does Mr. Barnum sleep in?" said the little bantam, in a petulant tone of voice.

His question was answered; the young eaves-droppers scampered to their sleeping apartments, and the Commodore soon came to my room, where he found me indulging in the foolish habit of reading in bed.

"Mr. Barnum, does Tom Thumb board here?" asked the Commodore, sarcastically.

"No," said I, "Tom Thumb does not *board* here. I invited him to stop over night, so don't be foolish, but go to bed."

"Oh, it's no affair of mine. I don't care anything about it; but I thought he had taken up his board here," replied the Commodore, and off he went to bed, evidently in a bad humor.

Ten minutes afterwards Tom Thumb came rushing into my room, and closing the door, he caught hold of my hand in a high state of excitement and whispered:

"We are engaged, Mr. Barnum! we are engaged! we are engaged!" and he jumped up and down in the greatest glee.

"Is that possible?" I asked.

"Yes, sir, indeed it is; but you must not mention it," he responded; "we agreed to tell nobody, so please don't say a word. I must tell *you,* of course, but 'mum is the word.' I am going, Tuesday, to get her mother's consent."

I promised secrecy, and the General retired in as happy a mood as I ever saw him. Lavinia also retired, but not a hint did she give to the young lady with whom she slept regarding the engagement. Indeed, our family plied her upon the subject the next day, but not a breath passed her lips that would give the slightest indication of what had transpired. She was quite sociable with the Commodore, and as the General concluded to go home the next morning, the Commodore's equanimity and good feelings were fully restored. The

General made a call of half an hour Sunday evening, and managed to have an interview with Lavinia. The next morning she and the Commodore returned to New York in good spirits, I remaining in Bridgeport.

The General called on me Monday, however, bringing a very nice letter which he had written to Lavinia's mother. He had concluded to send this letter by his trusty friend, Mr. George A. Wells, instead of going himself, and he had just seen Mr. Wells, who had consented to go to Middleborough with the letter the following day, and to urge the General's suit, if it should be necessary.

The General went to New York on Wednesday, and was there to await Mr. Wells' arrival. On Wednesday morning the General and Lavinia walked into my office, and after closing the door, the little General said:

"Mr. Barnum, I want somebody to tell the Commodore that Lavinia and I are engaged, for I am afraid there will be a 'row' when he hears of it."

"Do it yourself, General," I replied.

"Oh," said the General, almost shuddering, "I would not dare to do it, he might knock me down."

"I will do it," said Lavinia; and it was at once arranged that I should call the Commodore and Lavinia into my office, and either she or myself would tell him. The General, of course, "vamoosed."

When the Commodore joined us and the door was closed, I said:

"Commodore, do you know what this little witch has been doing?"

"No, I don't," he answered.

"Well, she has been cutting up one of the greatest pranks you ever heard of," I replied. "She almost deserves to be shut up, for daring to do it. Can't you guess what she has done?"

He mused a moment, and then looking at me, said in a low voice, and with a serious looking face, "Engaged?"

"Yes," said I, "absolutely engaged to be married to General Tom Thumb. Did you ever hear of such a thing?"

"Is that so, Lavinia?" asked the Commodore, looking her earnestly in the face.

"That is so," said Lavinia; "and Mr. Wells has gone to obtain my mother's consent."

The Commodore turned pale, and choked a little, as if he was trying to swallow something. Then, turning on his heel, he said, in a broken voice:

"I hope you may be happy."

As he passed out of the door, a tear rolled down his cheek.

"That is pretty hard," I said to Lavinia.

"I am very sorry," she replied, "but I could not help it. That diamond and emerald ring which you made me present in my name, has caused all this trouble."

Half an hour after this incident, the Commodore came to my office, and said:

"Mr. Barnum, do you think it would be right for Miss Warren to marry Charley Stratton if her mother should object?"

I saw that the little fellow had still a slight hope to hang on, and I said:

"No, indeed, it would not be right."

"Well, she says she shall marry him any way; that she gives her mother the chance to consent, but if she objects she will have her own way and marry him," said the Commodore.

"On the contrary," I replied, "I will not permit it. She is engaged to go to Europe for me, and I will not release her if her mother does not fully consent to her marrying Tom Thumb."

The Commodore's eyes glistened with pleasure, as he replied:

"Between you and me, Mr. Barnum, I don't believe she will give her consent."

But the next day dissipated his hopes. Mr. Wells returned,

saying that Lavinia's mother at first objected, for she feared it was a contrivance to get them married for the promotion of some pecuniary advantage; but, upon reading the letter from the General, and one still more urgent from Lavinia, and also upon hearing from Mr. Wells that, in case of their marriage, I should cancel all claims I had upon Lavinia's services, she consented.

After the Commodore had heard the news, I said to him:

"Never mind, Commodore, Minnie Warren is a better match for you; she is a charming little creature, and two years younger than you, while Lavinia is several years your senior."

"I thank you, sir," replied the Commodore, pompously, "I would not marry the best woman living; I don't believe in women, any way."

I then suggested that he should stand with little Minnie, as groom and bridesmaid, at the approaching wedding.

"No, sir!" replied the Commodore, emphatically; "I won't do it!"

That idea was therefore abandoned. A few weeks subsequently, when time had reconciled the Commodore, he told me that Tom Thumb had asked him to stand as groom with Minnie, at the wedding, and he was going to do so.

"When I asked you, a few weeks ago, you refused," I said.

"It was not your business to ask me," replied the Commodore, pompously. "When the proper person invited me I accepted."

Of course the approaching wedding was announced. It created an immense excitement. Lavinia's levees at the Museum were crowded to suffocation, and her photographic pictures were in great demand. For several weeks she sold more than three hundred dollars' worth of her *cartes de visite* each day. And the daily receipts at the Museum were frequently over three thousand dollars. I engaged the General to exhibit, and to assist her in the sale of pictures, to which his own photograph, of course, was added. I could afford to give them a fine wedding, and I did so.

The little couple made a personal application to Bishop Potter to perform the nuptial ceremony, and obtained his consent; but the matter became public, and outside pressure from some of the most squeamish of his clergy was brought to bear upon the bishop, and he rescinded his engagement.

This fact of itself, as well as the opposition that caused it, only added to the notoriety of the approaching wedding, and increased the crowds at the Museum. The financial result to me was a piece of good fortune, which I was, of course, quite willing to accept, though in this instance the "advertisement," so far as the fact of the betrothal of the parties with its preliminaries were concerned, was not of my seeking, as the recital now given shows. But seeing the turn it was taking in crowding the Museum, and pouring money into the treasury, I did not hesitate to seek continued advantage from the notoriety of the prospective marriage. Accordingly, I offered the General and Lavinia fifteen thousand dollars if they would postpone the wedding for a month, and continue their exhibitions at the Museum.

"Not for fifty thousand dollars," said the General, excitedly.

"Good for you, Charley," said Lavinia, "only you ought to have said not for a *hundred thousand,* for I would not!"

They both laughed heartily at what they considered my discomfiture, and such, looked at from a business point of view, it certainly was. The wedding day approached and the public excitement grew. For several days, I might say weeks, the approaching marriage of Tom Thumb was the New York "sensation." For proof of this I did not need what, however, was ample, the newspaper paragraphs. A surer index was in the crowds that passed into the Museum, and the dollars that found their way into the ticket office.

It was suggested to me that a small fortune in itself could be easily made out of the excitement. "Let the ceremony take place in the Academy of Music, charge a big price for admission, and the citizens will come in crowds." I have no manner of doubt that in this way twenty-five thousand dollars could easily have been obtained. But I had no such thought. I had promised to give the couple a genteel and graceful wedding, and I kept my word.

The day arrived, Tuesday, February 10, 1863. The ceremony was to take place in Grace Church, New York. The Rev. Junius Willey, Rector of St. John's Church in Bridgeport, assisted by the late Rev. Dr. Taylor, of Grace Church, was to officiate. The organ was played by Morgan. I know not what better I could have done, had the wedding of a prince been in contemplation. The church was comfortably filled by a highly select audience of ladies and gentlemen, none being admitted except those having cards of invitation. Among them were governors of several of the States, to whom I had sent cards, and such of those as could not be present in person were represented by friends, to whom they had given their cards. Members of Congress were present, also generals of the army, and many other prominent public men. Numerous applications were made from wealthy and distinguished persons for tickets to witness the ceremony, and as high as sixty dollars was offered for a single admission. But not a ticket was sold; and Tom Thumb and Lavinia Warren were pronounced "man and wife" before witnesses.

Several thousand persons attended the reception of Mr. and Mrs. Tom Thumb the same day at the Metropolitan Hotel. After this they started on a wedding tour, taking Washington in their way. They visited President Lincoln at the White House. After a couple of weeks they returned, and, as they then supposed, retired to private life.

Habit, however, is indeed second nature. The General and his wife had been accustomed to excitement, and after a few months' retirement they again longed for the peculiar pleasures of a public life, and the public were eager to welcome them once more. They resumed their public career, and have since travelled several years in Europe, and considerably in this country, holding public exhibitions more than half the time, and spending the residue in leisurely viewing such cities and portions of the country as they may happen to be in. Commodore Nutt and Minnie Warren, I should add, usually travel with them.⎯

In June, 1869, the report was started, for the third or fourth time, in the newspapers, that Commodore Nutt and Miss Minnie Warren were married—this time at West Haven, in Connecticut. The story was wholly untrue, nor do I think that such a wedding is likely to take place, for, on the principle that people like their opposites, Minnie and the Commodore are likely to marry persons whom they can literally "look up to"—that is, if either of them marries at all it will be a tall partner.

Soon after the wedding of General Tom Thumb and Lavinia Warren, a lady came to my office and called my attention to a little six-paged pamphlet which she said she had written, entitled "Priests and Pigmies," and requested me to read it. I glanced at the title, and at once estimating the character of the publication, I promptly declined to devote any portion of my valuable time to its perusal.

"But you had better look at it, Mr. Barnum; it deeply interests you, and you may think it worth your while to buy it."

"Certainly, I will buy it, if you desire," said I, tendering her a sixpence, which I supposed to be the price of the little pamphlet.

"Oh! you quite misunderstand me; I mean buy the copyright and the entire edition, with the view of suppressing the work. It says some frightful things, I assure you," urged the author.

I lay back in my chair and fairly roared at this exceedingly feeble attempt at black-mail.

"But," persisted the lady, "suppose it says that your Museum and Grace Church are all one, what then?"

"My dear madam," I replied, "you may say what you please

about me or about my Museum; you may print a hundred thousand copies of a pamphlet stating that I stole the communion service after the wedding from Grace Church altar, or anything else you choose to write; only have the kindness to say something about me, and then come to me and I will properly estimate the money value of your services to me as an advertising agent. Good morning, madam,"—and she departed.

CHAPTER XXXV

POLITICAL AND PERSONAL

I BEGAN my political life as a Democrat, and my newspaper, the *Herald of Freedom,* was a Jackson-Democratic journal. While always taking an active interest in political matters, I had no desire for personal preferment, and, up to a late period, steadily declined to run for office. Nevertheless, in 1852 or 1853, prominent members of the party with which I voted, urged the submission of my name to the State Convention, as a candidate for the office of Governor, and although the party was then in the ascendancy, and a nomination would have been equivalent to an election, I peremptorily refused; in spite of this refusal, which was generally known, several votes were cast for me in the Convention. The Kansas strifes, in 1854, shook my faith in my party, though I continued to call myself a Democrat, often declaring that if I thought there was a drop of blood in me that was not democratic, I would let it out if I had to cut the jugular vein. When, however, secession threatened in 1860, I thought it was time for a "new departure," and I identified myself with the Republican party.

During the active and exciting political campaign of 1860, which resulted in Mr. Lincoln's first election to the presidency, it will be remembered that "Wide-Awake" associations, with their uniforms, torches and processions, were organized in nearly every city, town and village throughout the North. Arriving at Bridgeport from New York at five o'clock one afternoon, I was informed that the Wide-Awakes were to parade that evening and intended to march out to Lindencroft. So I ordered two boxes of sperm candles, and prepared for a general illumination of every window in the front of my house. Many of my neighbors, including several Democrats, came to Lindencroft in the evening to witness the illumination and see the Wide-Awake procession. My nearest neighbor, Mr. T., was a strong Democrat, and before he came to my house he ordered his servants to stay in the basement, and not to show a light above ground, thus intending to prove his Democratic convictions and conclusions by the darkness of his premises; and so, while Lindencroft was all ablaze with a flood of light, the next house was as black as a coal-hole. My neighbor, Mr. James D. Johnson, was also a Democrat, but I knew he would not spoil a good joke for the sake of politics, and I asked him to engage the attention of Mr. and Mrs. T., and to keep their faces turned towards Bridgeport and the approaching procession, the light of whose torches could already be seen in the distance, while another Democratic friend, Mr. George A. Wells, and I ran over and illuminated Mr. T.'s house. This we did with great success, completing our work five minutes before the procession arrived. As the Wide-Awakes turned into my grounds and saw that the house of Mr. T. was brilliantly illuminated, they concluded that he had become a sudden convert to Republicanism, and gave three rousing cheers for him. Hearing his name thus cheered and wondering at the cause, he happened to turn and see that his house was lighted up from basement to attic, and uttering a single profane ejaculation, he rushed for home. He was not able, however, to put out the lights till the Wide-Awakes had gone on their way rejoicing under the impression that one more Republican had been added to their ranks.

After the draft riots in New York and in other cities, in July, 1863, myself and other members of the "Prudential Committee" which had been formed in Bridgeport were frequently threatened with personal violence, and rumors were especially rife that Lindencroft would some night be mobbed and destroyed. On several occasions, soldiers volunteered as a guard and came and stayed at my house, sometimes for several nights in succession, and I was also provided with rockets, so that in case of an attempted attack I could signal to my friends in the city and especially to the night watchman at the arsenal, who would see my rockets at Lindencroft and give the alarm. Happily these signals were never needed.

It always seemed to me that a man who "takes no interest in politics" is unfit to live in a land where the government rests in the hands of the people. Consequently, whether I expressed them or not, I always had pronounced opinions upon all the leading political questions of the day, and no frivolous reason ever kept me from the polls. Indeed, on one occasion, I even hastened my return from Europe, so that I could take part in a presidential election. I was a party man, but not a partisan, nor a wire-puller, and I had never sought or desired office, though it had often been tendered to me. This was notoriously true, among all who knew me, up to the year 1865, when I accepted from the Republican party a nomination to the Connecticut legislature from the town of Fairfield, and I did this because I felt that it would be an honor to be permitted to vote for the then proposed amendment to the Constitution of the United States to abolish slavery forever from the land.

I was elected, and on arriving at Hartford the night before the session began, I found the wire-pullers at work laying their plans for the election of a Speaker of the House. Watching the movements closely, I saw that the railroad interests had combined in support of one of the candidates, and this naturally excited my suspicion. I never believed in making State legislation a mere power to support monopolies. I do not need to declare my full appreciation of the great blessings which railroad interests and enterprises have brought upon this country and the world. But the vaster the enterprise and its power for good, the greater its opportunity for mischief if its power is perverted. The time was when a whole community was tied to the track of one or two railway companies, and it was too truthful to be looked upon as satire to call New Jersey the "State of Camden and Amboy." A great railroad company, like fire, is a good servant, but a bad master; and when it is considered that such a company, with its vast number of men dependent upon it for their daily bread, can sometimes elect State officers and legislatures, the danger to our free institutions from such a force may well be feared.

Thinking of these things, and seeing in the combination of railroad interests to elect a speaker no promise of good to the community at large, I at once consulted with a few friends in the legislature, and we resolved to defeat the railroad "ring," if possible, in caucus. I had not even seen either of the candidates for the speakership, nor had I a single selfish end in view to gratify by the election of one candidate or the other; but I felt that if the railroad favorite could be defeated, the public interest would be subserved. We succeeded; their candidate was not nominated, and the railroad men were taken by surprise. They had had their own way in every legislature since the first railroad was laid down in Connecticut, and to be beaten now fairly startled them.

Immediately after the caucus, I sought the successful nominee, Hon. E. K. Foster, of New Haven, and begged him not to appoint as chairman of the railroad committee the man who had held that office for several successive years, and who was, in fact, the great railroad factotum in the State. He complied with my request, and he soon found how important it was to check the strong and growing monopoly; for, as he said, the "outside pressure" from personal friends in both political parties, to secure the appointment of the person to whom I had objected, was terrible.

Though I had not foreseen nor thought of such a thing until I reached Hartford, I soon found that a battle with the railroad commissioners would be necessary, and my course was shaped accordingly. It was soon discovered that a majority of the railroad commissioners were mere tools in the hands of the railroad companies, and that one of them was actually a hired clerk in the office of the New York and New Haven Railroad Company. It was also shown that the chairman of the railroad commissioners permitted most of the accidents which occurred on that road to be taken charge of and reported upon by the paid lobby agent of that railroad. This was so manifestly destructive to the interests of all parties who might suffer from accidents on the road, or have any controversy therefor with the company, that I succeeded in enlisting the farmers and other true men on the side of right; and we defeated the chairman of the railroad commissioners, who was a candidate for re-election, and elected our own candidate in his place. I also carried through a law that no person who was in the employ of any railroad in the State should serve as railroad commissioner.

But the great struggle which lasted nearly through the entire session was upon the subject of railroad passenger commutations. Commodore Vanderbilt had secured control of the Hudson River and Harlem railroads, and had increased the price of commuters' tickets from two hundred to four hundred per cent. Many men living on the line of these roads at distances of from ten to fifty miles from New York, had built fine residences in the country, on the strength of cheap transit to and from the city, and were compelled to submit to the extortion. Commodore Vanderbilt was a large shareholder in the New York and New Haven road; indeed, subsequent elections showed that he had a controlling interest, and it seemed evident to me that the same practice would be put in operation on the New Haven railroad that commuters were groaning under on the two other roads. I enlisted as many as I could in an effort to strangle this outrage before it became too strong to grapple with. Several lawyers in the Assembly had promised me their aid, but long before the final struggle came, every lawyer except one in that body was enlisted in favor of the railroads! What potent influence had been at work with these legal gentlemen could only be surmised. Certain it is that all the railroad interests in the State were combined; and while they had plenty of money with which to carry out their designs and desires, the chances looked slim in favor of those members of the legislature who had no pecuniary interest in the matter, but were struggling simply for justice and the protection of the people. But "Yankee stick-to-it-iveness" was always a noted feature in my character. Every inch of the ground was fought over, day after day, before the legislative railroad committee. Examinations and cross-examinations of railroad commissioners and lobbyists were kept up. Scarcely more than one man, Senator Ballard, of Darien, aided me personally in the investigations which took place. But he was a host in himself, and we left not a stone unturned; we succeeded by our persistence in letting in considerable light upon a dark subject. The man whom I had prevented from being made chairman succeeded in becoming a member of the railroad committee; but, from the mouths of unwilling witnesses, I exhibited his connection with railroad reports, railroad laws, and railroad lobbyings, in such a light that he took to his bed some ten days before the end of the session, and actually remained there, "sick," as he said, till the legislature adjourned.

The speaker offered me the chairmanship of any one of several committees, and I selected that of the Agricultural committee, because it would occupy but little of my time, and give me the opportunity I so much desired to devote my attention to the railway combinations.

In the spring of 1866, I was again elected to represent the town of Fairfield in the Connecticut Legislature. I had not intended to accept a nomination for that office a second time, but one of the directors of the New York and New Haven Railroad, who was a citizen of Fairfield and had been a zealous lobby member of the preceding legislature, had declared that I should not represent the town again. As the voters of Fairfield seemed to think that the public interests were of more importance than the success of railroad conspiracies, combinations, and monopolies, I accepted their nomination.

I was again chairman of the Committee on Agriculture, and on the whole the session at New Haven, in 1866, was very agreeable to me; there were many congenial spirits in the House and our severer labors were lightened by some very delightful episodes.

During the summer Governor Hawley appointed me a commissioner to the Paris Exposition, but I was unable to attend.

In the spring of 1867, I received from the Republican convention in the Fourth District in Connecticut the nomination for Congress. As I have already remarked, politics were always distasteful to me. I possess naturally too much independence of mind, and too strong a determination to do what I believe to be right, regardless of party expediency, to make a lithe and oily politician. To be called on to favor applications from office-seekers, without regard to their merits, and to do the dirty work too often demanded by political parties; to be "all things to all men" though not in the apostolic sense; to shake hands with those whom I despised, and to kiss the dirty babies of those whose votes were courted, were political requirements which I felt I could never acceptably fulfil. Nevertheless, I had become, so far as business was concerned, almost a man of leisure; and some of my warmest personal friends insisted that a nomination to so high and honorable position as a member of Congress was not to be lightly rejected, and so I consented to run. Fairfield and Litchfield counties composed the district, which in the preceding Congressional election, in 1865, and just after the close of the war, was republican. In the year following, however, the district in State election went democratic, although the republican State ticket was elected. I had this democratic majority to contend against in 1867, and as the whole State turned over and elected the democratic ticket, I lost my election. In the next succeeding Congressional election, in 1869, the Fourth District also elected the only democratic congressman chosen from Connecticut that year, although the State itself was republican again by a considerable majority.

I was neither disappointed nor cast down by my defeat. The political canvass served the purpose of giving me a new sensation, and introducing me to new phases of human nature,—a subject which I had always great delight in studying. The filth and scandal, the slanders and vindictiveness, the plottings and fawnings, the fidelity, treachery, meanness and manliness, which by turns exhibited themselves in the exciting scenes preceding the election, were novel to me, and were so far interesting. My personal efforts in the canvass were mainly confined to the circulation of documents, and I did not spend a dollar to purchase a vote.

When Congress met, I was surprised to see by the newspapers that the seat of my opponent was to be contested on account of alleged bribery, fraud and corruption in securing his election. This was the first intimation that I had ever received of such an intention, and I was never, at any time before or afterwards, consulted upon the subject. The movement proved to have originated with neighbors and townsmen of the successful candidate, who claimed to be able to prove that he had paid large sums of money to purchase votes. They also claimed that they had proof that men were brought from an adjoining State to vote, and that in the office of the successful candidate naturalization papers were forged to enable foreigners to vote upon them. But, I repeat, I took no part nor lot in the matter, but concluded that if I had been defeated by fraud mine was the real success.

On the thirteenth day of July, 1865, I was speaking in the Connecticut Legislature, in session at Hartford, against the railroad schemes, when a telegram was handed to me from my son-in-law, S. H. Hurd, my assistant manager in New York, stating that the

Harper's Weekly

THOMAS NAST CARTOON ("MUTUAL ADMIRATION"). IN THE
ORIGINAL CAPTION BARNUM IS TELLING JUMBO, "YOU ARE A
humbug AFTER MY OWN HEART. YOU HAVE EVEN BEAT ME IN
ADVERTISING."

Jumbo. St Thomas, Ontario. Sept. 15. 1885

THE DEATH OF JUMBO, ST. THOMAS, ONTARIO, SEPTEMBER 15, 1885

American Museum was in flames and that its total destruction was certain. I glanced over the despatch, folded it, laid it on my desk, and calmly continued my speech as if nothing had happened. At the conclusion of my remarks, the bill I had been advocating was carried, and the House adjourned. I then handed the telegram, announcing my great loss in New York, to my friend and fellow-laborer, Mr. William G. Coe, of Winsted, who immediately communicated the intelligence to several members. Warm sympathizers at once crowded around me, and Mr. Henry B. Harrison, of New Haven, my strongest railroad opponent, pushing forward, seized me by the hand, and said:

"Mr. Barnum, I am really very sorry to hear of your great misfortune."

"Sorry," I replied, "why, my dear sir, I shall not have time to be 'sorry' in a week! It will take me that length of time before I can get over laughing at having whipped you all so nicely in this attempted railroad imposition."

The Speaker of the House and my fellow-members all testified that neither my face nor my manner betrayed the slightest intimation when I read the telegram that I had received unpleasant intelligence. Immediately after adjournment that afternoon, I took the cars for Bridgeport, spending the night quietly at home, and the following morning I went to New York to see the ruins of my Museum, and to learn the full extent of the disaster. When I arrived at the scene of the calamity and saw nothing but the smouldering debris of what a few hours before was the American Museum, the sight was sad indeed. Here were destroyed, almost in a breath, the accumulated results of many years of incessant toil, my own and my predecessors', in gathering from every quarter of the globe myriads of curious productions of nature and art—an assemblage of rarities which a half million of dollars could not restore, and a quarter of a century could not collect. In addition to these there were many Revolutionary relics and other links in our national history which never could be duplicated. Not a thousand dollars' worth of the entire property was saved; the destruction was complete; the loss was irreparable. My insurance was but $40,000, while the collection, at the lowest estimate, was worth $400,000, and as my premium was five per cent I had paid the insurance companies more than they returned to me. When the fire occurred, my summer pantomime season had just begun and the Museum was doing an immensely profitable business. My first impulse, after reckoning up my losses, was to retire from active life and from all business occupation beyond what my large real estate interests in Bridgeport and my property in New York would compel. I felt that I had still a competence and that after a most active and busy life, at fifty-five years, I was entitled to retirement, to comparative rest for the remainder of my days. I called on my old friend, the editor of the *Tribune,* for advice on the subject.

"Accept this fire as a notice to quit, and go a-fishing," said Mr. Greeley.

"A-fishing!" I exclaimed.

"Yes, a-fishing; I have been wanting to go a-fishing for thirty years, and have not yet found time to do so," replied Mr. Greeley.

I really felt that his advice was good and wise, and had I consulted only my own ease and interest I should have acted upon it. But two considerations moved me to pause: First, one hundred and fifty employees, many of whom depended upon their exertions for their daily bread, were thrown out of work at a season when it would be difficult for them to get engagements elsewhere. Second, I felt that a large city like New York needed a good Museum, and that my experience of a quarter of a century in that direction afforded extraordinary facilities for founding another establishment of the kind, and so I took a few days for reflection.

Meanwhile, the Museum employees were tendered a benefit at

the Academy of Music, at which most of the dramatic artists in the city volunteered their services. I was called out, and made some off-hand remarks in which I stated that nothing which I could utter in behalf of the recipients of that benefit could plead for them half so eloquently as the smoking ruins of the building where they had so long earned their support by their efforts to gratify the public. At the same time I announced that, moved by the considerations I have mentioned, I had concluded to establish another Museum, and that in order to give present occupation to my employees I had engaged the Winter Garden Theatre for a few weeks, and I hoped to open a new establishment of my own in the ensuing fall.

I very soon secured by lease the premises, numbers 535, 537 and 539 Broadway, seventy-five feet front and rear, by two hundred feet deep, and known as the Chinese Museum buildings. In less than four months, I succeeded in converting this building into a commodious Museum and lecture room, and meanwhile I sent agents through America and Europe to purchase curiosities. Besides hundreds of small collections, I bought up several entire museums, and with many living curiosities and my old company of actors and actresses, I opened to the public, November 13, 1865, "Barnum's New American Museum," thus beginning a new chapter in my career as a manager and showman.

CHAPTER XXXVI

WHEN the old American Museum burned down, and while the ruins were still smoking, I had numerous applications for the purchase of the lease of the two lots, fifty-six by one hundred feet, which had still nearly eleven years to run. It will be remembered that in 1847 I came back from England, while my second lease of five years had yet three years more to run, and renewed that lease for twenty-five years from 1851 at an annual rental of $10,000. It was also stipulated that in case the building was destroyed by fire the proprietor of the property should expend twenty-four thousand dollars towards the erection of a new edifice, and at the end of the term of lease he was to pay me the appraised value of the building, not to exceed $100,000. Rents and real estate values had trebled since I took this twenty-five years' lease, and hence the remaining term was very valuable. I engaged an experienced and competent real estate broker in Pine Street to examine the terms of my lease, and in view of his knowledge of the cost of erecting buildings and the rentals they were commanding in Broadway, I enjoined him to take his time, and make a careful estimate of what the lease was worth to me, and what price I ought to receive if I sold it to another party.

At the end of several days he showed me his figures, which proved that the lease was fully worth $275,000. As I was inclined to have a museum higher up town, I did not wish to engage in erecting two buildings at once, so I concluded to offer my museum lease for sale. Accordingly, I put it into the hands of Mr. Homer

Morgan, with directions to offer it for $225,000, which was $50,000 less than the value at which it had been estimated.

The next day I met Mr. James Gordon Bennett, who told me that he desired to buy my lease, and at the same time to purchase the fee of the museum property, for the erection thereon of a publication building for the New York *Herald*. I said I thought it was very fitting the *Herald* should be the successor of the Museum; and Mr. Bennett asked my price.

"Please to go or send immediately to Homer Morgan's office," I replied, "and you will learn that Mr. Morgan has the lease for sale at $225,000. This is $50,000 less than its estimated value; but to you I will deduct $25,000 from my already reduced price, so you may have the lease for $200,000."

Bennett replied that he would look into the affair closely; and the next day his attorney sent for my lease. He kept it several days, and then appointed an hour for me to come to his office. I called according to appointment. Mr. Bennett and his attorney had thoroughly examined the lease. It was the property of my wife. Bennett concluded to accept my offer. My wife assigned the lease to him, and his attorney handed me Mr. Bennett's check on the Chemical Bank for $200,000. That same day I invested $50,000 in United States bonds; and the remaining $150,000 was similiarly invested on the following day. I learned at that time that Bennett had agreed to purchase the fee of the property for $500,000. He had been informed that the property was worth some $350,000 to $400,000, and he did not mind paying $100,000 extra for the purpose of carrying out his plans. But the parties who estimated for him the value of the land knew nothing of the fact that there was a lease upon the property, else of course they would in their estimate have deducted the $200,000 which the lease would cost. When, therefore, Mr. Bennett saw it stated in the newspapers that the sum which he had paid for a piece of land measuring only fifty-six by one hundred feet was more than was ever before paid in any city in the world for a tract of that size, he discovered the serious oversight which he had made; and the owner of the property was immediately informed that Bennett would not take it. But Bennett had already signed a bond to the owner, agreeing to pay $100,000 cash, and to mortgage the premises for the remaining $400,000.

Supposing that by this step he had shaken off the owner of the fee, Bennett was not long in seeing that, as he was not to own the land, he would have no possible use for the lease, for which he had paid the $200,000; and accordingly his next step was to shake me off also, and get back the money he had paid me.

My business for many years, as manager of the Museum and other public entertainments, compelled me to court notoriety; and I always found Bennett's abuse far more remunerative than his praise, even if I could have had the praise at the same price, that is, for nothing. Especially was it profitable to me when I could be the subject of scores of lines of his scolding editorials free of charge, instead of paying him forty cents a line for advertisements, which would not attract a tenth part so much attention. Bennett had tried abusing me, off and on, for twenty years, on one occasion refusing my advertisement altogether for the space of about a year; but I always managed to be the gainer by his course. Now, however, when new difficulties threatened, all the leading managers in New York were members of the "Managers' Association," and as we all submitted to the arbitrary and extortionate demands of the *Herald*, Bennett thought he had but to crack his whip, in order to keep any and all of us within the traces. The great Ogre of the *Herald* supposed he could at all times frighten the little managerial boys into any holes which might be left open for them to hide in. Accordingly, one day Bennett's attorney wrote me a letter, saying that he would like to have me call on him at his office the following morning. Not dreaming of the object I called as desired, and after a few pleasant commonplace remarks about the weather, and other trifles, the attorney said:

"Mr. Barnum, I have sent for you to say that Mr. Bennett has concluded not to purchase the museum lots, and therefore that you had better take back the lease, and return the $200,000 paid for it."

"Are you in earnest?" I asked with surprise.

"Certainly, quite so," he answered.

"Really," I said, smiling, "I am sorry I can't accommodate Mr. Bennett; I have not got the little sum about me; in fact, I have spent the money."

"It will be better for you to take back the lease," said the attorney seriously.

"Nonsense," I replied, "I shall do nothing of the sort, I don't make child's bargains. The lease was cheap enough, but I have other business to attend to, and shall have nothing to do with it."

The attorney said very little in reply; but I could see, by the almost benignant sorrow expressed upon his countenance, that he evidently pitied me for the temerity that would doubtless lead me into the jaws of the insatiable monster of the *Herald*. The next morning I observed that the advertisement of my entertainments with my Museum Company at Winter Garden was left out of the *Herald* columns. I went directly to the editorial rooms of the *Herald;* and learning that Bennett was not in, I said to Mr. Hudson, then managing editor:

"My advertisement is left out of the *Herald;* is there a screw loose?"

"I believe there is," was the reply.

"What is the matter?" I asked.

"You must ask the Emperor," said Mr. Hudson, meaning of course Bennett.

"When will the 'Emperor' be in?" I inquired. "Next Monday," was the answer.

"Well, I shall not see him," I replied; "but I wish to have this thing settled at once. Mr. Hudson, I now tender you the money for the insertion of my Museum advertisement on the same terms as are paid by other places of amusement; will you publish it?"

"I will not," Mr. Hudson peremptorily replied.

"That is all," I said. Mr. Hudson then smilingly and blandly remarked, "I have formally answered your formal demand, because I suppose you require it; but you know, Mr. Barnum, I can only obey orders." I assured him that I understood the matter perfectly, and attached no blame to him in the premises. I then proceeded to notify the Secretary of the "Managers' Association" to call the managers together at twelve o'clock the following day; and there was a full meeting at the appointed time. I stated the facts in the case in the *Herald* affair, and simply remarked that if we did not make common cause against any newspaper publisher who excluded an advertisement from his columns simply to gratify a private pique, it was evident that either and all of us were liable to imposition at any time.

One of the managers immediately made a motion that the entire association should stop their advertising and bill printing at the *Herald* office, and have no further connection with that establishment. Mr. Lester Wallack advised that this motion should not be adopted until a committee had waited upon Bennett, and had reported the result of the interview to the Association. Accordingly, Messrs. Wallack, Wheatley and Stuart were delegated to go down to the *Herald* office to call on Mr. Bennett.

The moment Bennett saw them, he evidently suspected the object of their mission, for he at once commenced to speak to Mr. Wallack in a patronizing manner; told him how long he had known and how much he respected his late father, who was "a true English gentleman of the old school," with much more in the same strain. Mr. Wallack replied to Bennett that the three managers were appointed a committee to wait upon him to ascertain if he insisted upon excluding from his columns the Museum advertisements,—not on account of any objection to the contents of the advertisements, or to the Museum itself, but simply because he had a private business disagreement with the proprietor—intimating that such a proceeding, for such a reason and no other, might lead to a rupture of business with other managers. In reply, Mr. Bennett had something to say about the fox that had suffered tailwise from a trap, and thereupon advised all other foxes to cut their tails off; and he pointed the fable by setting forth the impolicy of drawing down upon the Association the vengeance of the *Herald*. The committee, however, coolly insisted upon a direct answer to their question.

Bennett then answered: "I will not publish Barnum's advertisement; I do my business as I please, and in my own way."

"So do we," replied one of the managers, and the committee withdrew.

The next day the Managers' Association met, heard the report, and unanimously resolved to withdraw their advertisements from the *Herald,* and their patronage from the *Herald* job establishment, and it was done. Nevertheless, the *Herald* for several days continued to print gratuitously the advertisements of Wallack's Theatre and Niblo's Garden, and inordinately puffed these establishments, evidently in order to ease the fall, and to convey the idea that some of the theatres patronized the *Herald,* and perhaps hoping by praising these managers to draw them back again, and so to nullify the agreement of the Association in regard to the *Herald*. Thereupon, the managers headed their advertisements in all the other New York papers with the line, "This Establishment does not advertise in the New York *Herald*," and for many months this announcement was kept at the top of every theatrical advertisement and on the posters and playbills.

The *Herald* then began to abuse and vilify the theatrical and opera managers, their artists and their performances, and by way of contrast profusely praised Tony Pastor's Bowery show, and sundry entertainments of a similar character, thereby speedily bringing some of these side-shows to grief and shutting up their shops. Meanwhile, the first-class theatres prospered amazingly under the abuse of Bennett. Their receipts were never larger, and their houses never more thronged. The public took sides in the matter with the managers and against the *Herald,* and thousands of people went to the theatres merely to show their willingness to support the managers and to spite "Old Bennett." The editor was fairly caught in his own trap; other journals began to estimate the loss the *Herald* sustained by the action of the managers, and it was generally believed that this loss in advertising and job printing was not less than from $75,000 to $100,000 a year. The *Herald's* circulation also suffered terribly, since hundreds of people, at the hotels and elsewhere, who were accustomed to buy the paper solely for the sake of seeing what amusements were announced for the evening, now bought other papers. This was the hardest blow of all, and it fully accounted for the abuse which the *Herald* daily poured out upon the theatres.

But the more Bennett raved the more the people laughed, and the more determined did they seem to patronize the managers. Many people came to the Museum who said they came expressly to show us that the public were with us and against the *Herald.* The other managers stated their experience to be the same in this respect. In fact, it was a subject of general remark that, without exception, the associated managers never had done such a thriving business as during the two years in which they gave the *Herald* the cold shoulder.

Bennett evidently felt ashamed of the whole transaction; he would never publish the facts in his columns, though he once stated in an editorial that it had been reported that he had been cheated in purchasing the Broadway property, that the case had gone to court, and the public would soon know all the particulars. Some persons supposed by this that Bennett had sued me; but this was far from being the case. The owner of the lots sued Bennett, to compel him to take the title and pay for the property as per agreement; and that was all the "law" there was about it. He held James Gordon Bennett's bond, that he would pay him half a million dollars for the land, as follows: $100,000 cash, and a bond and mortgage upon the premises for the remaining $400,000. The day before the suit was to come to trial, Bennett came forward, took the deed, and paid $100,000 cash and gave a bond and mortgage of the entire premises for $400,000.

Had I really taken back the lease, as Bennett desired, he would have been in a worse scrape than ever; for having been compelled to take the property, he would have been obliged, as my landlord, to go on and assist in building a Museum for me according to the terms of my lease, and a Museum I should certainly have built on Bennett's property, even if I had owned a dozen Museums up town.

In the autumn of 1868, the associated managers came to the conclusion that the punishment of Bennett for two years was sufficient, and they consented to restore their advertisements to the *Herald*. I was then associated with the Van Amburgh Company in my new Museum, and concluding that the cost of advertising in the *Herald* was more than it was worth, we did not enter into the arrangement.

The foregoing was written in 1869, and three years later Mr. Bennett died. In these pages I have not been sparing of criticism upon his business plans and schemes, but cannot forbear acknowledgment of the extraordinary talent and tact of this great journalist. By enterprise and energy he attained a world-wide reputation and a fortune of large proportions. Let personal conflicts be buried in forgiving forgetfulness.

CHAPTER XXXVII

DURING the summer of 1866, Mr. Edwin L. Brown, Corresponding Secretary of the "Associated Western Literary Societies," opened a correspondence with me relative to delivering, in the ensuing season, my lecture on "Success in Life," before some sixty lyceums, Young Men's Christian Associations, and Literary Societies belonging to the union which Mr. Brown represented. The scheme embraced an extended tour through Pennsylvania, Ohio, Indiana, Illinois, Wisconsin, Missouri and Iowa, and I was to receive one hundred dollars for every repetition of my lecture, with all my travelling expenses on the route. Agreeing to these terms, I commenced the engagement at the appointed time, and, averaging five lectures a week, I finished the prescribed round just before New Year's. Before beginning this engagement, however, I gave the lecture for other associations at Wheeling, Cincinnati, Louisville, and Chicago. I may add that I have invariably, as a rule, devoted to charitable purposes every penny I ever received for lecturing, except while I was under the great Jerome Clock cloud in England, when I needed all I could earn.

My western tour was delightful; indeed it was almost an ovation. I found, in fact, that when I had strayed so far from home, the curiosity exhibitor himself became quite a curiosity. On several occasions, in Iowa, I was introduced to ladies and gentlemen who had driven thirty miles in carriages to hear me. I insisted, however, that it was more to see than to hear; and I asked them if that was not really the case. In several instances they answered in the affirmative. In fact, one quaint old lady said: "Why, to tell you the truth,

Mr. Barnum, we have read so much about you, and your Museum and your queer carryings-on, that we were not quite sure but you had horns and cloven feet, and so we came to satisfy our curiosity; but, la, me! I don't see but what you look a good deal like other folks, after all."

On my tour, in attempting to make the connection from Cleveland, Ohio, to Fort Wayne, Indiana, via Toledo, I arrived at the latter city at one o'clock, P. M., which was about two hours too late to catch the train in time for the hour announced for my lecture that evening. I went to Mr. Andrews, the superintendent of the Toledo, Wabash and Western Railway, and told him I wanted to hire a locomotive and car to run to Fort Wayne, as I must be there at eight o'clock at night.

"It is an impossibility," said Mr. Andrews; "the distance is ninety-four miles, and no train leaves here till morning. The road is much occupied by freight trains, and we never run extra trains in this part of the country, unless the necessity is imperative."

I suppose I looked astonished, as well as chagrined. I knew that if I missed lecturing in Fort Wayne that evening, I could not appoint another time for that purpose, for every night was engaged during the next two months. I also felt that a large number of persons in Fort Wayne would be disappointed, and I grew desperate. Drawing my wallet from my pocket, I said:

"I will give two hundred dollars, and even more, if you say so, to be put into Fort Wayne before eight o'clock to-night; and, really, I hope you will accommodate me."

The superintendent looked me thoroughly over in half a minute, and I fancied he had come to the conclusion that I was a burglar, a counterfeiter, or something worse, fleeing from justice. My surmise was confirmed when he slowly remarked:

"Your business must be very pressing, sir."

"It is indeed," I replied; "I am Barnum, the museum man, and am engaged to speak in Fort Wayne to-night."

He evidently did not catch the whole of my response, for he immediately said:

"Oh, it is a show, eh? Where is old Barnum himself?"

"I am Barnum," I replied, "and it is a lecture which I am advertised to give to-night; and I would not disappoint the people for anything."

"Is this P. T. Barnum?" said the superintendent, starting to his feet.

"I am sorry to say it is," I replied.

"Well, Mr. Barnum," said he, earnestly, "if you can stand it to ride to Fort Wayne in the caboose of a freight train, your well established reputation for punctuality in keeping your engagements shall not suffer on account of the Toledo, Wabash and Western Railroad."

"Caboose!" said I, with a laugh, "I would ride to Fort Wayne astride of the engine, or boxed up and stowed away in a freight car, if necessary, in order to meet my engagement."

A freight train was on the point of starting for Fort Wayne; all the cars were at once ordered to be switched off, except two, which the superintendent said were necessary to balance the train; the freight trains on the road were telegraphed to clear the track, and the polite superintendent pointing to the caboose, invited me to step in. I drew out my pocket-book to pay, but he smilingly shook his head, and said: "You have a through ticket from Cleveland to Fort Wayne; hand it to the freight agent on your arrival, and all will be right." I was much moved by this unexpected mark of kindness, and expressing myself to that effect, I stepped into the caboose, and we started.

At the invitation of the engineer, I took a ride of twenty miles upon the locomotive. It fairly made my head swim. I could not reconcile my mind to the idea that there was no danger; and intimating to the engineer that it would be a relief to get where I could not

Adam Forepaugh's "Light of Asia," Chief Rival of Barnum's Toung Taloung and Exposed by Barnum as a Fraud

Barnum and Twelve of His Elephants Testing a New Bridge at Bridgeport

P. T. BARNUM'S
New and Only Greatest Show on Earth.

IN WATER-PROOF TENTS, COVERING SEVERAL ACRES. $1,000,000 INVESTED.
A GREAT AND AMUSING ACADEMY OF OBJECT TEACHING.

Museum, Menagerie, Circus, and Hippodrome.

Will travel by rail, on 100 Steel Cars of its own, passing through New York, the Canadas, Michigan, Illinois, Minnesota, Wisconsin, Indiana, Iowa, Missouri, and Texas. The Museum contains 100,000 rare and startling curiosities, including the most remarkable Captain COSTENTENUS, a Greek nobleman, who was

TATTOED FROM HEAD TO FOOT

in Chinese Tartary, as punishment for engaging in rebellion against the King.

The **MENAGERIE** consists of by far the largest collection of living wild animals that ever travelled, among which are the $25,000 Hippopotamus from the river Nile, Sea Lions from Alaska, Giraffes, the African Lioness and her little royal Cubs, no larger than cats, a picture of which occupies a full page in HARPER'S WEEKLY of April 28th. The six beautiful jet-black $30,000 Trakene Stallions, from Paris, present amazing and ENTIRELY NOVEL performances, which have been witnessed with delight by over 200,000 ladies, gentlemen, and children this spring at Barnum's great Hippodrome Building in New York. This picture shows them

EXACTLY AS THEY APPEAR IN THE RING,

where also will appear twice each day one hundred peerless performers, funny clowns, and more than a hundred beautiful Arabian horses, ponies, elephants, camels, and other marvelously-educated performing animals. A Golden Street Procession a mile in length, full of startling features, with immense glittering Chariots, men in Armor, Bands of Music, curious Automatons, OPEN CAGES OF LIONS, in which AN INTREPID LADY PERFORMER APPEARS, and ENORMOUS SERPENTS, with their FEARLESS KEEPERS INSIDE THE CAGES, takes place daily from 9 to 10 o'clock A.M.

Cheap excursion trains, conveying passengers to the town where the exhibition takes place.

ADVERTISEMENT IN *Harper's Weekly,* MAY 26, 1877

see ahead, I was permitted to crawl back again to the caboose.

I reached Fort Wayne in ample time for the lecture; and as the committee had discreetly kept to themselves the fact of my non-arrival by the regular train, probably not a dozen persons were aware of the trouble I had taken to fulfil my engagement, till in the course of my lecture, under the head of "perseverance," I recounted my day's adventures, as an illustration of exercising that quality when real necessity demanded. The Fort Wayne papers of the next day published accounts of "Barnum on a Locomotive," and "A Journey in a Caboose"; and as I always had an eye to advertising, these articles were sent marked to newspapers in towns and cities where I was to lecture, and of course were copied,—thus producing the desired effects, first, of informing the public that the "showman" was coming, and next, assuring the lecture committee that Barnum would be punctually on hand as advertised, unless prevented by "circumstances over which he had no control."

The managers of railroads running west from Chicago pretty rigidly enforce a rule excluding from certain reserved cars all gentlemen travelling without ladies. As I do not smoke, I avoided the smoking cars; and as the ladies' car was sometimes more select and always more comfortable than the other cars, I tried various expedients to smuggle myself in. If I saw a lady about to enter the car alone, I followed closely, hoping thus to elude the vigilance of the brakeman, who generally acted as door-keeper. But the car Cerberus is pretty well up to all such dodges, and I did not always succeed. On one occasion, seeing a young couple, evidently just married and starting on a bridal tour, about to enter the car, I followed closely, but was stopped by the door-keeper, who called out:

"How many gentlemen are with this lady?"

I have always noticed that young newly-married people are very fond of saying "my husband" and "my wife": they are new terms which sound pleasantly to the ears of those who utter them; so in answer to the peremptory inquiry of the door-keeper, the bridegroom promptly responded:

"I am this lady's husband."

"And I guess you can see by the resemblance between the lady and myself," said I to Cerberus, "that I am her father."

The astounded husband and the blushing bride were too much "taken aback" to deny their newly-discovered parent, but the brakeman said, as he permitted the young couple to pass into the car:

"We can't pass all creation with one lady."

"I hope you will not deprive me of the company of my child during the little time we can remain together," I said with a demure countenance. The brakeman evidently sympathized with the fond "parient" whose feelings were sufficiently lacerated at losing his daughter through her finding a husband, and I was permitted to pass. I immediately apologized to the young bride and her husband, and told them who I was, and my reasons for the assumed paternity, and they enjoyed the joke so heartily that they called me "father" during our entire journey together. Indeed, the husband privately and slyly hinted to me that the first boy should be christened "P. T."

I fulfilled my entire engagement, which covered the lecturing season, and returned to New York greatly pleased with my Western tour. Public lecturing was by no means a new experience with me; for, apart from my labors in that direction in England, and occasional addresses before literary and agricultural associations at home, I had been prominently in the field for many years as a lecturer on temperance. My attention was turned to this subject in the following manner:

In the fall of 1847, while exhibiting General Tom Thumb at Saratoga Springs, where the New York State Fair was then being held, I saw so much intoxication among men of wealth and intellect, filling the highest positions in society, that I began to ask myself the question, What guarantee is there that *I* may not become a drunkard?

and I forthwith pledged myself at that time never again to partake of any kind of spirituous liquors as a beverage. True, I continued to partake of wine, for I had been instructed, in my European tour, that this was one of the innocent and charming indispensables of life. I however regarded myself as a good temperance man, and soon began to persuade my friends to refrain from the intoxicating cup. Seeing need of reform in Bridgeport, I invited my friend, the Reverend Doctor E. H. Chapin, to visit us, for the purpose of giving a public temperance lecture. I had never heard him on that subject, but I knew that on whatever topic he spoke he was as logical as he was eloquent. What Doctor Chapin said produced a deep impression upon my mind, and after a night of anxious thought, I rose in the morning, took my champagne bottles, knocked off their heads, and poured their contents upon the ground. I then called upon Doctor Chapin, asked him for the teetotal pledge, and signed it. He was greatly surprised in discovering that I was not already a teetotaler., He supposed such was the case, from the fact that I had invited him to lecture, and he little thought, at the time of his delivering it, that his argument to the moderate drinker was at all applicable to me. I felt that I had now a duty to perform,—to save others, as I had been saved, and on the very morning when I signed the pledge, I obtained over twenty signatures in Bridgeport. I talked temperance to all whom I met, and very soon commenced lecturing upon the subject in the adjacent towns and villages. I spent the entire winter and spring of 1851-2 in lecturing through my native State, always travelling at my own expense, and I was glad to know that I aroused many hundreds, perhaps thousands, to the importance of the temperance reform. I also lectured frequently in the cities of New York and Philadelphia, as well as in other towns in the neighboring States.

While in Boston with Jenny Lind, I was earnestly solicited to deliver two temperance lectures in the Tremont Temple, where she gave her concerts. I did so; and though an admission fee was charged for the benefit of a benevolent society, the building on each occasion was crowded. In the course of my tour with Jenny Lind, I was frequently solicited to lecture on temperance on evenings when she did not sing. I always complied when it was in my power. In this way I lectured in Baltimore, Washington, Charleston, New Orleans, Cincinnati, St. Louis, and various other cities. In August, 1853, I lectured in Cleveland, Ohio, and several other towns, and afterwards in Chicago, Illinois, and in Kenosha, Wisconsin. An election was to be held in Wisconsin in October, and the friends of prohibition in that State solicited my services for the ensuing month, and I could not refuse them. I therefore hastened home to transact some business which required my presence for a few days, and then returned, and lectured on my way in Toledo, Norwalk, Ohio, and Chicago, Illinois. I made the tour of the State of Wisconsin, delivering two lectures per day for four consecutive weeks, to crowded and attentive audiences.

My lecture in New Orleans, when I was in that city, was in the great Lyceum Hall, in St. Charles Street, and I lectured by the invitation of Mayor Crossman and several other influential gentlemen. The immense hall contained more than three thousand auditors, including the most respectable portion of the New Orleans public. I was in capital humor, and had warmed myself into a pleasant state of excitement, feeling that the audience was with me. While in the midst of an argument illustrating the poisonous and destructive nature of alcohol to the animal economy, some opponent called out, "How does it affect us, externally or internally?"

"*E*-ternally," I replied.

I have scarcely ever heard more tremendous merriment than that which followed this reply, and the applause was so prolonged that it was some minutes before I could proceed.

On the first evening when I lectured in Cleveland, Ohio (it was in the Baptist Church), I commenced in this wise: "If there are any ladies or gentlemen present who have never suffered in consequence of the use of intoxicating drinks as a beverage, either directly or in the person of a dear relative or friend, I will thank them to rise." A man with a tolerably glowing countenance arose. "Had you never a friend who was intemperate?" I asked.

"Never!" was the positive reply.

A giggle ran through the opposition portion of the audience. "Really, my friends," I said, "I feel constrained to make a proposition which I did not anticipate. I am, as you are all aware, a showman, and I am always on the lookout for curiosities. This gentleman is a stranger to me, but if he will satisfy me to-morrow morning that he is a man of credibility, and that no friend of his was ever intemperate, I will be glad to engage him for ten weeks at $200 per week, to exhibit him in my American Museum in New York, as the greatest curiosity in this country."

A laugh that was a laugh followed this announcement.

"They may laugh, but it is a fact," persisted my opponent with a look of dogged tenacity.

"The gentleman still insists that it is a fact," I replied. "I would like, therefore, to make one simple qualification to my offer; I made it on the supposition that, at some period of his life, he had friends. Now if he never had any friends, I withdraw my offer; otherwise, I will stick to it."

This, and the shout of laughter that ensued, was too much for the gentleman, and he sat down. I noticed throughout my speech that he paid strict attention, and frequently indulged in a hearty laugh. At the close of the lecture he approached me, and extending his hand, which I readily accepted, he said, "I was particularly green in rising to-night. Having once stood up, I was determined not to be put down, but your last remark fixed me!" He then complimented me very highly on the reasonableness of my arguments, and declared that ever afterwards he would be found on the side of temperance.

I may add that I have lectured in Montreal, Canada, and many towns and cities in the United States, at my own expense. One of the greatest consolations I now enjoy is that of believing I have carried happiness to the bosom of many a family. In the course of my life I have written much for newspapers, on various subjects, and always with earnestness, but in none of these have I felt so deep an interest as in that of temperance reform.

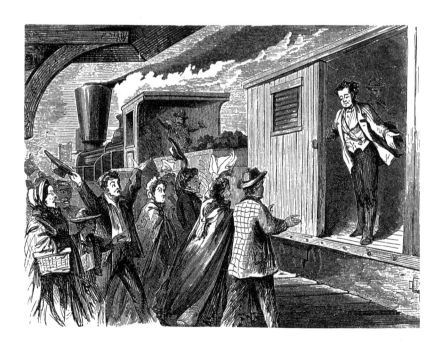

CHAPTER XXXVIII

THE NEW MUSEUM

MY new Museum on Broadway was liberally patronized from the start, but I felt that still more attractions were necessary in order to insure constant success. I therefore made arrangements with the renowned Van Amburgh Menagerie Company to unite their entire collection of living wild animals with the Museum. The new company was known as the "Barnum and Van Amburgh Museum and Menagerie Company," and as such was chartered by the Connecticut Legislature, the New York Legislature having refused us a charter unless I would "see" the "ring" a thousand dollars' worth, which I declined. I owned forty per cent and the Van Amburgh Company held the remaining sixty per cent in the new enterprise, which comprehended a large travelling menagerie through the country in summer, and the placing of the wild animals in the Museum in winter. The capital of the company was one million of dollars, with the privilege of doubling the amount. As one of the conditions of the new arrangement, it was stipulated that I should withdraw from all active personal attention to the Museum, but should permit my name to be announced as General Manager, and I was also elected President of the company. This arrangement gave me the comparative tranquillity which I now began to desire. I spent most of my time in Bridgeport, except in winter, when I resided in New York. I usually visited the Museum about once a week, but sometimes was absent for several months.

Meanwhile, immense additions were made to the curiosity departments of the new Museum. Every penny of the profits of this

Museum and of the two immense travelling menageries of wild animals was expended in procuring additional attractions for our patrons. Among other valuable novelties introduced in this establishment was the famous collection made by the renowned lion-slayer, Gordon Cummings. This was purchased for me by my faithful friend, Mr. George A. Wells, who was then travelling in Great Britain with General Tom Thumb. The collection consisted of many hundreds of skins, tusks, heads and skeletons of nearly every species of African animal, including numerous rare specimens never before exhibited on this continent. It was a great Museum in itself, and as such had attracted much attention in London and elsewhere, but it was a mere addition to our Museum and Menagerie, and was exhibited without extra charge for admission.

In the summer of 1867, I saw in several New York papers a thrilling account of an immense gorilla, which had arrived from Africa in charge of Barnum's agent, for the Barnum and Van Amburgh Company. The accounts described the removal of the savage animal in a strong iron cage from the ship, and his transportation up Broadway to the museum. His cries and roarings were said to have been terrible, and when he was taken into the menageries he was reported to have bent the heavy iron bars of his cage, and in his rage to have seized a poker which was thrust at him, and to have twisted it as if it had been a bit of wire.

For several years I had been trying to secure such an animal, and several African travellers had promised to do their best to procure one for me; and I had offered as high as $20,000 for the delivery in New York of a full-grown, healthy gorilla. From the minute description now given by the reporters, I was convinced that, at last, the long-sought prize had been secured. I was greatly elated, and at once wrote from Bridgeport to our manager, Mr. Ferguson, advising him how to exhibit the valuable animal, and particularly how to preserve its precious life as long as might be possible. I have owned many ourang-outangs, and all of them die ultimately of pulmonary disease; indeed, it is difficult to keep specimens of the monkey tribe through the winter in our climate, on account of their tendency to consumption. I therefore advised Mr. Ferguson to have a cage so constructed that no draught of air could pass through it, and I further instructed him in methods of guarding against the gorilla's taking cold.

A few days later I went to New York expressly to see the gorilla, and on visiting the Museum I was vexed beyond measure to find that the animal was simply a huge baboon! He was chained down, so that he could not stand erect, nor turn his back to visitors. His keeper could easily irritate him, and when the animal was excited he would seize the iron bars with both hands, and, uttering horrid screams, would shake the cage so fiercely that it could be heard and "felt" in the adjoining saloons. No doubt many of the visitors recalled Du Chaillu's accounts of the genuine gorilla, and were convinced that the veritable animal was before them. But I had been too long in the business to be caught by such chaff, and approaching the keeper, I asked him why he did not lengthen the chain, so that the animal could stand up.

"Because, if I do, he will show his tail," the keeper confidentially whispered in my ear.

The imposition was so silly and transparent that I did not care how soon it was exposed. As usual, however, I looked at the funny side of the matter, and immediately enclosed a ticket to my friend Mr. Paul Du Chaillu, who was then stopping at the Fifth Avenue Hotel, at the same time writing to the great African traveller that, much as he had done, the Barnum and Van Amburgh Company had done more, since he had only killed gorillas, while we had secured a living one, and brought the monster safely from Africa to America. I informed him, moreover, that all the gorillas he had seen and described were tailless, while our far more remarkable specimen had a tail full four feet long! Mr. Du Chaillu came into the Museum that afternoon, in great glee, with my open letter in his hand.

"Ah, Mr. Barnum," he exclaimed, "this is the funniest letter I ever received. Of course, you know your 'gorilla' is no gorilla at all, but only a baboon. I will not look at him, for when people ask me about 'Barnum's gorilla,' I prefer to be able to say that I have not seen him."

"On the contrary," said I, "I particularly desire that you should see the animal, and expose it. The imposition is too ridiculous."

"True; but I think your letter is more curious than your animal."

"Then I give you full leave to read the letter to all who ask you about the 'gorilla.'"

"Thank you," said Du Chaillu, "and I wish you would let me read it in my lectures at the West, where I am soon going on a tour."

I consented that he should do so, and I afterwards heard that he was delighting as well as enlightening western audiences on the subject of Manager Ferguson's management of the great "gorilla" in the Barnum and Van Amburgh Museum and Menagerie.

The menagerie of living animals was superior in extent to any other similar collection in America, embracing, as it did, almost every description of wild animal ever exhibited, including the smallest African elephant, and the only living giraffe then in the United States. The collection of lions and royal Bengal tigers was superb. There was a cage full of young lions that attracted great attention, and the whole menagerie was an exceedingly valuable one. When I say that to these attractions was added an able dramatic company, which performed every afternoon and evening, and that the admission to the entire establishment was but thirty cents, with no extra charge, except for a few front seats and private boxes, it is no wonder that this immense building, five stories high, and covering ground seventy-five by two hundred feet in area, was thronged "from sunrise to ten P. M.," and from top to bottom, with country and city visitors, of both sexes and all ages. The public was soon thoroughly convinced of the facts; first, that never before was such an outlay made for so great an assemblage of useful and amusing attractions, combining instruction with amusement, and thrown open to the people at so small a charge for admission; and second, that the surest way of deriving the greatest profit, in the long run, is to give people as much as possible for their money. That these facts were fully impressed upon our patrons is instanced in the monthly returns made to the United States Collector of Internal Revenue for the district, which showed that our receipts were larger than those of Wallack's Theatre, Niblo's Garden, or any other theatre or place of amusement in New York, or in America.

Very soon after entering upon the premises, I built a new and larger lecture room, which was one of the most commodious and complete theatres in New York, and I largely increased the dramatic company. Our collection swelled so rapidly that we were obliged to extend our premises by the addition of another building, forty by one hundred feet, adjoining the Museum. This addition gave us several new halls, which were speedily filled with curiosities. The rapid expansion of the establishment and the immense interest excited in the public mind led me to consider a plan I had long contemplated, of taking some decided steps towards the foundation of a great free institution, which should be similar to and in some respects superior to the British Museum in London. "The Barnum and Van Amburgh Museum and Menagerie Company," chartered with a capital of $2,000,000, had, in addition to the New York establishment, thirty acres of land in Bridgeport, whereon it was proposed to erect suitable buildings and glass and wire edifices for breeding and acclimating rare animals and birds, and training such of them as were fit for public performances. In time, a new building in New York, covering a whole square, and farther up town, would be needed for the mammoth exhibition, and I was not without hopes that I might be the means of establishing permanently in the city an extensive zoölogical garden.

It was also my intention ultimately to make my Museum the nucleus of a great free national institution. When the American Museum was burned, and I turned my attention to the collection of fresh curiosities, I felt that I needed other assistance than that of my own agents in America and Europe. It occurred to me that if our government representatives abroad would but use their influence to secure curiosities in the respective countries to which they were delegated, a free public Museum might at once be begun in New York, and I proposed to offer a part of my own establishment rent-free for the deposit and exhibition of such rarities as might be collected in this way. Accordingly, a week after the destruction of the American Museum, a memorial was addressed to the President of the United States, asking him to give his sanction to the new effort to furnish the means of useful information and wholesome amusement, and to give such instructions to public officers abroad as would enable them, without any conflict with their legitimate duties, to give efficiency to this truly national movement for the advancement of the public good, without cost to the government. This memorial was dated July 20, 1865, and was signed by Messrs. E. D. Morgan, Moses Taylor, Abram Wakeman, Simeon Draper, Moses H. Grinnell, Stephen Knapp, Benjamin R. Winthrop, Charles Gould, Wm. C. Bryant, James Wadsworth, Tunis W. Quick, John A. Pitkin, Willis Gaylord, Prosper M. Wetmore, Henry Ward Beecher, and Horace Greeley. This memorial was in due time presented, and was indorsed as follows:

"EXECUTIVE MANSION, WASHINGTON, D. C.
April 27, 1866.

The purpose set forth in this Memorial is highly approved and commended, and our Ministers, Consuls and commercial agents are requested to give whatever influence in carrying out the object within stated they may deem compatible with the duties of their respective positions, and not inconsistent with the public interests.

ANDREW JOHNSON."

I went to Washington myself, and had interviews with the President, Secretaries Seward, McCulloch and Welles, and also with Assistant Secretary of the Navy, G. V. Fox, who gave me several muskets and other "rebel trophies." During my stay at the capital I had a pleasant interview with General Grant, who told me he had lately visited my Museum with one of his sons, and had been greatly gratified. Upon my mentioning, among other projects, that I had an idea of collecting the hats of distinguished individuals, he at once offered to send an orderly for the hat he had worn during his principal campaigns. All these gentlemen cordially approved of my plan for the establishment of a National Museum in New York.

But before this plan could be put into effective operation, an event occurred which is now to be narrated. The winter of 1867-68 was one of the coldest that had been known for years, and some thirty severe snowstorms occurred during the season. On Tuesday morning, March 3d, 1868, it was bitter cold. A heavy body of snow was on the ground, and as I sat at the breakfast table with my wife and an esteemed lady guest, the wife of my excellent friend Rev. A. C. Thomas, I read aloud the general news from the morning papers. Leisurely turning to the local columns, I said, "Hallo! Barnum's Museum is burned."

"Yes," said my wife, with an incredulous smile, "I suspect it is."

"It is a fact," said I, "just listen: 'Barnum's Museum totally destroyed by fire.'"

This was read so coolly, and I showed so little excitement, that both of the ladies supposed I was joking. My wife simply remarked:

"Yes, it was totally destroyed two years ago, but Barnum built another one."

"Yes, and that is burned," I replied; "now listen," and I proceeded very calmly to read the account of the fire. Mrs. Thomas, still believing from my manner that it was a joke, stole slyly behind my chair, and looking over my shoulder at the newspaper, she exclaimed:

"Why, Mrs. Barnum, the Museum is really burned. Here is the whole account of it in this morning's paper."

"Of course it is," I remarked, with a smile, "how could you think I could joke on such a serious subject!"

It was indeed too true, and the subject was no doubt "serious" enough; in fact the pecuniary blow was perhaps even heavier than the loss of the other Museum, especially as there was probably no Bennett around who would give me $200,000 for a lease! But during my whole life I had been so much accustomed to operations of magnitude for or against my interests, that large losses or gains were not apt to disturb my tranquillity. Indeed, my second daughter calling in soon after, and seeing how coolly I took the disaster, said that her husband had remarked that morning, "Your father won't care half so much about it as he would if his pocket had been picked of fifty dollars. That would have vexed him, but he will take this heavier loss as simply the fortune of war."

And this was very nearly the fact. Yet the loss was a large one, and the complete frustration of our plans for the future was a serious consideration. But worse than all were the sufferings of the poor wild animals which were burned to death in their cages. A very few only of these animals were saved. Even the people who were sleeping in the building barely escaped with their lives, and next to nothing else, so sudden was the fire and so rapid its progress. The papers of the following morning contained full accounts of the fire; and editorial writers, while manifesting much sympathy for the proprietors, also expressed profound regret that so magnificent a collection, especially in the zoölogical department, should be lost to the city.

The cold was so intense that the water froze almost as soon as it left the hose of the fire engines; and when at last everything was destroyed, except the front granite wall of the Museum building, that and the ladder, signs, and lamp-posts in front were covered in a gorgeous frame-work of transparent ice, which made it altogether one of the most picturesque scenes imaginable. Thousands of persons congregated daily in that locality in order to get a view of the magnificent ruins. By moonlight the ice-coated ruins were still more sublime; and for many days and nights the old Museum was "the observed of all observers," and photographs were taken by several artists.

When the Museum was burnt, I was nearly ready to bring out a new spectacle, for which a very large extra company had been engaged, and on which a considerable sum of money had been expended in scenery, properties, costumes, and especially in enlarging the stage. I had expended altogether some $78,000 in building the new lecture-room, and in refitting the saloons. The curiosities were inventoried by the manager, Mr. Ferguson, at $288,000. I bought the real estate only a little while before the fire for $460,000, and there was an insurance on the whole of $160,000; and in June, 1868, I sold the lots on which the building stood for $432,000. The cause of the fire was a defective flue in a restaurant in the basement of the building.

Thus by the destruction of Iranistan and two Museums, about a million of dollars' worth of my property had been destroyed by fire, and I was not now long in making up my mind to follow Mr. Greeley's advice on a former occasion, to "take this fire as a notice to quit, and go a-fishing."

We all know how difficult it is for a person to stop when he is engaged in business, and how seldom it is that we find a man who thinks he has accumulated money enough, and is willing to cease trying to make more. An active business life, like everything else, becomes a habit, and the strife for success in business, through all the changes of fortune, and ups and downs of trade, becomes an infatuation akin to that which spurs the gambler. Hence, men often pursue their money-getting occupations long after the necessity therefor has ceased. Of course, by wedding themselves to this one ambition they forego many of the higher pleasures of life, and though they gave a vague idea of that "good time coming," when they are going to take things easy and enjoy themselves, that time never comes. Men who are entirely idle are the most miserable creatures in the world; but when by arduous toil they have secured a competence, and especially when they have reached a point in life where they are conscious of a waning of their vital energies, we must admit that they are unwise if they do not slip out of active business, and devote a large portion of their time to intellectual pursuits, social enjoyments, and, if they have not done so through life, to serious reflections on the ends and aims of human existence.

It is, perhaps, possible that notwithstanding the active life I have led, I have after all a lazy streak in my composition; at all events, I confess it was with no small degree of satisfaction that by this last burning of the Museum, notwithstanding the serious pecuniary loss it proved to me, I discovered a way open through which I could retire to a more quiet and tranquil mode of life. I therefore at once dissolved with the Van Amburgh Company, and sold out to them all my interest in the personal property of the concern. I was, however, beset on every side to start another Museum, and men of capital offered to raise a million of dollars if necessary, for that purpose, provided I would undertake its management. My constant reply was, "lead me not into temptation." I felt that I had enough to live on, and I earnestly believed the doctrine laid down in my lecture on "Money Getting," in regard to the danger of leaving too much property to children.

As I now had something like real leisure at my disposal, in the summer of 1868 I made my third visit to the White Mountains. To me, the locality and scene are ever fresh and ever wonderful. From the top of Mount Washington, one can see on every side within a radius of forty miles peaks piled on peaks, with smiling valleys here and there between, and, on a very clear day, the Atlantic Ocean off Portland, Maine, is distinctly visible—sixty miles away. Beauty, grandeur, sublimity, and the satisfaction of almost every sense combine to remind one of the ejaculation of that devout English soul who exclaims: "Look around with pleasure, and upward with gratitude."

During the year, Mr. George Wood, a most successful and enterprising manager, had been engaged in enlarging and refitting Banvard's building, at the corner of Broadway and Thirteenth Street, for a Museum and theatre; and wishing to avoid my competition in the business, he proposed that for a consideration, to be governed to some degree by the receipts, I should bind myself to have no other interest in any Museum or place of amusement in New York, and that I should give him the benefit of my experience, influence and information, and thus aid in advancing his interests and in building up and carrying out his enterprise. His proposition fully met my views, and I accepted it. Without incurring risk or responsibility, I could occupy portions of my time, which otherwise, perhaps, might drag heavily on my hands; my mind especially would be employed in matters with which I was familiar, and I might gratify my desire to assist in catering to the healthful, wholesome amusement of the rising generation and the public. I should not rust out; and, moreover, the new museum would afford me a pleasant place to drop into when I felt inclined to do so. Nothing in this arrangement compelled my presence in New York, or even in the United States; I could go when and where I chose, and could continue to be, as I hope to be for the rest of my life, "a man of leisure," which in my case, and according to my construction, is far from being a man of idleness.

While I was at the White Mountains, I received a telegram from Mr. George Wood, stating that he could not consider his list of curiosities complete unless I would consent to be present at the opening of his Museum, and I accordingly hastened to New York, making at Mr. Wood's request the opening address in his new establishment, August 31, 1868.

CHAPTER XXXIX

For nearly five years after our removal from Iranistan in 1855 my family had been knocked about, the sport of adverse fortune, without a settled home. Sometimes we boarded, and at other times we lived in a small hired house. Two of my daughters were married, and my youngest daughter, Pauline, was away at boarding school. The health of my wife was much impaired, and she especially needed a fixed residence which she could call "home." Accordingly, in 1860, I built a pleasant house adjoining that of my daughter Caroline, in Bridgeport, and one hundred rods west of the grounds of Iranistan. I had originally a tract of twelve acres, but half of it had been devoted to my daughter, and on the other half I now proposed to establish my own residence. To prepare the site it was necessary to cart in several thousands of loads of dirt to fill up the hollow and to make the broad, beautiful lawn, in the centre of which I erected the new house, and after supplying the place with fountains, shrubbery, statuary and all that could adorn it, I named my new home "Lindencroft." It was, in truth, a very delightful place, complete and convenient in all respects.

Meanwhile, my pet city, East Bridgeport, was progressing with giant strides. The Wheeler and Wilson Sewing Machine manufactory had been quadrupled in size, and employed about a thousand workmen. Numerous other large factories had been built, and scores of first-class houses were erected, besides many neat but smaller and cheaper houses for laborers and mechanics. That piece of property which, but eight years before, had been farm land, with scarcely six houses upon the whole tract, was now a beautiful new city, teeming with busy life, and looking as neat as a new pin. The greatest pleasure which I then took, or even now take, was in driving through those busy streets, admiring the beautiful houses and substantial factories, with their thousands of prosperous workmen, and reflecting that I had, in so great a measure, been the means of adding all this life, bustle and wealth to the City of Bridgeport. And reflection on this subject only confirmed in my mind the great doctrine of compensations. How plain was it, in my case, that an "apparent evil" was a "blessing in disguise"! How palpable was it now that, had it not been for the clock failure, this prosperity could not have existed here! An old citizen of Bridgeport used to say to me, when, a few years before, he had noticed my zeal in trying to build up the east side:

"Mr. Barnum, your contemplated new city is like a fire made with chestnut wood; it burns so long as you keep blowing it, and when you stop it goes out!"

I like now-a-days to laugh at him about his "chestnut-wood fire." Of course, I did blow the fire in all possible ways, but the result proved that the wood which fed the fire was not chestnut, but the best and soundest old hickory.

Up to the year 1865, the shore of Bridgeport west of the public wharves, and washed by the waters of Long Island Sound, was inaccessible to carriages, or even to horsemen, and almost impossible for pedestrianism. The shore edge in fact was strewn with rocks and boulders, which made it, like "Jordan" in the song, an exceedingly "hard road to travel." A narrow lane reaching down to the shore enabled parties to drive near to the water for the purpose of clamming, and occasionally bathing; but it was all claimed as private property by the land proprietors, whose farms extended down to the water's edge. On several occasions at low tide, I endeavored to ride along the shore on horseback for the purpose of examining "the lay of the land," in the hope of finding it feasible to get a public drive along the water's edge. On one occasion, in 1863, I succeeded in getting my horse around from the foot of Broad Street in Bridgeport to a lane over the Fairfield line, a few rods west of "Iranistan Avenue," a grand street which I have since opened at my own expense, and through my own land. From the observations I made that day, I was satisfied that a most lovely park and public drive might be, and ought to be, opened along the whole water-front as far as the western boundary line of Bridgeport, and even extending over the Fairfield line.

Foreseeing that in a few years such an improvement would be too late, and having in mind the failure of the attempt in 1850 to provide a park for the people of Bridgeport, I immediately began to agitate the subject in the Bridgeport papers, and also in daily conversations with such of my fellow-citizens as I thought would take an earnest and immediate interest in the enterprise. I urged that such an improvement would increase the taxable value of property in that vicinity many thousands of dollars, and thus enrich the city treasury; that it would improve the value of real estate generally in the city; that it would be an additional attraction to strangers who came to spend the summer with us, and to those who might be induced from other considerations to make the city their permanent residence; that the improvement would throw into market some of the most beautiful building-sites that could be found anywhere in Connecticut; and I dwelt upon the absurdity, almost criminality, that a beautiful city like Bridgeport, lying on the shore of a broad expanse of salt water, should so cage itself in that not an inhabitant could approach the beach. With these and like arguments and entreaties I plied the people day in and day out, till some of them began to be familiarized with the idea that a public park close upon the shore of the Sound was at least a possible if not probable thing.

But certain "conservatives," as they are called, said: "Barnum is a hair-brained fellow, who thinks he can open and people a New York Broadway through a Connecticut wilderness"; and the "old fogies" added: "Yes, he is trying to start another chestnut-wood fire for the city to blow forever; but the city or town of Bridgeport will not pay out money to lay out or to purchase public parks. If people want to see green grass and trees, they have only to walk or drive half a mile either way from the city limits, and they will come to farms where they can see either or both for nothing; and, if they are anxious to see salt water, and to get a breath of the Sound breeze, they can take boats at the wharves, and sail or row till they are entirely satisfied."

Thus talked the conservatives and the "old fogies," who unhappily, even if they are in a minority, are always a force in all communities. I soon saw that it was of no use to expect to get the city to pay for a park. The next thing was to see if the land could not be procured free of charge, or at a nominal cost, provided the city would improve and maintain it as a public park. I approached the farmers who owned the land lying immediately upon the shore, and tried to convince them that, if they would give the city free a deep slip next to the water, to be used as a public park, it would increase in value the rest of their land so much as to make it a profitable operation for them. But it was like beating against the wind. They were "not so stupid as to think that they could become gainers by giving away their property." Such trials of patience as I underwent in a twelvemonth, in the endeavor to carry this point, few persons who have not undertaken like almost hopeless labor can comprehend. At last I enlisted the attention of Messrs. Nathaniel Wheeler, James Loomis, Francis Ives, Frederick Wood, and a few

WINTER QUARTERS OF THE BARNUM-LONDON SHOW AT BRIDGEPORT

Loan Collection of Elizabeth Sterling Seeley

more gentlemen, and persuaded them to walk with me over the ground, which to me seemed in every way practicable for a park. These gentlemen, who were men of taste as well as of enterprise and public spirit, very soon coincided in my ideas as to the feasibility of the plan and the advantages of the site; and some of them went with me to talk with the land-owners, adding their own pleas to the arguments I had already advanced. At last, after much pressing and persuading, we got the terms upon which the proprietors would give a portion and sell another portion of their land which fronted on the water, provided the land thus disposed of should forever be appropriated to the purposes of a public park. But unfortunately a part of the land it was desirable to include was the small Mallett farm, of some thirty acres, then belonging to an unsettled estate, and neither the administrator nor the heirs could or would give away a rod of it. But the whole farm was for sale,—and, to overcome the difficulty in the way of its transfer for the public benefit, I bought it for about $12,000, and then presented the required front to the park. I did not want this land or any portion of it for my own purposes or profit, and I offered a thousand dollars to any one who would take my place in the transaction; but no one accepted, and I was quite willing to contribute so much of the land as was needed for so noble an object. Indeed, besides this, I gave $1,400 towards purchasing other land and improving the park; and, after months of persistent and personal effort, I succeeded in raising, by private subscription, the sum necessary to secure the land needed. This was duly paid for, deeded to and accepted by the city, and I had the pleasure of naming this new and great public improvement, "Sea-side Park."

In the summer of 1867, the health of my wife continuing to decline, her physician directed that she should remove nearer to the sea-shore. Lindencroft was sold July 1, 1867, and we immediately removed for a summer's sojourn to a small farm-house adjoining Sea-side Park. During the hot days of the next three months we found the delightful sea-breeze so bracing and refreshing that the season passed like a happy dream, and we resolved that our future summers should be spent on the very shore of Long Island Sound. I did not, however, perfect my arrangements in time to prepare my own summer residence for the ensuing season; and during the hot months of 1868, we resided in a new and very pretty house I had just completed on State street, in Bridgeport, and which I subsequently sold, as I intended doing when I built it. But, towards the end of the summer, I added by purchase to the Mallett farm, adjoining Sea-side Park, a large and beautiful hickory grove, which seemed to be all that was needed to make the site exactly what I desired for a summer residence.

But there was a vast deal to do in grading and preparing the ground, in opening new streets and avenues as approaches to the property, and in setting out trees near the proposed site of the house; so that ground was not broken for the foundation till October. I planned a house which should combine the greatest convenience with the highest comfort, keeping in mind always that houses are made to live in as well as to look at, and to be "homes" rather than mere residences. The first foundation stone was laid in October, 1868; and we moved into the completed house in June following. We formally christened the place "Waldemere,"—literally, but not so euphoniously, "Waldammeer," "Woods-by-the-Sea," for I preferred to give this native child of my own conception an American name of my own creation.

Having made up my mind to spend seven months of every year in the city, in the summer of 1867 I purchased the elegant and most eligibly situated mansion, No. 438 Fifth Avenue, corner of Thirty-ninth street, at the crowning point of Murray Hill, in New York, and moved into it in November.

CHAPTER XL

REST ONLY FOUND IN ACTION

AFTER the destruction by fire of my Museum, March 3d, 1868, I retired from business, not knowing how utterly fruitless it is to attempt to chain down energies peculiar to my nature. No man not similarly situated can imagine the *ennui* which seizes such a nature after it has lain dormant for a few months. Having "nothing to do" I thought at first was a very pleasant, as it was to me an entirely new sensation.

"I would like to call on you in the summer, if you have any leisure, in Bridgeport," said an old friend.

"I am a man of leisure and thankful that I have nothing to do; so you cannot call amiss," I replied with an immense degree of self-satisfaction.

"Where is your office down-town when you live in New York?" asked another friend.

"I have no office," I proudly replied. "I have done work enough, and shall play the rest of my life. I don't go down-town once a week; but I ride in the Park every day, and am at home much of the time."

I am afraid that I chuckled often, when I saw rich merchants and bankers driving to their offices on a stormy morning, while I, looking complacently from the window of my cozy library, said to myself, "Let it snow and blow, there's nothing to call *me* out to-day." But nature will assert herself. Reading is pleasant as a pastime; writing without any special purpose soon tires; a game of chess will answer as a condiment; lectures, concerts, operas, and dinner parties are well enough in their way; but to a robust, healthy man of forty years' active business life, something else is needed to satisfy. Sometimes like the truant school-boy I found all my friends engaged, and I had no play-mate. I began to fill my house with visitors, and yet frequently we spent evenings quite alone. Without really perceiving what the matter was, time hung on my hands, and I was ready to lecture gratuitously for every charitable cause that I could benefit. At this juncture I hailed with delight a visit from my English friend, John Fish and his daughter, who came to see the new world, and found me just in the humor to act as guide and exhibitor. I now resumed my old business and became a showman of "natural curiosities" on a most magnificent scale; and, having congenial and appreciative travelling companions, and no business distractions, I saw beauty and grandeur in scenes which I had before gazed on unimpressed. For the third time I visited Cuba, then New Orleans, Memphis, Louisville, Cincinnati, Baltimore and Washington, noting and enjoying the emotions of my English friends.

In April we made up a small, congenial party of ladies and gentlemen, and visited California *via* the Union and Central Pacific Railroads. We journeyed leisurely, and I lectured in Council Bluffs, Omaha and Salt Lake City, where amongst my audience were a dozen or so of Brigham Young's wives and scores of his children. By invitation, I called with my friends on President Young at the Bee-Hive. He received us very cordially, asked us many questions, and promptly answered ours.

"Barnum," said he, "what will you give to exhibit me in New York and the eastern cities?"

"Well, Mr. President," I replied, "I'll give you half the receipts, which I will guarantee shall be $200,000 per year, for I consider you the best show in America."

"Why did you not secure me some years ago when I was of no consequence?" he continued.

"Because, you would not have 'drawn' at that time," I answered.

Brigham smiled and said, "I would like right well to spend a few hours with you, if you could come when I am disengaged." I thanked him, and told him I guessed I should enjoy it; but visitors were crowding into his reception-room, and we withdrew.

During the week we spent in seeing San Francisco and its suburbs, I discovered a dwarf more diminutive than General Tom Thumb was when first I found him, and so handsome, well-formed and captivating that I could not resist the temptation to engage him. I gave him the soubriquet of Admiral Dot, dressed him in complete Admiral's uniform, and invited the editors of the San Francisco journals to visit him in the parlors of the Cosmopolitan Hotel. Immediately there was an immense furore, and Woodward's Gardens, where "Dot" was exhibited for three weeks before going east, was daily thronged with crowds of his curious fellow citizens, under whose very eyes he had lived so long undiscovered.

Speaking of dwarfs, it may be mentioned here that, notwithstanding my announced retirement from public life, I still retained business connections with my old friend, the well-known General Tom Thumb. In 1869, I joined that celebrated dwarf in a fresh enterprise which proposed an exhibition tour of him and a party of twelve, with a complete outfit, including a pair of ponies and a carriage, entirely around the world.

While I am about it, I may as well confess my connection, *sub rosa,* with another little speculation during my three years' "leisure." I hired the well-known Siamese Twins, the giantess, Anna Swan, and a Circassian lady, and, in connection with Judge Ingalls, I sent them to Great Britain where, in all the principal places, and for about a year, their levees were continually crowded. In all probability the great success attending this enterprise was much enhanced, if not actually caused, by extensive announcements in advance that the main purpose of Chang-Eng's visit to Europe was to consult the most eminent medical and surgical talent with regard to the safety of separating the twins.

We spent some time in the Yo Semite; stopping by the way at the Mariposa grove of big trees, whence I sent to New York a piece of bark thirty-one inches thick. Concluding a most enjoyable trip, we returned to New York, and on June 1st my family removed to our summer home, Waldemere. There the good and gifted Alice Cary, then in feeble health, and her sister Phoebe were our guests for several weeks.

In September, I made up a party of ten, including my English friend, and we started for Kansas on a grand buffalo hunt. General Custer, commandant at Fort Hayes, was apprized in advance of our anticipated visit, and he received us like princes. He fitted out a company of fifty cavalry, furnishing us with horses, arms and ammunition. We were taken to an immense herd of buffaloes, quietly browsing on the plain. We charged on them, and, during an exciting chase of a couple of hours, we slew twenty immense bull buffaloes, and might have killed as many more had we not considered it wanton butchery.

Our ten days' sport afforded me a "sensation," but sensations cannot be made to order every day, so, in the autumn of 1870, to open a safety-valve for my pent-up energies, I began to prepare a great show enterprise, comprising a Museum, Menagerie, Caravan, Hippodrome and Circus, of such proportions as to require five hundred men and horses to transport it through the country. On the tenth of April, 1871, the vast tents, covering nearly three acres of ground, were opened in Brooklyn, and filled with ten thousand delighted spectators, thousands more being unable to obtain entrance. The success which marked the inauguration of this, my greatest show, attended it the whole season, during which time it visited the Eastern, Middle and Western States from Maine to Kansas.

At the close of a brilliant season, I recalled the show to New York, secured the Empire Rink, and opened in that building November 13, 1871, being welcomed by an enthusiastic audience of ten thousand people. The exhibitions were continued daily, with unvarying popularity and patronage, until the close of the holidays, when necessary preparations for the spring campaign compelled me to close. One of the most interesting curiosities added at that time was a gigantic section of a California "big tree," of such proportions that on one occasion, at the Empire Rink, it enclosed two hundred children of the Howard Mission.

During the winter of 1871 and 1872, I worked unremittingly, re-organizing and re-enforcing my great traveling show. To the horror of my very able but too cautious manager, Mr. W. C. Coup, and my treasurer, Mr. Hurd, I so augmented the already innumerable attractions, that it was shown beyond doubt that we could not travel at a less expense than five thousand dollars per day, but, undaunted, I still expended thousands of dollars, and ship after ship brought me rare and valuable animals and works of art. Two beautiful Giraffes, or Camelopards, were dispatched to me (one died on the Atlantic), and a third was retained for me at the Zoölogical Gardens, London, ready to be shipped at a moment's notice. As no giraffe has ever lived two years in America, all other managers had given up any attempt to import them, but this only made me more determined to always have one on hand at whatever cost.

My agents in Alaska procured for me several immense sea-lions and barking seals, which weighed a thousand pounds each, and consumed from sixty to a hundred pounds of fish daily. My novelties comprised an Italian goat "Alexis," taught in Europe to ride on horseback, leap through hoops and over banners, alighting on his feet on the back of the horse while going at full speed. I had also many extraordinary musical and other automatons and moving tableaux, made expressly for me by expert European artists. But perhaps the most striking additions to my show were four wild Fiji Cannibals, ransomed at great cost from the hands of a royal enemy, into whose hands they had fallen, and by whom they were about to be killed and perhaps eaten.

Perceiving that my great combination was assuming such proportions that it would be impossible to move it by horse power, I negotiated with all the railway companies between New York and Omaha, Nebraska, for the transportation by rail of my whole show, requiring sixty to seventy freight cars, six passenger cars, and three engines. The result is well remembered. The great show visited the States of New Jersey, Delaware, Maryland, Pennsylvania, District of Columbia, Virginia, Ohio, Indiana, Kentucky, Illinois, Missouri, Kansas, Iowa, Minnesota, Wisconsin and Michigan, often traveling one hundred miles in a single night to hit good-sized towns every day, arriving in time to give three exhibitions, and the usual street pageant at eight o'clock A. M. By means of cheap excursion trains, thousands of strangers attended daily, coming fifty, seventy-five and a hundred miles. Thousands more came in wagons and on horseback, frequently arriving in the night and "camping out." The tenting season closed at Detroit, October 30th, when we were patronized by the largest concourse of people ever assembled in the State of Michigan.

At the close in Detroit of the great Western railroad tour, I equipped and started South a Museum, Menagerie and Circus, which, while it made no perceptible diminution in the main body, was still the largest and most complete travelling expedition ever seen in the Southern States. Louisville was designated as the rendezvous and point of consolidation of the various departments, and the new expedition gave its initial exhibition in the Falls City, November 4. Much of the menagerie consisted of animals of which I owned the duplicate, and hence could easily spare them without

FIRE AT BARNUM'S WINTER QUARTERS, NOVEMBER 20, 1887

Frank Leslie's Illustrated Newspaper

BARNUM AND BAILEY CIRCUS PARADE IN ENGLAND IN 1902

L. J. Currie Collection

injuring the variety in my zoölogical collection. I was aware, also, that many of the rare specimens would thrive better in a warmer climate, and as the expense of procuring them had been enormous I coupled my humanitarian feelings with my pecuniary interests, and sent them South.

In August, I purchased the building and lease on Fourteenth street, New York, known as the Hippotheatron, purposing to open a Museum, Menagerie, Hippodrome and Circus, that would furnish employment for two hundred of my people who would otherwise be idle during the winter. I enlarged and remodeled the building almost beyond recognition, at an expense of $60,000, installed in it my valuable collection of animals, automatons and living curiosities, and on Monday evening, November 18, the grand opening took place. It was a beautiful sight; the huge building, with a seating capacity of 2,800, filled from pit to dome with a brilliant audience, the dazzling new lights, the sweet music and gorgeous ornamentations completing the charm. The papers next morning contained long and eulogistic editorials.

Four weeks after this inauguration, I visited my Southern show at New Orleans. While seated at breakfast at the St. Louis Hotel and perusing an account of the flooding of my show-grounds in that city, the following telegram was handed me:

NEW YORK, *December 24.*

To P. T. Barnum, New Orleans:

About 4 A. M. fire discovered in boiler-room of circus building; everything destroyed except 2 elephants, 1 camel.

S. H. HURD, Treasurer.

The smaller misfortune was instantly forgotten in the greater. Calling for writing material, I then and there cabled my European agents to send duplicates of all animals lost, with positive instructions to have everything shipped in time to reach New York by the middle of March. I directed them further to procure at any cost specimens never seen in America; and through sub-agents to purchase and forward curiosities—animate and inanimate—from all parts of the globe. I then dispatched the following to my son-in-law:

NEW ORLEANS, *December* 24.

To S. H. Hurd, New York:

Tell editors I have cabled European agents to expend half million dollars for extra attractions; will have new and more attractive show than ever early in April.

P. T. BARNUM.

These details attended to, I resumed my breakfast, and took a calm view of the situation.

Returning to New York, I learned that my loss on building and property amounted to nearly $300,000, to meet which I held insurance policies to the amount of $90,000. My equestrian company, in which I took great pride, was left idle until the opening of the summer season. The members lost their entire wardrobes, a loss which can only be appreciated by professionals. The Equestrian Benevolent Society kindly gave them a benefit at the Academy of Music, on the afternoon and evening of January 7, 1873. Many stars in the equestrian, dramatic and musical firmament volunteered for the occasion, and the two entertainments were largely attended.

Before the new year dawned, I received tidings that my agents had purchased for me a full collection of animals and curiosities, and by the first week in April, 1873—but three short months after the fire—I placed upon the road a combination of curiosities and marvellous performances that by far surpassed any attempt ever made with a travelling exhibition in any country. Indeed, so wonderfully immense was "Barnum's Traveling World's Fair" in 1873, that its expenses greatly exceeded five thousand dollars per day, and my friends almost unanimously declared that it would "break" me. I suppose there is a limit beyond which it would be fatal to go, in catering for public instruction and amusement, but I have never yet found that limit. My experience is that the more and the better a manager will provide for the public, the more liberally they will respond. The season of 1873 was far from being an exception to this experience. My tents covered double the space of ground that I had ever required before, and yet they were never so closely crowded with visitors. Where thousands attended my show in 1872, numbers of thousands came in 1873. It visited the largest cities in Connecticut, Massachusetts, Rhode Island, Maine, New Hampshire, Vermont, and the Middle and Western States as far as St. Louis, Mo., taking Canada on the return route to New York.

In September, 1873, as I had not visited Europe since 1869, I concluded to run over and see the International Exhibition at Vienna, and visit other parts of Europe, to rest my over-worked brain, and see what could be picked up to instruct and edify my amusement patrons. On landing at Liverpool, I was met by my old friend, John Fish, the last friend who shook my hand as I left Liverpool in 1859, and the first to grasp it as I landed in 1873. After spending a few days at his house, in Southport, the "Montpelier of England," a delightful watering-place eighteen miles from Liverpool, I proceeded to London. I met many of my old English friends here, including, of course, my esteemed friend and faithful agent, Robert Fillingham, Esq., and then hastened on to Cologne, Leipsic, Dresden, and Vienna, which latter city I reached ten days before the closing of the great World's Fair. Those ten days I devoted most assiduously to studying the marvels of this great World's Exhibition, and I witnessed the ceremonies which terminated what is generally conceded to be the largest and best International Exhibition that the world ever saw. I proceeded leisurely back to Dresden, stopping at Prague on the way. Thence I went to Berlin, and, at each city, I took time to see all that was interesting. While at Berlin, I received letters from my manager, Coup, and treasurer, Hurd, saying they would be able to secure a short lease of the Harlem Railroad property in New

York, bounded by Fourth and Madison avenues and Twenty-sixth and Twenty-seventh streets, containing several acres, for the purpose of carrying out my long-cherished plan of exhibiting a Roman Hippodrome, Zoölogical Institute, Aquaria, and Museum of unsurpassable extent and magnificence. I immediately telegraphed them to take the lease, and within twenty-four hours from that time I was in telegraphic communication with seventeen European cities where I knew were the proper parties to aid me in carrying out a grand and novel enterprise. I visited all the zoölogical gardens, circuses, and public exhibitions, wherever I went, and thus secured numerous novelties and obtained new and valuable ideas. At Hamburg, I purchased nearly a ship-load of valuable wild animals and rare birds, including elephants, giraffes, a dozen ostriches, etc.

I had concluded all my purchases in Hamburg on the eighteenth of November, 1873, and was taking a few last looks around the city previous to starting for Italy, when, on the twentieth inst., I received from my son-in-law, Mr. Hurd, a telegraphic dispatch announcing the death of my wife on the day previous. After this sad blow I could not bear the thought of "sight-seeing," and I yearned to be where I could meet sympathizing friends and hear my native tongue. I therefore returned to London and spent several weeks in quiet.

At length, the continual letters from my manager roused me to action, and I went at it with a will. What I did is shown in the following extract from the London *Era:*

BARNUM'S NEXT SENSATION.

The greatest showman of the day is once more in London, completing preparations for the opening of the immense Hippodrome which he is erecting in New York. Some idea of the means which are being taken to create a sensation may be derived from the following facts: Mr. Barnum has not only sent agents to Spain and Africa to secure attractions, but has himself visited the Hippodrome in Paris, the Circus Renz at Vienna, Myers' Circus at Dresden, Salamonski and Carre's Circus at Cologne, the Zoological Gardens at Hamburgh, Amsterdam and other Continental cities, selecting and purchasing the choicest animals procurable, and engaging the most talented artists. He has secured what may fairly be called an endless variety of attractions, ranging from a race-horse to a Roman chariot. With the Messrs. Sanger alone he has done business to "the tune" of £11,000. He has already shipped to New York elephants, camels and horses, trained for every species of Circus performance. On the 25th a further "batch" will be dispatched, including sixteen ostriches, ten elands, ten zebras, a team of reindeer, with Lapland drivers, a troupe of performing ponies, monkeys, dogs, goats, &c., &c. The armor and costume makers of London are to be set to work immediately the pantomimes are off their minds and hands, and some portion of the paraphernalia which is to contribute to the gigantic whole will be shipped weekly. The Hippodrome will open in April next, and in the preliminary parade, we have no doubt, the citizens will find reason to say that their greatest and most popular showman has far outstripped all his former efforts. We may add that the New York enterprise will in no way interfere with the famous tent show everywhere known as "Barnum's Great Museum, Menagerie, Circus and Traveling World's Fair."

Already had we leased from the Harlem Railroad Company a plot of land in the center of New York valued at over a million of dollars, and on that land we were to erect buildings which would probably cost two hundred thousand dollars.

Curiosity impelled me to attend the Tichborne trial one day. I was told it would be useless to attempt it, as none were admitted without a court order. I, however, applied at the door of Westminster Hall, where a great crowd was waiting unable to get in. In reply to my request to be admitted, a policeman asked if I had an order from the court. Upon my answering in the negative he remarked: "Even if you had, you could not get in to-day, for every inch of room is occupied; but in no case can you ever get in without an order from the court." I asked for the inspector who had charge of the police. Inspector Deming was pointed out to me, and I handed him my card.

"Are you the great American Museum man?" he asked.

"Yes," I replied; "I am the Museum man, the Tom Thumb man, the Jenny Lind man, and the Showman."

"My dear sir," said the inspector, "I am glad to see you. Please write your name on the back of your card and I shall always prize it as a souvenir.   I am very happy that I can show the celebrated showman something he never saw before."

He then led me into Westminster Hall, secured me a good seat, pointed out the "claimant," Lord Chief Justice Cockburn, Justices Weller and Lush, Dr. Kenealy, Mr. Hawkins, and other prominent personages.

I arrived in New York from Liverpool by the steamer "Scotia," April 30, 1874, rejoiced to reach my native land again, and delighted to find my children and grandchildren in good health.   The great Roman Hippodrome had been open about a week, and on the evening of my arrival I was called out by the audience and was driven in my carriage around the immense arena and saw what, to me, was indeed a great "show"—the largest assemblage of people ever gathered in one building in New York.   I may be permitted to add, that my enthusiastic reception was at once a testimonial of the public appreciation of one of my greatest efforts in my managerial career, and a verdict that it was a complete and gratifying success.

This truly stupendous and superb spectacle, as the unanimous voice of the press pronounced it, opened every evening with an allegorical representation of a "Congress of Nations," in a grand procession of gilded chariots and triumphal cars, conveying the Kings, Queens, Emperors, and other potentates of the civilized world, costumed with historical correctness, royally surrounded, and accompanied and followed by their respective courts and splendid retinues.   The correctness and completeness of this historical representation required nearly one thousand persons and several hundred horses, besides elephants, camels, llamas, ostriches, etc.   The rich and varied costumes, armor and trappings, the gorgeous banners and paraphernalia, and the appropriate music accompanying the entrance of each nation produced an effect at once brilliant and bewildering.   The entire public, and the press, both secular and religious, declared unanimously, what is unquestionably true, that never before since the days of the Cæsars has there been so grand and so interesting a public spectacle.

Following this superb historical introduction were all kinds of races by highbred horses imported by scores from Europe and ridden and driven by accomplished experts of both sexes. To these succeeded various first-class entertainments, including the wonderful performances of the Japanese athletes, thrilling wire-walking exploits, athletic sports by non-professionals for prizes awarded as encouragements to such enterprises, semi-weekly balloon ascensions by Prof. Donaldson, the whole interspersed with a plenty of genuine fun in the monkey and donkey races and in "Twenty minutes of the Donnybrook Fair and Lancashire Races"—and with all was "thrown in" my magnificent menagerie.

Although the Hippodrome could accommodate ten thousand spectators, for weeks in succession all the best seats were engaged days in advance, and it is literally true that at every evening performance thousands were turned away. My patrons included the President of the United States and his Cabinet, Governors and Judges, the clergy of all denominations, and all the best people of our land, who expressed but one opinion, that the exhibition, as I intended it should be, far surpassed the most sanguine expectations of what managerial experience and endeavor could possibly accomplish. In the very midst of such success, the necessity of covering the central part of the Hippodrome with glass, putting in heating apparatus, and otherwise preparing the immense building for the winter campaign, compelled me to temporarily transfer the entire vast establishment to Boston for three weeks from August 3d, thence to Philadelphia, returning and reopening in New York about September 20th.

After the exciting scenes and unremitting labor of several weeks in New York, I retired to Waldemere for rest.

CHAPTER XLI

In July, 1874, immense canvas tents were made of sufficient capacity to accommodate all my great Roman Hippodrome performances. These tents, with the expense of removing the whole Hippodrome establishment to Boston for a three weeks' exhibition, cost me nearly fifty thousand dollars. During the three weeks' exhibiton in Boston, the tents were crowded each afternoon and evening with the most delighted audiences. Excursion trains on all the railroads leading to Boston brought thousands of visitors to the Hippodrome every day, and the Boston and New England papers, secular and religious, without exception, were loud in praise of what all acknowledged to be by far the most gorgeous, extensive, instructive and expensive travelling exhibition of which we have any record.

From Boston the entire Hippodrome was transported by railroad to Philadelphia, where a success was achieved fully equal to that in Boston. The Hippodrome afterwards visited Baltimore, Pittsburgh and Cincinnati, everywhere drawing immense crowds, and opened again in my great Hippodrome building in New York, in November, where, for several months, it afforded a treat to the American public that will probably not be witnessed again in this generation. I am confident that nothing less than my reputation for forty years as a liberal caterer for public instruction and amusement would have brought a paying response to my efforts. The great religious community aided mostly in sustaining this hazardous enterprise.

In the autumn of 1874 I married again. My second wife is the daughter of my old English friend, John Fish, Esq. We were married in the Church of the Divine Paternity, Fifth Avenue, New York, by my old and esteemed friend, the Rev. Dr. Chapin, in the presence of members of my family and a large gathering of gratified friends. After a brief bridal tour, our wedding receptions were attended at Waldemere.

In December, 1874, His Majesty, David Kalakau, King of the Sandwich Islands, visited New York. I invited the king and his suite to attend the Hippodrome, which they did on the afternoon of December 26th. During the entire performance I was seated by the side of the king, who kept up a pleasant conversation with me for a couple of hours. I took occasion to remind him that this was by no means the first time I had had the honor of "entertaining" royalty, as he would see from my book—a handsome presentation copy of which he had accepted from me on Christmas day. He expressed himself highly delighted with my entertainment, and said he was always fond of horses and racing. Some twelve thousand persons were present, and when the exhibitions were about half finished they called loudly "The King! The King!" Turning to me, His Majesty inquired the meaning of this. I replied: "Your Majesty, this vast audience undoubtedly wishes to give you an ovation. This building is so large that they cannot distinctly see Your Majesty from every part, and are anxious that you should ride around the circle in order that they may greet you."

The king looked surprised, and presently the audience commenced calling "The King! Barnum! Barnum! The King!" At that moment my open barouche was driven into the circle and approached where we were sitting. "No doubt Your Majesty would greatly gratify my countrymen," I remarked, "if you would kindly step into this carriage with me and ride around the circle." The king immediately arose, and, amid tremendous cheering, he stepped into the carriage. I took a seat by his side, and he smilingly remarked, *sotto voce:* "We are all actors." The audience rose to their feet, cheered and waved their handkerchiefs as the king rode around the circle, raising his hat and bowing. The excitement was indeed tremendous. The king remained till all the performances were finished, and expressed himself as greatly pleased with the whole entertainment.

It is said that "It never rains but it pours," and just at this time I was visited by a shower of royalty and nobility. The King of Hawaii had scarcely left New York before I received an invitation to breakfast with Lord Rosebery at the Brevoort House, Fifth Avenue. Lord Rosebery is a prominent member of the British Parliament, where he sits as Baron Rosebery. The invitation stated that his Lordship would sail for England on the twenty-seventh of January, and that having seen most of our country, and its "lions," he did not like to leave without having an interview with Barnum. I accepted the invitation. The breakfast came off at ten o'clock in the morning of January 26th, and I need scarcely say that it was a most dainty, delightful and *recherché* affair. Only one gentleman besides his Lordship was present. I found my host a very intelligent gentleman. He had been in America once before, and he seemed well "posted" in regard to our country and its institutions. He said he had read my autobiography, and had witnessed with amazement and delight the scenes at my Roman Hippodrome. These enhanced his desire to see "the man who was so celebrated throughout the world for the magnitude and perfection of his enterprises as a caterer for public gratification."

I accepted the compliment as gracefully as I could, and we were soon conversing socially without restraint on either side. Lord Rosebery is a good story-teller, and, what is still more pleasing to a loquacious old traveller like myself, he is a capital listener. While discussing the luxurious meal, we interchanged amusing anecdotes and personal experiences, some of mine so tickling his lordship's keen sense of humor that, more than once, he pushed back his chair from the table and gave vent to his hilarity in hearty, unrestrained laughter.

After a couple of hours we parted, exchanging photographs and autographs. His lordship expressed himself highly pleased with the interview, and politely added that he hoped to meet me in England, whenever I shall carry out my intention of taking a great show to that country.

In March, 1875, the nomination for Mayor of the city of Bridgeport was tendered me by a committee from the Republican party, but I declined until assured by prominent members of the opposition that my nomination was intended as a compliment, and that both parties would sustain it. Politically, the city is largely democratic, but I led the republican ticket, and was elected, April 5th, by several hundred majority.

My Hippodrome, in 1875, was transported by rail throughout the United States, going as far east as Portland, Maine, and west to Kansas City, Missouri. It proved a tolerably successful season, notwithstanding the depressed state of finances generally.

It gives me pain to record that our aeronaut, Professor Donaldson, having made his daily balloon ascension on Thursday, July 15, from our Hippodrome grounds at Chicago, was never heard from afterwards. He took with him Mr. N. S. Grimwood, a reporter of the Chicago *Journal,* whose body was found in Lake Michigan a few weeks afterwards. Prof. Donaldson was doubtless drowned during the terrible storm which occurred on the night of the ascension. He was a man of excellent habits, clear brain and steady nerve, fearless, but not reckless, and respected by all who knew him. His last was his 138th ascension.

During the autumn of 1875, under the auspices of "The Redpath Lyceum Bureau," in Boston, I delivered about thirty times a lecture on "The World and How to Live in It," going as far east as

Thomaston, Maine, and west to Leavenworth, Kansas, and including the cities of Boston, Portland, Chicago, Kansas City, etc.

On November 28, and following days, I offered all my show property at auction. This included my Hippodrome and also my "World's Fair," consisting of museum, menagerie and circus property. My object was to get rid of all surplus stock, and henceforth to have but one travelling show, which, as ever, should be as good as money and experience could make it. To this end my agent bid in all such property as I could use, in order to be properly prepared for our Centennial year. My travelling show consisted of Museum, Menagerie and Circus of immense proportions, and I introduced patriotic features that gave the people a Fourth of July celebration every day. My establishment travelled in three trains of railway cars. We took along a battery of cannon, and every morning we fired a salute of thirteen guns. We introduced groups of persons costumed in the style of our Continental troops, and supplemented with the Goddess of Liberty, a live eagle and some first-class singers who, with a chorus of several hundred voices, sang the "Star Spangled Banner" and other patriotic songs, accompanied with bands of music and also with cannon placed outside our tents, and fired by means of electricity. We closed our patriotic demonstration by singing "America" ("My Country, 'Tis of Thee"), the entire audience rising and joining in the chorus. At night we terminated our performances with fire-works, in which thrilling revolutionary scenes were brilliantly depicted. Our grand street procession was a gorgeous and novel feature. It began to move when the salute was fired, and I depended upon the patriotism of each town we visited to add to the effects of our National Jubilee by ringing of bells at the same time. My assistant managers were my son-in-law, Mr. Hurd, and Messrs. Smith Brothers, June and Bailey, late proprietors of the European Menagerie and Circus, which I purchased entire and added to my other attractions. My official term as Mayor expired April 3, 1876. I peremptorily refused a renomination, preferring to travel a portion of the time with my grand Centennial show, and meet face to face the millions of friends who, during the past year, had been my generous and I trust gratified patrons.

CHAPTER XLII

In December, 1876, I received a second invitation from Lord Rosebery to breakfast with him in New York. On parting with his lordship in 1874, his warm expressions of pleasure at having met me, and his assurances that he hoped and intended to renew our acquaintance, left no room for embarrassing misgivings on this occasion. Our meeting at the Brevoort House was very cordial. His lordship took me in his brougham to the New York Club, and there I first learned that our breakfast companions were Martin Farquhar Tupper and the chief editor of a prominent New York daily paper. Mr. Tupper and myself had held a correspondence previous to his leaving England, and the author of "Proverbial Philosophy" was apparently delighted at the unexpected meeting of his "dear friend Barnum." The occasion was an exceedingly enjoyable one, and if, as is said, laughter aids digestion, I am confident that three of the quartette were not troubled with dyspepsia after that delicious and *recherché* meal.

Among many other valuable additions to my travelling show of 1877 were six beautiful and remarkably trained black Trakene Stallions from Germany. My agents, Bailey and June, after scouring Europe in search of novelties, purchased them at large figures from James Myers, proprietor of the Great American Circus in Paris. They formed a novel and pleasing feature, and, with other startling novelties, aided to secure to me a still more profitable season than that of 1876.

On the 11th of April, 1877, my family were stricken with a heavy sorrow in the sudden death of my daughter, Pauline T. Seeley, at the age of thirty-one years, leaving a husband and three children. This blow would have been insupportable to me did I not receive it as coming from our good Father in Heaven, who does all things right.

In July, 1877, I sailed for England with my wife, in the Cunard steamer "Russia," returning home some eight weeks later in the "Scythia" of the same line. At the request of the captains and passengers, I gave a lecture on each steamer for the benefit of the Seamen's Orphan Institution in Liverpool. I also gave my lecture on "The World, and How to Live in It," several times in the Royal Aquarium Theatre, London, in Alexandra Palace, London, Southport Winter Gardens, and in Bolton. I likewise lectured on Temperance in Hawkstone Hall, London, at which the celebrated Rev. Newman Hall presided; and I gave a similar lecture in Hengler's Circus building, Liverpool. I was glad to meet many of my old friends in England after an absence of eighteen years.

In the spring of 1877 I offered $10,000 for the return of the kidnapped Charley Ross to his afflicted parents. But though my offer was published far and wide on both sides of the Atlantic, all efforts for his restoration proved unavailing.

In August, 1877, I visited Des Moines, and proceeded west with my show as far as Council Bluffs, Iowa, and thence to my cattle ranch in Colorado. I gave temperance speeches in Denver and Greeley, and also gave my lecture on "The World, and How to Live in It," in the former city and at Colorado Springs.

In November, 1877, I was elected to represent Bridgeport in the General Assembly of Connecticut. My majority was 212, although the political party with which I am identified is usually 700 in the minority. It was a personal sacrifice to me to leave my home to help make our State laws at Hartford, but I did not feel at liberty to refuse the demand upon my services, and I endeavored to fulfill my duty as a citizen of the Commonwealth without undue exertions party-wise. The Speaker, Hon. Chas. H. Briscoe, offered me the choice of chairmanship of half a dozen standing committees. I told him that on the two former occasions when I was in the Legislature I was Chairman on Agriculture (having plowed with an elephant), but I should now prefer to be one of the Committee on Temperance. He appointed me chairman of that committee. We succeeded in getting several favorable changes in our liquor laws, yet, like Oliver Twist, we asked for more. During the winter I gave a number of lectures in the vicinity of Hartford.

In April, 1878, my great travelling show opened for a fortnight at the American Institute building, in New York, and then proceeded to Philadelphia. The show, as usual, was transported through the country on nearly a hundred railway cars of my own, preceded a fortnight in advance by my magnificent advertising car, carrying press agents, the "paste brigade" of twenty men, and tons of immense colored bills, programmes, lithographs, photographs, electrotype cuts, etc., to arouse the entire country for fifty miles around each place of exhibition to the fact that "P. T. Barnum's New and Greatest Show on Earth," with its acres of tents and pavilions, could be reached by cheap excursion trains on certain days specified in the bills and advertisements. The show went East to Bangor, Maine, and West to Illinois, reaching New York and opening at Gilmore's Garden in October, for seven weeks to crowded houses.

In the summer of 1878, I expended some twenty thousand dollars in the purchase and reclamation of a large tract of salt marsh adjoining Sea-side Park and the grounds of Waldemere on the west. This marsh had been inaccessible from time immemorial, annually producing plentiful crops of mosquitoes. The times were hard, many laboring men in Bridgeport were suffering for want of employment, and although it was evident I should never be reimbursed for half my expenditures, I could see that the improvement would be a great

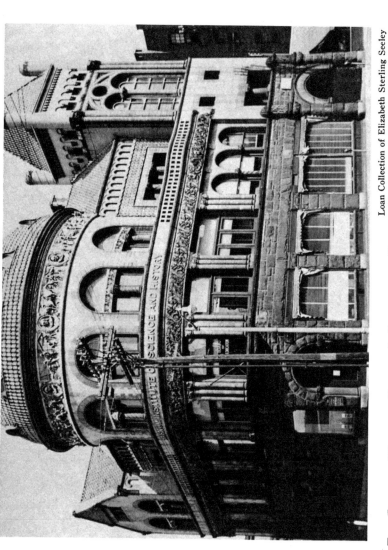

THE BARNUM MUSEUM, BARNUM'S GIFT TO THE CITY OF BRIDGEPORT

BARNUM IN HIS CARRIAGE IN FRONT OF WALDEMERE

public benefit, and remembering the dykes of Holland which I had
so frequently seen with astonishment and admiration, I determined,
as I told my neighbors, to "cheat my heirs," by expending a good
sum *pro bono publico.* I built this dyke straight across a channel
which let in the tide-water every twelve hours and covered an
immense tract of low salt meadow. I made the dyke seventy feet
wide at bottom, and of sufficient width on the top to form a fine
street leading from one of our city avenues to the beach on Long
Island Sound. This gives nearly a mile high and dry front on the
salt water connecting with Sea-Side Park.

In November, 1878, I consented, much against my will, to accept
another nomination to represent Bridgeport in the General Assembly
of Connecticut. I was re-elected by a majority of several hundred
votes.

Up to 1880, no travelling show in the world bore any comparison
with my justly-called "Greatest Show on Earth." Other show-
managers boasted of owning shows equalling mine, and some bought
of the printers large colored showbills pictorially representing my
marvellous curiosities, although these managers had no performances
or curiosities of the kinds which they represented. The cost of one
of their shows was from twenty thousand to fifty thousand dollars,
while mine cost millions of dollars. Their expenses were three
hundred to seven hundred dollars per day, while mine were three
thousand dollars per day. The public soon discovered the difference
between the sham and the reality, the natural consequences of mis-
representation followed; the small showmen made little or nothing,
some went into bankruptcy each season, while mine was always
crowded, and each succeeding year showed a larger profit.

My strongest competitors were the so-called "Great London
Circus, Sanger's Royal British Menagerie and Grand International
Allied Shows." Its managers, Cooper, Bailey & Hutchinson, had

adopted my manner of dealing with the public, and consequently their great show grew in popularity. On the tenth of March, 1880, while in Philadelphia, one of their large elephants, Hebe, became a mother. This was the first elephant born in captivity, and the managers so effectively advertised the fact that the public became wild with excitement over the "Baby Elephant." Naturalists and men of science rushed in numbers to Philadelphia, examined the wonderful "little stranger" and gave glowing reports to the papers of this country and of Europe. Illustrated papers and magazines of this and foreign lands described the Baby Elephant with pen and pencil, and before it was two months old I offered the lucky proprietors one hundred thousand dollars cash for mother and baby. They gleefully rejected my offer, pleasantly told me to look to my laurels, and wisely held on to their treasure.

I found that I had at last met foemen "worthy of my steel," and pleased to find comparatively young men with a business talent and energy approximating to my own, I met them in friendly council, and after days of negotiation we decided to join our two shows in one mammoth combination, and, sink or swim, to exhibit them for at least one season for one price of admission. The public were astonished at our audacity, and old showmen declared that we could never take in enough money to cover our expenses, which would be fully forty-five hundred dollars per day. My new partners, James A. Bailey and James L. Hutchinson, sagacious and practical managers, agreed with me that the experiment involved great risk, but, from the time of the Jenny Lind concerts, the Great Roman Hippodrome and other expensive enterprises, I have always found the great American public appreciative and ready to respond in proportion to the sums expended for their gratification and amusement.

In November of 1880, while in New York on business, I was suddenly attacked by an almost fatal illness, and laid for many weeks between life and death, unconscious of the tender solicitude shown me by countless good friends in this country, and the cable messages of inquiry that came thickly from others in foreign lands; the knowledge of which will be ever a bright and grateful memory. Dr. Chapin, then on his death-bed, sent a messenger daily; reporters besieged the house at all hours, and contributed bulletins of my progress or relapse to all the principal New York papers; while the Associated Press kept the remoter public informed by telegraph of my condition. When strong enough I went to Florida, to recuperate in that delightful climate, returning in April to take up my old avocations with the old zest and little less than the old strength.

The Barnum & London Circus opened in New York March 18, 1881, heralded by a torchlight procession through the city on Saturday night, March 16th, which was witnessed by more than half a million of people and pronounced the most brilliant display ever seen in America. Electric and calcium lights illuminated the whole. Windows were sold in New York, along Broadway, for five dollars, eight dollars and ten dollars, from which to view the pageant. So certain were we that this great street pageant and the marvellous combination of novelties to be produced throughout the season would totally eclipse any former show enterprise, that on Saturday, March 26th, we brought, in drawing-room cars, from Washington, D. C., and Boston, and all the principal cities on those routes, the editors of all the leading papers. These gentlemen, nearly one hundred in number, witnessed the torchlight procession Saturday night, and our opening performance at the Madison Square Garden Monday night, March 28th. They were lodged at hotels at our expense, and by us returned to their homes on Tuesday; a very costly piece of advertising, which yet yielded us a magnificent return in the enthusiastic editorial indorsements of so many papers of good standing, whose representatives had seen our show and exclaimed as did the Queen of Sheba to King Solomon, "The half was not told me."

Very early in the travelling season of 1881, we enlarged our already immense tents three different times, and yet so great was the multitude that attended our exhibitions—many coming on excursion trains twenty, thirty and even fifty miles—that at half the towns we visited we were unable to accommodate all who came, and we turned away thousands for want of room.   In every town we were patronized by the *élite,* and frequently the public and private schools, as well as manufactories, were closed on "Barnum Day," school committees and teachers recognizing that children would learn more natural history by one visit to our menagerie than they could acquire by months of reading.

In Washington President Garfield told me he always attended my shows, and when Secretary Blaine said, "Well, Barnum! all the children in America are anxious to see your show," the President smilingly added, "Yes! Mr. Barnum is the Kris Kringle of America."

For years showmen had asserted that I did not own my show; others assumed to be my relatives and representatives.   Determined to put down these false assertions and assumptions I sued the Philadelphia *Sun* for $100,000 damages in April, 1881, for saying that I merely hired out my name.   The publisher, convinced of his error, retracted the statement and apologized.   I withdrew the suit, having obtained all the redress I desired.   In May, 1881, the desire to acquire, for my show-season of 1882, attractions which only my personal negotiations could secure, I revisited England, sailing in the "Scythia."   After four pleasant weeks I returned in the "Gallia," successful in the object of my journey and invigorated by that finest of all tonics, a sea-voyage.   Desiring to aid in beautifying the village of Bethel, it being my birth-place, from which a busy checkered life has never alienated my interest, I presented to my old companions a bronze fountain eighteen feet high, made in Germany; the design a Triton of heroic size, spouting water from an uplifted horn.   It was a gala day for Bethel, the streets and residences were decorated with flags and bunting, a procession of police, fire companies with their engines, bands of music, citizens and invited guests in carriages, etc., paraded the town, and they formed in line around the square newly adorned by the fountain. From a grand stand many speeches were made, and as my old friends would not permit me to be merely a listener and looker-on, and as reminiscences of the old days presented themselves thickly in my mind, in wide and often amusing contrasts to the customs and conditions of to-day, I addressed them.

Our Great Barnum-London Show closed its season at Newport, Arkansas, November 12, 1881, from whence it came direct to its winter quarters, at Bridgeport, arriving on the morning of November nineteenth. The entire show travelled, during the season of thirty-three weeks, 12,266 miles.

CHAPTER XLIII

TWO FAMOUS ELEPHANTS

On February 2, 1882, "Queen," one of my twenty-two elephants, gave birth to a young one at our winter quarters in Bridgeport. The event had long been anticipated and thoroughly published throughout America and Europe. Scientists, all over the country, had been informed that the period of gestation being known to be about twenty months, a "Baby Elephant" might be expected early in February. The public press, naturalists, college professors and agents of zoölogical gardens in Europe were on the *qui vive,* and when the interesting event was imminent it was telegraphed through the associated press to all parts of the United States, and about sixty scientists, medical men and reporters arrived in time to be present at the birth. The next morning more than fifty columns of details of the birth, weight and name of the Baby Elephant appeared in the American papers, and notices cabled to London and Paris appeared in the morning papers. As this was the second elephant ever born in captivity, either in America or Europe, it created a great sensation. Its weight was only one hundred and forty-five pounds at birth. We named it "Bridgeport," after the place of its nativity and of my residence.

We opened our Great Show for the season of 1882 on Monday, March 13th, in Madison Square Garden, New York City, having given an illuminated street pageant the preceding Saturday evening, which eclipsed all similar exhibitions ever witnessed in America. The fame of the Baby Elephant had created quite a *furore* in the public mind, and from the very first night of opening, our efforts were crowned with success totally unprecedented in the show business. Day after day, and night after night, we turned away multitudes for want of room.

"Jumbo," the largest elephant ever seen, either wild or in captivity, had been for many years one of the chief attractions of the Royal Zoölogical Gardens, London. I had often looked wistfully on Jumbo, but with no hope of ever getting possession of him, as I knew him to be a great favorite of Queen Victoria, whose children and grandchildren are among the tens of thousands of British juveniles whom Jumbo has carried on his back. I did not suppose he would ever be sold. But one of my agents, who made the tour of Europe in the summer and autumn of 1881 in search of novelties for our big show, was so struck with the extraordinary size of the majestic Jumbo that he ventured to ask my friend, Mr. Bartlett, Superintendent of the Zoölogical Gardens, if he would sell Jumbo. The presumption of my agent startled Mr. Bartlett, and at first he replied rather sarcastically in the negative, but my agent pushed the question and said, "Mr. Barnum would pay a round price for him." Further conversation led my agent to think that possibly an offer of $10,000 might be entertained. He cabled me to that effect, to which I replied: "I will give ten thousand dollars for Jumbo, but the Zoo will never sell him." Two days afterwards my agent cabled me that my offer of $10,000 for Jumbo was accepted, I to take him in the Garden as he stood. The next day I dispatched Mr. Davis by steamer to London with a bank draft for £2000 sterling, payable to the order of the Treasurer of the Royal Zoölogical Gardens, London. From that time an excitement prevailed and increased throughout Great Britain which, for a cause so comparatively trivial, has never had a parallel in any civilized country. The council and directors of the Royal Zoo were denounced in strong terms for having sold Jumbo to the famous Yankee showman, Barnum. The newspapers, from the London *Times* down, daily thundered anathemas against the

sale, and their columns teemed with communications from statesmen, noblemen and persons of distinction advising that the bargain
should be broken at all risk, and promising that the money would
be contributed by the British public to pay any damages which might
be awarded to Barnum by the courts.   It is said that the Queen and
the Prince of Wales both asked that this course should be adopted.
I received scores of letters from ladies and children, beseeching me
to let Jumbo remain, and to name what damages I required and
they should be paid.   Mr. Laird, the ship-builder, wrote me from
Birkenhead that England was as able to pay "Jumbo claims" as she
was to pay the "Alabama claims," and it would be done if I would
desist and name my terms.   All England seemed to run mad about
Jumbo; pictures of Jumbo, the life of Jumbo, a pamphlet headed
"Jumbo-Barnum," and all sorts of Jumbo stories and poetry, Jumbo
Hats, Jumbo Collars, Jumbo Cigars, Jumbo Neckties, Jumbo Fans,
Jumbo Polkas, etc., were sold by the tens of thousands in the stores
and streets of London and other British cities.   Meanwhile the
London correspondents of the leading American newspapers cabled
columns upon the subject, describing the sentimental Jumbo craze
which had seized upon Great Britain.   These facts stirred up the
excitement in the United States, and the American newspapers, and
scores of letters sent to me daily, urged me not to give up Jumbo.

The editor of the London *Daily Telegraph* cabled me to name a
price for which I would cancel the sale, and permit Jumbo to remain
in London. I cabled back as follows:

NEW YORK, February 23, 1882.

To Lesarge, Daily Telegraph, London:
My compliments to Editor *Daily Telegraph* and British Nation. Fifty-
one millions of American citizens anxiously awaiting Jumbo's arrival. My
forty years' invariable practice of exhibiting the best that money could
procure, makes Jumbo's presence here imperative. Hundred thousand
pounds would be no inducement to cancel purchase.

P. T. BARNUM.

This dispatch was published in the London *Daily Telegraph* the next morning, and was sent by the London associated press to the principal newspapers throughout Great Britain, which republished it the following day, giving the excitement an immense impetus. Crowds of men, women and children rushed to the Zoo to see dear old Jumbo for the last time, and the receipts at the gates were augmented nearly two thousand dollars per day. A "fellow" or stockholder of the Royal Zoo sued out an injunction in the Chancery Court against the "councillors" of the Zoo and myself to quash the sale. After a hearing, which occupied two days, the sale was declared valid, and Jumbo was decided to be my property.

The fateful day arrived when Jumbo was to bid farewell to the Zoo, and then came the tug of war. The unfamiliar street waked in Jumbo's breast the timidity which is so marked a feature of elephant character. He trumpeted with alarm, turned to re-enter the Gardens, and, finding the gate closed, laid down on the pavement. His cries of fright sounded to the uninitiated like cries of grief, and quickly attracted a crowd of sympathizers. British hearts were touched, British tears flowed for the poor beast who was so unwilling to leave his old home. Persuasion had no effect in inducing him to rise, force was not permitted, and indeed it would have been a puzzle what force to apply to so huge a creature. My agent, dismayed, cabled me, "Jumbo has laid down in the street and won't get up. What shall we do?" I replied, "Let him lie there a week if he wants to. It is the best advertisement in the world." After twenty-four hours the gates of his paradise were reopened and Jumbo allowed to return to his old quarters, while my agents set to work to secure him by strategy. A huge iron-bound cage was constructed with a door at each end and mounted on broad wheels of enormous strength. This, with the doors open, was backed up against the door entrance to Jumbo's den, and the wheels sunk so that the floor of the cage was on a level with that of the elephant's.

A passageway was thus formed through which Jumbo must pass to reach the outer air. After much hesitation, he was persuaded to follow his keeper, Scott, through this cage to take his daily airing. For several days this ruse was repeated, then, as he entered the cage, the door behind him was swiftly closed, then the door in front of him, and Jumbo was mine.

Meanwhile Jumbo came up in Parliament, where the President of the Board of Trade was questioned in regard to precautions being taken to protect the passengers on shipboard. Mr. Lowell, our American Minister to the Court of St. James, in a speech given at a public banquet in London, playfully remarked, "the only burning question between England and America is Jumbo." The London *Graphic, Illustrated News, Punch,* and all the London papers published scores of pictures and descriptions of Jumbo, in prose and poetry, for several weeks in succession.

On the morning of his capture, March 25, 1882, the wheels of his cage were dug free of the ground, twenty horses attached, and in comparative silence of the following night, Jumbo was dragged miles to the steamship, "Assyrian Monarch," where quarters had been prepared for him by cutting away one of the decks. The Society for the Prevention of Cruelty to Animals hovered over Jumbo to the last, and titled ladies and little children brought to the ship baskets of dainties for Jumbo's consumption during the voyage. After a rough passage he arrived in New York, in good condition, Sunday morning, April 9th, and next day was placed on exhibition in the menagerie department of our great show, where he created such a sensation that in the next two weeks the receipts *in excess of the usual amount* more than repaid us the $30,000 his purchase and removal had cost us. Being a little wearied after the excitement of this achievement, and knowing well that there is no rest and recuperative like a sea voyage, I sailed with my wife in the

"City of Rome," for Liverpool, the latter part of May. We spent most of our time at the home of my wife's parents in Lancashire, making brief trips to London, visits made pleasant by the social attentions of old friends.

On account of the national interest manifested in "Jumbo," we presume the "British Lion" is for the time forgotten; and we therefore suggest the above as the most appropriate coat-of-arms for England.—*London Fun.*

CHAPTER XLIV

THE WHITE ELEPHANT

On the 9th of August, 1883, my wife and I made our usual summer trip to Europe, being met, as always, by my father-in-law, John Fish, who on this occasion said, "Mr. Barnum, I am always glad to see you set your foot on English soil, for I really believe that every voyage you make across the Atlantic adds a year to your life." "Then I will hereafter make two trips a year," I replied, which set my matter-of fact English father-in-law to practicing arithmetic, in order to discover how long I should live if I became purser of a steamship, and made a dozen trans-Atlantic trips a year!

In the summer of 1883 my little friend Tom Thumb died of apoplexy. He was at the time of his death a portly little man, of middle age, and in prosperous circumstances. His widow, the charming little Lavinia, has since married again, and is now known as the Countess Magri. In November I had the pleasure of entertaining at Waldemere Mr. Matthew Arnold, on the occasion of his lecturing in Bridgeport.

I was the recipient of a very novel compliment at Christmas. Labouchere, M.P., the publisher of *London Truth,* dubbed his Christmas number "Barnum in Britishland," and every line was devoted to imaginary interviews of P. T. Barnum with the most prominent Britishers, beginning with a hob-nobbing *tête-à-tête* with the Prince of Wales. It was a witty hit (done up in rhyme) at the foibles, follies, customs, fashions and sharp practices supposed to exist in Britishland. The sale reached a third edition, and exceeded by many thousands that of any previous season. The gratuitous advertisement was highly appreciated by me.

To add to the attractions of "The Great Combined Show" during the season of 1884, my agents in Africa and India and other parts of Asia, among whom were Messrs. J. B. Gaylord, Charles White, and Thomas H. Davis, after many months' residence in those lands, procured a number of additional ethnological specimens for exhibition in my "Grand Congress of the Nations." These novelties included specimens of the following tribes, namely. Nubian warriors, Zulu chiefs, Afghans, Hindus, Todas Indians, and Singing and Dancing Nautch Girls of India. A preliminary private exhibition of these ethnological rarities was given to members of the press and of the clergy in Madison Square Garden, New York, on the afternoon of March 15, 1884, which was attended with the customary success. In the evening of the same day they were introduced to the public as part of the Great Show.

The particular additional feature, however, by which the season of 1884 was made memorable, was the exhibition for the first time in any civilized country of that rare and beautiful animal which for ages has been recognized in Siam, Burmah, and other Buddhist countries as the "Royal Sacred White Elephant." This absolutely unique curiosity was accompanied by a Burmese orchestra and a retinue of Buddhist priests in full ecclesiastical costume, the sacred animal being surrounded by the same attendants and the like paraphernalia as during the performance of religious ceremonies in his native country. The priests were also supplied with documents, under the royal seal, attesting the sacred character of the beast, and with the royal bill of sale executed by King Theebaw's Master of Elephants, and also bearing the king's seal.

Until my agent first visited Bangkok, the capital of Siam, and there saw the king's "Sacred White Elephants," I had supposed that they were literally white, instead of technically so. Those who had not seen these animals, nor read authentic descriptions of them, had the same idea as myself. When, therefore, my Sacred Elephant arrived in London, a large portion of the public, having expected to see a milk-white elephant, were disappointed. The following article, which I clip from the New York *Tribune* of February 17th, gives the facts in the case:

> P. T. Barnum and his partners have dispelled a wide-spread popular illusion, that the so-called sacred white elephants of the kings of Siam and Burmah either are, or ever were, literally white. They say they have secured as perfect a specimen of this animal as exists anywhere and they do not claim that it is "white" in the strict sense of that word, yet it is the same species and exact counterpart of those white sacred elephants worshiped for centuries by the Buddhists. Up to this time, no European monarch has ever been able to procure "a sacred white elephant," or even get it into a Christian country, and in that Barnum has succeeded.

A rival showman, who labored under the "popular" illusion, had a common elephant painted milk-white, and so exhibited it for a time as a genuine specimen purchased in Siam. Two leading New York illustrated papers, early in 1882, were deceived into publishing pictures of this "pure white"-washed animal as a genuine Sacred *White* Elephant from Siam. The owner of this imposition soon announced that it had suddenly died. It was simply *un*-dyed! And thus another proof added to millions which have preceded it demonstrates that truth will always triumph over falsehood.

In his own land the white elephant is held in the utmost veneration; and as the people believe that if one of them leaves their country his departure will be the signal for dire calamities to them, and as, moreover, any person who is instrumental in sending one out of the country without the royal permission is liable to the penalty of death, the difficulty of procuring one for exportation has hitherto been so great as to have proved insurmountable. As, however, it has ever been my aim to bring together under our tents, utterly regardless of cost, the real marvels of this wonderful earth, I determined, if possible, even at the cost of half a million dollars if necessary, to procure a curiosity which centuries of unsuccessful endeavor had seemed to prove utterly unattainable. Unfortunately, just as my agents seemed on the verge of success, they were doomed to disappointment. A white elephant purchased by them in Siam many months before Toung Taloung was obtained, was poisoned on the eve of its departure by its attendant priests rather than that it should fall into the hands of profane Christians. Finally, however, after three years of patient persistence, and the exercise, on the part of half a score of our shrewdest agents, of wonderful tact, diplomacy, and untiring energy, often at the peril of their lives, and the outlay of a quarter of a million dollars, our efforts were crowned with victory. We now possessed and regularly exhibited *the first and only* animal of the kind that ever had been seen or that probably ever will be seen in a Christian land. So enormous were the difficulties which had to be conquered in order to get this only genuine White Elephant out of Burmah, that I am satisfied no other successful attempt to export one will ever again be made.

The Royal Sacred White Elephant, Toung Taloung, was purchased at Mandalay, in Burmah; and having been brought away under the royal warrant of King Theebaw, was shipped from Rangoon, in British Burmah, in the steamship "Tenasserim," December 8, 1883. After passing through the Suez Canal, and touching at Malta, it arrived safely at Liverpool, England, on January 14, 1884. Thence it was taken to London, where it was exhibited for several weeks at the Royal Zoölogical Gardens, Regent's Park, receiving the indorsement of many eminent scientists, prominent among whom was Professor W. H. Flower, President of the London Zoölogical Society and Curator of the Royal College of Surgeons. On March 13, 1884, it was shipped in the steamer "Lydian Monarch" for New York, and at that city it arrived on the 28th of the same month. On the 31st a special private exhibition of it was given to several hundred naturalists, scientists, Eastern travellers, scholars, leading physicians and clergymen, editors of New York and other papers, and other persons, whose closest scrutiny I invited, but who none of them doubted that the animal was what he was described to be, namely, a genuine white elephant from Burmah. Many certificates of his genuineness, now in our possession, were given by such eminent authorities as Colonel Daniel B. Sickles, late Minister to Siam; Colonel Thomas W. Knox, the only American to whom the King of Siam has ever presented the Order of the White Elephant; Mr. Edward Greey, author of "The Golden Lotus"; Mr. David Ker, Siamese correspondent of the New York *Times;* Frank Vincent, Jr., author of "The Land of the White Elephant," and many others.

As might have been anticipated, as a consequence of the exhibition of so unique a curiosity, not to speak of the other novelties, the tour of the "Greatest Show on Earth," during the season of 1884, was quite as successful as any previous one. The Show visited the principal cities of the United States as far east as Lewiston, Me., and as far west as Kansas City and Omaha.

The tour of the Great Show during the summer of 1884 was marked by an incident which is worthy of note here. The authorities of a thriving New England town, at which we were advertised to appear, demanded an exceptionally exorbitant sum as a license fee. Though our advance agent demurred to the imposition, the authorities, thinking no doubt that we would submit to it rather than pass by a town where the receipts for a day had averaged $10,000, were immovable. They reckoned without their host, however. We at once changed our plans, cancelled the date for their town, and announced instead that we would give the intended exhibition at a smaller town twelve miles off. The merchants, hotel-keepers and other business men of the larger town offered us four times the amount of the license-fee demanded if we would adhere to our original purpose and exhibit there. We, however, were immovable in our turn, and declined to change our plans a second time. On the day of the exhibition we ran a large number of excursion trains to the smaller town; the other town was nearly deserted; and the day's receipts for the exhibition were not $10,000, but $12,760.

Another incident, of a widely different character, by which the year 1884 was marked as a bright spot in my calendar, was the opening of the Natural History Museum of Tuft's College, near Boston, of which admirable educational institution I was a trustee at its foundation. The want of a natural history museum had long been felt, and some time ago my friend, President E. H. Capen, made an appeal to me to supply the need. To this appeal I responded; and the outcome has been the erection of a large and handsome stone structure, partially furnished with a fine collection of natural history specimens and other curiosities interesting and useful to students. The building was completed in the spring of 1884, and it was formally inaugurated at the Commencement exercises of the college, held on the 10th of June in the same year. The name of the founder had been kept a secret, but it was then publicly announced by President Capen in the course of his address.

When General Grant became financially embarrassed in 1884 he was specially anxious to secure Mr. W. H. Vanderbilt in the sum of $150,000, loaned to him under peculiar circumstances. The noble-hearted General and his wife made over to him all their personal property, including the valuable trophies and mementos presented to him not only in America but by monarchs, princes and other admirers during his celebrated trip around the world.

Recognizing the fact that people everywhere would feel interested in seeing these trophies, and that I could by exhibiting them in a most elegant and suitable manner throughout the civilized world gratify millions of persons of taste and appreciation, while I could afford to compensate General Grant so liberally for the privilege as to assure him a fine income, I wrote to him the following letter and sent it by special messenger:

NEW YORK, January 12, 1885.

To General U. S. Grant, twice President of the United States, etc.:

HONORED SIR: The whole world honors and respects you. All are anxious that you should live happy and free from care. While they admire your manliness in declining the large sum recently tendered you by friends, they still desire to see you achieve financial independence in an honorable manner. Of the unique and valuable trophies with which you have been honored, we all have read, and all have a laudable desire to see these evidences of love and respect bestowed upon you by monarchs, princes and people throughout the globe. While you would confer a great and enduring favor on your fellow-men and women by permitting them to see these trophies you could also remove existing embarrassments in a most satisfactory and honorable manner. I will give you one hundred thousand dollars cash, besides a proportion of the profits, if I may be permitted to exhibit these relics to a grateful and appreciative public, and I will give satisfactory bonds of half a million dollars for their safe-keeping and return.

These precious trophies of which all your friends are so proud, would be placed before the eyes of your millions of admirers in a manner and style at once pleasing to yourself and satisfactory to the best elements of the entire community. Remembering that the mementoes of Washingon, Wellington, Napoleon, Frederick the Great and many other distinguished men have given immense pleasure to millions who have been permitted to see them, I trust you will in the honorable manner proposed, gratify the public and thus inculcate the lesson of honesty, perseverence and true patriotism so admirably illustrated in your career.

I have the honor to be truly your friend and admirer,

P. T. BARNUM.

I called at General Grant's residence soon afterwards, and was politely received by him, his wife, and son, Colonel Frederick Grant. I said to the General, after our greeting: "General, since your journey around the world you are the best-known man on the globe."

"No, sir," replied the General, "your name is familiar to multitudes who never heard of me. Wherever I went, among the most distant nations, the fact that I was an American led to constant inquiries whether I knew Barnum."

Proceeding to the business on which I had called, the General informed me that the trophies were no longer under his control, as Mr. Vanderbilt, after refusing to take them, out of respect to the General, had finally accepted them on condition that after General Grant's decease they should be lodged in some safe public place in Washington, where all could see them.

"After all, Mr. Barnum," said General Grant, "under the present arrangements, everybody who visits Washington can see them."

"Yes, General," I replied, "but millions of persons who will never visit Washington will regret that I had never brought these historical relics where they would see them."

I shall always believe, regardless of any profit (or loss) which might have accrued to me, that my plan was one creditable to all concerned, and that it is to be regretted that it was not carried out.

I was reminded of General Grant's assurance of my name being known to the ends of the earth, when a few weeks later I received a letter addressed to "Mr. Barnum, America," and posted in Moulmein, British Burmah, on January 15th. It had been stamped seven times on its face and back, and bore the marks of the Post Office of Bombay, Brindisi, the "Sea Post Office," and the Post Office in New York, whence it was transmitted to Bridgeport. The envelope contained two letters in the Burmese language, to the attendants on the White Elephant.

CHAPTER XLV

OUR Great Barnum-London Show opened its season at Madison Square Garden, New York City, Monday, March 16, 1885, and closed at Newburg, N. Y., Saturday, October 24th, whence it was shipped directly to winter headquarters, Bridgeport, Conn. In the course of 192 days, exclusive of Sundays, it travelled 8,471 miles and exhibited in New York, Pennsylvania, New Jersey, Connecticut, Massachusetts, Rhode Island, Maine, New Brunswick, New Hampshire, Vermont, and the Provinces of Quebec and Ontario, Canada. The net profits were larger than those of the previous year.

The first event of note during the season—and a most lamentable one—occurred at Nashua, N. H., on Saturday afternoon, July 18th, when "Albert," a very large and treacherous Asiatic elephant, attacked James McCormick, one of the keepers, inflicting internal injuries which resulted in death the next day. For this, and to prevent further possible loss of life, Albert was sentenced to death, and executed in a ravine in the suburbs of Keene, N. H., on Monday, July 20th. After he had been chained to four large trees, and the location of his heart and brain marked with chalk, thirty-three members of the Keene Light Guard were marshalled in line at sixteen paces, and, at the word of command, discharged a volley into the huge culprit with such accuracy of aim that he fell dead, without a struggle. Albert was worth $10,000. His remains were presented to the Smithsonian Institute, Washington, D. C.

On Tuesday, September 15th, at St. Thomas, Ontario, Canada,

occurred a universally announced and regretted tragedy, by which the Show suffered a great and irreparable loss. At about 9 o'clock on the evening of that day, Jumbo, the biggest, noblest, most famous, popular, and valuable of beasts, was killed. While being led along the main line of the Grand Trunk Railway to his car, an unexpected special freight train rushed upon him. There was no time for escape, and the locomotive struck Jumbo with terrific force. The engine was badly broken and derailed, and Jumbo's skull fractured and internal injuries inflicted by his huge body being crushed between the freight train and a train of show cars standing on an adjacent track. He died in a few moments. The dwarf clown elephant, "Tom Thumb," had a leg broken, but has since recovered, retaining only an interesting little limp as a souvenir of his narrow escape.

The death of Jumbo was cabled all over the world, and, for the time, almost monopolized public attention, both at home and abroad. I received hundreds of telegrams and letters of sympathy. My first thought was of the many thousands who were counting on seeing the giant beast, the largest living creature in the world. Fortunately, in the case of Jumbo, science achieved a substantial victory over death. Professor Henry A. Ward, the distinguished head of Ward's Natural Science Establishment at Rochester, N. Y., was for many months engaged in the labor of preserving Jumbo's form, and also preparing his skeleton for exhibition. This great work has been successfully concluded, and the public can now look upon Jumbo, as majestic and natural as life, while beside him stands the prodigious framework of massive bones which sustained the vast weight of his flesh.

So many letters have been received by me from all parts of the world, asking the exact size of the lamented Jumbo, that I am impelled to print the measurements made by Professor H. A. Ward:

JUMBO'S SIZE.

Neck—Smallest circumference .... 11 feet, 6 inches.
Body—Circumference at shoulders .... 16 "   4   "
      Circumference at middle .... 18 "
      Circumference at hind legs .... 17 ⋅ "
Fore legs—Circumference of leg 3   feet above sole of foot 3 " 10 "
        "   "   5½   "   "   "   5 "   7 "
Hind legs—   "   "   2   "   "   "   3 "
        "   "   4   "   "   "   4 "   8 "
Length of tail .... 4 "   6 "
Length in all .... 14 "
Height to shoulder .... 12 "
Weight .... 7 tons.

Soon after Jumbo's death I succeeded in purchasing from the Directors of the Zoölogical Society's Garden, London, the great African elephant "Alice," for sixteen years the companion and so-called "wife" of the great Jumbo.   Alice, it will be remembered, was so sorrowfully excited when my agent attempted to remove Jumbo, February, 1882, that her groans and trumpetings frightened the wild beasts in the great zoo into such howlings and roarings as were heard a mile away.   When Jumbo was killed the English newspapers called Alice "Jumbo's widow," and several of the illustrated weeklies gave pictures of her wearing her "widow's cap."

Alice joined the Greatest Show on Earth in the early days of her widowhood, and was exhibited side by side with the skeleton and stuffed hide of Jumbo.   This pathetic juxtaposition did not apparently affect her spirits.   The dead Jumbo and the living Alice were among the most interesting features of the show season of 1886, both at the Madison Square Garden, from April 1st to April 24th, and in New York, Pennsylvania, Maryland, District of Columbia, Virginia, Ohio, Kentucky, Indiana, Tennessee, Michigan, Illinois, Iowa, Wisconsin, Minnesota, Nebraska. Missouri, Kansas, Georgia,

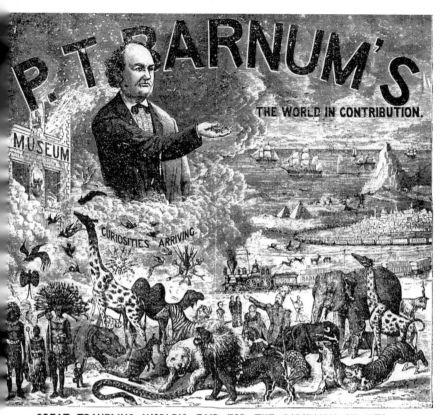

GREAT TRAVELING WORLD'S FAIR FOR THE CAMPAIGN OF 1873.

P. T. BARNUM TO THE PUBLIC.

GENTLEMEN, FAMILIES, CHILDREN, FRIENDS:

career for forty years as a public Manager of Amusements blended with Instruction is well You have all heard of my three New York Museums; my appearance before kings, queens, al courts, with Gen. Tom Thumb; my great triumphal tour with Jenny Lind, the Swedish gale; and my immense Traveling Exhibitions. Every body concedes that I give ten times ey's worth, and always delight my patrons. I now come before you with the **LAST D CROWNING TRIUMPH OF MY MANAGERIAL LIFE.**

ithstanding the burning of my last museum, in December (which, however, did not destroy y great traveling chariots, vans, cages, or horses, nor duplicates of most of my living wild which were then on exhibition in New Orleans), I have been enabled, through the aid of dispatches, electricity, and steam, and the expenditure of nearly a million of dollars, to on the road by far the largest and most interesting Combination of **MUSEUM, ME- RIE,** and **HIPPODROME** ever known. Indeed, it may fairly be called a great **ELING WORLD'S FAIR.**

scription will convey an adequate idea of its vastness, its beauty, and its marvelous collec- wonders. After our *Grand Opening* in the buildings of the American Institute, Monday, 1, where we will remain for about ten days, we shall commence the campaign of 1873. l travel entirely by railroad, and be exhibited this season in nearly every large town in gland, Canada, and the States east of the Mississippi River and north of the Ohio. It re- ore than one hundred cars, besides *fifty of my own*, made expressly for this purpose, and ix locomotives, to transport it. My daily expenses exceed $5000. We can only stop in rns, and leave it to those residing elsewhere to reach us by cheap excursion trains, which a easily get up.

g some of my novelties are a **FREE FULL MENAGERIE OF WILD ANI-** , including all, and more than are usually seen in a traveling menagerie, which I now be seen by every body, **WITHOUT ANY CHARGE WHATEVER.**

ngh I have consolidated more than twenty shows in one, containing nearly one hundred ly magnificent gold and enameled cages, dens, and vans, requiring the services of nearly IOUSAND MEN and OVER FIVE HUNDRED HORSES, the price of admission ntire combination of exhibitions is only the same as is charged to a common show, viz., ; children half price.

eat Hippodrome Tent comfortably seats 13,000 persons at one time, while my numerous ts cover several acres of ground.

The Museum Department contains 100,000 Curiosities, including Prof. Faber's wonderful **TALKING MACHINE,** costing me $20,000 for its use six months. Also a NATIONAL PORTRAIT GALLERY of 100 life-size Oil Paintings, including all the Presidents of the United States, our Statesmen and Military Heroes, as well as foreign Potentates and Celebrities, and the entire Collection of the celebrated John Rogers' Groups of Historical and Classic Statuary. Also an almost endless variety of Curiosities, including numberless Automaton Musicians and Mechanicians, and Moving Scenes, Transformation Landscapes, Sailing-Ships, Running Water-Mills, Railroad Trains, &c., made in Paris and Geneva, more beautiful and marvelous than can be imagined, and all kept in motion by a Steam-Engine. Here also are Giants, Dwarfs, Feejee Cannibals, Modoc and Digger Indians, Circassian Girls, the No-Armed Boy, &c.

Among the Rare Living Animals are **MONSTER SEA LIONS,** transported in great water-tanks; the largest **RHINOCEROS** ever captured alive, and 500 Wild Beasts and Rare Birds, Elephants, Elands, Gnus, Lions, Tigers, Polar Bears, Ostriches, and every description of Wild Animal hitherto exhibited, besides many never before seen on this Continent.

In the Hippodrome department are **THREE DISTINCT RINGS,** wherein three sets of rival performances are taking place at the same time, in full view of all the audience. Here will be seen performing elephants, horse-riding goats, educated horses, ponies, trick mules and bears, and three distinct equestrian companies (with six clowns), including by far the best male and female bare-back riders in the world, with numerous athletes and gymnasts who have no equal. Every thing is perfectly chaste and unobjectionable.

I regard this with pride as the culminating triumph of my amusement career, and I hazard nothing in saying that **the like will not be seen again in this generation.**

THE GREAT STREET PROCESSION, three miles long, takes place every morning at half-past eight o'clock. It is worth going one hundred miles to see. It consists of trains of elephants, camels, dromedaries, zebras, and elks in harness; nearly one hundred gold, enameled, and cerulean chariots, vans, dens, and cages; Arabian horses, trick ponies, three bands of music, and a most marvelous display of gymnastic, automatic, and musical performances in the public streets. ☞ THREE FULL EXHIBITIONS will be given each day at 10, 1, and 7 o'clock. Clergy- men of all denominations, and their wives, admitted free. Parties from the country are earnestly advised to see the Grand Procession, and attend the first morning exhibitions, while every thing is fresh, and seen to the best advantage, thus avoiding the immense crowds of afternoon and evening.

The public's obedient servant,

P. T. Barnum

438 FIFTH AVENUE, March 15, 1873.

ADVERTISEMENT IN *Harper's Weekly*, MARCH 29, 1873

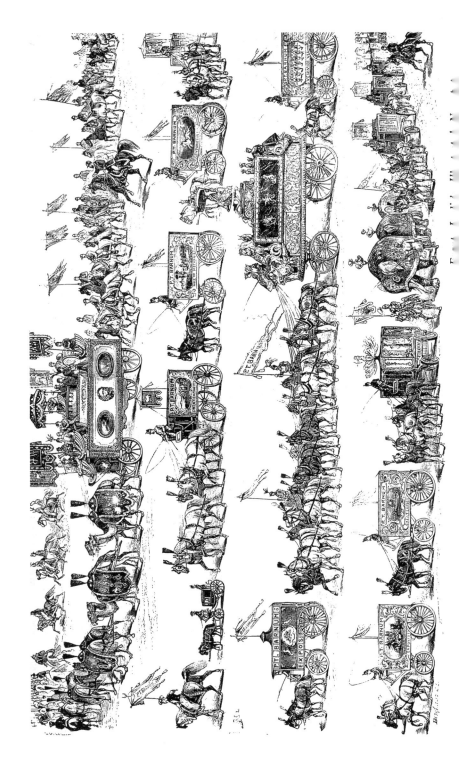

South Carolina and North Carolina. The show, as usual, was larger and better than ever before, and its financial success proportionate. This was the first visit of the great show to the Southern States, where it was received with the greatest enthusiasm. It visited, during its season of 1886, 21 States and 144 cities, travelled 10,447 miles, and gave 344 performances. Its longest single run was from Springfield, Mo., to Memphis, Tenn., 285 miles.

In pursuance of my custom of visiting my Great Show at such places as are railroad centers, where I know thousands will come in by excursion trains, in 1886 I met the show at Erie, Pa. I did not make myself known (for I like to mingle with the crowd *incognito,* and get information and pleasure listening to the various remarks, and especially criticisms, about the different details of the show) but seated myself among the audience, surrounded by the country people. It was a great satisfaction to witness their delight at the various exhibitions brought into the arena. One old farmer and his wife, who sat on the seat in front of me, attracted my attention.

"I declare, Sally," said the man, "I ain't seen a circus since I was twenty-one. I never did think it possible to do such wonderful things as I have seen here to-day."

"I have never," replied Sally, "seen a circus since I was a gal. But I was determined to see Barnum's, I had heard so much about it. It certainly beats all I had ever dreamt of."

"After all," said the husband, "there is one thing I would give more to see than the whole show, and that is Barnum himself."

"Well, perhaps, you may see him," replied the wife, "they say he sometimes goes with his show."

"I hope I will get a look at him," said the husband.

After a while, a young rider about three-and-twenty years of age, a perfect athlete and equestrian, came into the ring, riding four bare-backed horses. They were very spirited animals, and they went through their various evolutions with such perfection and celerity as to bring repeated thunders of applause. Presently the youthful rider turned a somersault, alighted upon his head, and in that position, with his heels in the air, rode several times around the ring. All were wondering at this extraordinary feat, when my old farmer friend jumped to his feet, wild with excitement, swung his hat in the air and exclaimed, "I'll bet five dollars that's Barnum. There ain't another man in America who can do that but Barnum." I did not disabuse his mind. He felt that he had gotten his money's worth, and I was satisfied.

During the six weeks of the exhibition in New York, I was a constant visitor in the afternoons and an occasional one in the evenings, at which times I renewed many old acquaintanceships. When it was not possible to attend both, I always gave the preference to the afternoon performances, so as to meet as many as possible of my little friends and patrons, to whose amusement and happiness it is such a pleasure to minister. To me there is no picture so beautiful as ten thousand smiling, bright-eyed, happy children; no music so sweet as their clear ringing laughter. That I have had power, year after year, by providing innocent amusement for the little ones, to create such pictures, to evoke such music, is my proudest and happiest reflection. Often, as I walked through the Madison Square Garden, I was the recipient of spontaneous bursts of applause and clapping of little hands from the multitude of children present. These incidents are among the pleasantest of my life and never to be forgotten.

The show left the city for its annual travelling season and travelled through the eastern states, closing the season in Hoboken on October 22, 1887. It was a most satisfactory season financially, although not quite as extensive as formerly. In its travels the show visited 175 cities, covering over 10,500 miles of territory, and meeting with but few accidents and none of any consequence. From Hoboken all the animals and material were safely transported to the winter quarters at Bridgeport.

At the close of the season, Messrs. Hutchinson, Cole and Cooper, feeling a desire for more leisurely lives than the terms of our partnership permitted, and being possessed of fortunes large enough to gratify all reasonable tastes, withdrew from the firm, with my free consent, and the show property was housed for the winter with myself and Mr. James A. Bailey as equal partners and proprietors, and under the name of the Barnum & Bailey Show.

The sad news of Jenny Lind's death in London, November 2, 1887, news which flashed across the world awakening universal sorrow and regret, appealed peculiarly to me. It was not only that the dead songstress was associated with one of the most successful business enterprises of my life, and one of which I am particularly pleased, but from the time of our first association I conceived for the woman and artist a warm regard which was not impaired by any subsequent events. Her impulses were always good, and if the somewhat abrupt termination of her engagement with me was not in keeping with the fine sense of justice which ordinarily regulated her actions, the blame must rest on her interested advisers, not on Jenny Lind.

In the years that have passed since then we have each held ourselves ready to do the other any friendly service possible, and have taken a mutual pleasure in recalling the many humorous and pathetic incidents of our concert season. I remember the glorious voice of the Nightingale, not alone in the raptures of unrivalled singing, but low and soft, with pitying tender words, as she sought to comfort one in trouble, or ringing out in the hearty laughter of blithe and vigorous young womanhood. From my very heart came the words of sympathy I sent to her devoted husband, and from his, I am sure, came the message he cabled from Malvern, England, where he had just laid the body of his worshipped wife:

P. T. BARNUM, New York:

Fully appreciate your condolences, coming from one who well knew my beloved wife, and was always remembered by her with sincere regard.

OTTO GOLDSCHMIDT.

So dies away the last echo of the most glorious voice the world has ever heard.

CHAPTER XLVI

On November 20, 1887, I was again, and for the fifth time, a heavy loser by fire. About ten o'clock on that night fire broke out in the great animal building of the winter quarters at Bridgeport, Conn., and in spite of strenuous efforts to subdue the flames it was entirely consumed, and so rapidly that there was not time to rescue the animals. Of the herd of thirty-four elephants thirty escaped. One lion, Nimrod, a fine specimen and great favorite, was led out by his keeper. With these exceptions, the entire menagerie perished in the flames. An immense quantity of properties, canvas tents, poles, seats, harness, etc., stored in the second story was also destroyed.

Many thrilling incidents of that night will long remain vividly in the memory of those who witnessed them. A terrified spectator, who did not realize that the released lion would obey the restraining hand of his keeper, tangled in his mane, shot at the beast, which, startled, broke away, outstripped his pursuers and entered a barn some distance from the scene of the conflagration. There he attacked a cow and calf, whose cries brought their owner, a Mrs. Gilligan. Mistaking the lion in the dim light for a huge dog, she stoutly belabored him with a broom-stick, saying, "Shoo! shoo!" The lion kept on making a meal of the cow and calf, but growled such a vigorous objection to being interrupted that the widow retreated precipitately, crying, "A bear! a bear!" A neighbor caught up his gun and ran to her assistance, and, little recking what noble game he was slaughtering, through the window of the barn he shot the trapped king of the forest dead.

The elephant "Gracie" rushed into the Sound, where she was found next morning swimming exhaustedly. She died of cold and exposure while being towed to shore. The white elephant determinedly committed suicide. Liberated with the rest of the elephants, he rushed back into the flames. Driven out again and again, each time he returned until the keepers were forced to abandon him to his fate. In the fiercest of the flames he was seen wildly thrashing his trunk in the air, then with one loud cry fell and was seen no more. The fire approached in a weird and picturesque way a very large portrait of myself painted on the end of the building overlooking the N. Y., N. H. & H. Railroad. For many minutes the picture glowed intact in an unbroken frame of flame.

As a strong force of water was suddenly turned into the fire hose, the great coils swelled and writhed and leaped along the ground, and many of the excited on-lookers fled in horror, and told honest stories of the huge boa constrictors that were wandering about seeking whom they might devour. At two o'clock in the morning the telegraphic despatch telling the dire news reached my rooms at the Murray Hill Hotel, New York, and was received by my wife, who is authority for the following story:

"I roused Mr. Barnum, who turned on his pillow just enough to focus one eye at me as I stood shivering in the chill morning air.

" 'What is it?' said he.

" 'A telegram,' said I.

" 'What about?' said he.

" 'I'll read it to you,' said I.

BRIDGEPORT, Nov. 21, 1887.

" 'To P. T. BARNUM, Murray Hill Hotel:

Large animal building entirely consumed. Six horses in ring barn burned, together with entire menagerie except thirty elephants and one lion.

C. R. BROTHWELL.

" 'I am very sorry, my dear,' said he calmly, 'but apparent evils are often blessings in disguise. It is all right.'

"With that he rolled back into his original comfortable position, and I give you my word for it, in three minutes was fast asleep."

The loss by this fire was $250,000; the insurance only $31,000. Many people thought I would be deterred by this disaster from ever collecting another menagerie. Some even surmised that I would give up the show business altogether. But I am not in the show business alone to make money. I feel it my mission, as long as I live, to provide clean, moral and healthful recreation for the public to which I have so long catered, and which has never failed to recognize most generously my efforts. Mr. Bailey was as little dismayed as myself. From all parts of the world dealers in wild animals and our own hunters telegraphed, cabled and wrote what they had to offer us. Eleven days after the fire I found Mr. Bailey intently reading a pile of telegrams and letters, and making memoranda. To my inquiry as to what he was doing, he coolly remarked, "I am ordering a menagerie." "What! all in one day?" I ejaculated, somewhat surprised. "Certainly," he replied, "I know from these telegrams just where we can get every animal we want, and in six hours we shall own a much finer menagerie than the one we have lost."

Apropos of this fire it is a strange coincidence that four of the most famous elephants the world ever saw, elephants which contributed very largely to the reputation and prosperity of the show, have all come to untimely ends. The baby elephant, a most amiable and popular little creature, died April 12, 1886, at the tender age of four years, in the very spot where he was born. Jumbo was killed by a locomotive, and the white elephant and Alice perished tragically in the burning of the winter quarters.

As I close this volume I am more thankful than words can

express that my health is preserved, and that I am blessed with a vigor and buoyancy of spirits vouchsafed to but few; but I am by no means insensible to the fact that I have reached the evening of life (which is well lighted, however), and I am glad to know that though this is indeed a beautiful, delightful world to those who have the temperament, the resolution, and the judgment to make it so, yet it happily is not our abiding-place; and that he is unwise who sets his heart so firmly upon its transitory pleasures as to feel a reluctance to obey the call, when his Father makes it, to leave all behind and to come up higher, in that Great Future, when all that we now prize so highly (except our love to God and man) shall dwindle into insignificance.

WALDEMERE, BRIDGEPORT, CONN., 1888.

————————

The remaining three years of Barnum's life, from the point at which his autobiography ends, were not particularly eventful. In 1889 his partner Mr. Bailey persuaded him to the plan of taking their circus to England. Barnum accompanied the show, and appeared in his carriage at each performance. In spite of his eighty years, he still continued to devote a good deal of time to business affairs after his return to this country; but in larger part his last two years were spent quietly in his Bridgeport home, writing, reading, and entertaining a host of friends—American and foreign—who came to see him there. In November, 1890, he suffered an attack of acute congestion of the brain. Although he rallied after an interval, and never gave up hope of his recovery, the attack finally brought about his death, in the early evening of April 7, 1891. His last words were a request to know what the circus receipts had been during the day at Madison Square Garden in New York. After his death it was said that more newspaper space had been devoted to his career than to that of any other American not a President of the United States. In his will Barnum disposed of an estate amounting to more than four million dollars.